JAMES MADISON

The Nationalist

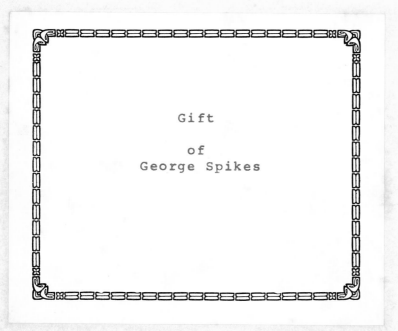

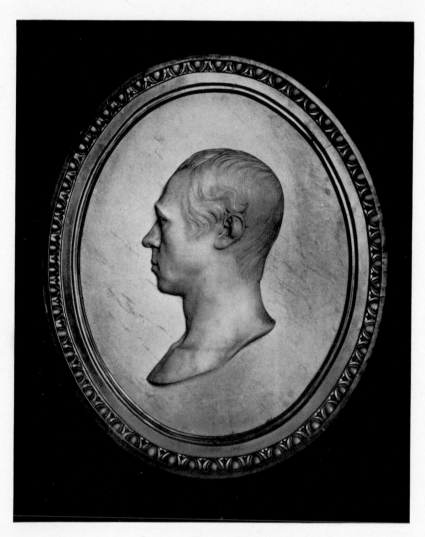

Ceracchi Bust of Madison

JAMES MADISON

The Nationalist

1780-1787

BY

IRVING BRANT

AUTHOR OF

James Madison: The Virginia Revolutionist

ILLUSTRATED

THE BOBBS-MERRILL COMPANY

PUBLISHERS

INDIANAPOLIS   NEW YORK

First Edition

CONTENTS

CONTENTS—*continued*

LIST OF ILLUSTRATIONS

MES MADISON

The Nationalist

CHRONOLOGY

1653. Great-great-grandfather John Maddison patents tidewa[ter]
Mattaponi River.

1723. Grandfather Ambrose Madison buys nucleus of Montp[elier]
near Orange.

March 16, 1751. James Madison born to James and Nell[y]
Madison, at his maternal grandmother's home, later Por[t]
on the Rappahannock.

About 1760. Central structure of Montpelier mansion built.

1763-1767. Madison studies at Donald Robertson school, in [King and]
Queen County.

1767-1768. Studies at home under the Reverend Thomas Ma[rtin.]

1769-1772. Attends college at Princeton, graduating in 1771, [stays]
for postgraduate work.

1772-1774. Continues studies at home, in ill health.

May, 1774. Visits Philadelphia, Princeton, New York and A[lbany.]

December, 1774. Becomes a member of revolutionary Oran[ge]
Committee, headed by his father.

1776. Delegate to Virginia Convention which declared for ind[ependence]
and set up state government. Drafts Virginia guaranty o[f religious]
liberty.

1776-1777. Attends legislature, supports Jefferson's reform p[rogram.]

1777. Defeated for re-election because of refusal to treat voters [to drink.]

1777. Elected by legislature to Virginia State Council, a nine-[man body]
controlling the acts of the governor.

1778-1779. As a member of the council, helps to direct Virg[inia]
in the Revolution.

December 14, 1779. Elected by the legislature to represent V[irginia in]
the Continental Congress.

CHAPTER 1

Youngest Delegate

Through heavy March rains which followed the intensely cold winter of 1779-1780, James Madison rode to Philadelphia to begin his service in the Continental Congress. The two-wheeled chaise driven by his Negro servant Billey lurched into mudholes. His three horses splashed red clay onto the stumps among which they threaded their precarious way. Around the northern flank of the "little mountains," out of the Blue Ridge foothills, they came down through farm and forest to tidewater. After crossing the Rappahannock by ferry at Fredericksburg, they turned north and skirted the Potomac. Then to Baltimore, the Susquehanna ferry and northward beside the Delaware. "The extreme badness of the roads and frequency of rains" delayed his arrival until March 18— twelve days of travel.[1]

The War of the Revolution had not visibly touched the greater part of the country Madison traveled through. Washington's army, then encamped near Morristown, New Jersey, might be half-starved and ragged, unable to move for lack of wagon transport. But there was plenty of food on the farms of Virginia and Maryland. The people were comfortable in homespun suits and jeans. Only in the region about Philadelphia itself, from which both British and American armies had drawn supplies during the occupation of the city by General Howe, had the country been stripped by purchases, impressment or the more violent ravages of war.

The conflict itself was in a transition stage, disquieting in prospect, but calm enough at the time. The major British attempt to quell the Revolution by subduing New England and New York had ended in failure. It failed, indeed, because of Howe's advance on Philadelphia in 1777, which left Burgoyne's Canada-drawn army subject to defeat and capture at Saratoga. All of the encounters in the center had been indecisive in effect if not in outcome—

Washington's victories at Trenton and Princeton and his failures at Brandywine and Germantown; the drawn battle at Monmouth during the enemy's retirement to New York; the capture of Stony Point by "Mad Anthony" Wayne. France had entered the war in 1778 and the arrival of a French fleet and army was looked for with eager longing. On the northern and western periphery the American cause was gaining. General Sullivan, at what is now Elmira, New York, had smashed the Loyalists who ravaged the Mohawk Valley. George Rogers Clark had reduced the Indian menace and strengthened American territorial claims by capturing Kaskaskia and Vincennes.

Military news at the moment was cheering—a bit too much so. On the day of Madison's arrival an express slushed in from South Carolina with news of terrible British losses in a storm at sea. Three ships had foundered, many were dismasted, four captured and thirteen were reported lost on the rocks of Bermuda. The wary observer might have noted that Sir Henry Clinton's invading army held four solid positions in front of Charleston and undamaged British warships were blocking up the harbor. The *Pennsylvania Journal* quoted a gleeful London account of the shrinking of Washington's army and in reply called on all Americans to exert themselves against enemies who, "after so many defeats, are still straining every nerve to reduce us to slavery and misery."

Philadelphia was a city of close to 40,000 population, the largest in America. Its broad, straight streets and wide sidewalks, its regular rows of uniform brick houses, set it quite apart from the winding lanes of Boston and the sprawl of Southern cities. At the western edge were new public buildings—prison, hospital, poorhouse—the pride of the Quaker community. Congress held its meetings at the eastern extreme, no longer in Carpenters' Hall, but on the second floor of the near-by State House, now called Independence Hall, which it shared with the Pennsylvania government. Its tower, later replaced, was called by Franklin a microscope half out of its case. Near by were the slave mart and the field of honor, where army officers and politicians engaged their kind "in a fury of fighting, incredible and scandalous," the former often with bullets in their guns, the latter with priming powder.[2]

It was with better-than-average spelling that a Pennsylvania delegate wrote of "young Madeson" entering Congress on Monday, March 20, 1780.[3] He was four days past his twenty-ninth birthday—the youngest man in that legislative body—and looked and acted younger than his years. Of slight build, five feet six inches tall, with delicate features which bore the stamp of scholarship, he suggested the schoolboy, and this impression was heightened by his shyness. There was nothing about him to reveal how thoroughly his previous four years of public service—in the convention which framed the Virginia Constitution and Declaration of Rights, in the ensuing legislative session, in the daily war work of the governor's council—had prepared him for the larger responsibilities of the national scene. During his first half year in Congress his shyness prevented him from taking the floor in debate, even though speeches in that small body were in a conversational tone. When he did assume the open leadership made inevitable by his intelligence, zeal and talent for political strategy, the effect was startling upon those who did not know him well. He had been a delegate for just one year when Thomas Rodney, of Delaware, writing his impressions of members he had known for ten days, made this entry in his diary:

"I take notice of a Mr. Madison, of Virginia, who with some little reading in the law is just from the College, and possesses all the self conceit that is common to youth and inexperience in like cases—but it is unattended with that gracefulness and ease which sometimes makes even the impertinence of youth and inexperience agreeable or at least not offensive."[4]

Rodney, a shallow egotist, was as poor a judge of character as any man who ever sat in Congress. But he must have recorded the exact impression Madison made on him. Since the young Virginian was known even in 1776 as a talented conversationalist, too diffident for public speaking, it is evident that Rodney judged him by his early uneasy forensic efforts. To such a critic, the self-consciousness of a gifted youth struggling against excessive modesty could easily become graceless impertinence. The words "just from the College," applied to one who was graduated ten years earlier, reveal the lingering mark of immaturity.

A final measure of Madison's talents is found in the sketches of delegates made by the Chevalier de la Luzerne, upon the eve of his return to France in 1784. The French minister placed him first among all the men who sat in Congress during his stay in America—a verdict the more notable because Luzerne had a low opinion of some who were friendly toward his own country. Of the young Virginian he wrote:

"James Madison junior—of a sound and just mind. A man of learning, who desires to do good works and to improve himself, but who is not overly ambitious. Of honest principles; zealous, without going to excess, for the honor of the thirteen states. He is not free from prejudices in favor of the various claims of Virginia, however exaggerated they may be; but that is a general failing. He appears to be devoted to us, and it is said that his behavior in Congress proves it. He is regarded as the man of the soundest judgment in Congress. He did not begin to take part in debate until he had been there two years and he speaks nearly always with fairness and wins the approval of his colleagues."[5]

Luzerne was mistaken as to the two years' delay in entering debates. Madison took a recorded part in them on October 6, 1780. But the error is in itself evidence of a reputation for reticence. Another four years passed and Chargé d'Affaires Louis Otto, who had been Luzerne's private secretary in 1780, sent his government this characterization of Madison:

"Well-educated, wise, temperate, gentle, studious; perhaps more profound than Mr. Hamilton, but less brilliant; the intimate friend of Mr. Jefferson and sincerely devoted to France. He entered Congress very young and seems to have concerned himself particularly with public affairs. He may one day be governor of his state, if his modesty permits him to accept that office. Not long ago he refused the office of President of Congress. He is a man one must study for a long time in order to make a fair appraisal of him."[6]

By the time he entered Congress, Madison was escaping from the chronic illness of his earlier youth. David Jameson, his former colleague on the Virginia council, responded to letters of August, 1780, with the remark that he was "very glad to find you were getting into better health." Three years later, hearing that Madison enjoyed a good state of health, Jameson remarked that "a close and constant application to business seems not to have been so prejudicial to you as I feared it would." In the interval Madison had made an all-time record for continuous attendance in Congress, passing untouched through epidemics which smote the community with disaster. There is no indication that he still was subject to the epileptiform hysteria which afflicted him just after his college years, but he continued to regard it, mistakenly, as a disease of his constitution.[7]

There were few in Congress to give Madison the greeting of old friendship when he took up his duties there. William Churchill Houston, under whom he studied at Princeton, but only five years his senior, was a mild and scholarly member from New Jersey. The more redoubtable President Witherspoon of that same school, who always wore cap and gown in congressional sessions, was out for a year because he could not stand the expense of commuting. Probably the only other member Madison knew was Cyrus Griffin, who for five months had been Virginia's sole representative in the national council. Winter absenteeism was the bane of Congress, but Virginia had of late been offering a year-round variety. Sixteen men held credentials from that state during 1779. Seven resigned, four failed to serve or went home, four delayed their attendance until the following spring.

Lamenting the low caliber of Virginia's representation, Washington urged various notables to offer their services—Jefferson, Wythe, Nicholas, Pendleton, Mason, Nelson, Benjamin Harrison. Not one responded to his call. In December the legislature cut the delegation to five members and filled the vacancies with James Henry, Joseph Jones, James Madison and John Walker, elected in that order. Jones, friend and confidant of Washington, had been a member in 1777. Madison's talents were known to legislative leaders, but the full list hardly suggests that the assembly was in quest of genius. Held at Montpelier by the most severe winter in the memory of living men, Madison employed his time in a study of the country's financial problems. The trunks he carried with him to Philadelphia, one may believe, were no heavier with coats and knee breeches than with the books and papers which were his weapons in the mingled enterprise of war and government.

After spending two days at a public inn, Madison took up his residence in the boarding establishment of Mrs. Mary House. Located at the corner of Fifth and Market Streets, barely a stone's throw from the hall in which Congress met, it enjoyed a well-deserved patronage from delegates to that body. "Our family," those who lived there called themselves, with the landlady's household included in the circle. Its presiding angel was Mrs. Eliza Trist, daughter of Mrs. House. Without the brilliance of one who conducts a *salon,* she mingled qualities of head and heart which wrought lasting ties with the Virginians who, following Madison's lead, established themselves in this domicile. Her husband, Nicholas Trist, came from a dying strain of clergymen who had contributed notably to populating the ancient English towns of Totnes and Torquay in Devonshire. Their young son, Master Browse Trist, became the surprised beneficiary of a thousand-pound windfall (as Madison described it) when all his uncles died off in England shortly after the end of the war. Completing the household was the landlady's son, Samuel House, a merchant who traded in the westerly counties of Virginia.[8]

Jefferson spent a few months in the House-Trist home in 1782-1783, then asked Madison to obtain Mrs. Trist's advice on a boarding school for "Patsy." To the latter he wrote: "As long as Mrs. Trist remains in Philadelphia [she was about to follow her husband down the Mississippi to Louisiana] cultivate her affection. She has been a valuable friend to you, and her good sense and good heart make her valued by all who know her, and by nobody on earth more than me."[9] By all the rules of romance, Browse Trist and Martha Jefferson should have developed an interest in each other. Instead, it was delayed a generation. Nicholas P. Trist (the diplomat who secured California for the United States) married Virginia Randolph, one of Martha Jefferson's eleven children. They went to live with Jefferson at Monticello. There Eliza Trist made her home in her old age, and her grandson Nicholas nursed Jefferson on his deathbed.

Toward Madison, Mrs. Trist adopted a protective attitude which throws light on his character and reveals the impression he made on sympathetic friends. Hearing from Jefferson that Madison could be elected governor of Virginia if he wished, she replied:

"He deserves everything that can be done for him, but ... I think it rather too great a sacrifice for a man to make when he accepts the office of governor under the present forms of government in America. ... He has a soul replete with gentleness, humanity and every social virtue and yet I am certain that some wretch or other will write against him. You I am sure would not advise him to it. I have no idea that men are to live only for the public; they owe something to themselves. Mr. Madison is too amiable in his disposition to bear up against a torrent of abuse. It will hurt his feelings and injure his health, take my word."[10]

Hot-tempered John Mathews, of South Carolina, whose influence was ruined by his unbridled tongue, was one of the guests of Mrs. House when Madison arrived there. William Floyd, of New York, lived there with his wife and three children, the youngest of them thirteen-year-old Kitty. Joseph Jones moved in when he arrived on April 24—three days after the coming of James Henry, a month ahead of John Walker, his wife and daughter Milly. The last two had just made a perfect recovery from smallpox, which decorated Milly with thirteen patriotic postules.[11]

Board and room were costly in Philadelphia in 1780. Madison's bill from Mrs. House, from March 20 to September 20, came to just $21,373 ⅔. Besides this he spent $2,459 for liquors, sugar and fruit; he paid $1,776 for washing and $1,020 to a barber. Two cords of wood cost $605. His horses in the congressional stables ran up a bill of $6,611.[12] All these items were chargeable to the state.

Such fantastic bills reflected the runaway inflation of the Continental currency, then in hard gallop down the slope of vanishing value. This was due to the issuance of $200,000,000 of unbacked bills of credit in five years; or, to state it in terms of basic responsibility, to the refusal of state governments to levy taxes for carrying on the war, and the inability of Congress to do so. Paid for in Spanish coin, Madison's $21,000 room-and-board bill hardens into about two specie dollars a day.

The first bit of congressional news Madison heard in Philadelphia was of the drastic step taken, on the day of his arrival, to halt inflation by devaluation of the dollar. Estimating that forty dollars in Continental currency were then equal in buying power to one dollar in specie, Congress voted on March 18 to make that the legal rate of exchange between the two. Only, having no coin or bullion, they decreed that the forty dollars in old paper money should be exchanged for one dollar in new paper, to be redeemed in specie within six years.

This new money, though authorized and guaranteed by Congress, was to be issued by the individual states. They would print one dollar in new money for each twenty dollars of the old turned in. Since the redemption rate was forty for one, that would limit the face value of the new money to twice the cash value of the old. This new federal-state money was to draw five per cent interest, payable by the United States. Having no money for this purpose, Congress ordered it paid in bills of exchange drawn on the American diplomats in Europe. That is, the interest would be paid by the French government, though France did not yet know it.[13]

The immediate effect of this act of Congress was to reduce the national debt of $200,000,000 to the modest sum of $5,000,000. The expected effect was to produce $10,000,000 in paper money which was to be divided, as fast as issued, in a forty-sixty ratio between Congress and the states issuing it. The states were to spend their $6,000,000 on war supplies, while the $4,000,000 delivered to Congress was to be credited to the issuing states' shares of the costs of war. The states were to lay specific taxes to redeem the whole $10,000,000 in specie.

Madison reserved his opinion of this new measure, against which Griffin, of Virginia, and all other Southern delegates voted. It was enacted, he told his father, because the depreciation of paper currency caused disorder in public affairs and threatened the United States with an intolerable burden of debt. He expected it to "create great perplexity and complaints in many private transactions," but the real disaster would ensue from its failure.[14] The whole national picture filled him with apprehension. He outlined it in these words to Governor Jefferson when he had been in Philadelphia one week:

"Among the various conjunctures of alarm and distress which have arisen in the course of the Revolution, it is with pain I affirm to you, sir, that no one can be singled more truly critical than the present.

"Our army threatened with an immediate alternative of disbanding or living on free quarter;

"The public treasury empty;

"Public credit exhausted, nay the private credit of purchasing agents employed, I am told, as far as it will bear;

"Congress complaining of the extortion of the people; the people of the improvidence of Congress; and the army of both;

"Our affairs requiring the most mature and systematic measures, and the urgency of occasions admitting only of temporizing expedients, and these expedients generating new difficulties;

"Congress from a defect of adequate statesmen more likely to fall into wrong measures and of less weight to enforce right ones, recommending plans to the several states for execution, and the states separately rejudging the expediency of such plans, whereby the same distrust of concurrent exertions that has damped the ardor of patriotic individuals must produce the same effect among the states themselves;

"An old system of finance discarded as incompetent to our necessities, an untried and precarious one substituted, and a total stagnation in prospect between the end of the former and the operation of the latter. . . . Believe me, sir, as things now stand, if the states do not vigorously proceed in collecting the old money and establishing funds for the credit of the new, that we are undone."[15]

Fearing interception by the enemy, Madison hesitated to entrust a letter of this kind to the post. Even after his death, the reference to "a defect of adequate statesmen" was considered so shocking that it was deleted from his published writings.[16] The criticism, though sharp, was by no means unjust. A few men of strength and standing were delegates at this time—General Philip

Schuyler, of New York, unjustly deposed from his army command; Robert R. Livingston, of New York, specialist in foreign affairs; Roger Sherman, shrewd, narrow-visioned Connecticut Yankee; Oliver Ellsworth, principal framer of the March 18 revenue plan; Thomas Burke, of North Carolina, able, vain, opinionated, who wrote state sovereignty into the Articles of Confederation. In a total attendance of less than thirty, the fingers of one hand would number the delegates who measured up to the standards of 1775. President Samuel Huntington, of Connecticut, glowed much less luminously than John Hancock, whom he resembled chiefly in the alacrity with which he failed to retire. "Damnation seize such sycophants" as keep him in office, the explosive John Mathews cried.[17]

Madison's criticism of the states for rejudging the plans of Congress was directed squarely at the Virginia legislature, which had just proclaimed a right either to approve or reject.[18] Using almost the language of this resolution, he gave fair notice that he did not intend to be subservient to the legislature to which he owed his office.

In these opening days of his congressional service Madison sensed the vital connection between financial power and political power in general—the first producing the second, and the loss of the first resulting in the destruction of the second. All powerful in the early days of the Revolution, the national assembly had undergone a total change. As long as Congress exercised an indefinite right of emitting money on the credit of their constituents, Madison observed to Jefferson, "They had the whole wealth and resources of the continent within their command, and could go on with their affairs independently and as they pleased." With the passage, in September, 1779, of a resolution to print no more federal money, this power was "entirely given up, and they are now as dependent on the states as the King of England is on the Parliament." Washington but a few weeks later described the same transformation without probing for its cause: "I see one head gradually changing into thirteen. . . . I see the powers of Congress declining too fast for the consequence and respect which is due to them as the grand representative body of America, and am fearful of the consequences."[19]

This fact of early congressional power, followed by a decline into impotence, has been ignored by those who look upon the Continental Congress as a mere advisory body to thirteen separately independent states, possessing no common sovereignty. To Madison and Washington, the United States in 1780 was a four-year-old nation disintegrating into thirteen parts because of the declining powers of its central government.[20] Madison's ability to see this determined the whole course of his congressional career. He would work at all times to support national dignity and prerogatives, against undermining attacks at home and abroad. He would search for means to restore the lost powers of Congress, if possible by asserting them as a matter of right, otherwise by new grants from their constituents. Without sacrificing the legitimate interests of his own state, he would not hesitate to resist and criticize the narrow views of a state legislature which had power to recall or supersede him. He would stand for the interests of the country as a whole.

CHAPTER II

AT THE VIRGINIA TABLE

No GREAT stir was created when Madison took his place at the Virginia table in the lofty room which formed the meeting place of Congress. In ultimate bearing on the perpetuation of the Union, his entry into that body warranted Bancroft's placing of it among the great events of the Revolution. Those present had no such thought. As competent and patriotic Charles Thomson read his credentials, Madison may have glanced from him to James Searle, of Pennsylvania. Perhaps they still showed marks of the little meeting described by the French minister four days earlier: "We saw, some weeks ago, a delegate and the Secretary of Congress attack each other with canes in open Senate, wound each other in the face, and on the morrow peaceably retake their seats."[1]

Monday was an unexciting day after the crucial monetary decision of Saturday. Madison's onetime teacher, William C. Houston, followed it up with a resolution asking the states to revise the laws which made Continental currency a legal tender for debt. This, Madison thought, foreshadowed a proposal to repay loans according to the state of depreciation at the time they were made. Nobody should cheat his neighbor or be cheated.

On the following day the destined-to-be-famous Olmstead Case came before Congress. Pennsylvania had defied the act of Congress which allowed an appeal from state admiralty courts to a federal court of appeals, in cases of captures at sea. This was no time to antagonize a powerful state, so Congress rejected Thomas Burke's committee report that Pennsylvania be charged with the amount of the federal court award and costs of appeal. Madison voted against Olmstead, for Pennsylvania. He would have been astonished beyond measure had somebody told him that three decades later he, as President of the United States, would enforce this same award to Gideon Olmstead by a show of force against

22

the resisting state, after the original appeal had been affirmed in the United States Supreme Court.[2]

The federal and Pennsylvania governments were on bad terms generally. Under a resolve adopted on December 3, 1779, Congress was to leave Philadelphia at the end of April and go to ———. It would have been easy enough for sardonic critics to fill in the blank, but there was doubt whether Congress could do so. The majority for removal had been produced by a combination of Northerners who wanted to move Congress north and Southerners who wanted to move it south. Some wished to escape the amazing expense of a city where "the devil was with all his emissaries let loose" to ruin money, as Delegate Floyd put it. Pennsylvania officials were jealous of a federal body exercising authority superior to their own. Life too was a trifle insecure in the City of Brotherly Love. Political factions rioted in the streets. Men died by gunfire when a mob laid siege to the home of Delegate James Wilson because he had acted as attorney for Quakers accused of treason. Some members felt as the French minister did that "a rich commercial city offering the most frequent opportunities for pleasure and dissipation is not suitable to the representatives of an infant republic which can sustain itself only by economy, activity and application to work."[3]

Now, however, General Clinton's landing in South Carolina made it impossible to take Congress south, so Griffin moved to repeal the resolution to leave Philadelphia. Madison helped to defeat his colleague's motion, thereby letting it be known, two days after his entry, that he was thinking and acting for himself. He helped later to defeat every specific motion to move Congress northward, the result being that it remained where it was.[4]

On the third day of Madison's service he was elected a member of the Board of Admiralty, a body set up three months earlier to replace the Marine Committee of Congress. Consisting of two delegates and three paid commissioners, it just matched, in numbers, the five ships that still remained in the shrinking United States Navy. But with two commissioners declining to serve, and Delegate Forbes of Maryland on his deathbed, it had been unable to produce a quorum since March 4. No doubt Madison was named because a new member of Congress was a convenient victim, but his belief in the need of sea power, to halt the movements of enemy troops by water, made him receptive.[5]

On the board Madison found himself with Commissioner Francis Lewis and Delegate William Ellery, of Rhode Island. The latter was a congenial spirit, much given to the kind of rough humor Madison had indulged in when writing pornographic poems for the American Whig Society at Princeton. Their first report demanded "that the flag of the United States shall be protected from insult" in neutral harbors. The words were a foretaste of Madison's ceaseless emphasis on national dignity.

Next came the problem of completing new ships to recoup the losses, by storm and enemy action, which had almost swept that same flag off the sea. The *Saratoga* was out of the slip but had no fittings. The *Bourbon* was close to launching, lacking only a bit of rigging, but the eastern naval office was still closer to its last shilling. Then there was the great naval headache, the 74-gun *America,* which had been on the stocks in New Hampshire since 1777. Lewis, Ellery and Madison reported that failure to complete these ships would lead to their destruction by weather or the enemy. They asked that three hundred hogsheads of sugar and rum, held by the Continental agent in Boston, be sold to finance them. Twenty hogsheads of sugar and a bit from wine sales was all that Congress voted them.[6]

Thus matters stood when the Marquis de Lafayette returned from France with the electrifying news that a French fleet and army were on their way to America. The Admiralty Board members promptly called on the Chevalier de la Luzerne and reported his "earnest wish" that the 74-gun *America* be completed. A congressional committee which discussed military co-operation with the minister brought back the same request. But there's many a slip 'twixt the ship and the dip. It would be a fine thing, Madison's group hinted to Luzerne, if France bought the unlaunched *America* and completed it with cannon, rigging and sailors. Luzerne fell in with this but his government replied that it was easier to put cannon and sailors on a vessel in France than to find space for their shipment to America. Renewing their request for sugar and rum Ellery and Madison finally obtained fifty hogs-heads of the former to sweeten the work on the *America*. The *Bourbon* was left to rot.[7]

By this time Madison had enough of being a half-time member of Congress and full-time assistant secretary of a nonexistent navy. On June 6 he resigned from the Board of Admiralty, but not from the 74-gun ship. Almost a year later, following Spain's entry into the war, he proposed that the still landbound leviathan be sold to that unpopular near ally. By this means Congress might get back the sixty thousand specie dollars that had been put into the mon-ster and avoid spending forty thousand more to finish it. Con-gress tacked both ways. It authorized the sale to Spain, then ordered the ship completed and appointed John Paul Jones cap-tain of it. Another year passed. The *America*, weathered like New Hampshire granite, was still on the Portsmouth ways, unrigged, uncannoned and unmanned. Then came a bit of good luck. The huge French warship *La Magnifique* was wrecked and beached in Boston harbor. Why not replace her with the *America?* Mad-ison wrote a resolution which Congress adopted the day it was offered:

"Whereas the *Magnifique*, a 74-gun ship belonging to the fleet of his Most Christian Majesty, commanded by the Marquis de Vaudreuil, has been lately lost by accident in the harbor of Boston, and Congress are desirous of testifying on this occasion to his Majesty the sense they entertain of his generous exertions in behalf of the United States: Resolved, That the agent of Marine be, and he is hereby, instructed to present the *America*, a 74-gun ship, in the name of the United States, to the Chevalier de la Luzerne, for the service of his Most Christian Majesty."

To Edmund Randolph, Madison wrote: "Independent of the motive of gratitude it was certain that our resources could not launch the ship before the winter; that before the spring she would be scarcely worth launching." A ship on the stocks, however, was better than one on the rocks. New Hampshire carpenters bit their teeth into French silver, and their gimlets into pine. *L'Amérique,* thundering the cannon of *La Magnifique,* took her dual place in the French line of battle and in bright pages of American history—a monument to our generosity toward an ally.[8]

If Madison did not succeed in building a navy, he at least helped give it a seal. There is no actual proof that he was the author of the device submitted by the board and adopted by Congress on May 4, but he was less buried in routine than other members, and the action was suggested by the appointment of his friend Houston to report a great seal for the United States. The naval seal, used until 1798, presented "thirteen bars mutually supporting each other, alternate red and white, in a blue field, and surmounting an anchor proper. The crest a ship under sail. The motto *Sustentans et Sustentatus*. The legend U.S.A. Sigil Naval." The Latin motto is almost a Madison signature.

Madison's retirement from the Board of Admiralty was timed to suit the convenience of Ellery, who had failed of re-election to Congress. His salary would cease when his successor arrived, and he needed $20,000 to replace a dead horse and pay his overdue board bill so that he could leave the city. But why leave when there were vacancies in the paid membership of the Admiralty Board? Ellery and Madison resigned from the board on the same day, and the former was re-elected to it as a salaried commissioner. Thus, as far back as 1780, the institution of the lame-duck congressman came into being.[9]

Madison and his fellow Virginians were beginning by this time to have their share of money trouble—nothing so serious, perhaps, as that caused by the death of a horse, but impressive enough. At Richmond, Madison received £2,000 in Virginia currency, amounting to $6,666 ⅔ in Continental money. It was worth exactly £32/5, specie, when he got it, and amounted to $166 under the forty-for-one devaluation plan. It was supposed to hold that value. But as soon as people heard that money had been stabilized in this manner, they took it as proof that it had not been stabilized, so down it went—sixty for one within a few days, seventy-five for one in August, one hundred for one in December, two hundred twenty for one in March of 1781, while everybody raged against the Tories and speculators whose wicked cunning was responsible for the calamity.[10]

Being a foresighted youth, Madison waited barely two weeks before moving to replenish his vanishing pile of paper. Starving delegates, he found, could obtain warrants on the federal Treasury, the amount to be charged to the states and settled for some day. So Madison on April 5 asked for a warrant for $8,000. Apparently Griffin was in trouble too, for they took instead a warrant for $15,000 and divided the money. At the same time they found a business house rash enough to take their warrant for $30,000 on the Virginia auditor. In the midst of poverty they were rolling in riches—$22,500 apiece, or about $375 in hard cash, minus $5,000 which Madison lent to Walker. Two months later the Virginia delegates disposed of a draft on the auditor for $23,312. By the end of summer they were broke, but Madison was better off than Jones. He had paid his board bill.

The delegation by this time was changing. Cyrus Griffin was elected a judge of admiralty in Virginia. James Henry went home for a visit and resigned when the state was unable to finance his return. Theodorick Bland, taking Griffin's place, arrived in Philadelphia at the end of August, bringing his gay and beautiful young wife, Martha Dangerfield Bland, and $66,666 ⅔ which looked even more attractive. Then, succeeding Walker, back to Congress came Meriwether Smith, known for his enmity to the faction headed by Samuel Adams and the Virginia Lees. "Fiddle-head" or "The Bass Viol," this group called him, a tribute to the peculiar physical graces with which nature endowed him.

Bachelor Madison got along better than his fellows. He lent Jones $10,000 to enable him and his wife to go back to Virginia and gave part of his own remittances to Bland. The latter, blessed with the socially ambitious Martha, was soon crying that his funds "evaporated like smoke" and left him "without the means of buying a dinner or . . . a bait of oats for my horses." Lacking relief, the delegates told their governor, they must sell their personal possessions or return home.[11]

All of this bore less resemblance to finance than to importing and exporting print paper. It was also fine mental discipline. The delegates were paid in Virginia currency—pounds, shillings and pence. Their expenses were reckoned in Continental currency based on Spanish dollars (ninety cents to the dollar) and their purchases were in Pennsylvania pounds, shillings and pence of a different value from Virginia's. The values of all these currencies changed from day to day and the final settlement was based on the level of depreciation at the time of each receipt or disbursement. This was what led to adoption of the decimal system, which Jefferson said would cause people's minds to weaken for lack of exercise.

On the country at large, the money collapse had the effect of an unplanned social revolution. Virginia approved the plan of March 18, but refused to repeal the law making the old Continental money legal tender. Instead, the legislature issued £2,000,000 in state currency without a penny's worth of taxes for its redemption. The result was that when Continental money stood at sixty to one against specie, Virginia currency slumped to forty for one against Continental. One Spanish dollar would pay a $2,400 debt. Huge farm mortgages were discharged with the price of a barrel of tobacco. Continental money stood at five hundred for one when Virginia finally outlawed it as legal tender. The state's own currency continued to discharge debts, at face value, until the assembly devalued it late in 1781 at one thousand for one. The *one* was but a new certificate at which the people shuddered.[12]

Americans looking back on the monetary inflation of the Revolutionary period are prone to think of it in federal terms, blaming Congress for issuing too much money and charging lack of faith in its devaluation. Madison and others of that period placed the main responsibility upon the states, first for refusing to levy taxes with which to redeem the federal currency, or to authorize Congress to levy them; then for issuing state money with even less regard to its value; and finally for passing or retaining legal tender laws with no other object than the wholesale wiping out of debt. Here is the genesis of the clauses in the United States Constitution forbidding the states to issue bills of credit or pass laws impairing the obligation of contracts.

Congressmen's horses might go hungry,[13] creditors might be reduced to bankruptcy, but the real effect of the money crisis was felt in the Continental Army. It virtually paralyzed Washing-

ton's effort to carry on the war. For Madison this was the paramount concern, both as an American patriot and as a probable
defendant in a treason trial if the war was lost. Two weeks after
he entered Congress, word arrived from General Washington that
the enemy was about to send 2,500 men southward by sea,
presumably to reinforce the siege of Charleston. Having only
10,400 men in his own army and enlistments expiring for 2,800
of these, he dared do no more than dispatch Major Henry Lee's
corps of partisans to the South and order the Maryland and Delaware lines to be ready to follow. Madison and John Mathews
must have been winning the war every evening at Mrs. House's,
for when a motion was offered to approve these measures for reinforcing the Southern army, the South Carolinian offered an
amendment, seconded by Madison, to make it read "immediately
reinforcing." That would have been a virtual order to Washington to carry out his tentative plan without delay. Six Northern
states voted it down. Within a few days Washington sent word
of so formidable a threat in New Jersey that he had ordered the
return of Lee.[14]

Lighthorse Harry's well-mounted guerrillas were camped on
the Philadelphia commons at the time, and Congress flared into
sectional battle over them. Northern delegates, moved by the
menace in New Jersey, upheld the sacred orders of the commander in chief. Southerners wanted to keep Lee moving south. June
1 brought a climax. Rivington's *Gazette* came in from New York
with what Madison called "a positive and explicit account of the
surrender of Charleston," although, he added to Jefferson, that
publisher's notorious character for lying left some hope that it was
fictitious. On that day, too, a letter from Governor Rutledge of
South Carolina was read in Congress, desperately appealing for
help. It was referred to Carolinians Kinloch and Burke, and Madison—the Virginian's first nontrivial committee assignment.

These three had no doubt about what to do. They offered a
resolve that Major Lee proceed immediately to South Carolina with
his corps. This was adopted, then rescinded and modified. Washington was notified that Congress desired Lee to proceed to that
state unless it would "counteract or embarrass" his plans. The

commander in chief stood by his order, but the Board of War, dominated by ex-members of the Conway Cabal, failed to carry it out. Washington then sent Congress General Nathanael Greene's description of a battle near Springfield, New Jersey, a bare two days' march from Philadelphia. The delegates instantly issued an order—not to Washington, but to the Board of War: Send Lee's corps back to New Jersey.[15]

It was in this period that Congress made its biggest military blunder of the war—the appointment of General Horatio Gates as independent commander of the Southern army, exempt from the control of General Washington. The Kinloch-Burke-Madison committee provided the occasion for this action, by moving that a day be set aside to consider the state of the Southern department. The Gates appointment, however, was planned before Madison entered Congress, aided by the general's astuteness in sending a plan of Southern defense to Southern delegates. Unanimous support was given by panic-stricken Southerners and by Northern delegates who worshiped Gates as the hero of the Battle of Saratoga, which he entered just in time to receive Burgoyne's sword. The final driving force behind it was confirmation of the surrender of Charleston.[16]

This critical state of affairs—disaster in the South piled on danger in the North, and a broken supply system—was debated at many a dinner table as well as on the floor of Congress. New members were given a round of dinners in the get-acquainted process. "Mr. Maderson and Mr. Killosh dined with us," Samuel Holten wrote in his diary on March 30, thereby indicating that James Madison and Francis Kinloch, wealthy young South Carolina planter, were guests of the Massachusetts delegates in the Dolley-Clark boardinghouse at the corner of Chestnut and Front streets.[17] It must have been a strange encounter—these two eager newcomers, zealous to build up the country's military power, and their New England hosts who reflected all the fears and jealousies of Samuel Adams, their temporarily absent leader. Holten himself, mediocre and virtuous, was a silent foil for the scholarly polish and biting wit of ex-schoolmaster James Lovell, chairman of the Committee of Foreign Correspondence, who spoke French and hated Frenchmen. They were united, these men of Massachusetts, by their quiet courage and their fears. Fear of the army, fear of Washington, fear of the French, fear of spending, fear of a government strong enough to do its work, yet with a completely patriotic devotion to the cause of liberty and independence—that was the New England paradox in the latter days of the Revolution.

The center of Philadelphia society, in 1780, was the French legation, a great house owned by John Dickinson, set in the center of a grassy square between the built-up western section of the city and the public buildings beyond. The Chevalier de la Luzerne, who succeeded Minister Gerard in 1779, had proved his diplomatic mettle at Munich, in helping to keep France out of a continental war (and therefore free to help America) during the crisis over the Bavarian succession. His military background—aide de camp, colonel of dragoons—served him well in dealing with American affairs. A wise and tolerant man, friendly to America, with as much friendship for republican government as was safe for a Bourbon diplomat, he wielded tremendous influence over Congress. He won this influence by offering sound advice with deference, backed by the decisive fact of America's military and financial dependence on France. Without making the faintest suggestion of a threat, he knew how to let congressional committees know what difficulties America would face if the anti-Gallic faction succeeded in weakening the alliance. He was ever ready to open his expense account to Americans who wielded a friendly journalistic pen—Dr. Cooper, of Boston, 4,800 livres a year; fifty guineas at a time to Thomas Paine; 1,200 livres to Hugh Henry Brackenridge, Madison's classmate at Princeton. If delegates hesitated to tell him all the secrets of Congress, 6,000 livres a year to Delegate and Brigadier-General John Sullivan would fill the gap.[18] Luzerne knew the value of his weekly dinners to groups of delegates—Southern delegates one week, Northern the next. Even before the French army arrived, Philadelphia was bright with the uniforms of overseas volunteers and the silk and lace of diplomatic attachés, while afterward——

"I am taken up by the gay scenes of Philadelphia ... the balls at the French minister. . . . Oh my dear! Such a swarm of French beaux ... marquises, counts, viscounts, barons and chevaliers." So rhapsodized Martha Bland to her sister-in-law as she told of her zestful entry "into the dissipations of the place" and of her greatest favorite, the Chevalier de la Luzerne, "one of the most amiable, the politest, easiest behaved men I ever knew." Inquired a colleague: "Are the French and Spanish ministers still at Mrs. Bland's feet?"[19]

The Spanish "minister" was an observer, sent to report on American territorial ambitions toward the Mississippi. So wonderful were his Havana cigars that congressional delegates lost their taste for any other kind of smoking.[20] Public officials, merchants and women in billowy silk and muslin came to the concerts and balls which Luzerne, who hated music and did not dance, gave on alternate weeks in his spacious home. In it was one of the marvels of Philadelphia—an imported iron bed, verminproof. The marvel was no less when, to the roll of the greatest clap of thunder ever heard in Philadelphia, the bed was melted one night by a bolt of lightning, the house shattered, and Luzerne—— With true foresight, he was sleeping that night in another bed, in Williamsburg, Virginia.[21]

Then there were the democratic social functions at the College of Philadelphia—theatrical performances at which shoemakers' wives and members of Congress, ship chandlers and Presidents' wives, fought and tore their way into the inadequate hall. Not all the handholds of three gallant escorts, François de Marbois and Louis Otto, the French *petits ministres,* and Don Francisco Rendon, could drag Mrs. Bland and Miss Shippen through one such mob. What sights to remember! Men climbed on the heads of others to get in. One lady lost her cap, another her drop curls, another her shoes. They saw a chief justice's lady seize an obstructing gentleman by the queue of his hair and break her fan on him. Another lady "full as large as Betty Wommack" was pulled through a trap door no bigger than a chariot window. "Oh, Fanny! What would I give to have you in a corner at some of those scenes of high life below stairs."

The Marquis de Chastellux wrote of enjoyable talk with Delegates Madison and "Flowy" at one of Luzerne's dinners for the Southern members. The name "Flowy" has long been cudgeled over. It was of course Colonel Floyd, of New York, whom Luzerne described as of the party of the South.[22] Madison was at his best, socially, at a small dinner party of congenial guests. He could feel at ease with some women—with honest and friendly Mrs. Trist, with little Kitty Floyd as she approached and passed the age of fourteen. He fitted no better into the ballroom scene at the French legation than into the good opinion of Martha Bland. With her beautiful moth wings still fluttering in front of the screened French candle, Mrs. Bland described Madison and all of his Virginia colleagues of the day except her husband. She wrote to Fanny Tucker:

"Virginia is most curiously represented—taking *one* out. Here are the completest trio I ever saw. Mr. Madison, a gloomy, stiff creature, they say is clever in Congress, but out of it he has nothing engaging or even bearable in his manners—the most unsociable creature in existence. Mr. Jones, who looks like a Presbyterian priest, his complexion as sable as his habit; he always wears black. Your cousin M[eriwether] Smith with all the grimace of a baboon, and exactly like one in figure. I often laugh at Mr. B——d and tell him it is absolutely necessary he should display all his pleasing qualities to make up for the amazing deficiencies of his brethren."

To which one may add the Chevalier de la Luzerne's appraisal of Theodorick Bland—"a braggart, having pretensions to eloquence . . . little character . . . vain, imprudent"—and feel no doubt as to how he got that way. The gay Martha froze Madison up inside, but from the same social set came Tom Shippen's verdict: "Madison is charming." The diffident stripling who entered Congress in 1780 was not so different from the man of seventy-seven whom Margaret Bayard Smith visited in 1828—one whose talk was "so rich in sentiments and facts, so enlivened by anecdotes and epigrammatic remarks, so frank and confidential as to opinions on men and measures, that it had an interest and charm which the conversation of few men now living could have." Yet, Mrs. Smith added, "This entertaining, interesting and communicative personage, had a single stranger or indifferent person been present, would have been mute, cold and repulsive."[23] A social defect, no doubt, but those who drew it into operation testified to their own deficiencies.

CHAPTER III

The Southern Campaign

James Madison had a brilliant flair for diplomacy. He had creative wisdom in governmental finance and in promotion of the general welfare. So in Congress he devoted himself for many months to military matters.

This was not wholly a case of the shoemaker sticking to the gunsmith's anvil. Congress went beyond its province only when it interfered with military operations. Both the organization and support of the army depended on this handful of congressional delegates, acting either as a national legislature or as a council drawing out the resources of the states. Speed and certainty in such work could win battles. Lack of them could lose the war.

Three weeks after Madison entered Congress, a committee was appointed to reside near Washington's headquarters and reform the army supply system. Its chairman, General Philip Schuyler, was the most competent man on military affairs in a Congress which had ousted him from his army command for alleged incompetence. John Mathews, of South Carolina, tried so hard to reform Congress that he seemed a good man to reform the army. Nathaniel Peabody, of New Hampshire, won third place with a demand, apparently plagiarized from the twentieth century, that government payrolls be purged of countless civilian employees "who appear in swarms like locusts [and are] rioting upon the blood and treasures of the virtuous citizens (if any such there be) in these United States."[1]

Peabody was not so far wrong. An economy bloc in Congress, to avoid paying salaries, had put governmental buying on a commission basis—the higher the price, the larger the commission. Nine thousand men, the French minister reported to his government, were engaged in depredations in the management of munitions, forage, clothing, hospitals, tents, barracks and wagons.

34

Profiting enormously, they "devoured the substance of the army, while it was tormented by famine and excessive want."[2] That almost equaled Washington's army—ten military wasps to each nine locusts.

With French aid coming, Washington wanted action of a different kind—fill up the regiments and feed the men. The committee was all right, in personnel. Give it power (he wrote for the "private ear" of Joseph Jones) to draw out men and supplies of every kind and give its sanction to military operations inside or outside the United States. Such a proposal—similar to giving emergency war powers to the President today—was enough to fill Congress with terror. This burst out, with anger added, when the Headquarters Committee, seeking to aid Washington's move, was rash enough to use the phrase "dictatorial powers" in asking for them. The debate on the proposal was secret—so secret that the only record of it is the one Minister Luzerne promptly sent to France. Let such a committee, cried Burke, Houston, Lovell and others, come within the already too great influence of Washington, and it will place Congress and the thirteen states at the mercy of the army. Was not Washington too virtuous for that? Why, said the objectors, the more virtuous he was, the greater the cause for alarm.[3]

Madison felt no shaking of the earth under military boots. It was on this occasion that, with Ellery, he composed what William C. Rives described as "a joint and playful letter" to the Committee at Headquarters. This was no doubt a lampoon on the subject of dictatorship, but hardly one based on alarm or hostility, for Madison, unlike Ellery, voted consistently to strengthen the committee. He praised the Pennsylvania legislature right at this time for investing the executive "with a dictatorial authority from which nothing but the *lives* of their citizens are exempted" and hoped the resulting good would offset the risk of the experiment. The weakness of Washington's army was what impressed him. If French forces did come, he told Jefferson, American inability to co-operate with them would add to our distress and disgrace.[4]

"Scarce a week, and sometimes scarce a day," he declared, "but brings us a most lamentable picture from headquarters. The army

are a great part of the time on short allowance, at some times without any at all, and constantly depending on the precarious fruits
of momentary expedients." A mutinous spirit was rampant, "engendered by hunger and want of pay"; and all Washington's endeavors "could not prevent an actual eruption of it in two Connecticut regiments, who assembled on the parade with their arms and
resolved to return home or satisfy their hunger by the power of
the bayonet."

Madison had a clear idea of the probable actions of the enemy.
Resisting an appeal from the Virginia legislature for Northern
troops to save the South from subjugation, he agreed that this was
Clinton's object but told Jefferson (June 6, 1780) that he could not
think it would be pursued at a risk of losing New York. The
enemy, he believed, would leave a strong garrison at Charleston
and carry back the rest of its forces. Washington within a week
gave the same prediction plus a warning. When the enemy united
its forces and attacked him, he would be compelled to retire toward
his main source of supply—Pennsylvania—instead of toward his
strongest defensive position, the Hudson highlands above New
York. That would mean the loss of West Point. Within the month
Clinton did return and Madison repeated his warnings to Virginia
that first thought must be given to central defense. Washington
"is weak in numbers beyond all suspicion," said Madison, "and
under as great apprehension from famine as from the enemy."[5]

The first need was for strength in government. "Certain I am,"
the commander in chief wrote to Joseph Jones, "that unless Congress speaks in a more decisive tone; unless they are vested with
powers . . . or assume them as a matter of right; and they and the
states . . . act with more energy . . . our cause is lost." Jones and
Madison saw no cheer on the federal side. Having frittered away
its powers to the states, the former replied, Congress would find it
very difficult to recover them. With Continental finance broken
down, the supply system disrupted and the former powers of
Congress dissipated, Madison saw no hope "but in the prompt and
vigorous supplies of the states."[6]

This was no mere generality. Printing no money, and getting
none from the states, Congress in the previous February had in-

stalled the "specs" system.[7] The states were called on for specific quantities of flour, salt, grain, hay, rum and other supplies, to be transported to army camps. There being no means of transport and no storage facilities, army provisions were now rotting, mildewing and being stolen wherever an effort had been made to collect them. Also, with the states doing the buying, the commission system was obsolete. Either the quartermaster and commissary staffs must be paid salaries or they would disintegrate.

Quartermaster General Nathanael Greene, high-strung, aggressive, blunt and uncompromising, had been angering Congress for months by combining offers to resign with demands for draft horses, storage warehouses, transportation agents, salaries for em-employees and other little luxuries. To get back at Greene, Congress put the framing of a new system largely in the hands of former Quartermaster General Thomas Mifflin, who had been fired after Washington said his management left the army no choice but to starve, dissolve or disperse. Mifflin was tied up with remnants of the Conway Cabal and—just to make it absolutely certain that the new system would be a bad one—he got his ideas for it from General Gates. The plan he submitted was so bad (Schuyler said it would "starve the army in ten days") that Congress was in a dilemma. It got out by referring the plan to the new Committee at Headquarters, which meant to Schuyler himself, under the eyes of Washington and Greene. Schuyler's plan reached Congress on June 17, and was immediately riddled with amendments.[8]

This was the state of affairs when General Greene asked Congress for an immediate explanation of the strange, new and unexpected doctrine, of which he had heard rumors, that he was to be held personally liable for the financial actions of his subordinates. His duty, he said, was to demand an accounting of all public money delivered to underagents, but if his best endeavors failed to secure it, the public must suffer the loss. No man, he declared, could safely be subject to a greater degree of responsibility, "nor would I hold the office a moment upon any other footing."[9]

This virtual ultimatum was referred to the veterans Ellsworth and Duane and the freshman Madison. Two days later the first two left for home. Livingston and newly returned Samuel Adams replaced them, but the change made Madison chairman of a crucially important committee. Writing its report, he made a microscopic review of financial accountability as practiced during the Revolution. He found it "essential to the public interest as well as incident to the nature of all offices entrusted with money for public uses, that those who exercise them should be accountable for its due application." This applied to agents, because their superior could and should require bond of them. He concluded with a resolution, adopted by Congress on July 24, holding Greene completely responsible, but promising such allowances as justice might require.

This was virtually a counterultimatum to Greene to back down or resign. Two days afterward, before he heard of this action, but with knowledge that the decision was coming, and disgusted with the reorganization of his department, he wrote a letter of resignation which nearly resulted in his summary discharge from the army. What he said sounds innocent enough today. He referred to Congress twice, as "administration." To any American revolutionist that word meant King George, Lord North and Parliament rolled into one. "What can have tempted him," wrote one delegate, "to treat Congress with sneer and sarcasm. He applies to them the odious term, Administration, and is so fond of the conceit as to repeat and reiterate his wit." Washington, meanwhile, was telling the Committee at Headquarters that a British move forced him to march toward the Hudson River and if Greene and his aides dropped out it would produce "such a scene of confusion and distress, that it will be impossible to remedy the evil."[10]

The Headquarters Committee, by this time, had entered the dispute over Greene's financial responsibility, expressing full approval of the stand he had taken. When Congress learned of this, its anger extended to the committee. Greene's resignation was accepted. The Headquarters Committee was censured. All that emerged unscathed was congressional dignity, and not much was left of that when Mathews replied to the resolution of censure. Approaching that "august body" with all deference, he ventured to submit a request—provided the committee's interference would not "retrench from the high prerogatives" of Congress—that a certain army officer be allowed to keep a favorite horse which had been taken by appraisement. Washington gave public notice of confidence in Greene by making him temporary commander of the main army.[11]

Throughout these developments, Madison's course was free of animus, but not of error. His report on Greene's financial liability took no account of the actual conditions under which the army was supplied. Subagents had to make instantaneous decisions, in remote places, often in violation of state laws, to save the army from disaster. Bonds were a drop of security in a bucket of risk. Greene was being asked to assume responsibility when he could not protect himself without injury to the country. What Madison and others failed to see was that fraud was a war cost, to be assumed by the government, not a risk to be borne by one man. With different associates on his committee, he might have given weight to Greene's side of the case. But Samuel Adams feared army officers and was a zealot for economy. Livingston, who affected friendship for Greene, was called a "snake in the grass" by the general's closest confidant in Congress.[12]

Showing balanced judgment, Madison helped to defeat a motion to reduce the quartermaster general's salary. He resisted a picayune decision that forage masters should not receive a ration of forage for their horses. When injured congressional pride swelled into a decision to recall the Headquarters Committee, he was one of five delegates who voted against the motion.[13]

Tension was added to the contest over Greene, but tension of a pleasing sort, by dramatic news which came from Washington in mid-July. A fleet, sighted off Providence, had answered private identity signals. The French were here. The cynical Lovell sneered his doubts; others waited expectantly for the confirmation which followed. Admiral de Ternay was at Newport with eight ships of the line, three frigates and two "bumketchers." Five thousand spick-and-span French regulars under the Count de Rochambeau came with them. The visitors brought diplomacy too, the art of thrilling a young nation with pride. Washington was to be honored and obeyed as a marshal of France. American officers of equal rank and date would have precedence over their allies. Here was national recognition.[14]

The coming of the French gave Madison his first chairmanship. He was to draft a reply to a gracious letter from Rochambeau, telling how New England militia rushed to block a British stab at his debarking forces. Madison threw himself into the writing of the letter. He praised the zeal of the French troops, the vigilance of their chief, the benevolence of their illustrious sovereign. Then he thought of the weakness of the American army, of the fact that Ternay could not take the sea until his belated second division arrived. What of that? "We persuade ourselves that sufficient amends will be made by the vigor of the combined operations and by the mutual emulation that must be felt by the allied troops fighting side by side." This carried him to a peroration:

"The citizens of the United States and the French nation, already bound together by the ties of interest, of honor and the most solemn engagements, want nothing to perfect their coalition, but the endearing circumstance of having mutually contributed to acquire for each other the glory of triumphing over a ruthless and powerful enemy to the rights of mankind."

Madison wrote this fulsome eulogy with shrewd knowledge of the glow it would produce in Gallic breasts. Delivered in duplicate to Luzerne, and sent in translation to Versailles, it might enable Benjamin Franklin to pull an extra 5,000,000 livres out of Louis XVI's war chest. Congress judged it with Anglo-Saxon acerbity. It was discarded for a perfunctory resolution acknowledging the vigilance and prudence of the French commanders and approving the spirit and discipline of their troops.[15]

Madison's fear that the American army would be unable to cooperate with the French was verified. Washington sent the advancing Pennsylvania militia back home lest they "come foward to starve." He lacked provisions for even half of the intended Franco-America operations. Congress had named an efficient man, Timothy Pickering, to succeed Greene, but no QMG could do anything with a supply system (the "specifics") which Washington described as "the most uncertain, expensive and injurious that could be devised."[16]

In Philadelphia, congressional delegates mopped their brows. "The wather," John Folsom, of New Hampshire, wrote on August 15, "hase bin so hot that when out of Congress we have had full imploymant to find air enough to breathe in." News from the South made them mop harder. Gates was short of food and fodder. Well, let King Louis help! Madison joined in ordering the drawing of $100,000 in bills on Franklin, to be sold in the South for supplies, then sent to Paris and made good by the French treasury. The rich taxpayers of France could mop their brows too.

On the last day of August came news, big and bad, from the congressional military idol in the South. Young officers on mud-lathered horses arrived with letters from Gates. In phrases of excitement and despair, the hero of Saratoga told of the utter rout of his army at Camden, South Carolina. The militia, untrained, half-starved, had run away; the Continentals were cut to pieces; Smallwood, Gist and Armand were dead, De Kalb wounded and a prisoner. Gates had gone to Hillsborough, North Carolina, to ask the legislature to help raise another army.[17]

A numbed Congress soon began to recover. John Mathews tried to give Washington dictatorial power, but "the rancor of these demagogs" was such that his proposals "were in the lump rejected." De Kalb died, but Smallwood, Gist and Armand rose sufficiently from the dead to write descriptions of the fighting—especially the orderly resistance of the Maryland Continentals—after Gates dashed away to raise a new army.

"We have the comfort to find from every successive account from the southward," Madison wrote to Edmund Pendleton within a fortnight, "that the late unfortunate affair in that quarter, although truly distressing, is by no means so fatal as was at first held up to us." The shame of the militia, he believed, would lead them to extraordinary exertions.[18]

As nerves relaxed, some men in Congress began to do a bit of figuring. The battle of Camden was fought on August 16. General Gates wrote on that date from Charlotte, on the twentieth from Hillsborough. Seventy miles traveled on the day of the battle, two hundred miles in four days—where did that put him in relation to the fleeing militia? The idol with feet of clay wore seven-league boots. Delegate William Sharpe arrived from North Carolina with his state's demand that Gates be ousted. Congress ordered a court of inquiry on his conduct and, eating a second mess of crow, directed Washington to name a new commander.[19]

At this moment there came a great emotional drawing together of all men loyal to the Revolution. The treason of Benedict Arnold came like a thunderbolt from West Point. Like everybody else, Madison reacted with vigor to the treasonable plot and approved the prompt hanging of Major André as a spy. "Clinton made a frivolous attempt to save him," he wrote to Pendleton on October 10, "by pleading the passport granted by Arnold. He submitted to his fate in a manner that showed him to be worthy of a better one." Arnold himself, "although he may for the present escape an ignominious death, must lead an ignominious life, which if any of his feelings remain will be a sorer punishment." Such thoughts, however, were byplay. The answer to Arnold must be given in gunfire and generalship in the South.

On that point, some reverse English from Madison's earlier course came into play. Thanks to the upheaval in the quartermaster department, Washington had just the right man available for the southern command—Nathanael Greene, a general, as his chief described him, of abilities, bravery and coolness, of comprehensive knowledge, fortitude and resources.[20] Appointed, he tactfully informed Congress that he was coming to Philadelphia for a consultation, and was confirmed in his new position three days after his arrival. Transferring to him the powers previously given to Gates, Congress made one exception. He was to be "subject to the control of the Commander-in-Chief." On the heels of this action came word that an enemy fleet with two thousand soldiers on board had dropped down toward Sandy Hook, en route to either Virginia or North Carolina. There was no mistaking that sign. The war was moving toward a Southern crisis. To clinch the proof of it, a letter was then on its way to Madison telling him that a British force under General Leslie had already landed in Chesapeake Bay.

This renewed emphasis upon southern operations brought three men forward in Congress—Mathews, Sharpe, of the Carolinas, and Madison. Mathews was the only member left of a standing committee appointed in 1779 to correspond with the commanding officer in the South and report defense measures for that region. Madison and Sharpe were added to the committee on October 23, 1780. All three lived in the House-Trist house, where they could work together. All were heartily in favor of General Greene's appointment.[21] For many months, after this, they were in constant touch with Greene, giving him all the information they could scrape up about military affairs and general conditions in the North.

It fell to Madison's lot to tell Greene of the mutiny in the Pennsylvania line which began in New Jersey on New Year's Day, 1781. Written at a time of anger and excitement, his letter is notable for its calm description of the conduct and grievances of the mutineers. Two officers had fallen victims to their fury and fear was felt because many of the troops were foreigners or deserters from the British army. His emphasis, however, was on the orderliness of their march toward Philadelphia, their determination to secure satisfaction, the decorum with which they treated General Wayne while holding him captive, their instantaneous seizure of two enemy agents who arrived "with a flattering invitation to them to take sanctuary from their miseries" by joining General Clinton. The grievances Madison listed—forcible detention beyond terms of enlistment, lack of food and clothing, long arrearages of pay— made it a miracle that only two regiments revolted. A committee of Congress, meeting with the mutineers, was close to a settlement of the grievances, and Clinton's two agents were slated to be hanged the day before he wrote.[22]

The Mathews-Sharpe-Madison committee left Greene in no doubt about its approval of his conduct of the Southern campaign— his skillful fadeaways before the superior forces of Cornwallis, his sudden advances that threw the enemy off balance. Mathews and Madison put through a resolution, written by the former, informing the general that his military measures "afford such proofs of his judgment, vigilance and firmness, as recommend him to the entire approbation of Congress." Toward the fallen Gates, a fellow Virginian, Madison showed no forgiveness. Just a week after this praise of Greene, Gates wrote to Jefferson that a motion to cancel his court-martial "has been several times made in Congress, but once to my astonishment was prevented from being carried by a Mr. Madison of this state, a gentleman I do not know, and who I am satisfied does not know me." In that one sentence can be seen the root of most of the trouble Gates caused and suffered in the Revolution. He could not think of public policy except in personal terms. Madison's intolerant feeling toward incompetent generals was impersonal. It reflected his patriotism and the fact that he was a revolutionist whose life or liberty depended on the outcome of bloody battles.[23]

Madison's appointment to the Southern committee came on the day of a great tonic to American hopes. Two words were on all lips —King's Mountain. Nine hundred North Carolina militiamen, commanded by five colonels, had surrounded and killed or captured virtually the whole of eleven hundred British regulars and Tories. Expresses, postmen, lawyers on horseback and farmers in carts, carried the news from town to town. On the back of Madison's letter telling Joseph Jones about Arnold's treason, one may read today an account of this battle penned by some unknown person (initials W.S.) as the missive was being forwarded.[24] The news in reality barely crept along. A victory won on October 7 became known to Congress on the twenty-third. But there was nothing slow about the sweep of joy that attended it.

In appearance, and in many later interpretations, this victory verified Madison's prediction that the Carolina militia would seek to redeem itself. But these men who won at King's Mountain were no untrained citizens suddenly sprung to arms. They were flint-and-iron mountaineers just back from a merciless war of extermination against the Cherokee Indians, and showed their gentleness by hanging or flogging the Tories under Colonel Ferguson, who surrendered to them. The victory, Madison believed, would thwart a junction between Cornwallis and Leslie and thus hamper an invasion of Virginia. But he saw little cheer in the general condition of the American army. Winter stores must be built up before roads became impassable. "But instead of magazines being laid in, our army is living from hand to mouth. . . . How a total dissolution of it can be prevented in the course of the winter is . . . utterly inexplicable, unless the states unanimously make a vigorous and speedy effort to form magazines for the purpose." At that same moment messengers were carrying Washington's warning to the states that the army was dwindling to nothing, the men were almost naked, there were no supplies for the winter and nothing but gloomy reports from the officers collecting them.

Madison believed that Cornwallis intended a pincers movement based on Charleston and Portsmouth. He thought the British defeat at King's Mountain would cause Clinton to build up his Carolina forces rather than strengthen those in Virginia. This seemed to be verified when Leslie's troops were withdrawn from Chesapeake Bay and taken south. The British could regain their footing in Virginia at any time, Madison remarked to Pendleton, "but every retrograde step they take towards Charleston proves fatal to their general plan."[25]

The Mathews-Sharpe-Madison committee sent word to Greene of all the enemy sailings from Sandy Hook. "Arnold at the head of his motley crew" was on his way, followed in a fortnight by another force of twenty-five hundred sea-borne redcoats. In return they heard of the dire condition of the defensive forces in Carolina —the regulars so naked and destitute (those from Virginia literally naked, Greene repeated) that no more than half were fit for any duty; part of the country stripped by the enemy, the rest of it so pillaged and plundered by American militia that it could produce nothing for the regulars. Charleston, the committee thought, was Arnold's destination. Rumor corrected this to Portsmouth, from near which, on the very day Madison was reporting a probable landing, the West Point traitor marched unopposed to burn the city of Richmond. Among the papers given to the torch were records of the governor's council during his membership on it.[26]

Madison's belief that Arnold would land farther south had nothing wrong with it except an underestimate of the enemy's capacity for blundering. Until Virginia was subdued, Cornwallis wrote to Clinton, his hold on the Carolinas would be difficult, if not precarious. Washington saw, on the contrary, that predatory invasions of Virginia meant little, compared with the danger from

British conquest of the states to the southward, and he appealed to Governor Jefferson to let nothing divert him from reinforcement of the Southern army. Both Jefferson and the Virginia delegates in Congress upheld this policy, even when they saw marauding raiders overrunning their country with torch and sword. Madison, indeed, upheld it so strongly that it led him and Mathews into another of their periodic efforts to order Washington to carry out policies which were actually his own. Mathews moved on November 21 that Washington be "informed" that he ought to take personal command of the Southern army, that he be "required" to order Pennsylvania troops south and "directed" to take measures for immediate Franco-American co-operation. This lay without action until the first day of 1781, when it was recommitted. Madison then moved that the commander in chief be informed of the desire of Congress "that he should immediately make such a distribution of the forces under his command, including those of our allies under the Count de Rochambeau, as will most effectually counteract the views of the enemy and support the Southern states." This was altered to a request that Washington give his opinion on a shift of French troops to Virginia, and passed.

The difficulty, Madison well knew, was not hesitancy on Washington's part to aid the South. It was "the want of subsistence, arms and clothing which results from the want of money." That, he told Pendleton next day, was the real cause of alarm. To know the cause gave little comfort to Virginia, where an agitated legislature under the leadership of Patrick Henry was taking steps which indicated lack of confidence in its delegates in Congress.

CHAPTER IV

Spyglass on Arnold

Deep uneasiness was felt by Madison in the fall of 1780, as he heard of enemy landings in Virginia and of the week-after-week failure of the legislature to assemble. Such tardiness, he declared to Joseph Jones, was "unfortunate and inexcusable at the present critical moment." Quite apart from the hazards created by the incursions of Leslie and Arnold, Virginia's Continental line needed to be reorganized to conform with the new system of long enlistments adopted by Congress on October 3. No longer, Washington hoped, would he have to support two armies—one coming, the other going. The Virginia militia had turned out in high spirits to face the enemy (shaking off a vicious apathy, Richard Henry Lee said) even though it lacked guns, ammunition, tents and blankets on the verge of winter. The new army plan called for three thousand additional regulars from this state enlisted for the war. Long-term soldiers didn't grow on trees, or, if they did, could only be shaken out of them by large bounties or the draft.[1]

When the assembly finally came together in November, there was no lack of vigor. It voted unanimously to recruit soldiers for the duration—an auspicious beginning, Madison commented, and a measure "which all the states ought to have begun with." He protested, however, against one feature of the pending bill—a proviso that every recruit should be given a Negro slave as part of his bounty.

"Would it not be as well," he wrote to Joseph Jones in Richmond, "to liberate and make soldiers at once of the blacks themselves, as to make them instruments for enlisting white soldiers? It would certainly be more consonant to the principles of liberty, which ought never to be lost sight of in a contest for liberty."[2]

Madison was not thinking of immediate universal emancipation. Freeing of some slaves, he added, would be safe because freedmen

47

at once lost sympathy with their former fellows. But he made it plain that he looked upon Negro slavery as contrary to the principles of human equality stated in the Declaration of Independence.

Jones replied with an economic argument, sound enough in wartime, yet showing the way to the firm fastening of slavery upon the South. The freeing of these people was "a great and desirable object," but must be attempted by some gradual course. The sudden drawing off of the best farm laborers would ruin individuals and distress the state and perhaps the continent.[3]

This difference between the two men was carried into their personal attitudes. When Jones's servant Cyrus ran away, his owner asked Madison to advertise for him in the *Packet*. "Let him be confined in prison until I come up, unless an opportunity present itself of shipping him for the West Indies, where if I recover him I mean he shall be transported and sold." When Madison's servant Billey ran away and was caught, the disposition of him became a major problem in ethics. It would not do to send him back to Virginia, because "his mind is too thoroughly tainted to be a fit companion for fellow slaves." Barring immediate liberation, the alternatives were to transplant him to the West Indies for a good price, or sell him at a low figure in Pennsylvania, where state law would set him free at the end of seven years. The latter course was chosen.

"I do not expect to get near the worth of him," Madison wrote to his father, "but cannot think of punishing him by transportation merely for coveting that liberty for which we have paid the price of so much blood, and have proclaimed so often to be the right and worthy the pursuit of every human being." Had that sentiment spread over the South, slavery would have disappeared without a civil war.[4]

The Virginia legislature, Jones reported, looked on the slave-bounty proposal as inhuman and cruel. It seemed less so as the invasion swelled. The law which emerged gave to each Continental recruit a bounty of $12,000 ($300 in hard money), three hundred acres of land and his choice of sixty pounds in gold or silver or a "healthy sound negro, between the ages of ten and thirty years." A slave, unlike paper currency, did not depreciate rapidly.[5]

Pennsylvania State House (Independence Hall), from a Drawing Made in 1796

CIPHERING BY JAMES MADISON, SR., ON BACK OF LETTER FROM JAMES MADISON, JR., DATED DECEMBER 24, 1785

Though Madison's proposal was ignored, the fighting value of black men was not. Within a month after he made his suggestion to Jones, the Board of War was asking that a contractor be paid for equipment for four hundred Negroes. "I cannot too frequently repeat," a French officer noted in his diary, "how much I was surprised at the American army. It is beyond understanding how troops who were almost naked, badly paid, composed of old men, negroes, and children, could move so well, both on the march and under fire."[6]

Madison's father, pursuant to the new Virginia law, took charge of the fitting out of soldiers in Orange County. He divided the county into forty-two districts, each of which was to furnish one suit of clothing, to wit: two shirts, a pair of overalls, two pairs of stockings, one pair of shoes and a hat or cap.[7] Add perhaps a feather, and that was what the Revolutionary soldier had between him and a state of nature, before he slid down a ravine or caught his second shirt on a broken sapling.

Rather say, it is what each soldier would have had if one county had been equal to the terrific task of turning up forty-two pairs of overalls. The attempt to do so produced a universal feeling that the new forces should be equipped by the King of France. At the moment this crisis developed, Madison and Bland were alone in Philadelphia. Patrick Henry, who was running the assembly, put little trust in nonorators. Madison, vocally, was nobody, while Bland's voluminous gift registered favorably only upon his wife. Under Henry's urging, the assembly named a delegate extraordinary to lay the state of the war before Congress, solicit aid from sister states or European allies, and concert necessary measures "with Congress, the minister of France and General Washington." Speaker Benjamin Harrison got the place, but not until after a tie vote with Richard Henry Lee had so disgusted him (because he could not very well break it in his own favor) that it was believed for a time he would refuse to go.[8]

Madison regarded this action as a vote of lack of confidence in himself. Cannot the facts, he asked Joseph Jones, be laid before Congress as well by the regular delegation as by a special messenger? "And will not the latter mode in some measure imply a distrust in the former one, and lower us in the eyes of Congress and

the public?" He hoped that the return of his influential colleague
to Philadelphia would cause the project to be dropped, but Jones
came down with malaria and also had to care for his wife, who was
reduced by it to a skeleton.[9]

Despite his chagrin, Madison did all in his power to aid Harrison.
He was one of a committee of six named on February 13 to confer
with the delegate extraordinary. Its report, written by Brigadier
General Sullivan, encroached on Washington's province (though
he approved it later) and resurrected a tone of authority toward
the states not heard since the money presses stopped. To create a
Southern force of ten thousand regulars, Congress placed all from
Pennsylvania to Georgia in Greene's army, and directed Washington to order the Pennsylvania line into Virginia. It resolved that
all states south of Pennsylvania "be, and hereby are required" to
furnish their quotas of supplies. With Pennsylvania, they must
complete their troop quotas and send them south.[10]

Madison was ready enough to issue such orders to the states. He,
like Washington, saw in them a proper reflection of national
sovereignty. But joining him now was Thomas Burke, the mighty
champion of state rights. There really was no anomaly about it.
Burke never questioned federal supremacy within the compass of
a clearly delegated power.

A tone of authority was easier to use, in this instance, because
Congress was not asking the states to equip the new army. It had
the same idea as Virginia: "Lean on Louis." Bills were ordered
drawn on Franklin, which meant on the King of France, to cover
the cost of 10,000 suits of clothes, 5,000 muskets, 8,000 blankets and
other equipment. These being for 10,000 men, and exclusive of
articles already provided, it would seem that half of the men lacked
guns and all were open to February winds.[11]

With the Continental Army theoretically clothed and armed,
Harrison, Madison, Bland and Jones (now back in Congress)
turned to the other part of the Harrison mission—the purchase of
arms, ammunition and clothing from France by Virginia. What
they actually bought was a two-year headache, paid for in kind.
Luzerne fell in with the plan the more readily because Maryland
made a similar application. These requests, combined with the

inability of Congress to secure money or supplies from the states, led the French minister into one of his few major misinterpretations of American affairs. If the states in the midst of pressing danger will not put effective means into the hands of Congress, he wrote to Vergennes, that body will be still more destitute after the war. Better then, he said, loan to the states individually than collectively. That, however, involved discrimination, so he added: Let the arms be paid for by Virginia and Maryland, but let the supplies go to Congress, for use of the Continental lines of those two states.[12]

One can imagine the roar with which Virginia and Maryland would have greeted this proposal. It was never emitted, however, for the Count de Vergennes turned the proposal squarely around. Let the goods be delivered to the two states, for their use, he suggested, but charge them to Congress and deduct their value from the current loan. Then it was that Congress roared, and none more loudly than the delegates from Virginia and Maryland.

Luzerne had remarked at the outset that, in dealing with these applications, he would "act with the circumspection which is required by the jealousy of a party in Congress toward all relations between the king's minister and the individual states." Outraged protests from thronging delegates now informed him how strong that feeling was. They ask, he said, "if because it pleased some particular state to address us contrary to the spirit of their Confederation, we believe on that account that it gave us the right to give them an extraordinary part of what had been granted to the thirteen United States in general." The minister calmed their spirits a little by telling them that Congress was free to do what it pleased with the goods. "But they continue to make all sorts of comments on this arrangement . . . it has not the approval of anyone, not even of the two states interested, which, despite the turn I have given to the affair, believe themselves compromised with their sister states." Even Harrison, by this time become governor, wrote to Luzerne that he was mortified at what had resulted from his request. Bland drafted a congressional protest against it. Financier Robert Morris rejected and denounced it.[13]

Vergennes refused to budge from his position, saying that he could not understand a country which would subordinate the winning of a war to questions of state and federal sovereignty. Luzerne, his lesson thoroughly learned, begged the foreign minister to accede to the views of Congress. During the tumult Madison was forced to give at least nominal support to the basic request, though nobody was more averse than he to state relations with foreign powers. The Virginia delegates met with Luzerne again and again to discuss financing. Unity was not heightened when the Virginians got the idea that Luzerne wanted payments to begin at once, and the minister concluded that Virginia did not expect them to begin at all. Vergennes settled the issue at last by throwing both the Virginia and Maryland schemes out of the window. "I will not inquire," he wrote finally, "whether the American Constitution declares our engagement inadmissible. I will limit myself to observing that the King, assisting the United States collectively, does not owe them a separate assistance." Thus ended a diplomatic enterprise whose inception (with nothing said about its termination) has been cited again and again to prove that the thirteen states during the Revolution were separately independent nations with no sense of common sovereignty.[14]

While all the Virginia delegates were smarting under the affront given them by the Harrison mission, Madison faced something a bit similar inside the delegation. This came from Theodorick Bland, who either used a thin-bladed knife on him, or, more likely, was led by his own excessive vanity into the appearance of an effort to discredit his colleague. It concerned French naval assistance in Chesapeake Bay.

If there was one military factor to which Madison was fully alert, it was the relation of sea power to Southern safety and ultimate American victory. From the spring of 1780 onward, after Lafayette brought the promise of naval aid, Madison sent to Virginia every scrap of fact, rumor or conjecture about it that reached Philadelphia. "Ternay is yet unreinforced, Graves at sea no one knows where." "The main French fleet under Guichen left the West Indies." "Rodney has sailed from New York with twenty ships."[15] Such reports and rumors were part of the nerve strain of the Revolution.

American hopes were brought very low, Madison reported in September, by news that Ternay's long-awaited second fleet was blockaded in Brest. They flared up again at "sundry concurring information that a large French fleet from the West Indies is on our coast." Alas! It was Rodney arriving from Europe. The lift and letdown of the false report shook even Joseph Jones, to whom Madison sent the mortifying correction. "Where for God sake is Count de Guichen?" he cried to Washington. Doubts about the French were spreading in Virginia. Were they able to help? Did they really intend to? Jones urged Madison to visit the French minister and get some explanation of the delay and inactivity, which would enable him "to satisfy the doubts of some and to silence the insinuations of others."[16]

Madison replied that he was aware of the advantage which secret enemies took of the situation, but since the French minister knew of this and said nothing, it was to be inferred that he could not stop the mischief. He appealed for continued trust in the French. Having experienced so many proofs of their wisdom and goodness, he admonished Edmund Pendleton, "we ought not on slight grounds to abate our faith in them." He was sensible, he added, of the great difficulties Virginia would have to contend with in facing Leslie's invasion, "and that no practicable exertions can save the state from much injury whilst the enemy have a total command of the bay and rivers."[17]

At this juncture, Madison and Bland were asked by Governor Jefferson to secure the transportation to Virginia of a shipload of French arms which had reached a New England port. They joined in asking Luzerne to forward the goods in a fast, blockade-running frigate from the fleet in Rhode Island.[18] The minister promised to do what he could, but nothing happened until, on January 22, 1781, a sudden winter gale struck four British war-ships off Newport, sinking one and damaging others. Combined with Rodney's departure, this shifted the balance of gun power to the French and gave them freedom of movement. Chef d'Escadre Destouches, in command since the death of Admiral de Ternay in mid-December, seized the opportunity with zeal, if not with wisdom.

The Virginia delegates ordinarily wrote joint letters to the governor about their public activities. But on February 9 Bland wrote one of his own. Recalling his and Madison's report on the application for a frigate to carry war supplies, he went on to say that since then "my personal application, singly [no help from Madison] has been unremitted . . . to have a line of battle ships and one or two frigates sent into our bay. Now," said Bland, "the minister of France has communicated to me, and charged me with secrecy to every soul but your excellency" that Destouches was going to blockade the British and send a small squadron into Chesapeake Bay. He concluded by praising Luzerne's cordial promotion of "every measure that we have jointly, and I have individually had the honor to propose to him."

To be trusted by the minister with the destination of the fleet thrilled Bland beyond measure. "It was so profound a secret," he boasted a few weeks later to Richard Henry Lee, "that no one in Philadelphia except him and myself knew it was sailed." In reality, Chairman Mathews of the Mathews-Madison-Sharpe committee sent simultaneous word of the sailing, also in deep confidence, to General Greene, with the added detail of a proposed feint off Charleston. Joseph Jones gave Jefferson a cryptic hint to be ready for co-operation with the fleet. Neither he nor Madison, however, sent anything specific until ten days later, at which time Bland preserved his aloof superiority by failing to sign a delegation letter duplicating his earlier one.[19]

The expedition did in truth result chiefly from the importunities of Bland. His hour of glory lasted until an icy letter from Washington reached Congress. The splitting of the French fleet had utterly ruined his plan of action against Benedict Arnold. The expedition would fail, he told Rochambeau, because Arnold's ships would lie under shore batteries and nothing could be done without a landing force. He urged that the remainder of the fleet be sent south at once, laden with troops. At this moment, unluckily, a supposedly dismasted sixty-four-gun British ship (the *America*) sailed back to Long Island from the open sea, unharmed. The enemy fleet once more was superior. The French could not move. And Rochambeau disclosed that Destouches acted on a congressional request.

Washington's letter to Congress was in answer to an appeal

which formed a final fillip to the Harrison mission. Three members, including Madison, were instructed to urge him to send the French forces south. To receive such an appeal, just after Arnold had escaped him through congressional meddling, disgusted Washington beyond measure. He told in reply how he had ordered Lafayette and twelve hundred men to Virginia, as soon as he heard of the results of the storm, then asked for the whole French fleet and part of their land forces. He specified the cause of the failure—an application through Luzerne which divided the fleet. Bitterly, to Joseph Jones, Washington lamented the blunder which prevented the destruction of Arnold's army. With quiet satisfaction, Madison placed a copy of this letter among his papers. Bland wrote no more to Virginia about his remarkable prowess as a naval strategist, or Madison's failure to support him in that field.[20]

Returning from the futile venture into Chesapeake waters, Captain Tilly had the good luck to encounter and capture the large frigate *Romulus,* cut for fifty guns. At Newport the energetic Destouches promptly announced that he would convert her into an eighth ship of the line and return in full force to the Chesapeake. He did so. The British followed in two days with eight heavier and faster ships. They met six days later (March 16, 1781) outside the capes. The French by good marksmanship put three of the enemy out of action, but when the seventy-four-gun *Conquerant* hoisted a distress signal Destouches slowed the pursuit ("afraid of the court," Commissary Claude Blanchard remarked) and Admiral Arbuthnot escaped into the bay. News of this second failure reached Madison when a French frigate came to Philadelphia with the Virginia arms consignment, twice carried to the Chesapeake and twice turned back. The delegates undertook to forward the goods by land—a matter of such infinite importance, Madison wrote to Jefferson, that he planned to pledge the faith of the state to instantaneous payment of the wagoners in real money when they arrived in Virginia.[21]

These French failures caused deep discontent in Virginia. The second was modified by the glow of a brave venture against odds, but left the ally sensitive. Madison was called on to spread a bit of salve. Mathews and Sullivan came to him on April 4 with identical letters from Washington, suggesting that Congress, both for political reasons and because the French attempt had been bold and enterprising, pay a compliment to Destouches and Rochambeau. "It may have a happy effect," he concluded. Madison at once drafted a resolution which Congress adopted. Unluckily he omitted Rochambeau, who had nothing to do with the action but whose feelings needed soothing because of Washington's tilt with him. Next day, therefore, the resolution was broadened to include the land commander, and was further strengthened by a toning down of too ebullient phraseology. The "ardor" of the naval forces suffered a sea change to "firmness," with room enough between the words for Arbuthnot to slip into Chesapeake Bay. "Unfortunate casualties" became, in two jumps, "unforeseen events"—no less potent in frustrating the expedition. The battle now did honor, instead of "so much honor" to the arms of King Louis, and perhaps did more in not trying to do so much.[22]

While the French were being led into these abortive naval ventures, Madison found openings to urge the basic need of strengthening the fleet. Hearing from Marbois that the French naval department had a new head, he told how enemies of the alliance were exploiting the nonarrival of a second fleet. He was much less astonished than many others, he remarked to Pendleton, at Arnold's audacious attack on Richmond: "To those who are strangers to the sparse manner in which that country is settled, and the easy penetration afforded by its long, navigable rivers, the rapid and unopposed advances of the enemy appear unaccountable, and our national character suffers imputations which are by no means due to it." That he urged the cure for this on Luzerne is evident from the latter's remarks to Vergennes a few days afterward:

"The Virginians, who have so often exaggerated the power of their state, are very humiliated to see it ravaged by a handful of soldiers, but they tell me that these successes of Arnold were due to the advantage he has from being near the sea. This invasion gives occasion to renew the urgings that are made on all sides to

Congress that it solicit from the King's bounty adequate naval assistance and I also receive frequent suggestions of the same nature."[23]

The tendency to rely on France would have been fatal had it not been paralleled by that other phenomenon of the American Revolution—the strengthening of popular resistance as the enemy came closer. With the southward shift of battle, the Northern states lost that zeal which made them for five years the bulwark of independence. They now wanted independence, peace and normalcy, at no cost. In the once apathetic and still Tory-ridden Carolinas, ragged guerrillas crept through the forests and crawled through swamps. In Virginia, especially in the middle and back counties, courage revived and lassitude was shaken off. A few months earlier the effort to raise troops had been like "the stirring of a man between sleeping and waking." So wrote James Madison of William and Mary College to his cousin James before the British landed. How different now: "Old men, who had long laid aside the musket, even half Tories caught the flame, and I believe had [Cornwallis] crossed the Dan, his fate would have been glorious for America. But *guns!* not men were wanting."[24]

At the center of danger the spirit of continental unity revived. "For God's sake my countrymen," cried Timothy Standfast in the *Virginia Gazette,* "rouse from your lethargy, look into consequences and return to your pristine vigor." Other thoughts were in the minds of some Americans. The day after Preacher James Madison wrote of the resurrected zeal of backwoods Virginians, the *Pennsylvania Gazette* published a subtly insinuating discussion of the alleged indolence and imbecility of Benjamin Franklin, coupled with a hint that members of Congress were selling out to the enemy.[25] Delegate James Madison soon found himself in the thick of that controversy, as he was sure to be in any which involved justice and the effective conduct of national affairs.

CHAPTER V

BATTLE OF THE DIPLOMATS

IN THE American Revolution, the diplomats outran the generals on the road to a victorious peace. This gave them time to conduct a vigorous civil war among themselves. Better say, it gave time for most of them to gang up on Benjamin Franklin, who was busily engaged in minding his own and the country's business. James Madison entered the congressional end of American diplomacy at a time when this conflict was momentarily quiescent, but it was merely a lull during which new positions were being taken.

The diplomatic structure in 1780 can be understood only by noting its development. Silas Deane, Connecticut merchant and congressional delegate, was sent to Paris in 1776 as purchasing agent of the Secret Committee of Congress. His instructions were to buy goods for the Indian trade, taking a commission of five per cent for himself. Posing as a private merchant, he was to buy arms, ammunition and clothing for the army, to be paid for later in American goods. Deane entered into an agreement with the playwright Beaumarchais, secret agent of France, for the purchase of surplus war goods from French arsenals.[1] Aiming at a military alliance, Congress then elected Deane, Franklin and Thomas Jefferson joint commissioners in Paris. Jefferson declined and his place was taken by Dr. Arthur Lee of Virginia, law student in London, and youngest of the eleven children produced by the persevering industry of Thomas and Hanna Ludwell Lee of Stratford Hall.

Lee was a patriotic and fanatically honest man who saw dishonesty in all who differed with him. Ambitious, jealous and given to intrigue, he found ample stimulus in Paris for his pathological suspicions and wholesale hatreds. Franklin's private secretary Bancroft and Lee's secretary Thornton were both in enemy pay, also using their secret knowledge for speculative profit. Lee was suspicious of Bancroft, but denounced Thornton's critics even when the evidence they furnished forced his discharge. His successor was the Reverend Hezekiah Ford, of Virginia, who was denounced by the Virginia executive council, during Madison's membership in it, as a notorious Tory who had fled to England early in the war. This secretary soon vanished, along with confidential documents given him by Lee.[2]

Silas Deane was made to order as a Lee target. His dual position as a diplomat and private merchant was enough in itself to invite distrust, and his extravagant living gave prima facie support to suspicions of large-scale speculation. Lee had talked with Beaumarchais in 1775 and understood that his supplies were to be a gift from France—a claim disproved by the fact that the playwright borrowed privately to enlarge the purchases financed by the court. Lee charged that Deane and Beaumarchais, aided by Franklin, were engaged in a fraudulent conspiracy against the United States. Congress joyfully accepted the army supplies which streamed across the ocean, and let the payments go. These shipments equipped the army which won the battle of Saratoga, while Beaumarchais went bankrupt and died in poverty. Deane was recalled to answer Lee's charges. Lee was recalled to answer Deane's. John Adams, who succeeded Deane, teamed up with Lee in common hatred of Franklin, but came home in 1778, when the regularizing of diplomatic relations made Franklin sole minister to France.

The confidence of the French court in wise old Benjamin Franklin proved a bastion of strength to the Revolution. The French people idolized him. But to Arthur Lee he was the image of all things evil. Abuse and accusations came in a steady flow from Paris. The victim of the assault made neither defense nor countercharge, but wrote to a friend that he considered Arthur Lee the most malicious enemy he ever had.[3]

Whipped into Lee and Deane factions and torn by passions, Congress in 1779 barely refrained from including Franklin in its recalls. Samuel Adams and two of Lee's brothers were seeking to put Arthur in charge of peace negotiations. It was at bottom an anti-Gallic movement, but could succeed only if Lee's supporters persuaded Congress that he enjoyed the confidence of France. The so-called Paca-Drayton Information, slipped to two delegates by French Minister Gerard, destroyed that illusion. *"Je crains M. Lee et ses entours,"* Vergennes had written to Gerard.[4] Knowledge of Vergennes' fear of Lee fortified Franklin, but the peace negotiations were assigned to John Adams, who also was commissioned to secure a commercial treaty with Great Britain. The same political trade that sent Adams back to Europe also made John Jay minister to Spain.

Lesser diplomats strummed their fingers in Paris cafés. Ralph Izard, refused admittance to Tuscany, drew bills on Franklin for the tuition of his children and demanded that he be consulted in Franco-American diplomacy. Brother William Lee waited for the Emperor of Germany to invite him to Vienna. Henry Laurens, former President of Congress, sailed in 1780 to negotiate a loan in Holland, but a British cannon ball deflected his course to the Tower of London.

Thus, at the time Madison came into contact with foreign affairs, Franklin, Jay and Adams were the American figures in Europe. Deane had gone back to France to gather his papers and prepare a reply to Lee. Izard had just reached the United States and Arthur Lee was on his way home. The United States had no department of foreign affairs. Diplomatic decisions were made and papers were written in Congress itself, while a standing committee handled routine correspondence. It had not even a secretary after Tom Paine was fired for attacking Silas Deane with confidential French papers.

Madison's aptitude for foreign affairs seems to have been recognized even before he took formal part in them. His cousin James Madison wrote to him on August 3, 1780: "We hear that you have refused an important place in a foreign embassy. If so, your refusal does you honor, but . . . [had you accepted] no doubt all the honors America could confer would in time have succeeded." The post probably was that of secretary to Franklin, which Congress had been trying to fill for the better part of a year. Trying, that is, to decide whether he should have a secretary to help him, hobble him, or perform his duties. Franklin, envious John Adams

EDMUND RANDOLPH

PRESIDENT SAMUEL HUNTINGTON   BENJAMIN HARRISON

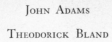

JOHN ADAMS   SAMUEL ADAMS

THEODORICK BLAND   ARTHUR LEE

wrote to a delegate, "knows too little of American affairs, of the politics of Europe . . . to be ambassador, secretary, admiral, consular agent, etc. . . . He is too old, too infirm, too indolent and dissipated."[5]

Madison's first diplomatic assignment was to deal with a report from Adams that England looked toward a truce with America. The committee advised that a long truce could be agreed to, with French concurrence, provided it included the removal of all British land and naval armaments from the United States. They relied on Adams, in such a case, "to hold up the United States to the world in a style and title not derogatory to the character of an independent and sovereign people."[6]

This report, presented by James Lovell, appears to be the joint work of Lovell and Madison. The opening is in Lovell's lucid public style—very different from the cryptic staccato of his letters—while the rest is in the thought, style and even the wording of other writings by Madison. Before the year ended, in an effort to secure diplomatic recognition and the support of Empress Catherine's "armed neutrality," Francis Dana was elected minister to Russia. Duane, Witherspoon and Madison instructed him to sign a treaty "consistent with the dignity and sovereignty of the United States as a free and independent nation." He was to impress upon Her Imperial Majesty "the nature and stability of our union, and the solemn engagements by which not only the states, but his most Christian Majesty, are reciprocally bound to maintain the sovereignty, rights and jurisdiction of each of the thirteen states inviolably." The purpose of that final statement was to reject *"uti possidetis"*—a peace in which each nation keeps what it holds.[7]

Practically every American statesman called the United States a nation during the Revolution. Every treaty refers to "both nations," "the two nations," etc.[8] But here is something to gaze upon—a defense of both national and state sovereignty in the same document, put forth by three of the country's foremost students of government and approved by Congress, three months before the Articles of Confederation came into effect. What does this leave of the theory that national sovereignty is a belated concept derived from the Constitution of 1787? Here, in 1780, is the dual sov-

ereignty of states and nation, rising to the relative heights suggested by the wording—"the sovereignty, rights and jurisdiction
of each" of the states, and "the dignity and sovereignty of the
United States as a free and independent nation." These instructions are in the handwriting of Duane, but the same words were
used by Madison within the next year, calling on Congress to
defend "the dignity of the United States as a sovereign and independent nation."[9]

The more heated aspect of foreign relations came before Madison a week after his diplomatic baptism in August. Along with
Thomas McKean and Lovell, he received Ralph Izard's report on
affairs in Europe. They heard a violent attack upon Franklin for
being too soft-spoken in asking aid of the French court. The
proper course, Izard declared, was to scare France with fear of an
American-British coalition. The foresighted Luzerne already had
warned members of Congress "against such insidious councils,"
and Izard got no satisfaction from the committee. Its report, he
lamented, "contained simply an approbation of my conduct, without mentioning anything respecting Dr. Franklin." Next came
Arthur Lee, home from Europe, and Madison was made chairman
of the committee to deal with him.[10]

Lee opened with an innocent little personal request. He wished
Congress either to accept for itself, or expressly authorize him to
retain, a "picture of the king of France set with diamonds, which
the minister of that monarch presented to me as a mark of his
majesty's esteem upon my taking leave of the court of Versailles."
He then asked for a full hearing to prove the untruth and malice
of the insinuations which led to his dismissal.

The Count de Vergennes must have been a mind reader. Eight
months earlier he wrote to the Chevalier de la Luzerne: "It is possible that Mr. Lee, to deceive them [Congress] again, may make
a big showing of the present which he has received from the king.
If this happens, you will simply remark that this present was given
to Mr. Lee, not as a special mark of the king's satisfaction in his
conduct, but because he signed the treaties of commerce and alliance."[11]

The Lee forces planned to rush an approving resolution to passage on the day his letter was read. One delegate, probably Duane, forced a day's postponement and (Luzerne being in Boston) hastened to tell Marbois what was happening. The chargé d'affaires, not feeling free to make use of Vergennes' warning, repeated the Paca-Drayton Information to President Huntington, with such good effect, he informed Vergennes, that before the day was over "the mere knowledge of your lack of confidence in Mr. Lee sufficed to cause a rejection."[12] To put these motions and votes in the *Journals of Congress* would have created an impression that all was not peace and harmony in the temple of government. Nothing is found there but the reference of Lee's letter to Madison, Bee and Clark, and a direction that he lay his information about Europe before Congress.

Madison's desire was to prevent a revival of the old factionalism. There was no charge that could rightfully be made against Lee, in the absence of a medical examination for paranoia, except that his virtuous emotions were so distorted by ambition and envy that he was temperamentally unfit to hold public office. The committee sought to exonerate him without reflecting on anybody else. Their report authorized him to retain the picture presented "as a mark of his Majesty's esteem," and assured him that "his recall was not intended to fix any kind of censure on his character or conduct abroad." The intricacy and deftness of this report mark it as the work of Chairman Madison, but it came before Congress in the handwriting of Thomas Bee, whose plodding style held neither sting nor honey. A Virginian unprepared to spread superlatives on Arthur Lee could well let fainter praise come from South Carolina.[13]

Weeks passed without action on this resolution. Lee charged that Duane (known to the Lee faction as "Swivel-Eye") was blocking it. What he did not know was that Luzerne told President Huntington of Vergennes' warning against misuse of the king's picture on a snuffbox. Madison had fallen just far enough into Lee's trap on that point to make his report internationally embarrassing.[14]

Delay gave the ex-diplomat time to dig his own pitfall. "We hear Dr. Lee and Mr. Izard are with you and are open and unreserved in their abuse of Franklin," Edmund Pendleton wrote to Madison at the end of October. The latter confirmed the report and added: "I have had great anxiety lest the flame of faction . . . should be kindled anew, but as far as I can judge the temper of Congress is in general by no means prone to it, although there may be individuals on both sides who would both wish and endeavor it."[15] The Lee forces planned to move for Franklin's recall, but the motion was not made, Luzerne reported, because Southern delegates, jealous of a Northern monopoly in the three principal missions, feared that John Adams would replace Franklin.[16]

With Lee's attacks becoming known over the country, it was no longer possible to praise and exonerate him without that action being construed as support of his anti-Franklin campaign. Congress on December 3 approved his "retaining the picture" (not even identified now), struck out a reference to his zealous and faithful exertions and merely assured him that there were no charges against him and no censure intended. "A cold ceremonial adieu," one of his supporters called it.[17]

Arthur Lee replied with such a diatribe against Franklin that the very magnitude of his falsehoods gave them the weight and hue of truth. He charged the minister with misconduct in the purchase of supplies, neglect of public business, devotion to pleasure despite his age (some truth in that), use of public money to make immense fortunes for himself and others, association with notoriously unfit persons, and such violence upon the persons and properties of Americans as would disgrace "the worst of men in the worst of times."[18]

The charge that counted most was an accusation that Franklin tied up the frigate *Alliance* through a fraudulent detention of prize money by his agent Chaumont (who was actually the French government's purchasing agent for the American army) resulting in the bitterly lamented failure of that ship to bring clothing and other supplies when it finally sailed. "Fraudulent detention" was Lee's way of saying that the crew refused a distribution of prize money under French law, which alone could be immediate, since American law required prior sale of the prizes. He was also fortifying himself against the coming accusation of Commodore John

Paul Jones that upon being admitted to the *Alliance* as a passenger, Lee stirred up a mutiny of its crew against Jones, on the prize money issue, and caused the ship to be seized by its former commander, Captain Landais.

There was another part of the story Lee did not tell. He did not reveal that Franklin had ordered Captain Landais court-martialed for failure to support the *Bon Homme Richard* in its duel with the *Serapis*. Nor did he say that as he strolled the decks of the *Alliance,* homeward bound, he walked above the heads of the non-mutineers who lay in irons in the hold. And who were these men in irons? They were the heroic seamen of the *Bon Homme Richard,* the men who captured the *Serapis* as their own ship went to the bottom. Arthur Lee could not hear the clanking of their prison chains.[19]

Shocked by these charges against Franklin, Congress named an investigating committee. Its chairman was Lee's alter ego, Theodorick Bland. With him were Dr. Witherspoon, pro-Lee and anti-Franklin, and Lee's enemy Duane. The bias of the majority was the best evidence of the impact of Lee's charges. This shattering of faith in Franklin came at a crucial moment for his mission. Shortly before, Duane had drafted a letter informing our good friend King Louis that the United States stood ready to raise an army of 35,000 regulars. For this a loan of 25,000,000 livres was indispensably necessary, and there was nobody more fit to furnish it than "a prince who nobly asserts the rights of mankind"—the same prince whose head was cut off twelve years later for denying those rights to his own people.[20]

Duane, Madison and Houston prepared instructions to Franklin to reinforce this appeal. Written by Duane, they followed the outline of his letter except for an important addition which apparently was proposed by Madison. The latter, for some weeks past, had been pointing to the need for specie throughout the country. "One or two millions of guineas properly applied," he declared to Pendleton, "would diffuse vigor and satisfaction throughout the whole military departments, and would expel the enemy from every part of the United States." Now Franklin was told that the loan must prove ineffective unless actual specie was remitted. Also, there was the strongest need for dispatching an effective naval armament and these warships could carry the specie in safety.[21]

After this action came the thunderclap of Lee's accusations. Could a minister sunk in corruption and senility (save as he rallied from the latter for iniquitous pleasure) be entrusted with the fate of the next campaign? The day after Lee's letter was read, Congress ordered an envoy extraordinary sent to Versailles to solicit the huge new loan and secure the materials to be bought with it. Young John Laurens, son of Henry Laurens and aide to Washington, was elected to the post.[22]

That Madison opposed this step is evident from his comment to Joseph Jones: "I leave the measure to your own reflection." His doubts were increased when Luzerne protested against the éclat of the proposed mission. To send a man with the overstuffed title of envoy extraordinary, and a letter of credence addressed to the king, would do nothing to aid his work and would seriously damage American prestige if he failed. If somebody must be sent, he advised, appoint a simple minister and let Franklin present him to Vergennes.[23]

Having voted against the original resolution, Madison was ineligible to move a reconsideration. However, just at this moment Dr. Witherspoon returned from Princeton, panoplied in his black scholastic gown. Madison and his former teacher followed up their warm reunion with a bit of teamwork. Witherspoon moved to reconsider the motion creating the mission. Southern enthusiasm for the mission upset their plan, but ten days later they found the climate changed. On Madison's motion Congress struck out "envoy extraordinary" and inserted "minister." At this point somebody seems to have crossed Madison up. The reconsideration was limited to "the style and title of the minister," yet a motion was made and carried to strike out a clause which required Laurens to act in conjunction with Franklin. Since Witherspoon was a Lee partisan and opponent of Franklin, the theologian may have finessed a card from his sleeve on this occasion.[24]

Madison owed much to Witherspoon. The old doctor started him on his studies of government and international law and pointed the way to his lifelong fidelity to freedom of conscience.

Nothing, however, is more naïve than the conventional assumption that the young Virginian expanded in Congress under the benign eye and helpful hand of the man who taught him moral philosophy at Princeton. They were in truth two of the shrewdest political strategists in that body and far more often in conflict than in partnership. One need not accept the prejudiced statement of Thomas Rodney that Witherspoon "has all the design and arch cunning" needed in a Scottish kirk without "that candid integrity, honesty and wisdom" required in government. The friendlier Luzerne called him a man of talents and intrigue, not one to lose ground, though "attention bends his inflexibility."[25]

Smitten with his own weapon, Madison looked for a way to repair the damage to Franklin. He and General Sullivan were to draw up Laurens' credentials. Madison wrote the commission and Sullivan used it (as shown by marked-out duplications) as a guide in writing the instructions. Laurens was ordered to communicate with Franklin "and avail yourself of his information and influence." On the floor, Madison secured an additional instruction to Laurens to confer with Washington, Luzerne, Lafayette and the French army and fleet commanders. These men gave him powerful letters of support, though Luzerne concealed the extent of his help. He warned Congress to expect nothing but told Vergennes that a refusal of Laurens' request might bring about a fatal revolt in the American army.[26] Thus the young army officer, enthusiastic and inexperienced, was sent to Europe (Tom Paine accompanying him) to perform the work of which shrewd old Benjamin Franklin was thought incapable.

All this came on the heels of Arthur Lee's sensational attack upon Franklin's integrity and ability. The prejudiced committee on those accusations was soon ready to report. It centered its inquiry on the charge that Franklin delayed the sailing of the *Alliance* and caused it to leave France half-empty. Chairman Bland knew from the Marquis de Lafayette, whose private secretary came across in that vessel, that "the *Alliance* was taken from Captain Jones by Captain Landais . . . Landais refused to take military stores offered in the name of the French court. . . . But Mr. Arthur Lee, who was on board, must know of this matter." To be sure he must, since he had engineered the mutiny, so why ask a Frenchman about it? Bland's report, based on "the most impartial testimony," advised the recall of Dr. Franklin.[27]

With Lafayette's letter pointing to the untold story, Madison and other defenders of Franklin staved off action on Bland's report until John Paul Jones arrived in February in the *Ariel*. Things changed fast after that. Landais was court-martialed and "broke," with comedy added to his trial by disclosure of a violent controversy between him and Lee, on the way home, over the diplomat's demand for fresh water for his bath and his protest against common seamen dipping their drinking cups into the same barrel used by officers and passengers. The Board of Admiralty reported that Landais' seizure of the *Alliance,* "contrary to the express orders of Dr. Franklin," was the cause of the failure in procuring war supplies. The Bland report stayed in its pigeonhole.[28]

Out on the Atlantic, perverse winds held back the impatient Laurens, but gave swift wings to a set of duplicate instructions to Franklin. These, arriving a month ahead of the special minister, directed Franklin to do everything in his power to promote the requests should a time gap of this kind occur. All that Franklin did, in the interval, was to secure an outright gift of 6,000,000 livres from France and nearly that much as a loan. He obtained a promise of immediate naval reinforcements (the De Grasse fleet, whose arrival won the war), and presented an argument for specie which led to the shipment of 2,500,000 livres in silver bullion.[29]

When Laurens came there was no mistaking his honest zeal, but his brusque and threatening manner would have wrecked his mission had not seventy-five-year-old Franklin soothed the wounds he made. Laurens bought goods with the money Franklin obtained for him, and when these were lost at sea, the decrepit old minister persuaded the French government to replace them by a new loan to the United States. Then, just to round things off, he tapped the French treasury for nearly a million livres to pay for excess goods which Laurens had bought in Holland, and for 3,500,000 to cover unauthorized bills drawn on him by Congress.[30]

Writing to Congress, Franklin praised the "indefatigable endeavors" of John Laurens, but of the offense he had given to the

French court, not one word. Prior to this, however, he said a few words about himself. "I have passed my seventy-fifth year," he wrote. "I do not know that my mental faculties are impaired; perhaps I shall be the last to discover that; but . . . I have been engaged in public affairs and enjoyed public confidence, in some shape or other, during the long term of fifty years, and honor enough to satisfy any reasonable ambition; and I have no other left but that of repose, which I hope the Congress will grant me by sending some person to supply my place."[31]

All knew that Franklin interpreted the sending of Laurens as a declaration of lack of confidence in himself. But what can you do when a man offers to retire on the score of unfitness and puts the offer in the same mail packet with a ten-million-livre addition to the country's war fund? The stunning fact was that this whole outline of French aid for America—all that was promised for the crucial year of 1781—was dispatched before John Laurens arrived in Paris.

For Madison, the discomfiture of Lee and Landais in the affair of the *Alliance* was a political blessing. Clothing for Virginia troops had been expected in the John Paul Jones convoy and its failure to arrive was one of the bitterest blows of the war. There was risk in standing by Franklin on this issue before the truth became known. If the reversal of the picture ended this risk, it increased the likelihood that Madison would soon be included among the enemies of Arthur Lee and righteousness. There was value, however, in these political conflicts. They speeded up Madison's release from the handicaps imposed upon by him his natural, or unnatural, modesty. Toughening his sensitive skin and sharpening his strategic talents, they made him the readier to lead in framing the major policies of the government, domestic as well as foreign.

MADISON's most famous paper on foreign affairs, his letter of instructions to John Jay in defense of Western territories and the right to navigate the Mississippi, was written barely six months after he reached Philadelphia. The subject was not new to him. On the day he began his duties in the Virginia executive council (January 14, 1778) he voted approval of a message from Governor Patrick Henry to the governor of New Orleans, proposing a Spanish-American military alliance and the use of New Orleans as a free port for American trade. Entering Congress, he carried the instructions of the Virginia legislature to seek an express stipulation, in any treaty with Spain, for free use of the Mississippi to the sea and a free port in Spanish territories.[1]

To Virginians, this was both a state and a continental issue. The whole transmountain country, north of the present state of Tennessee, was regarded by them as a part of the Old Dominion—a claim violently disputed by other states which either claimed it for themselves or for the United States collectively. However that might be, everybody visualized this real estate as part of the American empire. It was included in the boundaries fixed in the peace ultimatum drafted by Congress in 1779. Here too the United States asserted a right to navigate the Mississippi, but this was not an ultimatum. By the peace treaty of 1763, Spain owned both banks of the lower river, while farther north it formed the boundary between British and Spanish territories. When Spain again became a belligerent, late in 1779, everybody looked to see whether she would act as a well-behaved ally or selfishly seek those advantages which nature, law and destiny had earmarked for the new American republic. The answer came quickly. Spain notified Congress, through Luzerne, that none but Spaniards could navigate the lower Mississippi. She challenged the title of the United

States to any territories which had been closed to colonization by a British crown edict in 1763—an edict forbidding land grants west of the headwaters of rivers flowing into the Atlantic. As Spain saw it, all lands draining westward were "possessions of the crown of Great Britain, and proper objects against which the arms of Spain may be employed, for the purpose of making a permanent conquest for the Spanish crown." France agreed with this, but said so formally only to Spain.[2]

To give this policy the shock of reality, Agent Miralles slipped a story into the *Pennsylvania Gazette* of February 23, 1780, describing General De Galvez' capture of three British posts at Natchez, one hundred forty miles above New Orleans. With fantastic exaggeration, he treated this as an occupation, for Spain, of territories running fifteen hundred miles up the river. In the ensuing ferment, Southern delegates informed the French minister that they intended to raise the issue in Congress. He persuaded them that the cementing of a union with Spain was too important to be jeopardized by such a dispute.[3]

Following the death of Miralles, Luzerne talked privately with practically all of the delegates, getting their views and trying to soften them up in advance of a Spanish ultimatum. Those of New England and New York, he reported to Vergennes on June 11, agreed with him that Spain had an incontestable right to conquer these territories. So did South Carolina. Delegates from New Jersey, Delaware and Pennsylvania were little interested (their states having no Western lands) but thought the American claim should not be reduced except under the most absolute necessity. Tough-minded Thomas Burke, of North Carolina, clung stubbornly to the Western claims. But what of Virginia and Maryland, the two great antagonists on the subject of Western lands?

Luzerne found the Virginians more moderate than he expected. Western independence movements threatened to dismember their state. It was injurious (this came from Joseph Jones)[4] to have too distant and too extended possessions. Maryland, however, showed the most reasonable sentiments. "A delegate of that state, one who has great influence, does not hesitate to say," Luzerne reported, "that not only can Spain make this conquest without any opposition, but that, not having entered into any engagement with Congress, if today she swept the English out of the state of Georgia, which is in their hands, she would have the same right to the preservation of this conquest as England has. Maryland, to tell the truth, has no immediate interest in this discussion. But the opinion of a member as important as Mr. Jenifer serves at least to prove that the delegates of Congress disagree upon this matter."

A clear majority, Luzerne thought, would concede Spain's right of conquest in the West. Nevertheless, when it came to revising the instructions to Jay, the Northern states probably would support the South in order to gain Southern support for the conquest of Canada. Spain, therefore, should continue her conquests and destroy the chimerical hopes which the Americans had conceived of acquiring these lands by conquest or by the treaty of peace.

Luzerne mistook the temper of the Virginia delegates. The moderating of their interest in the West as part of Virginia did not lessen their desire to retain it as American territory. National patriotism accounted for that in men like Madison and Joseph Jones, but in the state there were other incentives. The country west of the Alleghanies was being settled by Virginia families. It was shot through with the speculative landholdings of Virginia planters, lawyers, doctors and politicians, and was looked to for the land bounties of Revolutionary soldiers. Blood ties and land ties could leave no doubt of Virginia's fidelity to the American claim.

A dispatch from John Jay, read on August 22, brought the matter to a climax. Unyielding as Madrid seemed to be, he believed that if Congress adhered firmly to its navigation demand, Spain would agree to use of the river under regulations suppressing contraband. On territories, the Spanish court asserted a full right of conquest. Jay saw no reason to diminish American claims, but asked for additional instructions.[5]

With Spain's ambitions clarified, the French minister decided to move in on the committee in charge. Starting with Chairman Joseph Jones, he was able—so he informed Vergennes—to establish the rights of Spain so completely that the Virginian could make no defense except expediency and the fact that he was bound by his state's instructions. That was plenty, for Jones told Luzerne that nothing but force would cause the states to expropriate these lands. Talking with others, Luzerne concluded that Congress would give Jay instructions with which the Spanish court could be content. Then, alas, he found that delegates who were quite tractable individually became excited when they returned to Congress. "Mr. Jenifer is absent," the minister lamented. "The presence of this Maryland delegate would be very useful under the circumstances."[6]

The committee itself now began a fade-out. Thomas McKean took leave of absence. He was a busy man, being, all at the same time, a member of the Delaware legislature, delegate of that state in Congress, and chief justice of the Pennsylvania Supreme Court. Jones delivered a report, then went back to Virginia. That left only the wavering Walton, of Georgia, and the effect was to force leadership upon Madison—the first open assumption by him of a major responsibility in Congress.

The *Journals* tell nothing of the fight that followed. They record only that the committee report, "being amended, was unanimously agreed to" on October 4. Not one amendment or motion on the subject is preserved in the "Papers of the Continental Congress." The letters of members are silent. Fortunately, no such delicate regard for harmony restrained the dispatches of Luzerne and Marbois.

Early in September, a member of the committee told the French minister that Jay was to be given a little more latitude on the Mississippi—free use subject to restrictions on contraband. The obscurity of Jay's letter made it impossible to give him new instructions on boundaries. The effect was to uphold American territorial claims as far as the Mississippi.

This report pleased neither set of extremists. Two delegates of great influence (unnamed by Luzerne) proposed to cede to Spain all lands between the Mississippi and Appalachicola rivers, south of the Chickasaw. Dismemberment! cried Southerners, and dug out an old resolution in which Congress pledged indissoluble union and the integrity of every state. They asked Congress to define the boundaries of the states according to their charters and apply this guaranty. A motion was made that Jay be recalled, in case Spain held to her territorial demands. Both motions were beaten, chiefly because the American defeat at Camden increased the feeling of need for Spanish aid. With a violent and damaging debate in prospect, the backers of the report decided to postpone action as long as possible. Since Jay already had firm instructions, they lost no ground in doing so.[7]

Thus matters stood until Daniel of St. Thomas Jenifer came back to Congress shortly after mid-September and took charge of the campaign to abandon the American claim. Or, as Chargé d'Affaires Marbois described it:

"But Mr. Jenifer, delegate of Maryland, decided that propriety, the regard due to Spain and the interests of the thirteen states, required that they take up this matter without delay. He therefore made a motion to this effect, that Mr. Jay be authorized to promise satisfaction to Spain upon the points in question. The motion, which had not been adequately prepared, was feebly supported, and the eloquence of Mr. Jenifer could not effect its passage. The opponents were mainly aided by Mr. Jay's opinion on the necessity of not appearing to buy the support of Spain nor lightly to abandon solemn contracts."

In the indignant rebound from Jenifer's effort, ten states voted to adhere to the original instructions to Jay. "It has been established," said Marbois, "that they should not let the least doubt of the validity of the charters appear; that the thirteen states could not flourish and could not hope to enjoy any tranquility without the navigation of the Mississippi, or without this river as a boundary as far as the thirty-first degree of latitude." Spain, the majority argued, wished to take advantage of the present military situation to force onerous and unjust conditions on the United States. If Congress agreed that Spain had a right to conquer all that was held by Great Britain, His Catholic Majesty would set up claims to Georgia and South Carolina. And if concessions were made in the West? The people, discontented with so unequal a treaty, would undertake to reconquer what Congress had given away in precipitation and weakness. Finally, since most treaties were based more on expediency than on right, it was enough for the United States to show that the lands in question could not so fittingly belong to any other country on earth.[8]

These arguments, strangely enough, came particularly from New Englanders. But they were Southern arguments, and the later choice of Madison to put them in writing leaves little doubt that they emanated largely from him. And what of the defeated Jenifer? "Mr. Jenifer is not disheartened by this failure," Marbois assured Vergennes, "and intends to revive the question when the committee named to prepare the reply of Congress to Mr. Jay makes its report. In the meantime he will take some measures which he has communicated to me."

Thus Madison and Jenifer became the opposing generals, the latter in league with the French minister. How did these two men look to that diplomat? Madison, we have seen, was rated by Luzerne at the top, in ability and integrity, among all the delegates of his five years' acquaintance. Of Jenifer he wrote:

"Rather enlightened, he has influence in Congress; according to some a man of faith, and according to others entirely guided by his interests and his ambition. He will be an excellent Whig if public affairs turn out as well as we have a right to believe, otherwise he will find a way of regaining the favor of England. . . . He is considered to be self-interested."[9]

Part of that self-interest, Luzerne indicated, grew out of Jenifer's position as guardian of the minor heir to the enemy-alien House of Baltimore. The remainder was stated by Marbois in reporting these very maneuvers. Sending his foreign minister a Virginia resolution condemning unnamed Marylanders for uniting with former British royal governors in huge land speculations northwest of the Ohio, the chargé commented: "Mr. Jenifer is one of the persons to whom the act alludes." A year earlier Jenifer had told Minister Gerard that the Appalachian Mountains formed the proper western boundary of the United States.[10] And how did that affect him? Such a limit could be imposed only by a teaming up of Spain and England at the peace conference. If Spain secured the Southwest, England would retain the Northwest. A land company which had British Governors Dunmore and Tryon among its stockholders was in a better position to secure a grant from Great Britain than from the American Congress. At the same time, such an outcome would help to realize Maryland's desire to cut down Virginia.

The measures Jenifer planned to take were not merely "communicated" to Marbois. They were a joint product. Marbois had in his hands a defense of Spanish territorial claims just given him by Francisco Rendon. Not wishing to use it publicly, he told Vergennes a week later, "I contented myself with speaking confidentially to Mr. Jenifer, and the observations which I have the honor to attach were redrafted in concert with this delegate. He gave it to his most influential colleagues to read and they united to persuade Congress to reconsider the question."[11]

A condensed English version of the Marbois-Jenifer paper is among the Madison Manuscripts, marked "by de Marbois."[12] Jenifer's hand is evident in the opening sentence of the French text (not copied by Madison) declaring that only the states totally cut off from a possible boundary with Spain were capable of impartial judgment. In other words, leave it to Maryland. It was evident also in the heavy assault made on state charters as the basis of the American claim—the same attack made by land speculators who were asking Congress to validate the huge concessions rejected by Virginia. The memorandum opened with an urgent plea for a triple alliance to retrieve the Charleston and Camden defeats, then listed and answered eight American arguments against the Spanish territorial claims. To protect Jenifer, these American arguments were described as having been offered to Luzerne by a congressional committee in the preceding January. Actually, some of them reflected later events and the January arguments recorded in the *Journals* were not so much as mentioned. The force of the document to Americans was not in the answers, but in the French sponsorship of them. This heightened the apparent need of concessions to secure a Spanish alliance, and weakened the prospect of enforcing American claims at the peace conference. Had it been known that the paper was jointly drafted by Jenifer and Marbois, from a Spanish memorandum, the reaction might have been very different.

As it was, the maneuver upset the southernmost delegates. "The northeastern delegations," Marbois reported, "were as much opposed to this reconsideration as if they had an immediate and direct interest in the question. The southern states on the contrary seconded the proposition, and it passed by a majority of two states."

Not one word of this was entered in the *Journals*. There all was peace and unanimity. Not so among the delegates, and least of all after they handed Madison this setback. The new coalition fell to pieces. Motions were made and rejected. Conflicting state interests produced a welter of contradictory arguments.

The New England states, except Rhode Island, continued to offer the firmest support to Southern territorial claims, which were opposed by Jenifer's middle block. "Then," wrote Marbois, "one of the delegates asked them if they had the means and intention of making war on Spain and consequently on its ally France. This question brought into full view the feebleness of the reasoning offered by the eastern states." Still they clung to their position, moved, the French diplomat believed, by their old thought of postponing peace until Canada and Nova Scotia should be liberated. Also, if they departed from the ultimatum as to Southern boundaries, might not the South desert the defense of Northern boundaries at the peace conference? As to the South: "Virginia, whose vote is directed by Mr. Madison, of English stock, well-informed and moderate, but bound by the orders of his constituents, maintained an unvarying adherence to the old instructions." Delegates from farther south took the position as individuals that concessions should be made to Spain, but they could not vote to sacrifice the territories of their states.

This reasoning did not protect the Mississippi navigation. New York and Pennsylvania, terming the use of the river unimportant, voted that it be not insisted on. They were influenced, said Marbois, by the fact that the opening of the Mississippi would deflect commerce from the Hudson and upper Ohio. However, having Western land claims, New York stuck by the ultimatum as to territories.[13]

The question was now in a state which required compromise.
What followed is not made clear in the French dispatches, but can
be surmised by comparing them with the recorded actions of Congress. Apparently Madison, Duane and Sullivan joined in putting
through a set of instructions which fully upheld those already in
effect, except that, as originally planned, Jay was authorized to
accept contraband control and a free port if he could not secure
explicit recognition of a free Mississippi. One delegate, presumably Jenifer, planned to cut the heart out of the new instructions
by moving to drop free navigation and authorize Jay to omit the
territorial stipulation. Marbois was uncertain whether this plan
had completely succeeded. It had not. Madison recorded his victory with all that exuberance of detail and regard for the dramatic
which habitually characterized his accounts of his own work. "The
instructions relating to the Mississippi," he wrote to Joseph Jones,
"have passed entirely to my satisfaction." That, and nothing
more.[14]

Madison's leadership in the battle is evident enough in what followed adoption of the instructions on October 4. Two days later
Sullivan and Duane moved that a committee be appointed to draft
a letter to Jay and Franklin, backing up the instructions and explaining the reasons and principles on which they were founded.
Madison was elected chairman of this committee, Sullivan and
Duane its other members. Those seeking concessions intended to
continue the fight, they told Marbois, should the new paper be
unsatisfactory to the Spanish court.[15]

Madison's aim, in the letter to Jay, was to state the American
case as strongly and persuasively as possible, using especial caution
not to offend Spain. Marbois followed the work of the committee
closely, enabled to do so by his "particular connections" with two
of its members—probably Sullivan and Madison. Sullivan, vain,
gullible, patriotic and ethically obtuse, was the habitual spiller of
congressional secrets to the French legation, but did not go on
Luzerne's pay roll until two months later. Madison was on confidential terms with Marbois and showed him the completed draft
of the letter, which contained a bid for French support of the
American position. Marbois responded, not with support, but with

advice to Madison to revise the letter. "At first," the chargé reported to Vergennes, "it showed a little too much of the ambitious aims pursued by Virginia, which he represents. His intelligence and his moderation aided me in inspiring him with sentiments more conformable to the circumstances. . . . It has been carefully drafted to avoid all expressions which could displease his Catholic Majesty."[16]

The best testimonial to Madison's skill is the fading out of opposition when his final draft, submitted on October 10, came up for action seven days later. It was far too positive to be satisfactory to Spain but no more was heard of the plan to prevent its adoption. "The final deliberations," Marbois wrote, "were marked by calm and moderation." Carrying self-effacement to its usual incredible length, Madison reported as before to Joseph Jones: "This letter also passed in a form equally satisfactory."[17] No mention that he was chairman of the committee. No mention that he wrote the letter. Not a word about its contents. This combination of satisfaction and reticence, in writing to the presumptive author of the original report, makes it all the more evident that Madison furnished the guiding hand from the start.

The letter to Jay[18] opened with a defense of American territorial rights east of the Mississippi. By the Treaty of Paris in 1763, all of the territory now claimed by the United States was ceded by France to the king of Great Britain. The benefits of that cession devolved upon the United States by virtue of the revolution in their government. It is fundamental in all lawful governments, and particularly in the Constitution of the British empire, Madison declared, "that all the rights of sovereignty are intended for the benefit of those from whom they are derived, and over whom they are exercised." When Americans were British subjects, it was their invariable principle that the sovereignty, rights and powers of the king of England did not extend to them by virtue of his being king of the English people, but because of American obedience to him "as king of the people of America themselves." This was the basis of their abolition of his authority. It followed that "all the territory lying within the limits of the states, as fixed by the sovereign himself," was held for their particular benefit and devolved on them "in consequence of their resumption of the sovereignty to themselves."

This argument was intended to refute the Marbois-Jenifer contention that the West lay open to Spanish conquest because France ceded the land in 1763 to the king, not to the colonies. Madison's reply was good John Locke doctrine against the divine right of kings, skillfully adapted to the revolt of crown colonies. To almost any American it would be convincing. To many Englishmen it might be plausible. But how could it be expected to impress the Bourbon potentate who sat by heaven's grace upon the throne of Spain?

Madison hit next at the Spanish contention of a right to conquer specific parts of this territory still held by Great Britain. Such spots were few and small. A right founded on conquest extended only to the object conquered—no fifteen-hundred-mile Natchez hinterland. Or, if the capture of British posts carried title to the entire territory in which they were located, the United States had a more extensive title than Spain could acquire, "having by the success of their arms obtained possession of all the important posts and settlements on the Illinois and Wabash, rescued the inhabitants from British domination, and established civil government in its proper form over them." American forces were also near the mouth of the Ohio. If Spain had a right of conquest based on British occupancy of lands within the charters of American states, she could conquer any other part of the United States so occupied—New York City, Long Island, South Carolina, Georgia. Such a claim, Madison suggested, would leave Spain's own seaports or maritime provinces open to seizure by any third power, should they be occupied by an enemy during war. Next to be refuted was the contention that American claims were estopped by the royal proclamation of 1763, forbidding colonial grants west of the Appalachian Divide. Both the title and tenor of that order, he declared, showed that the purpose was to prevent Indian disputes and cut off irregular land appropriations to individuals. There was no intent to renounce the land cessions of the Treaty of Paris, nor to alter the ancient charters. On the contrary, the document expressly declared that these lands "were within the sovereignty and dominion of that crown."

Madison was skating on thin ice here. Spain's contention was that the royal proclamation of 1763 nullified claims based on colonial charters. She did not deny British crown sovereignty, but specifically affirmed it.[19] Madison had no good defense of the ancient charters, with their indefinite, extravagant, overlapping grants to the South Sea. So he defended former British sovereignty against an attack which had not been made upon it, and treated this as a justification of charter claims. In fact, as he must have known, it was the opposite, because the king had asserted his sovereignty for the purpose of restraining the individual colonies.

The most effective reply to Spain's attack on the state charters would have been a claim that the king's title had devolved on the United States collectively. Madison rejected that idea in his next argument. The lands east of the Mississippi were so fertile and convenient that the transfer of them to Spain would lead to American intrusions, difficult to restrain and dangerous to the harmony of the two countries. No less would be the danger to domestic harmony, with resulting aid to the common enemy, should Congress relinquish a territory which "lies within the charter limits of particular states, and is considered by them as no less their property than any other territory." He then swung back to the federal position by citing the reliance of the United States upon this Western land as a source of funds for the prosecution of the war. The territorial defense concluded with a detailed argument that France was required to uphold the American claim by virtue of the territorial guaranty in the treaty of alliance—an argument far too circumstantial (the territories not being specified) to put any compulsion on France or to worry Spain.

In truth, not one of Madison's arguments was likely to impress Spain, unless it was the warning of turbulent intrusions upon Spanish conquests. The discussion of British sovereignty and state charters reflected the conflict in his own thinking on state and federal titles to the Western lands. He realized the essential justice of Maryland's demand that the Western country be a common pool for the general good. But he resented the hypocritical misuse of that slogan by Maryland, New Jersey and Pennsylvania speculators seeking to rob the public of this common pool, and he objected—he was compelled to object—to the forcible stripping of his state of lands to which it had a better title than rival claimants. Nevertheless, in emphasizing British crown sovereignty, over lands sought for national purposes, Madison weakened the state titles which he was upholding. It can hardly be assumed that he was unaware of this.

Far more powerful, as a reasoned argument, was Madison's exposition of the American demand for free navigation of the Mississippi. Instead of putting this on the basis of favor, thus admitting Spain's right to close the river, he boldly asserted its freedom under international law. The usage of nations, coinciding with "the clear indications of nature and Providence, and the general good of mankind," gave those living above the mouth of a river the right to navigate it to the sea, subject only to moderate tolls to cover expenses. Backing this, which he supported from Vattel, was the claim that a similar right guaranteed to Great Britain by the treaty of 1763 had devolved upon the United States. If this treaty right did not exist, he suggested finally, the generosity of His Catholic Majesty would not suffer American citizens to be put in a worse condition, by an "alliance with him in the character of a sovereign people," than they were as subjects of a hostile power. Jay was then told that, without abandoning this American right, he might omit its positive recognition, and agree to regulations against contraband, provided a free port was established near the mouth of the river.

Turning from questions of right to those of policy, Madison pointed to the vast trade which would flow down the Mississippi after postwar settlers swarmed into the Ohio country. Matching it would be the upward movement of manufactures. France and Spain would feel the benefit of this trade. Close the Mississippi, and trade would pursue another channel—up the rivers and by portage to the Great Lakes, down the lakes and the St. Lawrence to the sea. Should this great advantage go to Britain, rather than to France and Spain, the loss of her exclusive American trade rights "might prove a much less decisive blow to her maritime pre-eminence and tyranny than has been calculated."

According to Marbois, great hopes were entertained from this part of the letter.[16] It was thought that by picturing the advantages Spain would derive from American use of the Mississippi, added effect would be given to the slight toning down of American demands. Probably Madison did not tell the French diplomat that his chief aim in this argument was to win French support by inspiring trade hopes and naval fears.

With this hard-won victory behind him, the young man who directed Virginia's vote thought that all would remain quiet until Jay was heard from again. "It now appears that I was mistaken," he wrote to Joseph Jones late in November. Threatening news from Europe, giving new force to old fears, caused the Georgia and South Carolina delegations to move that, if an alliance could not be otherwise obtained, navigation of the Mississippi be ceded to Spain, together with that part of Georgia extending from the Mississippi to the Mobile. That little hissing Latin phrase, *uti possidetis,* wrought this mischief. It had been heard all year, but now, Walton, of Georgia, reported, "it circulates with terrors, as it is pretended to be drawn from the armed neutrality." Catherine of Russia and other neutrals were reported ready to impose a peace which would give every belligerent the territory it held. A sad change from Madison's earlier hope that Britain's violations of neutral rights would embroil her with this formidable league. British maneuvers in Madrid, to detach Spain from the war, extended the alarm.[20]

As Luzerne described the new development, the four southernmost delegations decided to seek a reconsideration of the Spanish negotiations. Virginia was divided—which meant, with Walker going home, that Madison stood firm, Bland went over to the other side. If Spain rejected the American terms, they were to be submitted to the king of France and whatever the king approved would become the definitive instructions to Jay. The French minister exhorted the Southern delegates to make further concessions. Madison's propositions, he told them, did not go far enough to secure an alliance. The Georgia motion followed, without the proviso for reference to the king.[21]

The mere offering and debating of such a motion, Madison thought, carried much of the harm of its passage. The fact of it could not be concealed from Spain "and the weight which our demands would derive from unanimity and decision must be lost." When Walker left, he carried a delegation letter to Governor Jefferson, written by Bland, which Madison refused to sign. Rather, it started out as a "we" letter, then shifted to a continuation by Bland alone, upon Madison's refusal to request new instructions authorizing them to abandon the navigation of the Mississippi. "I am sorry to say," Bland wrote of his colleague, "that notwithstanding the high idea I entertain of that gentleman's good sense, judgment and candor, I feel myself irresistibly impelled by a sense of my duty, to state a matter and to communicate it." State and communicate it he did, in a single sentence several hundred words long, containing twenty-seven verb forms, largely on the subject of the applause or censure of his constituents. He must have been a trifle excited, for the original wording invited applause for doing wrong or censure for doing right—a feature of American political mores not commonly carried back to the eighteenth century.[22]

Madison urged Bland not to send the letter. The Virginia legislature had given the instructions after mature deliberation. Their constituents knew the bad war news as well as they. Spain's opposition had been expected. Jay's dispatches were hopeful. If the Virginia instructions were revised, that action could not be concealed and Spain would insist on everything Jay was authorized to yield. Bland was obdurate. "He has embraced an opinion," Madison declared to Jones, "that we have no just claim to the subject in controversy . . . and that it is the interest of Virginia not to adhere to it."

Madison discounted the danger of *uti possidetis* and the reported British intrigues at Madrid. These, he remarked to Jones, were probably artifices of Spain for obtaining her object on the Mississippi. Unluckily, a letter from Jay received on December 4 informed Congress that Mississippi navigation was proving a very serious difficulty and British emissaries were active against the United States in Madrid.

This so alarmed the Georgia delegates that they demanded a vote on their motion. "Both my principles and my instructions," Madison wrote, "will determine me to oppose it. Virginia, and the

United States in general, are too deeply interested in the subject of controversy to give it up, as long as there is a possibility of retaining it." Bland too was bound by instructions, and obeyed them, but stated on the floor that his opinion was to the contrary. The motion fell one state short of adoption but Bland's open defection completely undermined the stand taken by Madison and the New Englanders. In vain did they argue that Spain had not stated her demands, that Congress was running the risk of giving more than Madrid wanted, or of inspiring that court to enlarge its claims. These arguments, coming with especial stubbornness from Massachusetts, formed so singular a contrast to the yielding attitude of the South that they aroused the suspicion of a desire to prolong the war. Madison staved off the Georgia motion only by securing a gentleman's agreement to wait until the Virginia legislature could be consulted. Now he himself drafted a letter to the legislature, which Bland signed with him, asking for the "precise, full and ultimate sense" of their constituents on the navigation claim. Madison's finger pressed lightly on the scales as he stated the alternatives—either strengthen the position of the delegates by reaffirming the instructions, or change them if an alliance with Spain ought to be "purchased even at the price of such a cession."[23]

The answer came, in effect, from Benedict Arnold. Hours, not days, after excited messengers brought news that his armada was sailing up Chesapeake Bay, the terrified assemblymen voted to rescind the old instructions. Madison's fears about lack of secrecy were more than realized. The motion was debated and passed in open session before a full gallery, on January 2, 1781, after which the legislators galloped away to Albemarle County.

Placing Virginia's shotgun acceptance before Congress, Madison was directed to consummate the Spanish-American union with a new epistle to Jay. He produced against his will the instructions of February 15, authorizing the minister, in case of necessity, to recede from the directions of October 4 as to the Mississippi. Forty years later, Madison was shocked to read in Ramsay's *History of the American Revolution* that Congress abandoned the Mississippi on the recommendation of Virginia. To refute this, he wrote for Niles's *Register* a detailed account of what led up to the February

15 action. He told of the disagreement of two Virginia delegates, but did not name Bland as the one who gave way to Spain. Nor did he mention his own part in the framing and defense of the original instructions. The instant the menacing crisis was over, he added, Virginia and Congress returned to their original positions. That was telescoping time a bit. Cornwallis had surrendered, fighting had stopped, the need for a Spanish alliance had evaporated, before Virginia receded or the American stand was restored.[24]

The fear-inspired revocation of Madison's work by no means destroyed its effect. According to Marbois, delegates expressed the belief that no minister would dare to relax such important American claims when the necessity of that action was left to his judgment. The original principles Madison laid down furnished a goal to return to. In addition, a comedy of errors in Spain prolonged their official effectiveness. Three or four copies of dispatches were always sent on different ships to lessen the risk of miscarriage. The Spanish government had the dainty habit of lifting one set, but never more than one, from the mails between Cádiz and Madrid. Having also obtained the American ciphers, they never knew less about Jay's affairs than he did. In this instance, they knew more, for the copy they took of the February 15 resolution was the only one that reached Spain. For months, the Spanish foreign minister gave broad hints to Jay that he had better talk frankly, as the orders of Congress were known. The mystified Jay concluded that he was being given a run-around to escape fulfillment of a promised loan. He became so skeptical of Spanish aid that when a private letter finally told him of the new instructions, he put a time limit on the offer to give up the Mississippi. That upset the Spanish plan of referring all American claims to a general peace conference, in which they could be ignored. Nothing could be gained anyway, Jay told Congress, by offering to give up the navigation, because Spain was in the war for her own objects and would fight as hard for them as for American objects. Finally, he feared that if he yielded on this issue, "little half-created doubts and questions" would be cultivated in America as to the necessity of it. Thus the invisible defense foreseen by the Madison forces did its work.[25]

At the time Jay wrote this, he had received a third letter of Madison's drafting. Written in the spring of 1781, it was intended as a morale builder. Congress praised the address and discernment with which Jay had reconciled "the respect due to the dignity of the United States with the urgency of their wants" and gave entire approval of his conduct. It directed him to express the gratitude of the states to His Catholic Majesty for the measures he had taken to maintain their credit, and to assure His Majesty that it was the inviolable purpose of the United States to keep their engagements with the monarchs of France and Spain.[26]

Jay's response to these three papers of Madison's authorship must have stirred a quiet pride in the Virginia delegate. The minister made good use, he reported to Congress, of the exposition of October 17, 1780, which stated "particularly and ably the right of the United States" to free navigation of the Mississippi. He had from time to time pressed every argument in it, except that of France's territorial guaranty to the United States. The French ambassador's adverse reaction to that held him back. Jay's dislike of the second paper was matched by that of its unwilling author. The third touched him deeply.

"I do not recollect to have ever received a letter that gave me more real pleasure," he replied to the President of Congress. Considering his painful perplexities and embarrassments, the constant danger "of either injuring the dignity and interest of my country . . . or trespassing on the overrated respectability and importance of this court . . . I say sir that on considering these things the approbation of Congress gave me most singular and cordial satisfaction." His manner of using the letter was no less a compliment to Madison. Since the communication to the Spanish court "could not be better made than in the very words of this letter," he recited them in a communication to Minister Florida Blanca.[27]

For the fourth time, upon the reading of this narrative from Jay, Madison found himself commissioned to frame the reply. A year had passed since Congress undermined his defense of the Mississippi. At Madrid, the American claim had been only partially impaired, and he saw a chance now to re-establish it in fact if not in form. He wrote, therefore, completely approving the time limit upon the surrender of navigation. That concession was meant

to secure an alliance in war, and every day's delay reduced the
incentive to adhere to the offer. Jay was instructed, therefore, to
allow further delay in signing a treaty only in exchange for added
advantages—either a larger grant of money, use of the Mississippi
by Americans, "or some peculiar indulgences in the commerce of
the Spanish colonies in America."[28]

Since Spain was known to be virtually bankrupt, and jealous
of her colonial trade above all else, this was virtually a categorical
choice of opening the Mississippi or signing a treaty of alliance at
once. Furthermore, if fear for his reputation made Jay hesitate
to surrender the Mississippi when he was explicitly authorized to
do so, there was even less likelihood of that action when the congressional sanction was reduced. Thus, aided by the kindred outlook of the minister to Spain, Madison virtually destroyed the
instruction to give up navigation of the Mississippi before the
Virginia legislature authorized him to return to its defense.

CHAPTER VII

PUBLIC LANDS—HERITAGE OR SPOILS?

HAD DYNAMITE been invented a century earlier, the issue of Western lands would have been filled with it. For a dozen years, after 1775, they furnished the source of bitterest contention among the states, producing alignments which had a lasting effect upon the structure of American government.

The Union consisted in the beginning of four-sided and three-sided states. Maryland, Delaware, New Jersey, Pennsylvania, Rhode Island and South Carolina had definite boundaries which, save in Pennsylvania, furnished no "waste lands" for settlement or speculation. The three-sided states—Virginia, North Carolina, Georgia, New York, Massachusetts and Connecticut—claimed an indefinite right of westward expansion by reason of colonial charters to the South Sea, royal grants or Indian treaties. New Hampshire disputed with New York and Massachusetts over a tract called Vermont, whose rifle-bearing inhabitants disclaimed the authority of all outsiders except Jehovah and the Continental Congress. To complicate the situation, Virginia's northern boundary ran northwest, cutting its disputed way across territories claimed by New York, Massachusetts, Connecticut and Pennsylvania.

Claiming the most, having the most rivals and facing secession movements west of the Alleghanies, Virginia was the storm center of the land struggle. It was chiefly against her that Maryland hurled the plea and challenge of 1776, "that the back lands claimed by the British crown, if secured by the blood and treasure of all, ought in reason, justice and policy, to be considered as a common stock, to be parcelled out by Congress into free, convenient and independent governments, as the wisdom of that body shall hereafter direct." It was against Maryland that Benjamin Harrison shouted that same year in the Continental Congress: "By its charter Virginia owns to the South Sea . . . [nobody shall] pare away the colony of Virginia."[1]

The highest morality underlay these contentions. Marylanders, Pennsylvanians and Jerseyites knew from John Locke and the Psalms of David that God had given the earth to mankind in common. So, to supervise the distribution, leading citizens formed the Indiana Company, the Vandalia Company, the Transylvania Company, the Illinois and Wabash companies. From the Six Nations, who did not own it, they bought the present state of West Virginia, paying with a receipt for damage inflicted by other Indians on Western traders. Still other Indians, northwest of the Ohio, sold them millions of acres which belonged to the Six Nations.[2] First from the British crown, then from state governments, finally from the Continental Congress, these advocates of a common fund for the general good sought validation of their speculative claims. British royal governors were made partners in the enterprise. Shares were given to American legislators and to French Minister Gerard. But Viginia was displeased.

Virginians saw clearly that justice and morality forbade the monopolizing of the West by the big speculators of Maryland and Pennsylvania. But if individual Virginia planters, lawyers and legislators, from George Washington down, chose "to acquire at a very low price immense lands of great fertility, which . . . ought . . . to triple the funds of the speculators,"[3] that was a different matter. It took nothing from any man (unless Indians were men), gave homes to the homeless and put much-needed money into the state treasury.

Speculators might mouth the phrases of morality, but the issues themselves were deep and vital. What would happen, Maryland asked Congress, if Virginia established her title to the West? Cheap land in that state, and low taxes made possible by the sale of it, would drain Maryland of her most useful inhabitants; she would sink in wealth and importance.[4] Never, never would Maryland ratify the Confederation—so swore Governor Thomas Johnson, Daniel of St. Thomas Jenifer, Samuel Chase and their speculator brethren, until Virginia abandoned her monopoly. What would happen, Virginia asked in reply, if the land companies made good their nefarious Indian titles? Lands expected to pay the national debt, and to provide bounties for Revolutionary soldiers, would go to enrich a handful of monopolizers. Thoughtful men asked questions about political organization. Could Virginia, with wagon and horseback transportation, maintain republican government over territories stretching a thousand miles to the northwest, through trackless mountain ranges, forests and Indian-peopled plains?

Relying on the candor and justice of the several states, New Jersey and Delaware finally ratified the Confederation without waiting for a correction of territorial injustice, but that "froward hussy" Maryland still held out. Insults, sailing through the air like George Washington's dollar, were hurled across the Potomac by the Virginia and Maryland legislatures. Maryland's big speculators, through their state assembly, denounced "the avarice and ambition of individuals" (in Virginia) and urged Congress to lay out the back lands into "free convenient and independent governments." Otherwise Maryland might soon be "securing their independence" by withdrawing from the Confederation.[5]

At that very moment, Virginia was proposing that the Confederation be forever binding on such states as chose to confederate. Get in or get out, Maryland was told.[6] Then, declaring Indian land purchases void, the Virginia legislature struck at the titles of the great land companies, but made a conciliatory offer to set aside Western lands to satisfy soldier bonuses throughout the country. Finally, Virginia set up a public land office. As soon as it should open its doors, a westward torrent of lawful migration would follow the hordes of lawless squatters. Also, a horde of Virginia speculators would slip their covetous fingers under the huge, grasping fists of the outstate companies. These sent petition after petition asking Congress to restrict the states and validate their claims.

In the fall of 1779, riding roughly over Virginia's denial of federal jurisdiction, eight states put through a Maryland motion earnestly recommending that the land office not be opened. The landless states then undertook to forbid the sale or cession of Indian lands except to the federal government or with its consent.[7] This threw the New Yorkers into terror. In their state the Indians still had a lot of land to lose. They blocked a vote by pleading that the proposed action would alarm the Indians, then went home and alarmed their own state legislature so thoroughly, by their account of the "violent inclination" of Congress to federalize the West, that New York decided to save a little by sacrificing the remainder. All New York lands from the Erie region as far as the Mississippi —the same territories claimed by Virginia—were ceded to Congress "as a common fund for the expenses of the war." The act of cession was read in Congress on March 7, 1780, two weeks before Madison took up his duties there.[8]

James Madison had no part in Western land speculations. He had already put into effect the strict rule of personal conduct described in his autobiography, "never to deal in public property, land, debts or money, whilst a member of the body whose proceedings might influence these transactions."[9] Equally disinterested, and less inclined than Madison to emotional support of Virginia against attack, was his colleague Joseph Jones. Together they undertook to solve the problem of Western lands.

Their first step, in April, 1780, was to present a violent protest adopted by the Virginia Assembly in the previous December, against the right of Congress to consider the petitions of the Indiana and Vandalia companies (claiming West Virginia). If Congress assumed such jurisdiction, the territory, sovereignty and government of the states would be in peril and the country threatened with an intolerable despotism. George Mason, who wrote this protest, was top man in the moribund Ohio Company, which had been granted the same lands in 1749. His wrath gained force as he turned to the Illinois-Wabash speculators. It was notorious, he declared, that men of great influence in neighboring states (he could have named Johnson, Jenifer, Charles Carroll, Paca and Chase of Maryland, Wilson, Morris, Gratz and Franks, of Pennsylvania) were partners of the Earl of Dunmore and other British subjects claiming vast Indian purchases between the Ohio and Mississippi. The scheme in Congress was to dupe the public "under color of creating a commond fund" and convert the public lands to private purposes. Virginia would "make great sacrifices to the common interest of America." She would listen to any just and reasonable propositions but must protest against any right of adjudication in Congress.[10]

When all the wordy violences were pared away, this was an ungracious invitation to Congress to make a deal with Virginia. Jones and Madison presented the paper, not to support its intransigent tone, but to initiate a plan they had worked out with Duane of New York. On the latter's motion, a committee was appointed to consider both the Virginia protest and New York's land cession. Jones then made a plea to his state. "The present," he declared to Governor Jefferson, "is the season for accomplishing the great work of confederation. If we suffer it to pass away, I fear it will never return. The example of New York is worthy of imitation. Could Virginia but think herself as she certainly is already full large for vigorous government, she too would moderate her desires, and cede to the United States, upon certain conditions, her territory beyond the Ohio." From George Mason, whose support was vital, Jones asked with flattering deference for advice about the conditions Virginia ought to impose. Mason advised that the state cede soil and sovereignty northwest of the Ohio, provided Congress guarantee Virginia's title south of that river, pay the cost of the George Rogers Clark expedition, lay out the ceded territory in two or more states and reserve part of it for Virginia soldiers. He then offered a stinger for Maryland, whose crafty declaration for a common fund was so worded as to protect the Illinois-Wabash speculators. Let Virginia require that all Indian purchases be declared void.[11]

Two months later Congress adopted the Duane-Jones report, urging the landed states to a liberal surrender of territorial claims which could not be maintained without endangering the Confederacy. Reminding these states that permanent federal union was essential "to our very existence as a free, sovereign and independent people," they praised New York for its effort to remove "the only obstacle to a final ratification" of the Confederation, and earnestly requested the Maryland legislature to authorize the signing of the articles.

The instant this report was adopted on September 6, Jones and Madison offered a motion covering the terms of cession and administration of the Western lands. It was in effect an effort to have Congress impose on the ceding states the very terms which Virginia desired to impose on Congress. More broadly, it undertook to set up a government of the Western territories and admit them into the Union as "separate and distinct states at such time and in such manner as Congress shall hereafter direct." Here was the germ cell of the famous Ordinance of 1787—with no hint, in Madison's sponsoring of it, that he regarded it as beyond the powers of Congress.

Though devoted to safeguarding Virginia's interests, as well as those of the nation, the Jones-Madison motion reversed that state's historic position by adopting a constructive attitude toward a land cession. It even used Maryland's favorite phrase, "a common fund," which made Virginia flame with anger. But there was a different flame in it for the speculative gentry of Maryland, Pennsylvania and New Jersey. Within all parts of such ceded territory, the motion provided, all purchases and deeds from Indians "which have been or shall be made for the use of any private person or persons whatsoever, shall be deemed and taken as absolutely void." The words "have been" would knock out every existing landcompany claim; "shall be" would foreclose the future. Marylanders who talked about a common stock of Western lands could now say whether that was what they wanted, or loot for big speculators.

The day after he offered his motion, Joseph Jones went back to Virginia, to work in the state legislature for a land cession. As in the related controversy with Spain, this threw the burden upon Madison, and he soon saw that he had his hands full. Virginians, offering lands to the nation, were looked upon as Greeks bearing gifts. We are "contriving how to *buy* some portion of that western world which the *Big Knife* pretends to *give* us," remarked the cynical Lovell to an absent Massachusetts colleague.[12]

The situation was not improved by evidence of congressional leaning toward the independence of Kentucky, Virginia's lusty Western province. Madison saw a connection between this and the growing support of Vermont's similar aspirations. With New Hampshire, New York and Massachusetts losing hope of holding that territory, they need no longer stand by Virginia to win support in turn.[13]

To cope with this, Madison worked out a deft resolution. The conflicting claims of New Hampshire and New York furnished proof that each one reached to the boundary of the other. There was no space between them. Vermont, therefore, was both within the general boundaries of the United States and of one or more individual states. Congress should decide what state or states Vermont was in. To satisfy the basic complaint of the Vermonters, that New York was aiding its speculators to steal their lands, he proposed that the state or states obtaining final jurisdiction confirm the titles of the inhabitants to the lands they held, regardless of defects in the grants on which they depended. For Madison, the core of his motion was a resolve "That every attempt by force to set up a separate and independent jurisdiction within the limits of any one of the United States, is a direct violation of the rights of such state, and subversive of the union of the whole, under the superintending authority of Congress." His purpose was to set up a precedent against the secession of Kentucky or Vandalia. With his colleague Bland upsetting his plan by opposition, Madison made his first recorded speech in Congress, expressing surprise at a charge of unfairness to Vermonters. His motion aimed at the true question, the fixing of Vermont's place within a state. Congress, by the original union of the states, must have a superior power of decision, and that authority should be utilized to settle the controversy. No final vote was taken, but a preliminary one revealed a tie.[14] The flaw in Madison's position was that, recognizing the deep and genuine grievances of the people of Vermont, he subordinated them to the political requirements of a Virginia imperialism with which he had no sympathy.

While this was going on, Madison got the Jones-Madison land-cession motion through the committee with only minor changes. Not until it came up on September 18 did the land companies show their hand. The clause annulling Indian purchases, its sponsor reported to Joseph Jones, "was postponed, with an intention, I believe, of not resuming it." Congress, the opponents argued, had no power to satisfy the land jobbers, therefore it need not be forbidden. This plea came from the land jobbers themselves—offered, Madison believed, with "the real view of gratifying private interest at the public expense." To thwart this scheme, he advised, Virginia should place conditions in her act of cession, to guard against misapplication of the ceded lands.[15]

The Illinois-Wabash speculators and those Siamese twins, the Indiana and Vandalia companies,[16] were now clamoring to be heard against the Jones-Madison resolution.[17] Observing the hostile trend in Congress, Madison refrained from pressing for final action, with the result that the opponents did so themselves. Countering his effort to restore the Indian clause, they sought to bring up the hostile petitions of the Illinois-Wabash and Indiana-Vandalia groups. Madison challenged this maneuver as unconstitutional. Congress had no right to pass upon memorials which dealt with lands still belonging to Virginia. Apparently he did not realize, or was unwilling to admit, that his own motion undermined this defense. If Congress had power to set up new states and admit them to the Union, it must have power to inquire into eligibility for statehood.

The argument on Indian purchases was a repetition of the earlier debate—the people (soldiers, settlers, little speculators) against the monopolists. The division was close, so close that the vote of Virginia became decisive. Once more Bland turned against Madison, and this time took Walker with him, carrying their state into the hostile camp. The result was a tie, five states to five, with two divided, and the clause was out. With greater ease, over Virginia opposition, Congress struck out the federal guaranty of nonceded state lands. The resolutions then were passed without recorded opposition.[18]

Madison's feeling was one of unmixed chagrin. His first thought, he told Joseph Jones, was to propose to his colleagues that they state the whole matter to the Virginia Assembly. On cooler reflection, he decided to pass the facts along to Jones and leave the use of them to his discretion. Not a word did he say, however, about the defection of Bland and Walker, either of whom, by voting with him, could have restored the clause annulling purchases from the Indians.

In choosing this moderate course, Madison showed judgment as well as charity. A statement to the legislature would have pilloried poor muddleheaded vanity-ridden Bland, who, Madison

felt sure, had no deliberate intention of aiding the land companies.[19] Beyond that, the disclosure of congressional subservience
to the speculators and hostility to Virginia might produce a flare-
up of passion in the assembly, fatal to a land cession.

Sensitive over minor setbacks, Madison failed to sense the victory he actually won in the proceedings of October 10. Ceded territories were to be settled and formed into distinct republican
states, their lands to be disposed of for the common benefit of
the United States. Those two principles, added to the basic policy
of federal ownership of the public domain, furnished the permanent core of the territorial policy of the United States. Under it
the West acquired its population, state after state was added to
the Union, while forested mountains and vast grazing lands remained the property of the whole American people. With the
passage of the Jones-Madison resolutions, the heart of the mid-
continent began to beat.

The land companies, in spite of their victory on Indian purchases, were now thoroughly alarmed. William Trent protested to
Congress against Madison's effort to prevent consideration of the
Indiana and Vandalia petitions. This question of jurisdiction, he
declared, was of infinite consequence to the American Union.
Apparently he saw nothing of consequence in the demand that
Congress administer these lands for the whole people instead of
delivering them to a group of speculators. George Morgan, for
the same group, cheekily proposed to the Virginia delegates that
the dispute between the companies and Virginia be submitted to
impartial arbitrators chosen by Congress, as in a dispute between
state and state. Madison made himself a bit taller than his five feet
six in sending back the frigid rejoinder. Even if Virginia had not
already decided the matter, they could not reconcile the respect
due to a state's own sovereignty and honor with an appeal to a
foreign tribunal "in a case which involves the pretensions of individuals only, and not the rights or pretensions of any foreign
state."[20]

Watching the reaction of Congress to the petitions with which
it was "much infested," Madison concluded that there was no
serious design "to gratify the avidity of land mongers," who seemed

to him "equally alarmed and perplexed." However, the best security for keeping Congress virtuous was to put it out of their power to be otherwise. He urged Joseph Jones, therefore, not only to press for a land cession by Virginia as a means of ratifying the Confederation, but to remind the assembly of the conditions which prudence called for. Bland, justifying Madison's belief that he was not an ally of the land jobbers, helped with a delegation letter to the governor warning against their influence.[21]

At Richmond, Joseph Jones, Richard Henry Lee and George Mason were leading the movement for a cession. Able friends to it, Lee warned, would leave the assembly at the year's end. In Edmund Pendleton, Madison uncovered a dangerous psychological hazard. Answering the plea that he join in winning Maryland's ratification of the Confederation and thus offset British military victories, Pendleton replied that he would not hesitate to yield a very large part of the state's back lands "except for the reason which Shakespeare has put into the mouth of his Hotspur."

> I'll give thrice so much land
> To any well-deserving friend;
> But in the way of bargain, mark ye me,
> I'll cavil on the ninth part of a hair.

Indignation swelled in Pendleton's breast as he declared, with gross exaggeration, that "the title of Virginia to the western territory can no more be questioned than to any other spot in it." One state was setting herself against twelve. "Yield to her on this, may she not play the same game to gain any future point of interest?" In truth it was not one state against twelve, for Maryland had a majority with her. So extreme and passionate a statement by a man noted for his moderation testified to the wisdom of Madison's effort to concentrate on the issue of national unity. On that point he won Pendleton, who feared that further delay in completing the Confederation might implant suspicions abroad of secret disunion.[22]

Vitally important was the attitude of Virginia's past and incumbent governors, Patrick Henry, now popular leader in the assembly, and Thomas Jefferson. The latter, in the congressional debates of 1776, had suggested that Virginia would some day limit herself. Now he told Washington that the exposed condition of the Western settlements imposed "a great and perpetual expense" upon the state. Patrick Henry had created that expense by sending George Rogers Clark to conquer the Northwest for Virginia. Would not his state imperialism put him into the opposition? By no means. The Indiana Company held his deposition upholding the validity of its Indian grant. He had a survey of his own on the Ohio and blossomed out later as one of the foremost land speculators of the country.[23] Either for these reasons, or because of a sudden secretion of continentalism in his endocrine glands, the fiery Patrick refrained from opposition.

As time passed without action in Virginia, Madison became alarmed. Further delay would prevent a communication to Maryland before the rising of their legislature. Unknown to him, a powerful ally was about to arrive on the legislative scene. Benedict Arnold, good old traitor Benedict, who needed one deed of inadvertent grace to mitigate his treason, decided this issue, as he did another, by his landing in Chesapeake Bay. On the same day —January 2, 1781—that Virginia moved to surrender the Mississippi River to Spain, the legislature gave in to Maryland on the question of public lands. While thirty-one enemy ships came sailing up the James, and slaves cinched saddles in Richmond's wintry streets, the Virginia Assembly ceded the American Northwest to Congress, under the terms and requirements laid down by Mason and advised by Madison.

What now would Maryland do? The speculator group, led by Jenifer and Johnson, still had reason to fight ratification of the Confederation. They needed bargaining power to block the annulment of Indian deeds, which formed one of the terms of Virginia's act of cession. Here Arnold once more worked better than he knew. In early January French Minister Luzerne received a joint appeal from Daniel of St. Thomas Jenifer, in his capacity as president of the Maryland Senate, and Speaker William Bruff, of the House, asking for French naval aid against Arnold. For a year the French diplomat had been exhorting Jenifer and other

Marylanders to accede to the Confederation. They not only spurned his advice, but refused even to transmit an appeal by Congress that Maryland ratify the articles for effect on Spanish military policy and at home they tried to establish a belief that France was opposed to the completion of the Confederation. "One especially among them," wrote Luzerne, "a man looked up to for his situation, his talent and his fortune, used all sorts of means to prevent it. He had even tried to persuade me that the alliance could not gain by it and that we should desire that Congress should not emerge from the impotence in which it finds itself today."[24]

This obviously was Jenifer, who also was encouraging the French to support Spain against the United States in the West. Marbois too urged on him that Maryland's accession to the Confederation would be the proper answer to Benedict Arnold's address to the American people, in which he claimed that the French treaty was invalid because the Confederation had not been completed at the time of its ratification by Congress. The Maryland delegate was not persuaded.[25]

Now the Jenifer-Bruff appeal for help, brought forth by Arnold's threat to Baltimore, allowed Luzerne to break the barricade. Knowing, as he told Vergennes, that Bruff favored ratification while Jenifer did not, he seized this chance to place an appeal for ratification where it was bound to reach the assembly. So fitting, he told the two men, was this step to give energy to the states, to strengthen their union, to destroy enemy hopes of sowing dissension, "that all good citizens can see only with satisfaction that the obstacles which have hitherto stood in the way of this accession have been at last removed."[26]

Pressed by Arnold's threat and Luzerne's plea, the Maryland House voted to accede. Jenifer in the Senate still fought on and the bill was beaten. Former Governor Johnson, House leader, partner of British governors in the Illinois-Wabash speculation, now sent a message which the Senate could understand. The pressure value of Maryland's refusal to confederate had disappeared. Justice in the Western land policy (that is, a validation of Indian purchases) could better be secured from the good will of confederated states than from the outside. To which was added the desirability of pleasing the French ally. The Senate reversed itself. The Confederation was completed.[27]

For Madison, this was just the beginning of the fight over Western lands. It was a surprise to him that Virginia's liberal cession did not meet with early acceptance. His optimism was rudely jolted when Congress referred the Virginia, New York and Connecticut cessions to a committee of seven without a Virginian on it, headed by the shrewdest opponent of the Virginia title, Dr. Witherspoon, of New Jersey. New York delegates then served notice that their state's Western cession would be withdrawn unless New York received the same guaranty of remaining territory that any other state (meaning Virginia) might receive. With this, to the Witherspoon committee, went three land-company memorials—a notice of congressional jurisdiction in Western affairs.[28]

The Witherspoon committee advised against accepting any of the three cessions. Instead, Congress should "ascertain what vacant territory belongs to the United States in common," and plan for its division, settlement and sale to pay the national war debt. This was a direct challenge of the Virginia doctrine that no territory could belong to the United States in common without a prior cession by some individual state. The report lay without action until October, when it was transferred to a committee of five, no less hostile to Virginia and friendlier to the speculators.[29]

"The ingredients of this composition," Madison commented to Jefferson, "prepared us for the complexion of their proceedings." Their first step was to inquire into state titles to the ceded territory, after which they took evidence in support of land-company claims. "On this occasion," said Madison, "we renewed our remonstrances to the committee, and our complaints to Congress, but with as little effect as on the first occasion. The upshot of the whole was a report to Congress, rejecting the cessions of Connecticut and Virginia, and accepting that of New York; disallowing also the claims of the companies northwest of the Ohio, but justifying that of the Indiana company."

Historians have made many conjectures as to the reason for this discrimination between two companies with equally bad claims, the favorite one being that the Illinois-Wabash backers were in-

different because they looked to continued British sovereignty
over the Northwest. Some no doubt desired that, but the prospect
of it was too dim to warrant indifference to Congress. The true
explanation lies elsewhere. Madison stated that the committee
seemed to distrust the earlier doctrine of collective sovereignty
and chose instead to recognize the title of New York, "stretching
it over the whole country claimed by the other ceding states, and
then accepting a transfer of it to the United States." How did
New York come by this vast area? According to the committee
report, by acting for the British crown as protector of the Six
Nations. But the Illinois-Wabash Company held deeds to much
of this same land from Indian tribes whose claims were disputed
by the Six Nations. If Congress validated the company's title, it
would be a confession that the Six Nations did not own the land,
consequently New York had no jurisdiction over it and no power
to transfer it to Congress.[30]

To Madison's vexation, he found that the terms of his own
state's cession were turned against it. These furnished "a handle
for taking up questions of right, both with respect to the ceding
states, and the great land companies, which they have not before
ventured to touch." Congress and the committee turned deaf
ears to the protest that if the land lay within Virginia, that state
alone could deal with matters affecting it. Apparently Madison
held to the remarkable doctrine that Congress could accept conditions laid down by Virginia, thus writing them into federal law,
but could not previously inquire into their nature, necessity or
effect, nor into the existing ownership of the offered territories.
His own resolution of October 10, 1780, on which the Virginia
cession was grounded, presumed far broader powers in Congress.

Madison recognized the part played in this campaign by general
land hunger. "An agrarian law," he remarked, "is as much coveted
by the little members of the Union, as ever it was by the indigent
citizens of Rome." If there was disgust in that comment, it was
inspired not by the ambitions of the indigent, but by the machinations of little states in behalf of big speculators. The true policy
of Congress, he believed, was to accept all cessions and thus "bury
all further contentions by covering the territory with the titles of as

many claimants as possible." Instead, the committee asked Virginia to make a new cession, free of any conditions whatsoever. The purpose of that was plain—to make it possible for Congress to validate the Indian deeds. With everything else subordinated now to the need of fighting against the adversaries of Virginia, Madison urged Jefferson (by this time returned to private life) to prepare a complete documentary defense of the state's title to the West. Until that was done, he was helpless to contradict "the misrepresentations and calumnies which are daily leveled against the claims of Virginia." Angered though he was, his greatest anxiety was lest the congressional attack "exasperate the Assembly into measures which will furnish new hopes to the British court to persevere in the war." It would be particularly unhappy if any symptoms of disunion "should blast the golden prospects" opened by the victory at Yorktown. But Congress was so divided that neither side could produce an effective majority so it would "be impossible for the enemies of Virginia to obtain any positive injury to her rights." The issue could run along until time helped decide it.[31]

CHAPTER VIII

Fighting for Implied Powers

PHILADELPHIANS, if the *Pennsylvania Packet* portrayed their thoughts correctly, believed that Thursday, the first of March, 1781, would be "memorable in the annals of America to the last posterity." In Congress, on that earth-shaking day, took place the final ratification of the Articles of Confederation and Perpetual Union between the states. The American system of government was complete, to the joy of patriots and (said a delegate) "the mortification of the infamous Tories" who expected it to crumble to pieces.

The number thirteen was in the air. Thirteen shots rang out from artillery. Thirteen boomed from naval cannon in the Delaware. Church bells clanged the tidings to the public. "The *Ariel* frigate, commanded by the gallant Paul Jones, fired a *feu de joie* and was beautifully decorated with a variety of streamers in the day and ornamented with a brilliant appearance of lights in the night." Fireworks at the State House vied with the *Ariel*'s sky-peppering display, and the festivities ended, we may presume, with the usual smashing of windows in unlighted houses.[1]

Congress had a joyful day, externally and internally. The usual gustatory pleasures were increased by a ten o'clock collation at the home of Samuel Huntington, President of Congress. At two o'clock there was a larger one at the home of Samuel Huntington, President of the United States in Congress Assembled. His new title came with the noonday signing by the Maryland delegates. The whole celebration was planned by a committee consisting of Walton, Madison and Mathews. Madison apparently did not feel the full solemnity of the occasion, for when Walton wrote that the President's wine should be accompanied by "a keg of biscuit, in the room of cake," Madison facetiously underlined it with: "Does it mean the cake room."[2]

The United States, as two Philadelphia newspapers said in identical articles, was now growing up "into greatness and consequence among the nations." They did not see this as the creation of the American republic. A nation already in being was taking maturer form. Nobody, practically, regarded the new articles as adequate. Alexander Hamilton, that old-headed boy on Washington's staff, already had warned that the "uncontrollable sovereignty in each state" would defeat the powers given to Congress. On the day after Maryland voted to accede, John Witherspoon sought an amendment to give Congress power over commerce. Duane and Joseph Jones both hoped that in this moment of uplift, Congress would ask the states for additional articles, to give vigor and authority to government.[3]

Now that the new powers were in effect, how did they compare with those exercised during the previous six years? They were narrower, it was clear, than those originally given to delegates by the Revolutionary conventions of 1775 and renewed by the later-established states. But they were decidedly broader than the meager authority Congress had been able to retain in the face of rising state pride and jealousy.[4]

James Madison was one of a handful of delegates who saw that the primary question confronting Congress was its ability to transact business under the rules laid down in the articles. There were omissions in the expressed powers which could well prove fatal. Other powers, broadly interpreted and effectively utilized, might fill the gap. Nine states, however, must give their assent to many actions—to decisions of war and peace, to treaties, to requisitions of money from the states, to appropriations, borrowings, currency emissions or coinage. That meant that with nine states present, one could outvote eight. With eight present, Congress could not vote. The article on procedure than added: "nor shall a question on any other point, except for adjourning from day to day, be determined, unless by the votes of a majority of the United States, in Congress assembled."

The nine-state proviso was definite and inescapable. But what about other actions, including the preliminary steps to measures which required the consent of nine? Must they be supported by a majority of *all* the United States or merely by a majority of those assembled on any particular day?

Four days after the fireworks, Madison joined Duane, Lovell, Witherspoon, McKean and Root—an oddly mixed lot of delegates —in arguing for the latter construction. The plain and obvious meaning, they contended, was a majority of the old quorum of nine—only five of which need be present if all agreed. They cited the practice of the British parliament and of corporations. Congress would be able to do little indeed if seven affirmative states must be mustered for every incidental motion. Some went so far, the French minister said, as to contend that four out of seven, or even three out of five, was enough to establish a majority of a quorum. As reported by the hostile and prejudiced Thomas Rodney, the Duane-Madison group employed "much fine reason and sophistry . . . indeed no species of artful reasoning within the reach of a lawyer was left untried on this occasion." He saw the maxim verified that "all men would be tyrants if they could git the power."

Thomas Burke, the old war horse of state sovereignty, took the lead against them. He clearly remembered the debates in Congress when the articles were being drafted. The purpose was to require seven affirmative votes on all motions that did not require nine. The number was omitted because Canada was expected to enter the Union. If Congress "attempted so early to claim powers that were not expressly given by that charter, or began to pervert it to increase their power," Burke warned, "they would give a dreadful alarm to their constituents who are so jealous of their liberty." Allow five states to carry a motion and a junto or cabal of that number could ruin the majority of eight. Mathews of South Carolina, bound by instructions, came to the support of Burke, and state-minded Bland needed none to make him do the same.

The debate must have been a strenuous one, for Rodney reported that the delegates were too tired out next day to carry it on. Feeling also that a final decision was unsafe without a larger attendance, they agreed that for the present, seven states should be required to carry every ordinary motion. Since only a contrary decision would have been unsafe, it is evident that a majority favored the Duane-Madison interpretation, but feared to put it into effect. Hesitating, they were lost. It would be harder to change a temporary rule than to adopt the contrary one at the start.

Burke no doubt was right about the original intent of Congress, although Madison's view accords with the interpretation given to analogous provisions of the United States Constitution. But, as an effective lawmaking and executive body, the United States in Congress Assembled died right then, at the age of six days. The North Carolinian's talk about a cabal of five states ruining the other eight was a preposterous reversal of the truth. His own construction fastened minority rule on Congress and made absenteeism a weapon of negation. An absent delegation, in effect, voted No to every motion, and a state was absent, now, unless two or more of its delegates were present. If a two-man delegation divided, it was the same as voting No. With nine states present, three could outvote six, and if these nine had two delegates apiece, three delegates could outvote fifteen. Madison's interpretation, on the contrary, would have forced the states to send delegates for the protection of their interests, thus not only insuring majority rule, but furnishing the attendance needed for nine-state actions.[5]

For nearly a year, Congress was plagued with the fact that the seven-state rule produced one result directly contrary to its own principle. No change could be made in the wording of a measure, after it came from committee, without the approval of seven states. This meant, in a lean Congress, that a small minority could force the retention of obnoxious wording right up to the moment of the final vote. Suppose, for example, that in the framing of financial policy Congress had a resolution before it "That two plus two make five." With seven states present, one delegation could prevent a change from "five" to "six," or whatever figure the majority believed in. Not seven states, but one, would be determining the form of legislation. How remedy this without abandoning the seven-state requirement? Congress adopted an order that when a motion was made to strike out any part of a proposition, the question voted on should be "Shall those words stand?"[6] If fewer than seven states voted Aye, they were stricken out.

That was very fine, as far as "two plus two make five" was concerned. But what happened when a lean Congress undertook to inform tax-resisting states that "two plus two make four"? Some delegate, recalling that the purpose of the American Revolution was to abolish taxes, was almost sure to move that "four" be stricken out. On the question, "Shall that word stand?" out it went unless the affirmative mustered seven states. Without seven, they could not fill the hole.

Again and again, this technique was used by obstructive delegates to disrupt legislation, or by clever ones to reverse its meaning. When attendance was low, the seven-state rule almost paralyzed the routine process of putting motions in shape for passage. By making absenteeism a defense against adverse action, it fostered the condition which made the rule most damaging. By reducing the ability of Congress to do its work, it lowered that body in prestige and power. Measured by its results, this may justly be called the "chaos clause" of the Articles of Confederation.

Madison and Duane had met defeat, not from the hostility of Congress, but from the timidity of a friendly majority and the historic weight of the opposing position. Shifting its approach, this majority appointed Varnum, Duane and Madison "to prepare a plan to invest the United States in Congress assembled with full and explicit powers for effectually carrying into execution in the several states all acts or resolutions passed agreeably to the Articles of Confederation." Madison wrote the committee's report.[7] One might have thought it emanated from Alexander Hamilton or John Marshall, so far did it go in the assertion of implied federal power in the new articles of government.

Article two reserved to the states every power, jurisdiction and right which was not "expressly delegated" to the United States. However, Madison pointed out, Article thirteen required every state to abide by the determinations of Congress on all matters so delegated. By this article, he declared, "a general and implied power is vested in the United States in Congress assembled to enforce and carry into effect all the articles of the said confederation against any of the states which shall refuse or neglect to abide by such their determinations, or shall otherwise violate any of the said articles."

Because no specific provision was made to enforce this implied power, Madison feared that the states might question the legality of enforcement measures. Also it was "most consonant to the spirit of a free constitution" that there be explicit warrant for the exercise of powers, and that the penal consequences of a violation of duty be clearly understood. He advised, therefore, that the states be asked to confirm a new clause in the articles, authorizing Congress "to employ the force of the United States as well by sea as by land" to compel the states to fulfill their federal engagements. Congress should be authorized to seize the vessels and merchandise of citizens of the offending states and to prohibit their trade and intercourse with other states and foreign countries.

The significant fact is that Madison believed Congress possessed all these powers by implication, without any new grant from the states. The expediency of making the application, he wrote to Jefferson, "will depend on the probability of their complying with it. If they should refuse, Congress will be in a worse situation than at present; for as the Confederation now stands . . . there is an implied right of coercion against the delinquent party." As for enforcement of it against recalcitrant states, "two or three vessels of force employed against their trade will make it their interest to yield prompt obedience to all just requisitions on them."

How far did Madison think this right of coercion extended? Farther than to the measures outlined in his report, for he said also to Jefferson: "Without such powers, too, in the general government, the whole confederacy may be insulted, and the most salutary measures frustrated, by the most inconsiderable state in the Union. At a time when all the other states were submitting to the loss and inconveniency of an embargo on their exports, Delaware absolutely declined coming into the measure, and not only defeated the general object of it, but enriched herself at the expense of those who did their duty."

Delaware refused to renew a state embargo supporting the federal embargo of June 8, 1778. At the very least, therefore, Madison believed that the Articles of Confederation gave Congress implied power to lay a nationwide embargo, and to coerce individual states into acceptance of it. Let no one think he was unaware of this reasoning. At the time he wrote, a committee report was before

Congress advising "That the Board of Admiralty be directed to . . . seize all vessels in the river Delaware loaded for exportation" with banned articles and that "no vessel loaded with such provision be suffered to proceed to sea until the embargo shall be repealed by Congress."[8]

Five times, following the writing of Madison's report on federal coercion of the states, he and Joseph Jones asked Governor Jefferson to give his opinion of the proposal.[9] They received no reply. Six years later, after Madison repeated his suggestion, Jefferson made the proposition his own. Writing to Edward Carrington he said that it was not necessary to give Congress that power expressly; "they have it by the law of nature . . . a single frigate would soon levy on the commerce of any state the deficiency of its contributions."

This Jefferson letter was a godsend to William C. Rives when he faced the task of concealing the fact that Madison believed not only in federal coercion of the states, but in the existence of an implied power of coercion—doctrines anathema to the antitariff, proslavery South of the mid-nineteenth century, and contrary to Madison's own later state rightism. The most Rives would concede was that Madison, "habitually jealous of the exercise of constructive powers, appears to have favored, at this time, a specific amendment" expressly conferring coercive power on Congress. He then quoted part of Madison's 1781 letter to Jefferson, omitting the portion which declared that Congress already possessed such a right. He cited the existence of a congressional report on the subject, but failed to mention either that Madison wrote it or that it too upheld the doctrine of constructive powers. Jefferson's 1787 letter, however, was quoted at length, giving the impression that he, but not Madison, believed in powers by implication.[10]

All this means that as Madison approached the great task of his life—a leading and guiding part in the writing of the United States Constitution—he approached as a believer in a strong federal government, in federal coercion of the states, and in easy discovery of implied powers where none were expressly stated. His indorsement of military coercion has puzzled those few students of political behavior who have recognized the existence of it. E. M.

Burns comments: "Professor Parrington considered Madison's emphasis upon coercive government as marking a fundamental conflict between his philosophy and that of Jefferson. The difference can rather easily be accounted for by reference to Madison's more cynical and perhaps more realistic view of human nature."[11] Since Jefferson finally accepted Madison's view, the difference between them was hardly fundamental. This manner of thinking may have been a reflection of the "whiff-of-grapeshot" age in which they were living. It was more cynical than realistic. To say nothing of the hatred engendered by actual resort to military force, the fear of it almost certainly would have led to secret interstate alliances, converting attempted coercion into civil war.

Congress found Madison's report on coercion too hot for comfort. After debate on May 2, it was referred to a grand committee, to which each state delegation named one man. Varnum and Duane carried over, but Virginia put hostile-minded Bland in Madison's place. Since the delegation then present hardly would have done this against his wishes, he probably sensed the evasive purpose of the reference. The larger the committee, the weaker its action.

While this was going on, Madison was driving to the same end by specific legislation based on implied powers. Aiming at the West Indies trade, he offered a motion on March 16 "for putting a stop to all commercial intercourse between the inhabitants of the United States of America and the subjects of the king of Great Britain." This was a move to extend and strengthen the old embargo by revoking exceptions from it. Under what authority? The Articles of Confederation, which had superseded the indefinite earlier powers, said nothing about regulation of commerce. Madison's theory apparently was that the war power and the power over prizes, expressly delegated to Congress, included the implied power to regulate commerce for war purposes.[12]

Enlarged and strengthened on the floor of Congress, his proposal sailed through to passage. It received the title, "An ordinance relative to the capture and condemnation of prizes"—the first action of Congress to be called an ordinance. The tone of authority was unprecedented: "It is hereby ordained and ordered"—the

first time in the history of Congress that such words had been
used. National sovereignty rode high in it: "The United States in
Congress assembled . . . judging it inconsistent with their dignity
as a free and independent nation . . ." In the flush of its new
powers, Congress spoke for once as it wanted to.

This ordinance took no account of the theory, so often expounded in later years, that the authority of the Confederation
bore only upon states and not on individuals. After ordering general reprisals against enemy ships, goods and subjects, and providing for the disposition of prizes in admiralty courts, it "farther
ordained, that the citizens and inhabitants of these United States
be, and they hereby are, strictly enjoined and required to abstain
from all intercourse, correspondence or dealings whatsoever, with
the subjects of the said King of Great Britain, while at open war
with these United States, as they will answer the same at their
peril." State executives were "hereby called upon to take the most
vigilant and effectual measures" for enforcing this ban and bringing its violators "to condign punishment." The punishment was
to be under state laws which supported the old federal embargo,
but the concept of power was broad enough to sustain a federal
penal code. If Congress could validly ordain that citizens of the
United States should not do a thing, it could punish those who
violated the ordinance.[13]

That Madison wished to use state officers for the direct enforcement of federal law became evident a few days later, when he
offered an amendment to a newly adopted second ordinance, punishing piracies and felonies on the high seas. Congress had express
authority, under the Articles of Confederation, to set up courts
for this purpose. It decided instead to give the higher state courts
authority to conduct these trials under common law, with the
same punishment as for robbery or murder on land. Madison
moved to transfer piracy trials to the existing "Court of Appeals
in cases of capture," a federal court to which appeals were carried
from state courts of admiralty. In his amendment, the states were
"called upon to order their sheriffs and jailers to attend the said
court when necessary," and take accused persons to the jail most
convenient to it.[14]

Turning then to the main work of the Court of Appeals, Madison's motion called upon the states "to order their respective marshals to carry into immediate execution the decrees of judgment of the said court under the penalty of dismission by the said Court of Appeals and action for damages in the courts of common law at the suit of the party injured." This was a most extraordinary proposal. By joint action of Congress and of any individual state, state officers were to be given federal status and be made subject to total dismissal by a federal court for neglect of federal duties. By similar joint action, civil penalties of the unwritten common law of England were to be used to compel enforcement of federal law. While this fell short of a full-fledged effort to plant the common law in the Articles of Confederation, it ran in that direction, as did the resort to common law in the piracies trials.

This revamping of prize courts was dropped at the end of hostilities, but in the meantime Madison was called on to revise an ordinance on captures. He drafted twenty amendments, all accepted. One of them, by insertion of a few words, totally knocked out unchartered privateering. Distributing prize money was easy enough, when it came to allowing one-twentieth to the Treasury and one-tenth to the privateer's captain; not so easy to decide that each petty officer, from midshipman to cook, deserved one-twenty-second part of three-twentieths of the whole. When it was found desirable, a year later, to give the Treasury a bigger cut in the swag, Congress remembered Madison's immunity to mathematical headaches and turned the revision over to him.[15]

Having become such an expert on ships, on whose rolling decks he never set foot in his life, the Virginian was given the kindred task of dealing with recaptures on land. General Greene's council of war had ruled that certain South Carolina horses, recaptured from the enemy by Polish Colonel Kosciusko, became the property of the United States. Not so, said the state of South Carolina, they go back to their original owners. Madison's report upheld South Carolina in principle, for Congress had decreed that property captured on land and recaptured on water should revert to the original owners. But by failing to deal with recaptures on land, it had left that subject, over which it had exclusive jurisdiction, to the judgment of military commanders. The council of war, Madison held, could not be overruled by Congress, which possessed, in cases of captures, "a legislative only, and not a judicial authority." The remedy, therefore, was to exercise that legislative authority by passing a resolution (which Congress proceeded to do) remitting the animals to their original owners, minus a limited compensation promised to the recaptors.

These South Carolina horses, with Madison guiding them, trample heavily on John Adams' theory that the old Congress was a diplomatic and not a legislative body. That careless statement, which forms one of the underpinnings of the twentieth-century campaign to decry the early nationhood of the United States, was quickly challenged by Thomas Jefferson, with the result that Adams half abandoned it. Madison had knocked it out five years in advance, and Congress planted his words in the country's statutes.[16]

Madison's ban on trading with the enemy stirred up no tumult over federal power. That was because it depended on state officers for enforcement. Sharp as a knife edge, however, was his second move in the exercise of implied powers—an authorization and order to the army to impress food and forage for its southward march against Cornwallis.

Impressment had been simple enough in the early days of the Revolution. At the 1776 summit of its authority and prestige, Congress without a tremor gave General Washington "full, ample and complete powers . . . to take . . . whatever he may want for the use of the army . . . allowing a reasonable price for the same." A year later, when the half-starved Continentals crouched shivering at Valley Forge, Congress complained that the too sparing use of this power by Washington threatened the army with destruction and imperiled the general liberties of the country. It ordered that in certain military areas "every kind of stock and provisions . . . be taken from all persons without distinction, leaving such quantities only as he shall judge necessary for the maintenance of their families."

Washington had seen how impressment by the army built up jealousy of military power. He wanted it transferred to civil authority, which the people were accustomed to obey without question. That meant to the states. But when the states assumed this duty, in response to the request of Congress, their halfhearted laws seemed more to restrict impressment than to authorize it. In making this transfer, Congress allowed Washington's authority to lapse. It could be reasserted only in defiance of the new state laws. So the army got all it could from the civil magistrates, and took more by naked force, giving military certificates in payment.[17]

The earlier impressment order of Congress was defended by its author, William Duer, on the ground that congressional authority was not limited by any article of the yet unratified Confederation.[18] Now the articles were in effect. They said nothing about impressment. Did this power exist, by implication, in the authority given Congress to carry on war? If so, could Congress impress supplies in violation of state law?

Madison's answer was Yes. He was assisted to this conclusion by a double crisis as acute as that of Valley Forge—though the dark military shadow actually held the light of approaching victory. Cornwallis, smarting under Tarleton's defeat at the Cowpens (January 17, 1781) and infuriated at being outmaneuvered by General Greene, was cutting loose on a march to Virginia. Now, in May, he might at any moment make a junction with Arnold, who had been strongly reinforced by Phillips. Two thousand more British troops were reported sailing south from Sandy Hook.

To face these armies in Virginia were the meager forces of Lafayette and Steuben. "Mad Anthony" Wayne's little army of Pennsylvanians was under marching orders to reinforce Lafayette but it did not budge from York. For months, following their New Year's mutiny in Jersey, the sullen Pennsylvania regiments had stayed in their barracks, refusing to stir until paid what had been promised them. Congress at last took care of the pay by scraping up all of the forty-for-one money Pennsylvania was able to emit, and borrowing $13,740 from the state in addition. Still the troops remained motionless. They could not march without provisions which the penniless Board of War was unable to furnish.[19]

At this crucial moment, long-gathering pressures burst their paper-money wrappings and financial cataclysm swept the land. In the previous November the New Jersey legislature, to let nature (i.e., inflation) take its course, had repealed its forty-for-one devaluation law. Madison wrote a strong though conciliatory protest against this blow to the financial system but Congress did nothing with the report. In the spring (April 27, 1781) New Jersey fixed the exchange at one hundred fifty for one. That loosed the deluge. To protect itself against Jersey speculators, Pennsylvania set its own figure at one hundred seventy-five for one. Panic seized the populace. Down went the new paper money—"vibrating downward," as Madison described it on May 5, till it had less than one-fourth the value of specie. With speculators able now to buy four times as much old money with specie as they could with the new bills, down went the specie value of continental dollars—four hundred, five hundred, seven hundred, nine hundred to one in six days' time. Merchants refused the old money altogether and disorder swept the city. Hungry sailors roamed the streets, hammering people with clubs. A mob of Philadelphians, wearing cockade hats of continental dollars, led a tarred and dollar-feathered dog through the streets. And what of the speculators, loaded up with worthless money? By every road they streamed out of the metropolis, their saddlebags bulging with currency, hastening to swindle the inhabitants of distant states before they heard of the collapse. Passing them, on the road to Richmond, galloped an express sent by the Virginia delegates to give warning of the danger.[20]

This financial collapse anchored the Pennsylvania troops still more firmly in the little city of York. Washington's Northern army was starving, too. The desperate Q.M.G. was selling precious meat and flour to secure wagons with which to move what little he had left. The Treasury had not the means of moving a hundred barrels of flour. "Congress is at its wits' end," wrote Daniel of St. Thomas Jenifer, stirred for a moment out of his speculative schemes.[21]

Such was the state of affairs when Madison offered his impressment motion, two days after Cornwallis entered Virginia. It provided "that General Wayne be, and he is hereby, authorized and directed, in case the supplies of provisions and forage necessary for the immediate march of the detachment under his command to the southern department cannot be otherwise obtained, to impress the same," with their value credited to the states against the requisitions of Congress. Seven states voted Aye; Pennsylvania alone said No. Yet the decision was perilously close. Five out of the affirmative seven had two-man delegations. If a single delegate in any of these had voted No, the motion would have failed, even with a six-to-one majority in its favor. Seldom has so much depended on unanimity, seldom did the "chaos clause" come so near to working disaster without doing so.

This authorization of impressment proved to be one of the decisive steps of the war. Wayne was "rarin' to go," and his army was not so reluctant after he shot six of his men who thought differently about it.[22] His union with Lafayette near Culpeper, Virginia, led to a stand against Cornwallis at the point of his farthest advance and started him back to fatal Yorktown.

Passage of Madison's motion was hailed with shouts of joy by John Mathews, his associate in the committee on the Southern campaign. It would have been done six weeks earlier, Mathews wrote to General Greene, had not action depended on men "whose souls are confined within the compass of a nutshell." They have at last blundered across the Rubicon, he added, but most of them "did it with their eyes shut, as children do, when they walk in the dark, for fear of meeting the devil in their way."

Greene might laugh, Mathews thought, at such a fuss over impressment, since his army in the disorganized Carolinas was fed by scarcely any other means. "But remember there is no such power *literally* given to Congress by Confederation, and to act up to the spirit of it is a doctrine supposed to be big with many evils." With this point gained, he hoped that necessity would "oblige them to interpret the powers given by the Confederation in their utmost extent," or even strain them for the great purposes of the war. But he feared that "when these doughty heroes have opened their eyes, and looked back on the tremendous gulf they have passed, they will . . . examine their tender consciences . . . and apostatize."[23]

What could reveal more clearly the degeneration of Congress from its pristine strength than this hesitancy, even at a moment of supreme crisis, to resume powers which once had been freely exercised? Timidity alone could doubt whether power to feed an army was implied in the power to make war. Forced by necessity, Congress adopted one specific measure after another which Madison put before it, based on implications of power. But what of the general principles he was asking Congress to establish—his assertion of a general and implied federal power to enforce all the Articles of Confederation, including the implications he saw in them, against unwilling states? Mathews' description of the "doughty heroes" in Congress left little doubt about the fate of that report. The grand committee to which it was referred reported a substitute for it in July. It asked the states to authorize Congress to lay embargoes for sixty-day periods, and to earmark specific revenues for Congress. Such a masterpiece of negation, coming four months after the adoption of Madison's ordinance for a complete and unlimited embargo, was too much even for men hunting the Rubicon bridges. Congress referred both reports to a new and moderately nationalistic committee with additional orders to prepare an exposition of the Confederation, a plan for its complete execution and supplemental articles.[24]

The report of this committee[25] was likewise a masterpiece—in the art of going two ways at once. Echoing Madison, it declined to make an exposition of the Confederation because failure to enumerate any congressional powers would become an argument against their existence. It then listed twenty-one actions which ought to be taken by Congress under its existing powers, closing with Madison's coercive policy. Proving that it could find a giant-sized implied power of its own, the committee declared that the common guarantee to Americans, of the privileges and immunities of citizenship in all the states, gave Congress the power and duty of describing those privileges and immunities.

Having thus gone virtually as far as Madison did in the assertion of implied power, the committee went full distance on the opposite tack. It proposed to ask the states for power after power which had already been claimed or exercised under Madison's leadership. Authority was sought:

To lay wartime embargoes. (One had been laid on March 27, on Madison's motion.)

To prescribe rules for impressment. (Done on May 18, on Madison's motion, and again on June 4.)

To admit new states into the Union. (The Jones-Madison motion, adopted October 10, 1780, authorized their admission.)

To distrain the property of a delinquent state. (Madison's report on coercion declared that Congress had this power.)

To vary the rules of suffrage in Congress. (Madison and others on March 5 contended for the validity of a different rule.)

To give Congress exclusive control of foreign consuls. (Congress had this power by implication, and exercised it one week later.[26])

To authorize Congress to appoint collectors and direct the mode of accounting for taxes levied for its benefit. (Madison's doctrine of an implied power to collect taxes from the states by force would cover such matters.)

The contradictory nature of this report was enough to insure a quiet pigeonhole for it. With it, into lasting repose, went Madison's resolves on the implied power of Congress. Yet his campaign was not lacking in results. His specific legislation based on implied power set troops in motion for the final campaign of the war. The difficulty of maintaining the principle of it, in a government limited to powers expressly delegated and facing jealous and contentious states, aroused him to the danger of the word "expressly." Eight years later he omitted it from the Tenth Amendment to the United States Constitution—reserving undelegated powers to the states—and successfully opposed the effort to have it inserted.[27] By that 1789 victory, stemming from his 1781 defeat, he prevented the cutting down of the United States government to its Confederation level.

One can only guess at what would have followed had Madison

won on all points in 1781. He would have established the principle of implied powers in a one-house federal Congress chosen by the states, operating under workable voting rules, and unchecked by the courts. That would have been a weak structure at the time. But what would it have been after the gradual emergence of an appointed executive and the rise of political parties? The indirect election system—choice by legislatures instead of the people—might then have reared a cabinet and senatorial government, unified by national political organization, infinitely more powerful than anything the United States has known. That would not have been what James Madison wanted, but the germ of it was in his 1781 interpretation of the Articles of Confederation. Here too was more than the germ, here was the lusty growing embryo of that government of implied powers, derived from the United States Constitution, which developed by congressional action and judicial construction through later decades and centuries.

CHAPTER IX

EXPANDING THE GOVERNMENT

No SOONER were the Articles of Confederation in effect than Madison found himself projected into a new political struggle. From about the time he entered Congress, there had been a faltering movement to set up civil departments headed by secretaries, in place of the clumsy system of congressional committees and boards. Maryland's acceptance of the articles brought action. A Department of Foreign Affairs was created on January 10, 1781, followed on February 7 by Finance, War and Marine.

There wasn't any doubt about the man for Superintendent of Finance. Merchant, banker, importer, privateersman, lender and raiser of war funds—Robert Morris had been the financial mainstay of the Revolution from its beginning. If, as his critics said, he made a million or so for himself in the process, there could be no denying that he risked his fortune in the war, and his bitterest enemy could not name a substitute for him. Following the unanimous election of Morris on February 20, Madison supported the condition Morris laid down for acceptance—that he be allowed to continue certain business partnerships (presumably in privateering, importation of war goods and foreign exchange) to which he was "bound in honor and by contracts." A committee report by Madison fixed the number and salaries of his assistants—one eighteen-hundred-fifty-Spanish-milled-dollar deputy and two five-hundred-dollar clerks. "Tall Boy" Gouverneur Morris, unrelated to Robert, got the number two place. That was the Department of Finance at full strength.[1]

It took eight months to elect a Secretary at (not of) War, with Madison, Witherspoon and a few others opposing the delay. Samuel Adams didn't want any secretary at all—the old committee system was the republican way to ruin an army. Some wanted to avoid voting against Candidate John Sullivan, brigadier general

and member of Congress—not that they questioned his ability!
Oh, no, Sullivan explained, they just regarded him as an apostate
from the New England faith because he sometimes voted with the
South. Backers of Candidate Horatio Gates sought delay until he
should be acquitted of pending charges; hence, perhaps, that vexed
outburst of Gates against Madison for blocking the revocation of
his court-martial. The choice finally fell on General Lincoln, the
now exchanged surrenderer of Charleston. A Congress suspicious
of administrative authority rejected Madison's motion that the
assistant secretary be authorized, in the secretary's absence, to
transact business assigned to him by his chief. The navy disappeared, except for two ships, while Congress was seeking a head
for it, so it was put into the Department of Finance.[2]

The post that really caused trouble was Secretary for Foreign
Affairs. Arthur Lee and Chancellor Robert R. Livingston, of New
York, were promptly put in nomination, the one hostile to and
distrusted by France, the other pro-Gallic and desired by Luzerne.
A fortnight later Thomas Burke predicted the election of Madison
to the place. "He is a young gentleman of industry and abilities,
but I fear a little deficient in the experience necessary for render-
ing immediate service in that department," wrote the North Carolinian. "However his local situation makes him more desirable to
the southern gentlemen."[3] In other words, the South objected to
a Northern monopoly in appointive offices but didn't want Lee.

That Madison would have taken the place is doubtful. He had
too many legislative irons in the fire and control of foreign affairs
still lay in Congress. For Arthur Lee, however, here was ambition's feast and the sweet morsel of revenge. Once let him gain
this place and he would have the whip hand over Franklin; Luzerne and Vergennes would be at his feet. He was in a strong
position, too. Sam Adams' smooth-running New England machine was true to the old Adams-Lee alliance. Witherspoon and
McKean were for him, and he was a member of Virginia's most
powerful family. That gave Madison and Jones something to
think about. With all their distrust of Lee, how could they support a New Yorker against him? They decided to join Lee-wor-
shiper Bland in a state loyalty vote, presumably relying on the

seven-state rule—the "chaos clause" of the newly ratified Articles of Confederation—to prevent his election. The result was alarming: five states for Lee, only three for Livingston. A fuller Congress might elect the Virginia paranoiac.[4]

The French minister, reporting that Adams had "gone to work with all his resources of friendship and intrigue" to get Lee elected, went into action against him. Converts, he heard, were being made in a new burst of extraordinary activity. Luzerne proceeded not only to enlighten the delegates who had been led into error, "but also to declare to the President in a positive manner that it would be impossible for me to place the slightest confidence in this ex-minister, that in case the choice of Congress fell on him, I should be obliged to continue to transact affairs either directly with the President or by means of a committee." This produced such an effect, he said, that on the next test of strength only Massachusetts and Delaware (led by Adams and McKean) voted for Lee.[5]

That tells only part of the story. The question for Madison was: How take Virginia out of the Lee column—thus blocking his election—without laying himself open to Lee's fury and the charge of disloyalty to his state? He invented, for the occasion, a device best known for its later potency in presidential politics. To kill off one favorite son, bring on another. Dr. James McClurg, a Virginia physician who fancied himself as an expert in international affairs, was placed in nomination for foreign secretary and deadlocked the election in a three-way split.[6]

During this time Lee had been in Virginia. Returning in May, he rebuilt his strength to four states. "With inconceivable assurance," as Luzerne described it, he told wavering delegates that the French minister had not the slightest objection to his election. When Luzerne disabused them of this notion, Lee supporters argued that Livingston was so closely leagued with France that he should be excluded on that account. Months passed, while Congress waited for a large enough attendance to break the deadlock.

Late in July, the presence of all states except North Carolina encouraged the Livingston forces to a third ballot: Livingston five, Lee four, McClurg three. Lee understood the division. Virginia "was prevailed on to throw away its vote," he complained in a final summary to the absent Adams. But Madison kept his counsel so well that he fooled even Luzerne, who described McClurg as "a phantom put up by the friends of Mr. Lee, to prevent Mr. Livingston from having seven votes, and to delay the election to a time favorable for their candidate." Actually, the Lee and McClurg delegates could have produced a majority on this ballot merely by uniting. Madison's strategy was to keep Lee out until Livingston could secure seven states without Virginia.

Luzerne and Livingston now held a conference at which it was decided that the French minister should do what he had so far refrained from—work directly for the New York chancellor. Two states were needed. The minister picked on New Jersey as the key to the deadlock. Its vote was ruled by Dr. Witherspoon—pro-French and pro-Lee, a paradoxical combination. Arguing that Lee's election would work grievous injury to the good relations of the allies, Luzerne won his case. At the next balloting, Witherspoon stayed away and his colleagues changed sides. Still there was no election for Pennsylvania's Thomas Smith had been knocked senseless by a fall and the two other delegates divided. As soon as he could be moved, the half-recovered Smith (mentally injured for life) was carried into the hall and the final vote was tallied: two for McClurg, three for Lee, seven for Robert R. Livingston. Thus, on August 10, 1781, did virtue triumph over ambition and the United States secure its first Secretary for Foreign Affairs.[7]

Organization of the Department of Finance went far to overcome Madison's alarm at the crisis which brought it about. In a two-thousand-word review of the Revolution for Philip Mazzei, he told in July, 1781, of financial vicissitudes "as great as those of the war." The ambitious plan of March 18, 1780, for cutting a $200,000,000 national debt down to $5,000,000 by currency devaluation, had failed. The new money, still largely unissued, had suffered so great a depreciation that Congress and the states were determined to keep the issue as low as possible and lay taxes in specie. Hard money was coming in—Spanish dollars from Havana, to pay for flour shipped to the Spanish forces, and the silvery pay rolls of the French ally.[8] He swept on with surprising optimism:

"These advantages, as they have been and are likely to be improved by the skill of Mr. Robert Morris, whom we have constituted minister of our finances, afford a more flattering prospect in this department of our affairs than has existed at any period of the war."

This declaration of faith was the more surprising, since the principal step thus far taken by Morris had been the promotion of a federally chartered national bank, about whose constitutionality Madison had increasing doubts. Also, the Virginian was included by implication in a severe rebuke just handed out by the superintendent for an unorthodox finance proposal.

During the desperate effort to find money for the Southern army and its reinforcements, Madison put through a resolution ordering the drawing of $387,000 in warrants upon the continental loan offices of Virginia, Delaware and Maryland, to pay the troops from those states. As in a similar earlier action for Northern troops, there was a joker in this. The warrants were to be paid in new bills issued "in pursuance of the act" of March 1780—that is, if and when the old money was retired at forty for one. The Virginia pay warrant was for $237,279, but at last report only $15,985 in new money could be issued in that state.[9]

Two weeks later John Mathews offered a resolution, the first half of it in Madison's handwriting, that warrants be drawn at once for the full federal four-tenths ($4,000,000) of the new money, and that bills be printed immediately to cover them. The states, however, were forbidden to receive any part of their six-tenths until they had delivered and canceled enough old bills to cover the federal four-tenths.[10] This proposal, Madison wrote in his part of it, was aimed at "the remissness of the states" in failing to collect and retire the old money. In effect, it proposed a forcible seizure of $4,000,000 from the states before they collected the taxes to cover it.

Robert Morris' opinion of this proposal was brought to Congress by Committeeman Theodorick Bland, whose gusto may have been increased by knowledge that Madison was co-author. It was "absolutely improper," unavailing and "an unjustifiable breach of public faith." Instead of forming an enmity to Morris because of the exaggerated charge of breach of faith (the prior dereliction of the states left little of that element), Madison continued to give the financier wholehearted support. When Morris ran afoul of the neurotic suspicions of Arthur Lee and was charged in the Virginia legislature with using his national bank for that state's ruin, Madison came to his defense with sweeping praise:

"I am persuaded that he accepted his office from motives which were honorable and patriotic. I have seen no proof of misfeasance. I have heard of many charges which were palpably erroneous. I have known others, somewhat suspicious, vanish on examination. Every member in Congress must be sensible of the benefit which has accrued to the public from his administration. No intelligent man out of Congress can be altogether insensible of it. The Court of France has testified its satisfaction at his appointment, which I really believe lessened its repugnance to lend us money. These considerations will make me cautious in lending an ear to the suggestions even of the impartial; to those of known and vindictive enemies, very incredulous."[11]

The national bank proposed by Morris was approved by Congress on May 26, 1781. With three other delegates, Madison opposed the clause promising the bank a federal charter. At this significant point—foreshadowing his great controversy with Alexander Hamilton a decade later—he saw a limit to the implied powers of Congress. No power to establish a bank was set forth in the Articles of Confederation. Therefore no such power existed. But Madison voted for the resolution with this clause in it.

In the following December, after slow stock sales, Morris asked Congress to fulfill the promise of incorporation. By this time, as Madison reported the day after the bank opened its doors, the majority opinion was that the Confederation gave no such power. "The bank, however, supposing that such a sanction from Congress would at least give it a dignity and pre-eminence in the

Chevalier de la Luzerne   François de Marbois

Daniel of St. Thomas Jenifer   John Witherspoon

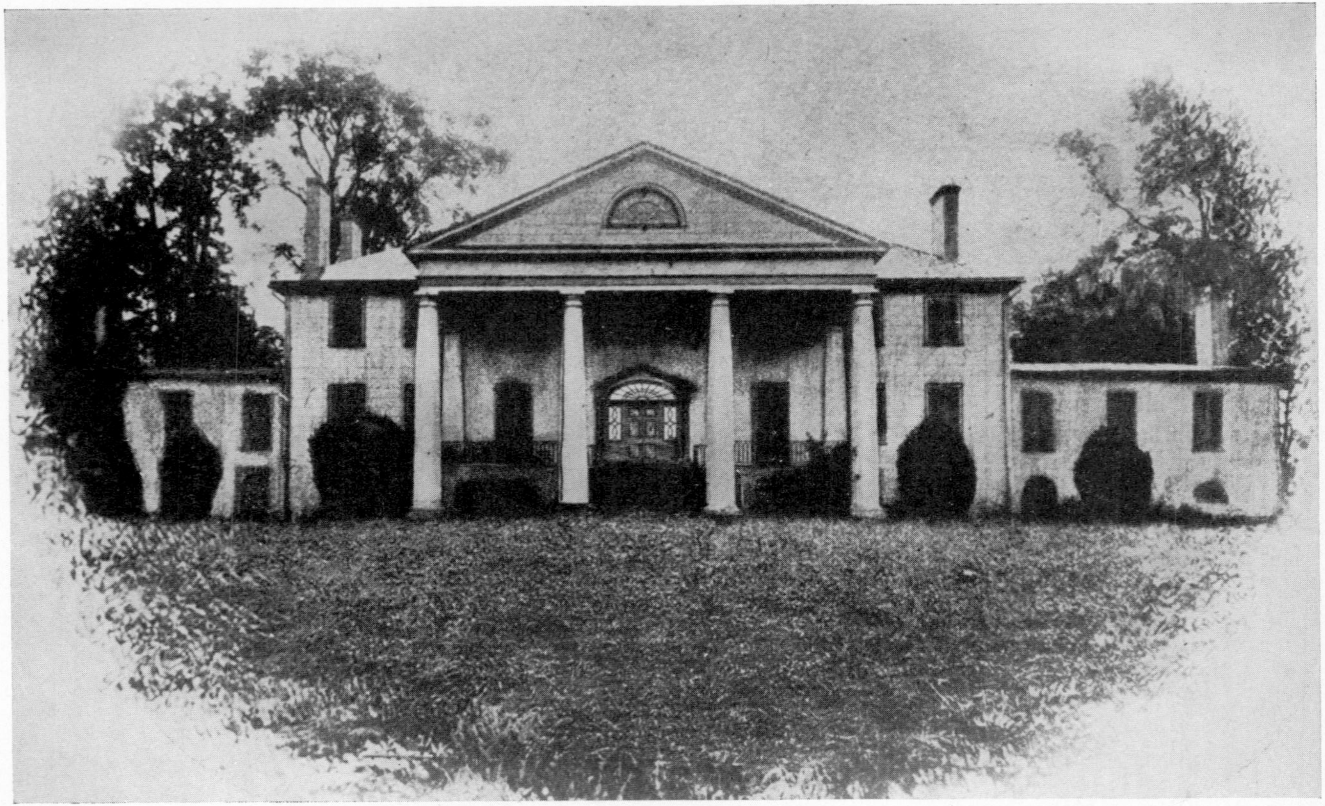

Montpelier in the Eighteenth Century

public opinion, urged the engagement of Congress." Failure to carry out the promise would leave subscribers free to withdraw their names. Also, Morris expected aid from the bank in paying the army. Immediate congressional action was needed, Madison said, because the adjournment of the Pennsylvania legislature made it impossible to obtain a state charter "which, it was the opinion of many, would have given them a sufficient legal existence in every state." In this dilemma, Madison joined in what he called "an acquiescing, rather than an affirmative, vote." Congress granted the charter, with a recommendation to the states to give it validity within their borders.

"As this is a tacit admission of a defect of power, I hope it will be an antidote against the poisonous tendency of precedents of usurpation."

This denunciation of usurpation leaves no doubt that Madison regarded his own excursions into implied power as constitutional and valid. The unenumerated powers which he invoked—coercion, embargo, impressment, territorial government—were not usurped. On everything except federal incorporation, he seems to have given the Morris Bank his full approval. He offered no objection and asked no roll call on any other point. In approving the bank, and regardless of who chartered it, Congress promised to "promote and support the same by such ways and means, from time to time, as may appear necessary for the institution and consistent with the public good." The notes of the bank were made receivable for all taxes, duties and debts payable to the United States. Madison summarized the relationship in this way:

"Its principal founder is Mr. R. M., who has certain prerogatives with respect to it in his quality of Superintendent of Finance. It is pretty analogous in its principles to the Bank of England. The stock subscribed is 400,000 dollars."[12]

And who subscribed the stock? One half of it—five hundred shares—was subscribed by the Superintendent of Finance from the Treasury of the United States. With this stock payment, which consisted of $200,000 in silver livres brought from France by John

Laurens, the bank issued notes and loaned $300,000 of them to the United States for army pay. Morris borrowed a total of $1,249,-975 for the government, and increased its stock holdings to $253,-394. He then turned in government stock to help pay off the loans, and cleared the books of both at the end of 1783.[13] Authority for these stock purchases did not arise from the federal charter, but from the earlier resolution of Congress to promote and support the bank. Constitutionally, it sprang from the power of Congress to pay expenses "incurred for the common defense or general welfare."

What did Madison think, in these early days, about the scope of the common defense and general welfare? By the end of the century, he had become the chief opponent of Hamilton's contention, upheld by the courts, that the power to spend for the general welfare extends to all objects which are for the general welfare. These words in the Constitution, said Madison, were picked up from the Articles of Confederation, and must have the same meaning in both documents. It will scarcely be said, he declared in 1800, that in the Articles they were ever understood to authorize expenditures for the common defense and general welfare "except in the cases afterwards enumerated, which explained and limited their meaning."

No bank was enumerated. Consequently, if he felt that way about it in 1782, he must have regarded the purchase of stock in the Bank of North America as unlawful. Why did he not protest? To get his actual view at the time, one must go back to 1780, when Philadelphia businessmen set up the nonprofit Bank of Pennsylvania to help in the purchase of army supplies. This bank had no federal charter, but the federal government was its only customer and Congress guaranteed the entire investment against "all deficiencies of losses and expenses." What was Madison's attitude toward this appropriation of public money to the common defense or general welfare? "Our greatest hopes of being able to feed [the soldiers]," he wrote to Jefferson, "are founded on a patriotic scheme of the opulent merchants of this city. . . . Congress for the support of this bank, and for the security and indemnification of the subscribers, have pledged the faith of the United States, and agreed to deposit bills of exchange on Europe to the amount of 150,000 pounds sterling" to support the pledge. Within a year Congress ordered enough of these bills sold to make up a deficiency of £3891.2.4 in repayments to subscribers.[14]

Openly in one case and by silence in the other, Madison supported the use of public money to sustain two banks. Even more thoroughly, the full record of Congress destroys his later narrow definition of spending for the common defense and general welfare. If, as he argued in 1800, those words must have the same meaning in the Constitution as in the Articles of Confederation, their meaning in the Articles must be the same as in the earlier period when they came into use. What expenditures did the Continental Congress make for these purposes?

In 1779, saying that its action was for "the promotion of the general welfare," it ordered the use of public funds to restore the value of money—the same purpose for which it afterward supported the Bank of North America.

It educated Indian children at Dartmouth and Princeton.

It moved a private printing office from Philadelphia to York.

It established government-owned tanyards for the manufacture of shoes.

It maintained a "Continental ferry" across the Delaware River at Trenton.

It built a road from the Penobscot River to Nova Scotia to "facilitate supplies of livestock to the eastern parts of the Union."[15]

Expand these projects sufficiently, without bringing in a single new kind of activity, and they add up to a complete federal system of education, national ownership of industry and transportation, a national system of roads and ferries—in short, to complete state socialism, within the compass of spending for the common defense and general welfare. Not from Alexander Hamilton, but from the actual appropriations of the Continental Congress, does one find the most convincing testimony to the meaning of those phrases in the Constitution. The James Madison of 1800 is more than answered by the James Madison who took part in the earlier spending.

The Bank of North America, as Madison saw it, was a useful

instrument of war and business. He gave no voice to the thought expressed by Morris and Hamilton that it would attach powerful moneyed men to the federal government (in the words of Morris) "by the strong principle of self-love and the immediate sense of private interest." That would have repelled Madison as surely in 1781 as it did when Hamilton made it the basis of his money policies after 1789. But the Virginian was quite willing that the bank's nine-per cent annual dividends should attach the moneyed men of Holland to the idea of a loan to America. "Will not this be very captivating to the avarice of the Dutchman?" he asked. It might be so indeed, especially if the Dutchman did not know that just before the initial dividend was paid, Minister Luzerne saved the bank from collapse in a Philadelphia business panic by a secret deposit of the pay roll of the French army in it.[16]

As long as Congress did everything itself, it never needed to investigate anything. It was different after departments were set up. Having helped to create five administrative branches—finance, foreign affairs, war, marine and post office—Madison saw the need for a periodic accounting of their activities. On his motion, Congress appointed five committees to make semiannual inquiries into their work. As chairman of the committee named to deal with the Department of Foreign Affairs, he reported that its business "appears to have been conducted with much industry, attention and utility, and without any errors or defects worthy of being taken notice of to Congress." The secretary, he was sure, would make use of various suggestions made directly to him.[17]

There was no hostility to public ministers in the policy Madison sponsored. The purpose, he told his friend Randolph, was not only to discharge the general duty of Congress but also to "shelter in some degree faithful officers from unmerited imputations and suspicions," as well as to censure their opposites. Having this dual or triple intent, he was little pleased to see the investigation of the Department of Finance fall into the hands of Morris' bitterest enemy, Arthur Lee, by this time in Congress. The ex-diplomat, after failing to gain a place in the Virginia delegation (headed by Madison) elected in June 1781, was named in December to fill a vacancy.[18] He opened at once a many-sided campaign of his own, having among his objects the recall of Franklin, the discrediting of Morris and the defeat of Madison for re-election in 1782.

In the investigation of Morris, according to Madison, Lee ignored the purposes of Congress and undertook to probe into old trade contracts authorized years before the Department of Finance was created. All of Lee's movements, he said, "are pointed directly or circuitously either to Morris or Franklin." The investigation stretched out through the fall of 1782 until three members of the committee, including Lee, found it necessary to go home. This gave the friends of Morris an opening. Madison, Samuel Wharton and Thomas Fitzsimons were named to succeed the absentees. Wharton was an organizer of the Indiana Company, Fitzsimons a Philadelphia merchant—both inside the Morris orbit. The committee proceeded to do nothing except get a renewal of its life. A few weeks later, in January, a new committee was appointed, not as a successor to the old one, but pursuant to the original Madison resolution for semiannual inquiries. So now there were two investigations, each covering a separate half year.

To make things a bit merrier, Arthur Lee came back and observed that three members of the new committee had gone home, including Wharton, a member of both old and new. He got himself elected to both committees, then went back to Richmond to manipulate other irons while his henchman Bland took his place on the old committee.[19]

Madison and others of this committee promptly secured an order of Congress transferring its work to the Leeless, Blandless new committee. Fitzsimons, a member of both committees, then wrote a report for the new one. Superintendent Morris, he found, had conducted his business "with great ability and assiduity, in a manner highly advantageous to the United States, and in conformity with the system laid down by Congress." The Treasury, in a year and a half, had paid out $404,712 more than it had taken in, and Morris had balanced the national budget by issuing his personal notes for the difference.[20]

Among other blessings derived from the Articles of Confederation was a presidential rotation clause ("in no instance less proper," said Madison) which lowered the caliber of presiding

officers by compelling a yearly turnover. Successive Presidents of
the United States in Congress Assembled, while he was in Congress, were Huntington, who resigned on account of illness in
July, 1781; Thomas McKean, of Delaware, who said "this honor
is going a begging" two days before he got it; John Hanson, of
Maryland, and Elias Boudinot, of New Jersey. Hanson got the
office, said Luzerne, because "they prefer to give themselves a
mediocre chief" rather than two in succession from the same state,
and New England delegates dared not face their constituents if
they elected the more capable Daniel Carroll, of Maryland, a
Catholic. Hanson, third President of the United States in Congress Assembled, held that chronological position until the advent
of the Age of Publicity, when Maryland experts brought him to
primacy by propounding the question: Who was the first President of the United States, George Washington or John Hanson?

A year later Madison voted for his fellow Virginian, Bland,
against Boudinot, while Bland and Boudinot (having each but
one colleague present) voted for themselves to make the state's
vote count. "As you were present at the last election," wrote Madison to Randolph, "I need not recite to you the motives" to this
one. Boudinot, he meant, like Hanson, was an enemy of Virginia's
Western land title and a friend of the big speculators. The President of Congress, it seems, was not wholly a figurehead in Confederation days, and the battle of the West must be fought on every
front.[21]

CHAPTER X

CLIPPING DIPLOMATIC WINGS

As THE American Revolution approached its military climax, the uncertainty of coming events produced a crisis in peace plans. The major issues—independence, territorial boundaries, fishing rights and navigation of the Mississippi—were all mixed up in an international welter of conflicting interests and desires. American aspirations entered into the quest for a Spanish alliance. They had a bearing on French war weariness and apprehension, and on the mediation efforts of neutral European monarchs.

For Americans, the question was how much they could gain in addition to independence. The aim of France was to weaken England by cutting loose her colonies. The less the United States demanded, in addition to freedom, the easier to make peace, and the smaller the drain on French wealth and man power; also, the less danger of losing through a military upset or unfriendly mediation.

French morale, including that of the Count de Vergennes, was at its lowest ebb at the end of 1780. Military disasters at Charleston and Camden, halfhearted recruiting, a broken-down supply system and the refusal of free citizens to pay taxes, furnished a gloomy portent of American efforts in the coming campaign. Russia and Germany were pressing for a *status quo* peace. French taxpayers were shrieking with anguish over an indecisive war. England too was half-bankrupt, but Parliament, encouraged by successes in Carolina, had given Lord North a full war chest.

To unsettle Vergennes still more, he was subtly assailed from an American source. Silas Deane, ordered to France to straighten out his accounts, found nobody authorized to review them. The ex-diplomat reputed to have made a fortune in war speculations was reduced to begging handouts from American friends and French officials. Embittered by poverty and neglect, he plunged

into a pessimism which ultimately turned to treason. Before that
stage was reached, Vergennes relayed Deane's tale of wavering uncertainty in the American people, their shaken zeal and patriotism,
the decline of Congress till it had neither authority, credit nor
consideration. "This picture, sir," the foreign minister remarked
to Luzerne, "is anything but a laughing matter, and what strikes
me more, is that it is made by a man whose patriotism and truth-
fulness I cannot suspect."[1]

Such was the state of affairs when Vergennes learned that Finance Minister Necker had made a secret proposal to Lord North
to end hostilities with a truce. The foreign minister smashed the
move at once because it made no provision for American independence. Then, thoroughly worried, he sat down and wrote a
memoir on a truce. How could one be framed without loss of
honor or national objectives? A long truce—twenty years—would
insure the one essential, independence, provided Great Britain
evacuated New York. Conciliation required sacrifices. South
Carolina and Georgia were unimportant—harborless, enervating
in climate, sparsely populated, but cherished by the most enlightened and zealous Americans. If they must be sacrificed, the
proposal should come from the mediators, not from France. Vergennes sounded out the British ministry on such a truce and met
with a rebuff, the British interpreting it as a confession of weakness. France then turned with new vigor to the winning of the
war, but continued to look on Russo-German mediation both as
a possible means of bringing the conflict to a favorable close and
as a potential threat of armed intervention if the mediators should
be rebuffed.[2]

These developments intensified a feeling already strong in Vergennes, that John Adams was not the man to negotiate peace for
the United States. The minister was astonished when Adams suggested to him, immediately after his arrival in France in February, 1780, that he should at once notify the British government of
his power to negotiate treaties of peace and commerce. Vergennes
advised him not to. Adams complied unwillingly and—unaccred-
ited to the French court—devoted himself to interfering in Franklin's business. On the basis of a private letter from Elbridge

Gerry, he notified Vergennes in June that French holders of loan certificates would be subject, along with Americans, to the forty-for-one devaluation of money. When Vergennes protested that devaluation was a form of taxation, and this was taxing Frenchmen for American war costs, Adams came back with a three-thousand-word argument, aggressive in tone, that foreigners engaging in American trade made themselves to that extent American citizens.

Having thus set the stage in personal relations, the peace negotiator chose the worst possible moment—following the bad news from Charleston—to set forth eleven reasons for speedy communication of his diplomatic powers to Great Britain. The North ministry, he granted, would return an insolent answer, or none, but think of the effect upon the British people! Hearing that he was empowered to discuss both peace and commerce, they would rise up in a new outburst of rioting against the war. "I know of no measure," wrote Adams (and this is history, not grand opera), "that will be more likely to increase the opposition against administration than communicating my powers." Vergennes replied that Adams was furnishing the house before the foundation was laid. To talk of a commerce treaty while war was raging would expose the United States to insult in London and make it the laughingstock of all Europe. As for effect upon the English people, his commission was known to everybody, as Adams himself had said in the previous February. What could he tell them that they did not know?[3]

Only one thing was lacking now—a final straw to break the camel's back. Adams found it right under his foot. Picking out, from an already answered letter, a remark by Vergennes that the king had sent his fleet to America "without being solicited by the Congress," he assailed the foreign minister's veracity. Naval aid had been requested in 1776 and 1778. Adding another back-breaker, he said he would take up with the foreign office, in the future, anything that seemed proper, "without the intervention of any third person." In other words, he would assume the work of a minister, ignoring Franklin.[4]

Vergennes' reply was swift and emphatic. He notified Adams

that he would neither see him again nor answer his letters. He demanded that Franklin inform Congress of this, sending them also the exchanges of letters on devaluation and communication of Adams' powers. He instructed Luzerne to talk confidentially with the president and leading members of Congress and let them know that Adams had revealed "a rigidity, a pedantry, an arrogance and a self-love that render him incapable of dealing with political subjects." His intemperate desire to show off his powers should be restrained by a positive order to take no step about his commission, "if they still wish to leave it in his hands," except in concert with the king's minister. Otherwise he was likely to compromise the alliance and the honor of his country.[5]

By a blend of good judgment and good luck, Adams got his story to Congress first. Franklin's dispatches were held back for months by the dismasting of the *Ariel*. Adams sent the correspondence on devaluation, then hitched up his horses and left for Amsterdam, from which place he forwarded a cogent plea for the appointment of some good man to be American minister to Holland, and with it the exchange of letters on his peace and commerce powers. But of the bad feeling between him and the foreign minister—nothing.[6]

A shocked and surprised Congress, which had barely finished rebuking Adams on devaluation and electing him minister to Holland, listened on New Year's day, 1781, to his account of the more important disagreement. It was decided that the matter should be kept secret from Luzerne until final action was taken. The diplomat readily fell in with this plan. "They were of one opinion," he wrote next day, "upon the imprudence of Mr. Adams . . . and upon the solidity of the arguments with which you have demolished his assertions." Since the minister was "supposed not to have any knowledge of it," he confined himself to impressing one delegate (presumably his paid informant Sullivan) with the necessity of speaking to Adams with both clarity and energy about his future conduct. The result was a moderate reprimand to Adams on January 10, informing him that his zeal and assiduity had led him astray.

It was not until late May that the impasse between Vergennes and Adams came squarely before Congress. Luzerne submitted memorials telling of French plans to aid the United States and asking Congress to join France in accepting Russo-German mediation on the basis of complete American independence. To a committee on these memorials, the French minister delivered a new warning from Vergennes against the desire of Adams to present his credentials to London. If Congress put any confidence in the king's friendship, they would direct Adams "to take no step without the approbation of his majesty." In his instructions, the important outlines should come from Congress, the manner of executing them should be directed by Vergennes. In all things except independence, American peace terms should be moderate.[7]

For the first time, now, the president, the committee and several other delegates heard what Vergennes thought of Adams—that he was no doubt a zealous patriot and faithfully attached to independence and the alliance, but possessed of "an inflexibility, an arrogance and a stubbornness which would lead him into a thousand vexatious incidents and drive his fellow negotiators to despair." It was likely, Luzerne reported to Vergennes on June 1, that Adams either would be given two associates, or would receive clear and precise instructions with orders "to be governed in their execution by your commands."[8]

The timing favored Luzerne's efforts. Cornwallis was at the peak of his offensive operations. Continental currency was plunging to destruction. From Europe came a rising threat of armed intervention by powers unfriendly to free governments and revolting colonies. More than ever before, the fate of America was in French hands. The committee personnel favored Luzerne too. Not only (due to an advance conference between the President and French minister) was it solidly composed of friends of France, including pensioner Sullivan, but Chairman Daniel Carroll, of Maryland, and Dr. Witherspoon, of New Jersey, were hostile to Virginia's western empire. Mathews of South Carolina was ready to sacrifice the West to save his state from *uti possidetis*. Only Joseph Jones, of Virginia, would stand by the old territorial ultimatum which Luzerne wished to get rid of. To make sure that the report would be exactly what the French minister wanted,

either Carroll or Sullivan stayed behind after a committee conference with him and wrote it under his very eyes. (Luzerne said
the chairman stayed, but the report is in Sullivan's handwriting.)
It revoked all former instructions but cited them as a guide to
American wishes, demanded the independence of the United
States, left a blank for the boundaries, and ordered Adams "in
all other points to conform yourself to the advice and opinion" of
the French peace negotiator.[9]

After this, things did not go according to plan. The actual legislation offered by the committee on June 6 was a resolution written by Madison, a nonmember. It instructed the American peace
negotiator to accede to no treaty of peace which did not "effectually secure the independence and sovereignty of the thirteen states."
Madison excluded *uti possidetis,* with its threat to South Carolina
and Georgia, by specifying the independence of *thirteen* states.
Sullivan had omitted that safeguard. Thus, although Madison
knew nothing of Vergennes' inclination to yield to the mediators
on southern territory rather than prolong the war, his resolution
made Congress no less stubborn on that point than Vergennes
feared Adams would be.[10]

The instant Madison's resolution was adopted, Witherspoon
moved in with a proposed addition to it, revoking former territorial instructions, but toning down the Sullivan report on French
control. As to "disputed boundaries and other particulars," the
American representative was to use his own judgment and prudence in securing his country's interest. He was to make "the
most candid and confidential communications upon all subjects"
to the ministers of France and "undertake nothing in the negotiations for peace without their knowledge and concurrence."

For the next two days Madison engaged in battle with his old
Princeton teacher, who had the vigorous support of Jenifer of
Maryland, chief spokesman for the land speculators. Aided by the
"chaos clause," Virginia and New England defeated the territorial portion of Witherspoon's motion, though seventeen delegates voted for it, eight against. The vote told Madison that he
was facing a powerful combination of middle-state opponents of
the Virginia land claims, Western speculators looking to England
for validation of their concessions, and Southerners driven by the

fear of European mediation. The resourceful Witherspoon came back with a committee report reoffering his original motion, together with three additional secret instructions. The peace negotiator was to (1) try to secure the limits demanded in the past; (2) failing that, leave the northern and western limits open to future discussion, or (3) if boundaries must be ascertained, get the best settlement possible.[11]

Luzerne by this time was in the thick of the battle, trying to convert the opposition. How could they hope to secure the West by treaty when the enemy held two or three of their states? If they put expediency in place of justice, they would revolt the mediators at the very start. The Virginians in reply cited their charters and the treaty and royal proclamation of 1763. If the American title did not reach north to latitude forty-five, no point could be fixed; the British could come clear down to Philadelphia. Very well, said Luzerne, present these acts as the basis of your claims. Then, if circumstances require moderation, draw in the boundaries. France, he warned, had not faced a Continental enemy for the remarkable period of eighteen years. Should that be changed, as it might be if American inflexibility provoked armed mediation, the United States would be left exposed to the full attack of England.[12]

Madison felt the weight of Luzerne's argument, but not to the extent of trusting American boundaries to a peace commissioner under French control. The first two of Witherspoon's three secret instructions were just what he wanted. After they had been adopted, Virginia and Massachusetts knocked out the third. Knowing that Congress would not stop at this point, and fearful of a positive relinquishment of the West, Madison drafted a compromise proposal. The American negotiator might give up the lands north of the Miami and Illinois rivers and a line connecting the mouth of the former and source of the latter. Not a single state stood with Virginia on the roll call. Next he sought an instruction forbidding the negotiator to relinquish lands south of the Ohio, or to recognize an exclusive British claim north of the river. Again Virginia stood alone. Congress would not even guarantee Vandalia and Kentucky to the Big Knife.[13]

Witherspoon pressed his advantage quickly. After New Eng-

land swung over, he put through his original motion, defeated
two days earlier by the Madison forces, leaving boundaries to the
discretion of the peace negotiator. Virginia alone voted No, but
joined in support of Witherspoon's order to Adams to undertake
nothing without French knowledge and concurrence. Massachusetts, home of Adams, cast the only opposing vote. Witherspoon
then made another attempt to complete his trio of supplemental
instructions, which in their bobtailed condition were favorable to
Madison's position. Falling one state short, he got rid of the first
two by a vote to reconsider.

On the territorial issue, Madison had met with a thumping defeat at the hands of the canny Scotch theologian under whom he
once studied morals, and who was now allied with land speculators and frightened Southerners. The toughness of the fight is
evident in Jenifer's comment: "Great obstructions [were] thrown
in the way by Virginia, Massachusetts and Connecticut, especially
the former. We were several times overthrown but regained our
feet again." Luzerne gave similar testimony. "Virginia, in spite
of the presence of the enemy, showed more obstinacy than ever,"
he reported to Vergennes. They finally "designated the Ohio as
a boundary they had at last decided to accept." This final compromise, Luzerne said, might have passed if he had given it his
support. Believing, however, that circumstances might call for a
shift from this boundary, he thought it best to fix nothing with
precision. Should circumstances force a sacrifice of everything west
of the Atlantic watershed, the peace would be ratified but "it
would chill our partisans and it would be hard to convince the
Americans that their interests had not been sacrificed." Rejection
of the Madison boundary left Witherspoon's indefinite instructions in force. The way was open to territorial retreat. Yorktown
turned it into a road on which to advance. Defeat of Madison's
attempt to save Kentucky made it possible to save the Northwest.[14]

During this time the reaction against John Adams was gaining
force. The Witherspoon instructions on French guidance, shown
confidentially to Luzerne by order of Congress, brought the reply
that they were too weak. Observing the absence of New Englanders from the committee, the minister hammered at Adams'

blind devotion to the fisheries. For this sole object he might "disrupt a negotiation upon which the welfare and tranquility of the whole continent depend. . . . Distant from the theater of war . . . he ignores the distress of the southern states. . . . Shall he be the one to decide whether we are in danger of a war upon the continent which would force us to leave you to the mercy of your enemies?" Recalling that Adams had once "brusquely withdrawn" from the French court, he asked the delegates to consider whether the delicate task of dealing with the pacificators should be left without check to the impetuosity of his character. "I do not hesitate to tell you," the minister concluded, "that the only means I see to prevent the inconveniences arising from the peculiar disposition of Mr. Adams is to place him entirely under the direction of the plenipotentiaries of His Majesty to the peace conference."[15]

To the chairman's protest that Adams could do nothing without the advice of the French court, Luzerne replied that the instructions gave France the power of preventing, but not of acting. No person of sense would supect France of preferring the interests of England to those of America. If concessions were made, it would be only because of the impossibility of avoiding them. Congress should remember that neither Great Britain nor the neutral mediators would receive Adams, except perhaps "as the agent of a rebelling people," unless the approach was made through the French court.

Under this heavy pressure, Congress inserted another clause in the instructions. In addition to consulting with the French ministers, the negotiator was told "ultimately to govern yourself by their advice and opinion." New Hampshire, New Jersey and five Southern states produced the necessary seven, with Massachusetts and Connecticut opposed and Pennsylvania divided. Madison, Jones and Smith of Virginia cast the crucial votes. Had any one of these joined Bland in opposition, the instruction would have been defeated.[16]

Prior to this action, Congress defeated a motion to join other persons with Adams in the negotiations. Now, with confidence in him thoroughly shaken, it voted to give him two associates. Jay was elected to one place. A sectional struggle over the other, combined with an anti-Franklin campaign by the followers of Arthur Lee, caused the total number to be raised to five. John Adams, John Jay, Benjamin Franklin, Henry Laurens (if released from the Tower of London) and Thomas Jefferson (if he would go) were to make the peace for America.[17]

No sooner was this done than it was realized that the reason for putting the negotiations under the control of France—distrust of Adams—no longer mattered. What should be done? Revoke the instruction or let it stand? Delaware alone joined the New Englanders in an attempt at reconsideration. Defending this instruction a year and a half later, Madison said it was adopted because a motion to enlarge the delegation had just failed, and the subsequent enlargement to five members "was not suggested until the measure had been adopted, and communicated to the Chevalier de Luzerne to be forwarded to France, when it was too late to revoke it." This explanation was truer to the feeling of Congress than to the factual record. Congress voted to have three members on the very day that it adopted the final French instruction. The instructions were not given to Luzerne for transmission to France. He himself wrote to Vergennes: "The President of Congress tells me that they were sent by the *Anna* . . . in cipher to Mr. Franklin, Mr. Adams and Mr. Jay."[18]

As Luzerne related it, delegates friendly to France came to him in distress about the instruction immediately after the delegation was enlarged. They had adjourned Congress to block a vote on reconsideration, but, to preserve harmony, wished to find some middle course. The minister at first "displayed the greatest surprise" at such an attempt to alter the decisions of Congress, but reversed his tactics when he saw the extent of the anxiety. American confidence in the king, he then said, ought to be spontaneous. They should regard the communication which had been made to him as null and void. France would make no use of a confidence "which was not unanimous among well-meaning persons." He then gave them something to think about. The peace would not satisfy everybody. Perhaps it was true that the states were all ready for independence. In that case, the more power the American plenipotentiaries had, the better for France, since she would escape

GEORGE WASHINGTON

BENJAMIN FRANKLIN

blame for what might happen. "The effect of this language, my lord, was to cause them to reconsider the resolutions, and confirm them, even as I firmly hoped."[19] This hit the basic truth, which was that the United States, at this moment of military and diplomatic hazard, was too dependent on France to deviate from French wishes as to the manner of negotiation, though some who felt that way—notably Madison—wanted Congress to continue its control of the substantive terms of peace.

Pursuant to this desire, Madison cast about for a method of restoring the territorial demands knocked out by Witherspoon. In the original 1779 instructions,[20] the Great Lakes-Mississippi boundary was made a *sine qua non* of peace, while Newfoundland fishing rights, though urgently pressed as a condition of peace, were made an ultimatum only of the treaty of commerce. Now that the territorial ultimatum was gone, the fisheries stood in a preferred position. The effect was to break the mutual dependence of Massachusetts and Virginia, the former feeling less need to woo, the latter losing the power to coerce.

The peace instructions were fixed, but Congress had ordered a revision of those on commerce. Madison moved that Adams be instructed to enter into no commerce treaty unless, in addition to the fisheries, it included all the objects of the peace ultimatum prior to its recent revisal. That is, territories and fisheries, or no treaty. Fishery advocates, opponents of Virginia land claims and terrified Southerners handed him a six-to-three defeat.[21]

This attempt to circumvent the peace instructions threw a scare into the more extreme supporters of France. They were alarmed still more by an article in the *Freeman's Journal,* to which Arthur Lee had easy access, revealing and attacking the secret peace instructions. A campaign to turn the people against the instructions might turn them also against the alliance. To thwart the anti-Gallicans, Marbois was informed, a motion would be introduced next day to unite the four other peace negotiators with Adams in making a commerce treaty.[22]

The motion was not offered. In one of the shrewdest pieces of strategy in congressional history, it was anticipated by another motion made by Madison. Dropping his original idea of using

Adams' powers for territorial protection, Madison outdid his fellows in emphasizing the danger, especially to the states suffering from enemy invasion, of leaving any power whatever in the unfettered hands of the New England egotist and fisheries devotee. He moved that Adams' commission for negotiating a commerce treaty be revoked and the peace negotiators use strenuous endeavors to obtain both the fishing rights and territorial boundaries originally called for. Southern delegates were worried by these provisions, also feared that the British would not make peace without a commerce treaty. Marbois (elated at Madison's move because he did not know its purpose) reassured them on the last point. The peace negotiators had power to write commercial clauses into the treaty. Madison took care of the first objection by dropping the final clauses. He reoffered a straight motion that Adams' commission to negotiate a commerce treaty be revoked. Outside of New England, the only delegate to vote No was Madison's arch opponent, Jenifer, of Maryland. Witherspoon, who might have penetrated his strategy, was absent.[23]

Madison was seconded, on the first day by Sharpe, on the second by Mathews, both of whom lived in the same house with him and were his fellows on the Southern war committee. Both, however, opposed him on Western territorial demands. It is evident, therefore, that he planned the move with them and won their support by playing up the ostensible reason for his motion—fear that Adams would use his commerce power to upset the peace negotiations—not by disclosing his underlying purpose.

What Madison achieved was a new parity between territories and fisheries. Repeal of Adams' commerce powers destroyed the fisheries ultimatum in the commerce instructions, just as the Witherspoon resolutions destroyed the territorial ultimatum in the peace instructions. They were equal now, on a lower level, merely as objects left to the discretion of the peace negotiators. If the fishing claim was to be lifted above that level, the territorial claim must go up too. Massachusetts once more must woo Virginia; Virginia had regained its power to coerce New England.

James Lovell of Massachusetts appeared to see only the personal side of these developments, as he reported them to John and Abigail Adams. "The whole of the proceedings here in regard to your two commissions are, I think, ill judged," he wrote to the former, "but I persuade myself no dishonor intended." And to Mrs. Adams: "There is no such idea here as any criminality in Mr. A——, he is much esteemed. But such is the uncouth way of proceeding here at times that unintended chagrin must arise."[24]

It was several months before the true reaction came, in the form of an act of the Massachusetts legislature. Congress was implored to instruct the peace commissioners to insist in the most pressing manner on American fishing rights. Lovell and Madison, with Daniel Carroll as a makeweight between them, were ordered to report on this appeal. Chairman Lovell confidently drafted a report restoring the fisheries to their old position, without regard to territories. "Alas, alas," he wrote to Samuel Adams after his recommendation was debated and recommitted, "I thought very little or no objection would be made, but I was greatly mistaken." The committee then turned the task over to Madison, who had been maneuvering for six months to get control of it.[25]

CHAPTER XI

National Domain

Directed to frame a new policy on fisheries, Madison immediately linked them with Western territories, in an extensive report submitted to Congress on January 8, 1782. Refraining from any enlargement of the peace ultimatum, he proposed that the king of France be informed of the extent and foundation of the desires and expectations which were "eventually submitted to his councils." The limits of the states, he declared, were established by the crown when they were colonies and "to these limits the United States, considered as independent sovereignties, have succeeded." The royal edict prohibiting private land grants west of the Appalachian Divide was intended to keep the Indians at peace, not to restrict boundaries. It would be dangerous to the United States, said Madison, if Great Britain retained territory bordering on the Mississippi, especially (this to alarm France) as it might be used as "a new nursery for her marine." From a full confidence that this western country lay within the United States, British posts had been seized; American government was being exercised, bounties had been promised to the army and land sales were relied on for discharge of the war debt.[1]

Turning to the fisheries, Madison declared that a common right of taking fish more than three leagues from the shore could not be denied "without a manifest violation of the freedom of the seas," save when that right had been given up by agreement or lost through long and silent acquiescence. The United States consistently exercised fishing rights off Newfoundland prior to the war. Though this was "not in the character of an independent nation," such a right was now incident to the United States as a free and independent community and could not be given up without a partial renunciation of that sovereignty which must be maintained entire.

Madison put in a word against restoration of confiscated property, after the wanton destruction inflicted by the enemy, and concluded with a warning against commercial clauses in the peace treaty. "The United States, as a free and sovereign nation, being the absolute masters as well of their commerce as of their government," could allow no outside claims based on right. Like most of his state papers, this report was shot through with references to national sovereignty. There was one conspicuous omission. It treated the Western lands entirely as national assets, but made no attempt to claim them on the theory that the United States, as a nation, had succeeded to the British crown sovereignty over them.

Madison wrote his defense of fisheries in the face of stiff warnings from Luzerne that France's commitment extended only to American independence, and the European mediators would reject these new doctrines. In reply the minister was told of threats by Lovell that Massachusetts would secede from the Union or come to "detest independence" if denied a fisheries guaranty. Luzerne, however, saw evidence of nationalistic ambitions swollen by the triumph at Yorktown. Instead of coupling French and American fishing interests, as Madison proposed, he sent his court a proposition—which Vergennes rejected—that France safeguard her position off Newfoundland by seizing Cape Breton Island.[2]

In Congress, Madison's work was caught in a crossfire. Lovell, bitter at the failure to make fisheries a *sine qua non* of peace, argued for no action at all, lest England be stirred to demand a positive exclusion of Americans from the fishing banks. On the other hand, the position taken was considered too strong by states little interested either in fisheries or lands. Congress finally took an affirmative course. It sent the peace negotiators a strong, brief directive to contend for fisheries and territories, and referred the report to a new committee (Carroll, Randolph and Montgomery) with orders to support it with facts and observations upon the American claims. The committee was willing to let Edmund Randolph (briefly in Congress from Virginia) perform this heavy task, with the result that it was done jointly by him and Madison.[3]

While this was going on, the Virginia delegates undertook to force a final vote on their state's land cession. The opponents, they discovered, were so fearful of its acceptance that they would not even vote on their own report rejecting it. Lee and Bland, aided by Madison, tried to smoke out the speculators by moving that "each member do declare upon his honor, whether he is, or is not personally interested" in any land-company claim. By a skillful use of the "chaos clause," the persons aimed at struck out successive clauses until it provided only for a postponement of the report. Other efforts to force a vote, Madison reported, "produced all the perplexing and dilatory objections which its adversaries could devise"—tactics imputable only to land-company influence.[4]

The majority against Virginia, it was evident to Madison, was increased by the strategy of the Vermont statehood advocates. "Their agents and those of the landmongers are playing with great adroitness into each other's hands," he reported to Randolph just before the postponement vote. To make his own task harder, he and Bland were now alone at the Virginia table, Bland was "still schismatical" as to Vermont (favoring its independence) and thought Virginia's charters unimportant to her Western title. "Is not my situation an enviable one?"[5] To clarify the situation he wrote out a set of "Observations Relating to the Influence of Vermont and the Territorial Claims on the Policies of Congress."[6] It was a shrewd examination of economic self-interest and political prejudices in the formulation of national policy in a swaddling-clothes republic—proof too of the early development of Madison's gift for realistic political analysis.

Rating Vermont first, Western territories second, he linked them as the two great objects in the politics of Congress. New England states desired Vermont's statehood. They were moved by ancient prejudice against New York, speculative interest in Vermont land grants, but chiefly by the desire to gain another Eastern vote in Congress. Pennsylvania and Maryland supported Vermont for trading purposes—to insure New England's opposition to Virginia's land claims. New Jersey, Delaware and Rhode Island had this same motive and the added one of swelling the number of little states.

These five states all opposed Virginia's Western title. They were influenced by a desire to share the lands for revenue, by envy and jealousy of superior resources and importance, but "principally by the intrigues of their citizens who are interested in the claims of the land companies."

This brought Madison to the trading alliance between Vermont backers and the big middle-state speculators. As soon as the Western claims were settled, Pennsylvania and Maryland would break away from New England on the subject of Vermont. To prevent this, Massachusetts and Connecticut were thwarting final action on the Western cessions. As for the Southern states, they opposed Vermont's statehood out of jealousy of the East, and supported the Western claims from self-interest.

One can search in vain for noble attributes in the motives Madison ascribed to the thirteen individual states. Self-interest, prejudice, envy, jealousy and the intrigues of speculators were the springs of their policies. It is noteworthy that he did not confine himself to economic motives, even though these predominated. Prejudice could offset them, if brotherly affection could not. It was this ability to judge actions by motives, combined with his own freedom from unworthy aims and harmful impulses, that lifted Madison's knowledge of government into a genius for the building of it, when the time came for the writing of a new constitution.

Plunging heavily into their study of territories and fisheries, Randolph and Madison produced a monumental set of "facts and observations" in the spring of 1782. Though Madison referred to it as Randolph's work, his participation is evident from a remark, after his colleague went home in March, about the discovery of pamphlets which had "escaped our researches." There is abundant internal evidence that it was written by them jointly.[7]

Once more the Virginians found themselves in the position of Greeks bearing gifts. Chairman Carroll, a mild opponent, blocked committee action by going home for four months. Seeking another avenue, Madison showed the yet secret document to his chief antagonist and close friend, Dr. Witherspoon, and easily convinced him both of "the innocence and expediency of it." Without revealing their purpose, they undertook to open the way to its use. After one or two abortive moves, Madison in early August was appointed, along with a friendly majority, to fill up and enlarge the committee. A few days later he and Witherspoon secured their own appointments to a committee to reinforce the peace demands. They would use this committee to guide the action of the other.[8]

This peculiar maneuver was due to a dilemma Madison was in. The "facts and observations" were anti-Virginian in net weight. With Lee and Bland on a rampage, he dared not submit them to Congress. So, as chairman of the new committee on peace terms, he submitted a report advising that "the committee to whom was referred the report of a previous committee" on American claims give the foreign secretary anything they "may have collected" and that the secretary perfect the same and transmit it to the peace commissioners in Europe. In personal terms, Madison was asking Congress to order him to make official use of his own observations on his own report of January 8, without first submitting them to Congress.[9]

If the enemies of Virginia intended to object, they were beaten to it. Theodorick Bland jumped up, his olfactory organs quivering with suspicion. He wanted to see this material before voting to deliver it to the foreign secretary. Madison explained, in his calm and reasonable way, that it was the design of the committee that "Congress should give no opinion or judgment in the matter." The papers should go to the ministers "merely as information, not as instructions." This would be impossible if Congress acted on them.

This added the curiosity of all to the suspicion of some. Seeing that his scheme had failed, Madison wrote an overnight report for the filled-up first committee, duplicating his proposal that the material be delivered to Secretary Livingston as information, not instructions. The instant this was submitted, Congress ordered a reading of the whole paper.[10]

For page after page the secretary droned along, through a document which fills fifty pages in the *Journals of Congress*.[11] At last came the words which all, without knowing it, were waiting to hear:

"Thirdly, That if the vacant lands cannot be demanded upon the preceding grounds, that is, upon the titles of individual states, they are to be deemed to have been the property of his Britannic Majesty immediately before the Revolution, and to be now devolved upon the United States collectively taken."

Here, from a Virginia source, was the doctrine of the landless states upon which Virginia's title to the West had been assailed since 1776. Bland and Lee were on their feet in an instant, moving to expunge this paragraph from the report. Writing in his super-secret cipher, Madison described the scene to Randolph:

"The business was going on smoothly . . . when the reading of the argument in favor of boundary drawn from the federal source presented to Bland a snake in the grass. This jealousy was sup-ported by Lee by suggestions which pointed to Franklin. The arguments used by these gentlemen raised up the advocates for the federal pretensions. . . . Nothing could have been more fatal to the report than to connect this dispute with it in the mind of Congress and I have no longer any hope of its success."[12]

In the debate (according to Secretary Thomson) Madison said that this clause was put in "for the purpose of reconciling all the states to the report, that though he was satisfied there was no solid foundation in the argument, yet he saw plainly if the clause was struck out sundry states would object to the rest of the report and therefore he should be for its standing." Adjournment came when Madison challenged Bland's right to interrupt a reading which was for information, not debate.

When the reading was resumed four days later, Lee and Bland found more to stir their anger. Following a long and intricate defense of individual state titles, the document returned once more to the federal theme. Our diplomats would not need to prove that the Western lands belonged to the king before the Revolution. His ministers would be quick to say that he was seized of them. Then:

"The character in which he was so seized was that of king of the thirteen colonies collectively taken. Being stript of this character, its rights descended to the United States for the following reasons:

"1. The United States are to be considered in many respects as one undivided independent nation, inheriting those rights which the king of Great Britain enjoyed as not appertaining to any one particular state, while he was what they [the United States] are now, the superintending governor of the whole.

"2. The king of Great Britain has been dethroned as king of the United States, by the joint efforts of the whole.

"3. The very country in question hath been conquered through the means of the common labors of the United States."

Lee and Bland managed to wait until the reading was concluded before they moved to strike out both sections advancing the federal title. The states individually, Lee declared, were sovereign and independent, and upon them alone the rights of the crown devolved. From what source was the sovereignty of the United States derived? "Is it in the Confederation? Is it in the treaty of alliance? Does it really exist?" This from the same man who wrote, a few months later: "The president of Congress being at the head of the sovereignty of the United States takes precedence of all and every person in the United States."[13]

Madison kept quiet, while Witherspoon ripped into Lee's argument. "The several states," declared he, "were known to the powers of Europe only as one nation under the style and title of the United States." It mattered little to European powers whether one state or another owned the uncultivated wilderness. The question with them was whether the security of the United States required that other nations, particularly Britain, be excluded from these territories.

Bland insisted on the yeas and nays, which meant that the facts and observations either would be defeated or become an act of Congress. Wanting neither of these alternatives, the Madison-Witherspoon forces chose a lesser evil, as Madison called it, and referred the papers to a new committee. The American peace negotiators were not wholly bereft of advice, for Secretary Livingston, taking time by a long forelock, had sent them a complete paraphrase of Madison's original report the day before he delivered it to Congress, seven months earlier.[14]

The "facts and observations" slept, but not in effect. The dead-lock over territories left New England clamorous for a new ulti-matum about fisheries. Then came an intimation from Luzerne that a pledge against a separate peace would have a useful effect in London. Seizing this opening, a committee including Madison presented a suitable declaration. Onto this they tacked an ap-peal to France to support the American claim to fisheries and the West—the precise line of action Madison had proposed in his January 8 report—and capped the resolution with a full return to the American demand for navigation of the Mississippi. For the Virginian, this held a multiple satisfaction. It marked final victory in his two-year effort to restore the Mississippi claim. It kept ter-ritories and fisheries on the parity he had established a year earlier, but at a higher level. At the same time he thought it had "appeased in some the rage" for an extension of the ultimatum. Luzerne had no liking for this part of the resolution. When the committee read it to him by order of Congress, Madison reported, "his emo-tion was betrayed by a strong and universal suffusion of the face." However, the declaration against a separate peace was expected to "sweeten the pill."[15]

The major effect of the disputed Randolph-Madison report was in the domestic territorial fight. The basic fact was almost in-credible. Two Virginians had prepared and presented the most forceful argument yet made for the collective title of the United States to Western lands claimed by Virginia. The shrewd Dr. Witherspoon lost no time in exploiting his advantage. A week after the flare-up over the report, Congress gave ear to a petition from Kentuckians who considered themselves "subjects of the United States and not of Virginia." Declaring that the rights of the British crown had devolved on the United States, they prayed Congress "to erect them into a separate and independent state and admit them into the federal Union."

This put Madison on the hottest kind of seat, and he lost no time in getting off. Kentucky, he agreed, should and would be made a separate jurisdiction, but Virginia and not Congress would judge when that was proper. "As to the supposition that the right of the crown devolved on the United States, it was so extravagant that it could not enter into the thoughts of any man." At this, Witherspoon's Scotch burr rolled through the room. He supposed Madison was merely indulging in a figure of rhetoric. Devolution of crown rights on the United States "certainly could enter into the thoughts of men." It had entered into his thoughts, the thoughts of the Kentucky petitioners, and of very many sensible men who had looked upon these lands, from the very beginning of the Revolution, as a fund for the discharge of the war debt. The collective powers of the United States, the New Jersey delegate declared, covered cases which must be decided by "the great law of necessity, which was admitted as a law of nations." One state might grow so powerful and ambitious that the law of necessity and self-preservation would "compel the others, by a sovereign act of authority, to abridge the power of that state, and even to divide it into two or more distinct and independent states." David Howell then asserted that there had been a common devolution, from crown to Congress, of land ownership and the right of setting off new governments. This was a telling shot at Madison, who two years earlier had sponsored the latter right in Congress. By inaction, Congress now rejected the motion to refer the Kentucky petition to Virginia.[16]

Madison was of course protecting himself against political assault in Virginia when he made his remark about the devolution of crown rights. Indications are that he himself placed this federal argument in the "facts and observations." The defense of state titles, in that paper, is in Randolph's florid legal style. Not only is there a sharp stylistic change to the federal argument, but all the rest of the document, beginning with this part of it, is a restatement of Madison's January 8 report and his 1780 instructions to Jay.

Regardless of actual authorship, Madison used all his efforts to promote the federal title for peace conference purposes. He knew as well as Witherspoon did that in European eyes the United States either was a nation or it was nothing. "A free and sovereign nation" he called it in his original report. He advanced the federal territorial argument with full knowledge of its political explosiveness—witness his effort to secure congressional sanction without a reading of it. Unlike Lee or Bland, he would neither reject the use of it out of state loyalty, nor let that feeling blind him to its value.

Madison may or may not have known that the argument for federal inheritance of crown rights, coming from Virginia, would pull the props from under his state's title to the West. It mattered little, for he wanted the lands transferred, and was moving along a new line toward that goal. "Every review I take of the western territory," he wrote to Randolph early in September, 1782, "produces fresh conviction that it is the true policy of Virginia as well as of the United States to bring the dispute to a friendly compromise." What gave force to this was his conclusion that Virginia had something stronger than charters to compel a compromise. It made no difference, he said during one of the ensuing jangles, whether the federal title was valid or not. No coercive force could be put behind it, but individual states "having both the will and the means" could open land offices, issue patents and go right ahead with their plans without any molestation except the clamors of individuals in and out of Congress. There must be a compromise on these Western lands or no advantage ever would be derived by the United States, no matter how valid their title to them might be.[17]

This blunt threat and forecast brought the opposition up short. Witherspoon moved a set of resolutions, apparently drafted in concert with Madison,[18] whose effect was to ask Virginia to revise its act of cession, and to strike down the land-company claims by a pledge to accept state decisions as to private property. The compromise won seven states on a first test, though Witherspoon was outvoted by his speculator colleagues and Madison by Lee and Bland. When Madison called the resolutions up, for a final vote, Indiana Company supporters knocked out the antispeculator clause, whereupon Madison turned against the mutilated resolutions. The opposition then upset him by accepting New York's cession—one more step in a war of nerves.[19]

At this point the trampling feet of the American people swept over the controversy. Men and officers of the Continental Army, civilians now, and other civilians with them, poured westward over the mountains, westward through Pennsylvania and Virginia, lured by the rich lands of the Ohio Valley. Nought they cared for this or that state's title or sovereignty. Land-company deeds meant as little to them as the rights of Indian owners. Unless Congress and the landed states reached a quick understanding, Madison warned his governor, neither the United States nor individual states would reap advantage from the vacant lands.[20]

This new menace moved Virginia to further compromise and enabled Madison to work out a new formula for acceptance of his state's cession. He would relinquish the clause striking down the Indian deeds, believing that land-company claims were tacitly excluded by a provision in the Virginia Act. The land companies feared he was right and shrieked about "common blood and treasure."[21]

By the end of the summer in 1783, the westward tide of lawless migration threatened to destroy the hopes of soldiers not yet on the march. With General Washington as their spokesman, veterans of the Revolution put such heat on Congress that only New Jersey and Maryland—that is, only the Indiana and Illinois-Wabash land speculators—continued to resist. Eight states to two, Congress accepted the compromise Madison had worked out. Its last sentence was a promise that if Virginia would make a cession conformable to its terms, Congress would accept it. Virginia did so, Congress did so, and the great fight was over.[22]

Madison's leadership in this three-year struggle was not of the spectacular variety. Had it been, he would have met defeat. Far more difficult, his task was to draw together two sets of truculent extremists. Passionate devotees of state policy, land speculators hiding their self-interest under a mountain of morality—these, or a majority torn from their fringes, must be won to a compromise which satisfied neither passion nor self-interest. Madison knew that Maryland's demand for common possession of the Western lands, no matter how grievously it was misused by speculators, voiced nevertheless the universal need and right of the American people. Ardent as he was in defense of Virginia's title, he placed the interest of the nation first and did not flinch from political risk in upholding it.

The trend of events made it certain that federal title to the Northwest would ultimately be enforced. What would have happened, though, had that claim been forcibly asserted? With Virginia, the Carolinas and Georgia holding everything from the Ohio River to the Floridas, and their general economic interests in conflict with the North, it might have been the one move needed to split the United States into two confederacies. Blending political skill with devotion to principle, Madison not only averted this danger to the Union, but gave it the cementing bond of a national heritage of Western lands.

CHAPTER XII

YORKTOWN

THE military situation looked better to Madison when he sent
his long account of it to Philip Mazzei in July, 1781. He gave his
friend in Europe a running narrative of enemy operations in the
South under Clinton, Cornwallis and "the parricide Arnold," the
misfortunes of Lincoln and Gates, the skillful exploits of Greene
and Lafayette, the vigilance and dash of Morgan. Goaded into a
rash undertaking, Cornwallis had advanced into Virginia, "abandoning his southern conquests to their fate."

Madison described Tarleton's cavalry foray into Charlottesville,
where, but for "a young gentleman who discovered the design and
rode express" with a warning, Governor Jefferson and the whole
legislature would have been captured. Their savior by an hour's
margin was young Jack Jouett, who proved once more what everybody knew—that a Virginian could outloaf and outride anybody
else in the world. Lounging in a tavern as the dragoons passed, he
guessed their purpose and sped by them on back roads. Tarleton
did succeed in capturing Madison's recent associate in Congress,
South Carolinian Francis Kinloch, who was taken "at Mr. John
Walker's, whose daughter he had married some time before."
Fifteen-year-old Milly had accompanied her father to Congress
only one year back. Romance flowered quickly in Philadelphia,
with its young legislators and budding daughters of older ones.[1]

Madison's account carried the breath of war to his own Montpelier doorstep, in the British pursuit of Lafayette through Orange
and into Culpeper County. It revealed (though he did not mention it) the decisive effect of his own impressment legislation,
which put Wayne on the march. Reinforced, the Marquis "faced
about and advanced rapidly on Cornwallis, who retreated to Richmond, and thence precipitately to Williamsburg, where he lay on
the 27th ultimo." The odds were shifting faster than Madison

knew, for just at this time the Virginia executive council, learning that Lafayette "has nothing to drink but very bad whisky,"
ordered the state commercial agent "to purchase a pipe of good
wine and a hogshead of spirit, to be presented to the Marquis as
a compliment from the state."[2] The prospect was "very flattering,"
Madison thought, in spite of the enemy's great advantage "in the
superiority of their navy, which enables them continually to shift
the war into defenseless places, and to weary out our troops by
long marches."

To Madison, the contest was being waged between men and
devils. He told the Tuscan grape grower:

"No description can give you an adequate idea of the barbarity
with which the enemy have conducted the war in the southern
states. Every outrage which humanity could suffer has been
committed by them. Desolation rather than conquest seems to
have been their object. They have acted more like desperate
bands of robbers or buccaneers than like a nation making war for
dominion. Negroes, horses, tobacco, etc., not the standards and
arms of their antagonists, are the trophies which display their
success. Rapes, murders, and the whole catalogue of individual
cruelties, not protection and the distribution of justice, are the acts
which characterize the sphere of their usurped jurisdiction."

These crimes, Madison went on, are a lesson to the American
people, who, when the pressure of local tyranny is removed, "rise
up as one man to avenge their wrongs and prevent a repetition
of them." Were these facts published to the world in their true
colors, "the British nation would be hated by all nations as much
as they have heretofore been feared by any," and all nations would
see the necessity of abridging their power.

Madison did not overdraw the picture of terrorism, as Cornwallis ordered and practiced it in the South. The Virginian's
reaction deepened an Anglophobia which ruled his mind and
emotions for years to come. It made him an uncompromising opponent of friendship with England after the war, increased his
hostility to the pro-British money party in America, affected his

attitude toward the French Revolution and Napoleonic wars, and made it harder to avoid the War of 1812.

Anger against the enemy rose to new heights in September, 1781, when word came that Benedict Arnold, transferred to Connecticut, had burned New London and Groton, while Cornwallis had reduced Georgetown, South Carolina, to ashes. Madison was made chairman of a committee to deal with various retaliatory motions. It had been proposed, at first, "to employ persons to reduce to ashes the towns of Great Britain." Also, if these acts were repeated, "to put to death all persons found in arms against these United States." That seemed a trifle extreme, even to the delegates (Mathews and Varnum) who proposed it, so they themselves toned it down to an order that the army and navy of the United States demolish enough cities and villages in Great Britain to retaliate for these deeds. If further burnings and murderings occurred, all persons concerned therein should be "immediately consigned to the flames," or, if captured later, be put to death.

Madison did not believe in burning people to death. He doubted also whether the American navy, consisting then of John Paul Jones and two ships, would have much luck burning the cities of Great Britain. His report took the form of a public manifesto. Not only did we lack the ships, he pointed out in this proposed proclamation, but it was "even more consonant to the spirit of justice and humanity" that those who did the burning should be the objects of vengeance, rather than "the remote and unoffending inhabitants of such towns and villages." Let Congress resolve and declare, he wrote, "that British officers now prisoners to the American arms, or which may hereafter be made prisoners, shall answer with their lives, for every further destruction by fire of any town or village" in the United States. On the first authentic notice of such a burning, the War Department was "to cause such and so many of the said officers as they shall judge expedient to be put to instant death."[3]

No doubt it was more humane to shoot the innocent than to burn the guilty, but what Madison's revision gained in humanitarianism it lost in justice. The manifesto, never voted on, was referred to a committee appointed to confer with General Washington, and the subject of atrocities was dealt with instead in a proclamation of thanksgiving and prayer. To the Reverend Doctor Witherspoon, to Roger Sherman, the Connecticut shoemaker, and to General Varnum, co-author of the proposal to throw British prisoners into the flames, it became evident that "Almighty God, the father of mercies," had been pleased "remarkably to assist and support the United States of America in their important struggle for liberty." His influence against the enemy had been clearly perceived through the whole of the contest, but "above all, in making their extreme cruelty to the inhabitants of these states . . . the very means of cementing our union, and adding vigor to every effort in opposition to them." It should please God, therefore, to pardon our offences, impart judgment and fortitude to our officers and soldiers, "bless all seminaries of learning; and cause the knowledge of God to cover the earth, as the waters cover the seas."[4]

All through that critical spring and summer of 1781, hope raced with apprehension among the members of Congress. What of the French navy? In August, Madison heard rumors of huge allied concentrations in the West Indies. Such a rendezvous, just ahead of the hurricane months, convinced him that operations were impending, but he feared that the ships would be deflected into selfish projects of Spain against Gibraltar and Minorca. (Spain, of course, had no right to be at war except for the benefit of the United States.) "Lying Jemmy" Rivington, the enemy propagandist, reported great numbers of American pilots taken to the Indies, pointing to a junction of De Grasse and the French squadron at Newport. "I wish he may guess right," was Madison's longing comment. On that very day, if De Grasse kept to schedule, he was one day out of port on his way to the Chesapeake. Before the month was out, word that he was coming reached Madison as a member of the committee to correspond with General Greene.[5]

The gala days of the Revolution, in martial color and festivities, came to Philadelphia in the first week of September. Out of the north rode Washington and Rochambeau. Dropping the siege of New York, the allied armies were moving against Cornwallis. On Sunday, September 2, three thousand American Continentals passed through—lean men in ragged, faded overalls, with General Lincoln at their head. Then, for two successive days, the French streamed in—mile after mile of bright-hued infantry, cavalry and artillery, bound for the tidelands of Virginia. The Philadelphia capital had in the past seemed full of Frenchmen—diplomats, army officers, visiting noblemen—but this was the first glimpse, for Madison and nearly everybody else, of that military force which for so many heartbreaking months had lain idle in Rhode Island. "Nothing," he wrote upon the arrival of the first division, "can exceed the appearance of this specimen which our ally has sent us of his army, whether we regard the figure of the men, or the exactness of their discipline."[6]

Through Front and Chestnut streets, to the sound of stirring music, up past the delegates at the door of the State House and out to the Commons, marched the French troops. Their officers greeted Congress with a royal salute. They "let fall the point of the sword, likewise the colors, and the members of Congress took off their hats." So one of the delegates described the scene. No ordinary hour this, the French explained. They had been ordered by Rochambeau "to salute Congress as a crowned head, and the President as the first prince of the blood." This dubious unrepublican distinction came to Thomas McKean. "How do you think friend Thomas felt?" exclaimed one of his chaffing fellow delegates. Festivities rose higher after the second division joined the bivouac on the Commons. There the Soissonois regiment held the populace spellbound with its brilliant public maneuvers. South then went the first division, but French officers stayed behind for the crowning event of the week—the great dinner given by the Chevalier de la Luzerne on Wednesday afternoon to more than eighty guests.[7]

French and American officers, members of Congress, federal officials and local dignitaries gathered for the feast. All the great were there except the greatest—Washington and Rochambeau—the whole cast of *Hamlet* without the Prince or Horatio. In a storybook version of history, it might be recorded that Washington missed this feast because his eager Continentals, ill-fed and ragged though they were, refused to let any blue-and-white French

regulars beat them on the road to Yorktown, and no heaped-up
platters could keep their commander from being at their head.
But some knew that Washington hurried after his troops that
morning to guard against a mutiny. Marching unpaid through
the financial capital of the country was too much for hungry men
to bear. On the day of the banquet an inner council met at the
French legation. Luzerne, Rochambeau and Chastellux heard
from Robert Morris the warning and plea of Washington. To
quell "great symptoms of discontent," the troops must be given a
month's pay, more than $20,000 in hard money, at once. Surely
the French could spare that out of their war chest. They were
willing, but what little specie they had was in Boston. De Grasse,
when and if he came, would bring more. In any event, they
would need the consent of the paymaster and he was on his way
south. Ride down with us this afternoon to Chester, Rochambeau
advised, and we'll see what can be done about it. So the two
Morrises (Gouverneur going as French linguist) likewise missed
the feast, while Washington, overtaking his troops, sent back a
new and more urgent appeal for money: "I wish it to come on the
wings of speed."[8]

For Madison and the other guests at the great French banquet,
the headiest wine was not in bottles. Glamour and excitement were
about them, and good news was everywhere. Among the guests
was John Laurens. Back from his Paris mission with four loaded
vessels, two and a half million livres in silver and a diamond-
studded snuffbox from the king, he asked that his sole reward be
an assignment to do some fighting. Americans and Frenchmen
talked of the naval news. De Barras, successor to Destouches, had
put to sea with his little French fleet, Graves and Hood followed
with nineteen ships (as Madison heard it). What could this mean,
he asked, except the impending arrival of De Grasse, and mighty
opposing efforts, on which the outcome of the war might hinge, to
achieve or block a union of the two French fleets?[9]

With the stage thus set for a climax, it came. Into the banquet
room, late in the afternoon, strode a courier from the South. De
Grasse had arrived! Twenty-eight French ships of the line were
in Chesapeake Bay. Three thousand men had joined Lafayette in

the siege of Yorktown. "Cornwallis, who found himself between the fleet and the land forces, was in danger of being captured." Writing thus in his journal of that day, French Commissary Blanchard testified to the full realization of the meaning of the news, received "with great joy by all the guests, French and Americans." By the people, too, for in the evening the citizens assembled and proceeded in a huge crowd to the home of the French minister. Silenced, now, were the anti-Gallic whisperers.[10]

On the road to Chester there was rejoicing too. The Morrises and Rochambeau met that same messenger with his naval news. The $20,000 was promised instantly. In the excess of his joy the financier promised to repay it in a month, something even more difficult than threading his way homeward through the baggage wagons of the second division.[11]

Madison, like others, was in a state of tension during the crucial weeks that followed. He heard of the "fortunate rencontre" between De Grasse and Graves off Cape Henry, but lack of confirmation kept up the public anxiety. The whereabouts of Barras was unknown. If his small squadron should be caught outside the capes—— Nobody knew that he had slipped inside while the incompetent Graves repaired his ships and the competent Hood tore his fingernails. As weeks passed, confidence grew. Madison scoffed at stories from New York that new British fleets were approaching. A trick of the enemy, he called them, "to buoy up the sinking hopes of their adherents, the most staunch of whom give up Lord Cornwallis as irretrievably lost." Some desperate naval experiment there well might be, since the British had twenty-nine ships of the line, but French "skill and bravery on the water forbid any apprehension of danger."[12]

On the day Madison penned these lines, the most powerful fleet the enemy could muster was sailing south for that desperate experiment. On the ensuing day, a drummer boy climbed the parapet at Yorktown and beat the signal for a parley. An officer joined him, raising a white flag. The army of General Cornwallis was capitulating. The War of the American Revolution was drawing to its victorious close.

Five days on its way, an express from Admiral de Grasse galloped into Philadelphia on October 22, bearing the first flash of the news. It was so overwhelming that even with full belief in its truth, Congress held back for Washington's official confirmation. That came in forty-eight hours, when Aide-de-Camp Tench Tilghman splashed in with the articles of capitulation. No slow rider, he, for he made the journey in four days. Congress in a burst of extravagance voted him a new horse and an elegant sword, for carrying such good news so swiftly.

Joy inconceivable now swept the city. Pennsylvania's legislature and executive, forgetting their feud with Congress, thronged into its meeting place, where Minister Luzerne joined in a triangle of congratulations. At noon artillery roared in the State House yard and in the harbor. President McKean, who had just resigned in order to take a ride in the country before presiding over the Pennsylvania Supreme Court, was so perked up that he consented to serve out the remaining two weeks of his term. Congress at two o'clock marched in a body to the Dutch Lutheran church, the largest and most beautiful place of worship in the city, where with other "great and respectable characters" they listened to the inspiring words of Chaplain Duffield and gave thanks to Almighty God for crowning the allied arms with success. Fireworks had to be postponed to a drier season, but it was a glorious evening for window illumination. Even the Quaker windows had candles in them that night—not through the will of their pacific owners, but placed there by friends and neighbors who ran ahead of the stone-throwing mobs.[13]

The "fervent congratulations" Madison sent to Virginia on the Yorktown victory were almost submerged in his rejoicing over the discomfiture of the enemy. "If these severe doses of ill fortune do not cool the frenzy and relax the pride of Britain," he wrote to Pendleton, "it would seem as if Heaven had in reality abandoned her to her folly and her fate." In other parts of the world the enemy had lost nearly everything but infamy. With what hope could they try the fortune of another campaign? "Unless they can draw succor from the compassion or jealousy of other powers [of which he saw no prospect] ... it seems scarcely possible for them much longer to shut their ears against the voice of peace."[14]

Congress followed the Yorktown surrender with a deluge of eulogistic resolutions—to Washington, Rochambeau, De Grasse, Greene (for the Eutaw Springs victory), Marion—everybody but Lafayette, who loved eulogies. Madison repaired the oversight a month later. Reporting on a request from the marquis for leave to go to France, his resolution ordered that Lafayette be given a proper conveyance and then proceeded to tell him where he stood in the minds and hearts of Americans. The high opinion Congress already held of his merits and military talents had been added to by new proofs of his "zealous attachment to the cause he has espoused, and of his judgment, vigilance, gallantry and address in its defense" against far superior numbers. Madison must have talked with the marquis before making his report, for the next section of it gave effect to a cherished ambition. It instructed the American ministers in Europe to confer with Lafayette, avail themselves of his information, and employ his assistance in accelerating French supplies.

This was no mere formalism on Madison's part. He wrote also to Virginia, asking that the assembly "pay some handsome compliments to the marquis for his judicious and zealous services." The result was an order by the legislature that a bust of Lafayette be made in Paris of the best marble and presented to him "as a lasting monument of his merits and their gratitude"—an order which the governor and council, as Madison discovered three years later, proceeded to ignore.[15]

The diplomatic toe hold which Madison obtained for the marquis was scooped deeper by Franklin. The wily old diplomat encouraged Lafayette to postpone his return to America and used him to present Vergennes with American loan arguments which would have more weight "as appearing to come from a Frenchman." Peace Negotiator John Adams, who saw his own jealousy in everybody but himself, wrote in his journal that Lafayette's activity "nettled Franklin, as it seemed an attempt to take to himself the merit of obtaining the loan, if one should be produced." Franklin's very different comment to Livingston was that he worked for the loan both directly and through the marquis, who "has employed himself diligently and warmly in the business."

The marquis, he remarked a year later, "loves to be employed in our affairs and is often very useful."[16]

The lull in military activities after Yorktown gave Madison his first opportunity to become more than casually acquainted with George Washington. Their past correspondence, apparently, was limited to an impersonal letter written by Madison for the Virginia delegation, in response to Washington's inquiry about the trustworthiness of young Peter Thornton, just returned from England.[17] Now, "our illustrious General" was back to receive in person the congratulations of Congress, and, as Madison described it, to give that body "very seasonable aid in settling the military establishment for the next year, about which there is some diversity of opinion." In those good old days, there was nothing ironic in the official invitation the commander in chief received to confer with congressional committees and "enjoy a respite from the fatigues of war." He stayed four months. Madison dealt with him on committee matters and was brought into closer association through the concentration of Virginians in the House-Trist ménage. The memory of this period must have been in Washington's mind, when, coming to the Constitutional Convention in 1787, he wrote in his diary that he "alighted through a crowd at Mrs. House's."[18]

Madison had been in Congress a year and a half when the fighting ended. It was noticeable, now, that he was called on for the most difficult and diverse jobs of public writing, especially when they involved appeals or admonitions to the public, or any deft handling of a delicate subject. Was Polish Count Beniowszky, adventurer, soldier, traveler and yarn spinner, to be told painlessly that Congress could not accept his generous offer to bring a Polish-German legion to the United States at the expense of the French government? Let Madison say it—not, of course, that Luzerne had slipped him a quiet denial of French backing. Instead, he declined the zealous and generous offer of the Polish nobleman in terms lavish enough for an obituary. The count, as Madison recorded his reaction, "betrayed a temper which is very far from enhancing our esteem for him." So violent a temper, indeed, that Luzerne persuaded him "to commune with himself" until he could be sent back to France at the minister's personal expense.[19]

Madison headed the committee which dealt with a warning from France that the British ministry was still bent on conquest (as indicated by its answer to mediators) and the Yorktown victory must not be followed by a military letdown. This information, he reported on May 1, 1782, should be sent in confidence to the states, that they might be stirred to expel the enemy and disprove his false assertions "that the people of these states are neither united nor determined in support of their national independence." Always Madison's emphasis was on national unity. His report led to an appeal by Livingston to the governors for soldiers, for taxation and for state resolutions of fidelity to the alliance. The resolutions poured in; the troops and money did not.

Blushing, according to Marbois, at the degradation into which Virginia was fallen, Madison sent his own personal appeals to Richmond. "Fidelity to our allies, and vigor in military preparation—these, and these alone, will secure us against all political devices."[20] This plea, Randolph replied, arrived just at the proper moment to quench anti-Gallic flames which were being set and fanned in the legislature by Arthur and Richard Henry Lee. The smoke of this fire reached Luzerne, who told Madison that Virginia correspondents reported "very unfavorable symptoms in a large party." Madison returned "a consolatory answer" and at once urged Randolph to seek a unanimous declaration by the legislature on this point. "Such a mode of announcing the sense of the people," he was forced to confess, "may be regarded as more authentic than a declaration from Congress." What a fall from the days of '76, when Congress alone was the voice of America! Yet Madison clung to constitutional appearances, adding: "The best form, I conceive, will be that of an instruction to the delegates." His appeal crossed a notification of the assembly's action. Peace proposals, directed to any body of men other than Congress, were declared to be insidious and inadmissible, and, if received by the assembly, would be rejected as "inconsistent with their national faith and federal union."[21]

Congress might have lost its ability to speak for the people, but it still had a keen sense of propaganda values. Something wonder-

ful had occurred in France. Queen Marie Antoinette, after twelve
blessedly uneventful years (girl babies didn't count) had given
birth to a dauphin. What should be done with the glad tidings?
Minister Luzerne worked out a deal by which they were held back,
officially, until some expected British peace commissioners reached
New York. On the day their arrival became known in Philadelphia, Congress announced a public reception of the French
minister to receive news of the birth of the royal babe, now seven
months old. The plan was to build up a roaring American jubila-
tion that would outdo colonial festivities over similar deliveries to
the House of Hanover. Madison was one of the committee of three
which drew up the announcement ceremonial. The French minister, arriving in his own coach, was to be conducted into the
State House by two delegates:

"As the minister enters, the president and the house shall rise,
the president remaining covered, the minister shall bow to the
president and then to the house before he takes his seat. The president shall uncover his head as he returns his bow. The minister
shall then seat and cover himself; the members conducting him
shall sit on each side of him. The members of the house shall seat
themselves."

Thirteen cannon shots and a musketry *feu de joie* were to end the
reception, followed in the evening by an entertainment for Luzerne at the City Tavern. To it Secretary Livingston was to invite "such general officers and foreigners of distinction in town
as the president shall approve." The American armies were to give
"such demonstrations of joy as their commanders shall respectively direct."

When Livingston read this, he exploded with a *feu de joie* in reverse. Not only, he informed Congress, had the committee disregarded his own suggestions, but he was called upon to direct an
entertainment at which he was not even a guest, and to which the
heads of departments were not invited. Could he make the world
believe that an officer whose position entitled him to some respect
had been placed "on a footing with the president's steward?" As-

suring Congress of his "veneration for their orders," he promised to carry them out if they were changed. They were changed— indeed the original record was blotted out—and Livingston so far recovered as to give an entertainment of his own after the grand display of fireworks at night.[22]

Luzerne soared skyward in describing for King Louis the dual triumph of fatherhood and diplomacy. The British peace overture found Congress "celebrating the birth of the heir of the crown of France with more éclat than the birth of a Prince of Wales ever elicited in the eras of British rule. These festivals, these marks of universal joy for an event which especially concerns us, unite the two nations more and more." Madison was more reserved about the spontaneous outbursts. "It was deemed politic at this crisis," he remarked, "to display every proper evidence of affectionate attachment to our ally."[23]

The crisis to which he referred—uncertainty over British moves—was unrelieved when the enemy commander sent word that same day that Lord North's ministry had fallen and by order of the new government he wished to talk peace. So patent an effort at separate negotiations was instantly rejected by Congress. Madison's concern was deepened when a rumored French naval victory in the West Indies turned into a severe defeat for De Grasse. This was followed by a report to Luzerne of secret British offers—very liberal ones—for a separate peace with France.[24]

"This insidious step," Madison hoped, would "not long be withheld from the public." It was not dangerous, having been rejected, but there was publicity value in it both for the alliance and against the seductive peace overtures from New York. More important still was the need to reassure France of American fidelity. Madison was given the task of replying to Luzerne's communication on the subject. Welcoming the "signal proofs of inviolable constancy" given by the French monarch, he wrote that Congress would harken to no propositions for peace which were not perfectly conformable to the alliance. If, in spite of "the insidious steps which the Court of London is pursuing," proper offers were made, Congress would adhere to past pledges to discuss them only "in confidence and in concert with his Most Christian Majesty." The resolves closed with a pledge of military exertions to match the redoubled efforts of France—a mild suggestion, perhaps, that French efforts be redoubled. The assembly was of one voice, said Luzerne in sending Madison's resolves to France, in demonstrating that the British naval victory had no effect on the constancy of Congress.[25]

The public, at this time, knew only from enemy sources of the defeat of De Grasse. Madison and Marbois worked out a plan for confirming it without scaring anybody, at the same time fulfilling Madison's desire to publicize French good faith and British duplicity. The Virginian put forward the idea "in an evening of promiscuous conversation" with the legation secretary. Marbois said he would think it over, and next day sent Madison the text of a letter, "with a request that I would revise and translate it for the press." According to Madison, he was only the translator of what appeared in the *Pennsylvania Packet* of June 11, 1782, as an "Extract of a letter, written from Philadelphia by a gentleman in office, to one of the principal officers in the State of New Jersey." If so, Marbois had a genius for uttering Madisonian thoughts. Treating the state resolutions against a separate peace as if they were a response to the bad naval news, the Marbois-Madison letter both admitted the defeat and minimized it. The British victory was a barren one, said Marbois in Madison's best style, since it had "afforded us an occasion of displaying a national character, a good faith, a constancy and firmness worthy of a people who are free, and determined to perish sooner than cease to be so."[26]

Two days after the publication of this letter Congress poured more cement, this time moistened with their tears, on the French alliance. They told their "great, faithful and beloved friend and ally, Lewis the sixteenth," of the extreme grief they felt at the death "of your most dear and beloved aunt, the Princess Sophia Philippina Elizabeth Justina. . . . We pray God, dear, great, faithful friend and ally, always to preserve and keep you under his holy protection."

Taking advantage of this moment of heartfelt sorrow over human suffering, Madison and Bland tried to persuade Congress to buy a cork leg for a Virginia veteran who had lost its living predecessor in a duel. All they got for Captain Cooper was a sixteen-dollar installment on his back pay.

CHAPTER XIII

War Crimes and Criminals

Madison's desire to retaliate against the enemy did not abate with the Yorktown victory, but was held in check by his scrupulous regard for national engagements. He joined with most of Congress in rejecting a South Carolina motion that Lord Cornwallis and other officers be detained in custody, in violation of the parole granted them under the terms of capitulation. He was eager, however, to invoke the weapon of imprisonment in behalf of a locked-up American, Henry Laurens. This public minister and former president of Congress, Madison pointed out in a motion offered on December 3, 1781, was imprisoned in London as a British subject suspected of high treason. Declaring that "the dignity of the United States as a sovereign and independent nation" required relief measures, he asked for the immediate imprisonment of a blank number of British officers "most eminent for birth and rank," chosen from prisoners of war not exempted by capitulation.[1]

This was a protest against the failure of Great Britain to respond to the six-months-old offer to exchange General Burgoyne for Laurens. The effect was to bring Cornwallis into the Laurens picture. Congress forbade his inclusion in a general cartel for exchange of prisoners, but modified the order, on Washington's protest, to permit the earl to be exchanged by composition (that is, for a composite group held equal to him) provided Laurens was set free also. This was an indirect proposal to exchange the two.[2]

This exchange was just what the British ministry was working for. Cornwallis was the idolized pet of Lord Germain, ministerial mismanager of the war, whose past support had enabled the earl's blunders to prevail over those of his immediate superior, Sir Henry Clinton. To clear the way, Germain rejected the Burgoyne-Laurens exchange and agreed to give one thousand forty-four

American privates in composition for the victim of Saratoga—a valuation more flattering to Burgoyne than to the privates.

As another result of the Yorktown capitulation, Madison was called on to defend the rights of a group he hated worse than Cornwallis—the Virginia Loyalists. At the time of Captain Tilly's naval dash into Chesapeake Bay, capture of a party of refugees induced Madison to ask Minister Luzerne that these men, "traitors who deserved exemplary punishment," be surrendered to the state to be treated as malefactors. This was in accord with a 1777 resolution of Congress, but the minister replied that they were French prisoners of war and not liable to American law because the French naval squadron, unlike Rochambeau's army, was not auxiliary to the forces of the United States. Traitors they still were, in Madison's view. But when Washington agreed at Yorktown that civilian prisoners might sell their goods in Virginia and have the proceeds remitted to New York, Madison was ready to support them, and to clash with his legislature and the powerful Lee brothers in doing so.[3]

The issue arose over method of payment. Since it was difficult and harmful to transfer specie, Finance Superintendent Morris arranged for the sale of Virginia tobacco in New York and asked Congress to authorize a passport for its shipment. Madison and two other delegates conferred with Morris and Washington and advised that the passport be issued.[4] Arthur Lee, always on the lookout for a weapon against Morris, saw one in this action. He went to Richmond, secured the oratorical aid of Richard Henry Lee and opened an assault in the House of Delegates.

The financier, Arthur whispered and Richard Henry declaimed, was using the Bank of North America to ruin Virginia. The tobacco passport was a scheme of Morris and the Secretary of Congress to reap speculative profits by trading with the enemy. Congress had no power to issue passports because no such power was set forth in the Articles of Confederation. Moreover, the exportation of tobacco to the British was forbidden by state law and by the Franco-American treaty, for which the Lees developed a sudden veneration.

Seeking to stem the tide, Attorney General Randolph appealed to Madison for a constitutional interpretation. The latter knew that he ran a particular risk at this time in crossing Lee. "From a review of certain characters and circumstances," he and Joseph Jones believed that Lee's purpose in going to Virginia was to work for Madison's elimination from Congress. In reply to Randolph, Madison not only asserted the right of Congress to issue flags, but defended the policy of shipping tobacco as a means of saving specie. He even wasted an argument on Arthur Lee while performing a financial favor for him: "If the goods included in the capitulation of York were sold, and are to be paid for, it would seem that a mode of payment, which affords to Virginia a vent for her staple, cannot be complained of by her."[5]

Arthur's answer came that same day, when Morris placed before Congress a savage attack on himself, the Bank of North America and the passport, adopted by the Virginia lower House and sent on without waiting for Senate approval. An unnoticed clause in the Articles of Confederation, forbidding Congress to interfere, by treaty, with state laws banning exportations, forced Madison to change sides on the question of power. On the basic issue he held firm: "As to the simple right of granting flags, it is impossible to shake it on any principle. It is a lesser power evidently involved in the major one of making peace. A flag is a partial truce as a truce is a temporary peace."

Congress now needed Virginia's help to fulfill the pledge to the Loyalists. The mass of falsehoods in the House resolution made it evident that the state lawmakers had been deceived. Two congressional delegates, going south on another mission, were ordered to explain the passports to the Virginians. Madison eased their task by a deferential rewording of their instructions and sent a private protest of his own to Randolph. A great personage was touched by the attack (it was unsafe to name Washington while Virginia letters were being intercepted and published) and he told of their conference on the subject. On all sides, he said, there was criticism of the state for raising such false issues, especially as Virginia herself had sought and obtained from Congress the right to ship tobacco instead of specie for the support of prisoners in New York. As to the assault of Arthur Lee upon Robert Morris:

"My charity, I own, cannot invent an excuse for the prepense malice with which the character and services of this gentleman are murdered." A eulogistic defense of the financier closed with this appraisal and interpretation of duty:

"The same fidelity to the public interest which obliges those who are its appointed guardians, to pursue with rigor a perfidious or dishonest servant of the public, requires them to confront the imputations of malice against the good and faithful one. I have, in the conduct of my colleague here [Bland], a sure index of the sentiments and objects of one of my colleagues who is absent, relative to the department of finance."[6]

Arthur Lee, right at this time, was furnishing no less sure an index of his feelings toward Madison. He suddenly challenged the right of his colleague to re-election to Congress on the ground that a Virginia law limited consecutive service to three years. Then (though both a state and federal legislator himself) he broadened the challenge by declaring that Edmund Randolph could not be both congressional delegate and attorney general. Launched in secrecy, Lee's campaign had its fullest effect, Randolph reported, "before it came to the knowledge even of our friends. But it may be triumphantly said that the wicked and malevolent did not dare to exclude from their most poisonous reports a respect for our characters. You were assailed under . . . such a fervor of compliment that it was unpleasant to distrust its sincerity. I too was declared to be ineligible after a preface overflowing with panegyric."

So big a bite was too much for even the well-exercised molars of Arthur Lee to masticate. Patrick Henry, perennial foe of the Lees, took the floor in defense of Randolph and "no man rose to assert the negative" except Richard Henry Lee. Recognizing his defeat, Arthur himself, under "an affectation of candor," turned around and spoke in opposition to the brother whom he had prodded into the first attack. The legislature took care of Madison, as had been intended all along, by repealing the three-year law, leaving in effect only the three-year federal limitation dating from ratification of the Articles of Confederation. In the election, Arthur Lee salvaged last place in a five-man delegation headed by the men he had plotted against. To fill his cup of gall to the brim, Rutledge and Clymer came from Congress with so logical a justification of the tobacco passports, as a benefit to Virginia and a federal necessity, that the legislature almost unanimously reversed its stand.[7]

That Madison knew he was choosing trouble, in supporting Morris against Lee, is evident in his comment after the embittered doctor returned to Philadelphia late in June—a comment which harmony-loving editors have seen fit to delete from his published letters:

"The prevailing temper of the present delegation is too little flexible to the factious and vindictive feelings of a particular member of it to be relished by him and his adherents. No delegate who refuses to league with him in the war against the financier must expect to be long at ease in his post. The disappointment in the affair of the flags will increase the venom against the minister. The first conversation I had with the doctor after his return betrayed how much it rankled."[8]

While Arthur Lee, for political purposes, pictured the fulfillment of Yorktown surrender terms as trading with the enemy, Madison devoted himself to money-hungry merchants who really were engaged in such operations. "The trade with New York," he averred to Randolph in June, 1782, "begins to excite general indignation, and threatens a loss of all our hard money. The continued drains which it makes from the bank must at least contract its utility, if it produces no greater mischief to it. [This was when Luzerne saved the bank by depositing French army funds in it.] The legislature of New Jersey are devising a remedy for this disgraceful and destructive traffic, and a committee of Congress are also employed in the same work."[9]

Madison did not mention that he himself was chairman of the committee, appointed on his own motion against illicit trade with the enemy. He had little hope of finding an adequate cure, as long as the naval blockade of Delaware and Chesapeake bays annihilated American commerce and the enemy kept a trade channel open through New York. This did not diminish the vehemence of his report, which denounced those who "by a sordid attachment to gain, or by a secret conspiracy with the enemies of their country, are wickedly engaged in carrying on this illicit traffic."

If blocking such trade was difficult, the means used should be strong. There was nothing halfhearted in Madison's suggestion. In addition to a request for state laws, he proposed that the commander in chief "be and hereby is authorized and directed to make such disposition" of his regular forces as will "aid in suppressing the pernicious traffic aforesaid." Living up to its reputation for timidity, Congress passed it with this resort to military enforcement stricken out.[10]

The original report stands as a revelation of the extent to which Madison, in this nationalistic period of his career, was able to discover implied powers in a government limited to those expressly delegated. The army was not to be used merely to stop sales to the enemy. By the very words of the preamble, the purpose was to regulate commerce and the flow of money. The action was designed to stop practices "whereby a market is provided for British merchandises, the circulating specie is exported from the United States, the payment of taxes rendered more difficult and burdensome to the people at large, and great discouragement occasioned to honest and lawful commerce." More specifically, as Madison wrote to Randolph, the desire was to protect the specie supply of the Bank of North America. Long after fighting had stopped, the war power was resorted to for purposes distantly related to war, but immediately concerned with the stability of governments and financial institutions and the welfare of merchants and taxpayers—objects normally associated with the regulation of commerce. Madison's strong federalism was outlasting the battles of the Revolution. He was able to see federal powers not enumerated in the Articles of Confederation, and he looked on the army as a handy agency for their enforcement. His views did not prevail, but it was by just such discoveries of power that a later American government of limited scope became adequate to its enlarging tasks.

Madison was helped to this resort to the war power by his feeling that the end of fighting did not mean peace. The enemy was still

the enemy. In this same month of June, 1782, he offered a motion
to force the British commander to pay overdue living expenses of
war prisoners in American hands by reducing their rations as
much "as the interests of the United States shall require, and the
preservation of the said prisoners will admit." It was a different
matter when the enemy cut down the diet of American prisoners.
Then Madison asked Congress to grant protection to a fishing
boat off Sandy Hook, for the benefit of seamen held "in loathsome
confinement" on a prison ship. To encourage these and other
"brave but unfortunate seamen" to continue their rejection of inducements to enlist against their country, he joined in committee
indorsement of an agreement by Franklin, militarily undesirable,
to exchange British soldiers for American sailors. "This bold step
at first gave much offense," he remarked to Randolph. "Compassion, however, for the patriotic captives stifled reproaches."[11]

German prisoners—Hessian mercenaries—were placed by Madison in a special category. These hapless conscripts, so hatefully
portrayed in American school histories, appealed to him as fine
material for the upbuilding of the United States. Many of them,
he reported to Congress, from a dislike of the military service into
which they had been forced, and from a desire to improve their
condition, were asking to be admitted to the Continental Army.
Others wanted to become indentured servants for a short period,
all "with a view of eventually becoming citizens and settlers."
Congress approved Madison's plan of recruiting Hessian volunteers into the army or allowing a three-year indenture "on such
conditions as will secure . . . a comfortable maintenance and be
most conducive to the public interest." What was the reaction of
the American people to this friendly policy? Did they respond
with violent outbursts of antiforeignism and punitive hatred?
Apparently not. For when the greedy Hessian monarch who sold
these conscripts to King George insisted on their return, and Congress was obliged by treaty to accede, there was a mass desertion
of those still in barracks and the French minister reported that "it
is impossible to find them in the homes of the inhabitants who are
all in agreement to hide them."[12]

Very different was Madison's attitude toward Americans who

voluntarily aided the enemy. On his motion, Congress approved Washington's refusal, while negotiating a general exchange of prisoners, to discuss the treason laws of the several states. The states of the Union being sovereign and independent, said Madison's resolution, "the laws respectively passed by them for their internal government and the punishment of their offending citizens, cannot be submitted to the discussion of a foreign power, much less of an enemy."[13] By treating this as an affair of internal government, he put it in theoretical harmony with his emphatic views on national sovereignty. It was a forced harmony, however.

The exchange of prisoners was a war function, therefore under the exclusive control of Congress. But, as Madison saw it, captured Loyalists were not prisoners of war at all. This case merely involved "two traitors, who, under the cover of a flag of truce, exposed themselves to arrest in New Jersey, and had sentence of death passed upon them." Such a curtailment of the war power, besides testifying to Madison's passion against Loyalists, disclosed the presence in him of a political frailty which has become an American characteristic. With all his intellectual honesty and analytical gifts, he was better able to discover constitutional power to do a thing if he wanted it done, than if he did not.[14]

With Loyalists out of it, Madison was ready enough to see national principles in the exchange of prisoners. During the negotiations, Congress voted to retain all prisoners until a general cartel should be agreed to. A fortnight later, apparently in Madison's absence, the exchange of two foreign officers was authorized. Securing a reconsideration, he denounced any such exchange as "highly dishonorable to Congress." It violated a resolution whose purpose was "to compel the enemy to a national convention with the United States" and enable Congress to assume a higher tone. As the British commander "either from a want of power or of will had declined treating of a cartel on national ground, it would be peculiarly preposterous and pusillanimous in Congress to return to the former mode." The authorization was repealed by a unanimous vote.[15]

The easy victory Madison won in this instance, compared with his numerous defeats in seeking national action in domestic affairs, tells a significant story of the trend of thought and feeling as the Revolution drew to a close. The sense of nationhood was growing in the relations of the United States with foreign nations. But as military victory made national unity less imperative, a weak government was driven to a lower tone in dealing with jealous, bickering states and their suffering or profiteering inhabitants. Madison strove along national lines in both fields, successfully in one, fruitlessly in the other, and often inflamed by the intense end-emotions of the Revolution.

Where these emotions were involved, consistency was not a Madison virtue. If a pair of New Jerseyites enlisted in the British Army to defend their old allegiance, and came to the American lines bearing a flag of truce, hanging them was a right and proper enforcement of treason laws. He did not appear to realize that his own doctrine, taken in reverse, would justify the hanging of every American soldier captured by the enemy, nor that each execution forged a link in the chain of endless savage reprisals.

It was vastly different when New Jersey refugees "perpetrated one of the most daring and flagrant acts that has occurred in the course of the war." Captain Joshua Huddy, of the New Jersey militia, after being "treated with every mark of insult and cruelty in prison," was taken out "and in cold blood hanged." General Washington, Madison reported, "has in the most decisive terms claimed of Sir Henry Clinton a delivery of the offenders up to justice as the only means of averting the stroke of vengeance from the innocent head of a captive officer of equal rank to the Jersey captain."[16]

The innocent prisoner, chosen by lot, was Captain Charles Asgill, whose condemnation to death for another's crime inspired five plays on the eighteenth-century French stage but has not yet brought forth an American epic. In Congress the cruel sentence won instantaneous and complete approval. On the very day that Washington reported it (April 29, 1782) and without an opposing vote, the delegates praised the commander's "firm and judicious conduct" and assured him "of their firmest support in his fixed purpose of exemplary retaliation." Madison's approval was natural enough. The congressional indorsement was in the very words with which, in the previous October, he had called on the general to "cause exemplary retaliation to be executed" for all acts of cruelty. That proclamation, though unadopted, had been placed before Washington by order of Congress and he wrote once that he was awaiting action on it as a guide to his own course.[17]

Huddy's hangman, Captain Lippincott, was court-martialed by the British commander, but Madison saw no prospect of a conviction in the dragged-out trial. "It is inferred," he remarked before the verdict was made public, "that this murderer will not be given up, and consequently a vicarious atonement must be made by the guiltless Asgill."[18] No longer a person of flesh and blood, that young officer had become a symbol of stern retributive justice.

The case seemed quite different to the condemned man's mother, Lady Theresa Asgill, who received word of it as her husband lay near death in their English home. Directing her appeal to the Count de Vergennes, she wrote:

"My son (an only son), as dear as he is brave, amiable as he is deserving to be so, only nineteen, a prisoner under the articles of capitulation of Yorktown, is now confined in America, an object of retaliation. Shall an innocent suffer for the guilty? Represent to yourself, sir, the situation of a family under these circumstances; surrounded as I am by objects of distress, distracted with fear and grief, no words can express my feelings or paint the scene. My husband given over by his physicians a few hours before the news arrived, and not in a state to be informed of the misfortune; my daughter seized with a fever and delirium, raving about her brother, and without one interval of reason, save to hear heart-alleviating circumstances.

"Let your feelings, sir, suggest and plead for my inexpressible misery. A word from you, like a voice from heaven, will save us from distraction and wretchedness. I am well informed General Washington reveres your character. Say but to him that you wish my son to be released, and he will restore him to his distracted family and render him to happiness."[19]

Barriers of war, and the slow reaches of Atlantic travel, lay between that plea and any possible effective action on it. Washington himself, meanwhile, sought the advice of Congress. The British court-martial, he reported in August, had found Captain Lippincott's defense of the Huddy killing inadequate, but acquitted him (in Madison's indignant paraphrase) "on the ground that no *malicious* intention appeared." The arrival of peace preliminaries removed the need to execute Asgill as a deterrent to other outrages, and left retaliation as the only motive for doing so. Should he carry out the sentence, the commander in chief asked. The general seemed to "lean to the side of compassion," Madison remarked, but there was no such feeling in the big congressional majority whose arguments he summarized. They contended that a departure from the resolution so solemnly adopted and ratified "would be an indelible blot on our character." If the enemy allowed the innocent Asgill to perish after the guilty Lippincott had confessed, "the blood would be on their hands, not on ours."[20]

Yet Washington was hesitant. Carleton had criticized the Lippincott verdict and promised further pursuit of the matter. Congress held back its final action: Theresa Asgill's son still lived, though except for the miracle of a delivery of the Huddy murderer, or the tenuous chance of French intervention, his fate was compressed between Washington's misgivings and the vindictive savagery of Congress.

While this was going on, the interlocked affairs of two more noted prisoners, Charles, Earl of Cornwallis, and Henry Laurens, continued to command the attention of Congress. Madison was one of a committee of three at whose instance (on a motion by Arthur Lee) Washington was ordered to recall the earl from England to the United States—though not into American custody—unless Laurens should be at once released and given passports or a general parole. There was a bit of shadowboxing in this action of July 11, for private information had come in April that Laurens was at liberty on a six-months' summons. That in turn followed publication by enemy propagandist Rivington of an extraordinary December petition from Laurens to Parliament (a petition denounced by his friends as a forgery) beseeching that body to pity his suffering and set him free.[21]

The subject came before Madison in September, when John

Rutledge of Laurens' home state, Duane and he were ordered to report on a no less extraordinary letter from the captured diplomat. Writing from Amsterdam on May 30, the South Carolinian told how, in December, he was asked by the ministry whether Franklin had authority to exchange Cornwallis for him. "I could give no positive answer, and there the subject dropped." On the last day of the year, without any foreknowledge or preconcert on his part, he was admitted to bail signed by Richard Oswald of the Foreign Office. In April, following Lord North's downfall, the new ministry gave him permission to go to Holland and offered him a full and unconditional discharge, to which he replied that "I dared not accept of it myself as a gift." But since Congress had once offered to exchange a lieutenant general (Burgoyne) for him, he had no doubt they would offer another of the same rank (Cornwallis) for his release. Three weeks later, he said, he made a peremptory demand for a court hearing and thereupon was given a full discharge. There was no agreement for the release of Cornwallis, but he had reason to believe, from his prior refusal to accept discharge as a gift, that the Secretary of State, Lord Shelburne, "understood and expected that such a return would be made." In consequence, he had written to Franklin and asked him to concur in discharging Lord Cornwallis, but as yet had received no answer. As for his diplomatic mission, he did not suppose all five commissioners were expected to attend, so he declined the honor and would soon come home.[22]

The resignation alarmed Rutledge and other Southerners, since in combination with Jefferson's refusal to go it would throw the entire peace negotiation into the hands of three Northerners.[23] Madison was puzzled rather than alarmed. Why did Laurens refuse an unconditional release? Why did he, on his own initiative and with no apparent need, create an expectation that Cornwallis would be released? He would have been less perplexed if Laurens had remembered the December conference in the Tower of London the way Richard Oswald did. The two men were friends and business associates of nearly thirty years' standing—Oswald as a Scotch trader carrying Negroes from Africa to South Carolina, Laurens as a distributor of the imported slaves. This naturally put them on good terms now that the elderly slave trader, seeking to fill his later years with good deeds, was endeavoring to raise the humanitarian level of British diplomacy.

As Oswald related the story, he carried from the Tower a promise "signed by Mr. Laurens' hand" that if released on parole he would apply to Franklin for an exchange in favor of Cornwallis, and failing that, would seek it of Congress, in consequence of which he "was soon after set at full liberty" on bail.[24] Lord Shelburne, who came into power with the new Rockingham ministry, had no part in this. Unsolicited, he offered Laurens his unconditional discharge to enable him to act as a peace negotiator. Saying nothing of this offer or his refusal of it, Laurens immediately asked Franklin to sanction his exchange for Cornwallis. Instead, Franklin requested Shelburne to give Laurens a discharge because of his commission for peace. Shelburne did so at once and notified Franklin of the fact. Franklin informed Laurens of this, adding that nothing was said about an exchange, but that, honoring his colleague's sensibility on that point, he would join him in seeking it. Oswald then told Franklin of Laurens' signed promise to work for the release of Cornwallis. Laurens followed with frantic pleas to Franklin to set the earl at liberty, lest some day in America there be "diabolically trumped up against me an imputation of having been discharged under a pardon." This fear was genuine— practically the only thing in the Laurens record that was.[25]

Madison felt from Laurens' own statement that something was wrong in his conduct. "Far from unexceptionable" was the way he described it. Rutledge, however, was concerned only over the sectional aspect of the peace negotiations. At the committee's request, therefore, Congress resolved that Laurens' services could not be dispensed with and directed him to go to Paris.[26]

On the day this action was taken, dispatches from Franklin were being decoded—the first of later date than March. Saying nothing of the agreement Laurens had signed, Franklin merely stated that his colleague had given the ministry such expectations about Cornwallis that he did not feel free to act in public affairs until the general was absolved. Accordingly, Franklin had given Cornwallis a discharge, "reserving to Congress the approbation or disallowance of it."[27]

Madison headed the committee named to deal with this unpleasant news.[28] It was not in this capacity, however, that he took the floor next day (September 19, 1782) to make a motion which would admit of no delay. His seriousness so impressed Congress that current business was postponed. Secretary Thomson took private notes of what followed. Madison had in his hands, he said, a copy of the *Parliamentary Register,* from which he wished to read the petition of Henry Laurens to the House of Commons. In terms of supplication, it set forth at great length his grief at the breaking out of war, his acts of kindness to "loyalists and quietists," his present illness and suffering, on account of which he "humbly prays your honors will condescend" to release him or grant such other relief "as to the wisdom and benignity of your honors shall seem fitting."

When published in Rivington's *Gazette,* that had been looked on as a forgery. Now, said Madison, there was evidence that it was genuine. If Laurens did actually sign and present it, "he had thereby wounded the honor and dignity of the United States in such a manner that he was no longer fit to be entrusted with the character of a public minister." No man, Madison said, would be readier than he to restore Laurens' character to its ancient splendor if the petition should be found spurious. If it was genuine, he was sure Congress would realize the effect in Europe should they press a man to remain in office after he had "prostrated the dignity of his country, wounded its honor, and as far as in him lay denied its sovereignty and independence."

Congress realized no such thing. Laurens' Southern friends, uniting with New Englanders who relied on him to support the fisheries, opened a furious attack upon Madison's motion not to transmit the order sending Laurens to Paris. Arthur Lee led the assault. The publisher of the *Parliamentary Register,* he averred, was an infamous person "who would ruin the character of any man for five shillings." Bland echoed Lee. From others came declarations that the petition was forged. In vain was the answer made that former publisher Almon was noted for his devotion to the American cause, his successor probably was of the same mind and in any case would not ruin the paper's high reputation by a falsehood so easily detectable. The attack struck so close to Madison that he had to take the floor again to defend "the purity of his motives." The dignity, honor and interest of the United States, he declared, required the passage of his motion, but when the opponents called eagerly for a vote his side secured an adjournment.[29]

Madison renewed the fight next morning, calling attention to the recorded debate on the petition in Parliament. Speakers were named, remarks summarized, orders set forth, the petition formally inserted—such marks of authenticity as could hardly be doubted. A petition like this would be unworthy of a private citizen. Far worse to have it come from a minister "commissioned to represent the sovereignty of these United States." The appeal, he pointed out, "is stated not as coming from a citizen of the United States but a native of South Carolina. What is this but indirectly relinquishing the claim of independence which we have so solemnly declared and pledged ourselves to maintain at the risk of our lives and fortunes?"

This so weakened the forgery contention that Rutledge of South Carolina swung to a defense of Laurens' conduct. It was true that he did not call himself a citizen of the free and independent states of America, "fine, high-sounding language," but who among those present would do so after fourteen months of imprisonment, illness, solitude and deprivation? As for the tenor of the petition, that was the way Congress itself used to address the king.

Laurens had in truth lapsed into pre-independence thoughts and phrases, but quite aside from this Madison distrusted his patriotism. During his captivity, Madison observed to Randolph, Laurens had shown such bias toward Britain and cordiality toward its new leaders that he dreaded his participation in the making of peace. On the margin of his copy of Laurens' petition Madison wrote: "I am informed that at the time of the Stamp Act his house was beset by a mob in consequence of his known heterodoxy."[30] Had the full story been known, the very facts which Laurens concealed might have helped to exonerate him. If he accepted a release without the discharge of Cornwallis to balance it, his petition to Parliament would furnish clinching evidence that he had sought and received a pardon. His overwhelming dread of such a development is enough to indicate that the humble supplication was a temporary reflection of illness and despondency.

Southern loyalty and New England fishing interests (to which Laurens was devoted) united to hand Madison a five-to-three defeat. Once again, sectional, personal and economic motives overrode the considerations of national dignity and sovereignty which bulked so large in the Virginian's thinking. His own delegation was split by the defection of Lee and Bland. Yet right in his own hands he still had the means of excluding the South Carolinian from the peace conference, and of winning applause for himself in the process.[31]

Franklin's discharge of Cornwallis was subject to ratification or rejection by Congress. Laurens would not act in the peace mission if the discharge was rejected. Madison was chairman of the committee upon that subject. His fellow member Rutledge was author of a motion to reject the discharge. Madison need but join him in asking Congress to overrule Franklin's action, and Laurens would be placed on a shelf. Instead, he united with Montgomery and wrote a contrary report.

Laurens, Madison declared, had authorized an expectation in the British ministry that Cornwallis would be absolved from his parole in exchange for his own freedom. The earl's peculiar barbarities in this most barbarous of modern wars should make him the last, rather than the first, object of indulgence, yet "it is upon the whole expedient for Congress to confirm the act by which he has been set at liberty." The report encountered a hostile Congress. Arthur Lee tried to make Franklin the villain of the piece, but the congressional animus was against Cornwallis. The report was fired back to the committee.[32]

Since inaction would amount to ratification, Madison and Montgomery proceeded to do nothing until Congress, after a couple of months, woke up to this strategy and asked for a report. To force an advance decision on the main issue, Madison moved that the committee prepare a proper act of ratification. He then proceeded to heap burning coals on anti-Cornwallis delegates who in September had been leading defenders of Laurens. By its actions at that time, Congress had insisted that the minister stay in office. He must therefore be supported. It would be "preposterous to retain him in so dignified and confidential a service, and at the same time stigmatize him by a disavowal of his conduct and thereby disqualify him for a proper execution of the service." It was far overrating the earl's importance to sacrifice all these considerations to the mere pleasure of prolonging his captivity.

The opposition squirmed. They heaped odium on Cornwallis, then turned on Laurens. No exchange had been necessary for his release. He was too friendly with Shelburne. He had been eulogized in Parliament. He had sent a reprehensible petition to the House of Commons (no forgery now). In short, everything Madison said in September, with other accusations added, was thrown against Laurens in order to injure Cornwallis, while Madison, distrusting one and hating the other, protected both in order to preserve the honor and prestige of the United States in Europe. Six states took a stand against the Cornwallis discharge. The lack of a seventh gave Madison the victory, for inaction made Franklin's decision final. Charles, Earl of Cornwallis, was free. And free to do what? Why, to go on, more openly now, with his arguments for abandoning a hopeless war.[33]

In this month of November, 1782, Madison began to make daily notes of the debates and proceedings of Congress, entering them in a fine hand in manuscript booklets with four-by-six-inch pages. This practice, which he continued for half a year, gave him the training and no doubt furnished the suggestion for the great work he performed four years later, in making a permanent record of the debates in the Constitutional Convention. The day on which he recorded the final discussion over Cornwallis—November 25— had another element of peculiar interest. It marked the entrance into Congress of twenty-four-year-old Alexander Hamilton, who within a few years was to become Madison's foremost political foe. Nothing but friendship and co-operation was visible at this time, when both were intent on the triumph of the Revolution and the establishment of a stable and effective national government. With a self-assurance which contrasted strongly with Madison's initial diffidence, Hamilton plunged into the debate over Madison's Cornwallis motion and "warmly and cogently espoused the ratification."[34]

And what of that other Charles, the condemned nineteen-year-old son of Theresa Asgill? Autumn produced no abandonment of the "fixed purpose of exemplary retaliation" to which Congress had subscribed in the spring. The Asgill death sentence, on which Washington had asked for new instructions, came up for a vote on October 28. Nineteen delegates, including the professor of Christian theology from Princeton, voted death to Asgill; seven said no. Madison was absent. But the majority had only five states. The death-sentence forces began work on a modified wording but the "chaos clause" had saved Asgill for a day at least.

While this was going on, a messenger from General Washington was spurring his horse through the winding valleys and over the hills of Jersey. For three days he rode, bearing a packet of letters, and arrived on the morning after the vote. A dazed Congress listened to the reading of them—the letter of Lady Asgill to Vergennes, one from Vergennes to Washington, one from Washington to the President of Congress. Vergennes told of the deep effect of Lady Asgill's letter upon the king and queen, to which he added his own solicitations as "a tender father who feels all the force of paternal love . . . in favor of a mother and family in tears." Washington wrote that he was sending "a very pathetic and affectionate interposition" for Captain Asgill without any observations of his own—as if that were not observation enough.[35]

The scene was described years afterward by a delegate who voted for the death penalty and succeeded in forgetting that he had done so. The reading, Elias Boudinot wrote in his *Reminiscences,* "operated like an electrical shock, each member looking on his neighbor, in surprise, as if saying here is unfair play. It was suspected to be some scheme of the minority. The president was interrogated. The cover of the letters was called for. The general's signature was examined. In short, it looked so much like something supernatural that even the minority, who were so much pleased with it, could scarcely think it real."[36]

Madison recorded the legislative effect of the Vergennes intercession, which, founded on "a most pathetic and importunate memorial" from Asgill's mother, arrived "in the midst of our perplexities." All agreed that retaliation could not be executed in the face of it. Some welcomed the intercession, looking on it as a lucky ground of retreat. Others saw a wounding of national honor in "such a public exhibition both of our obsequiousness to France and of her disapprobation of our views," and felt too that the revelation of it would be "an impeachment of the humanity of Congress." They preferred a spontaneous retreat based on Carleton's promise to pursue the Huddy murderer.[37]

Though he did not say so, Madison was leader of this second group, for after a committee cited the Vergennes intercession as grounds for the action, he drafted a substitute motion along the other line. The form finally adopted left people to draw their own conclusions. Congress resolved, on the report of a committee to whom certain listed letters were referred, that Asgill be set at liberty. The list revealed the stabbing of a guilty conscience. All the letters were there, from July to October, that had a bearing on the case, except one. Congress made no mention of the letter from Asgill's mother.[38]

On the heels of this action, Madison called up the second part of his substitute proposal, directing Washington to demand a fulfillment of Carleton's pledge to pursue the Huddy murderer. It fell short one state on the first vote, Madison reported, but he secured its passage next day on the plea that Congress would be more blamed for dismissing the innocent if it failed to pursue a promised vengeance on the guilty. Apparently, by this time, Madison had his fill of retaliation on innocent men. He joined Howell, of Rhode Island, leader of the pro-Asgill delegates, in toning down a sweeping grant of authority to military commanders to take retaliatory steps without the specific approval of Congress. Defeated in an attempt to soften it still further, they acceded to the final form only because of fear that the raging Carolinians might put through something more offensive. Madison's partnership with Howell in this work, combined with his general tendency to support Washington, affords some probability that he would have voted to rescind the death penalty had he been present on October 28.[39]

Aside from long-continued vindictiveness against the enemy, the outstanding feature of Madison's share in all these controversies was his invariable emphasis upon national dignity, honor and authority. The depth of this feeling is evident in the way it overruled personal considerations. He opened the fight in Laurens' behalf with a declaration that his imprisonment affronted "the dignity of the United States as a sovereign and independent nation." He charged that the minister had denied the sovereignty and independence of his country by calling himself a native of South Carolina instead of a citizen of the United States. He put national honor above his violent feeling against Cornwallis, against Virginia loyalists. He wished the exchange of prisoners to be on national grounds, to force the recognition of sovereignty to a higher level. In recovering from the passion of vengeance against Asgill, his primary concern was not for the cruelly condemned youth but for the threat to national honor in too abject submission to France. His objection to giving military commanders an un-controlled power of retaliation was not that they might abuse it, but that "political and national considerations" might require the intervention of the supreme authority.

Coupled with this increasing emphasis upon national dignity and sovereignty was a growth of forcefulness in Madison's ap-proach to congressional work. He was still primarily a winner of men by the art of reasoning, a strategist, a conciliator, but the vigor of denunciation came more often into his mildly spoken phrases. His self-effacing modesty and the chaste sobriety of his recorded utterances reinforce their logic and scholarship in producing the impression that they came from a half-embodied intellectual machine. Not so to those about him. Outside of Congress, in everyday relationships with his fellow delegates, he was known for his racy conversational skill, ribald wit and zest for salacious stories.

Madison's talent for personal friendliness and conciliation was not devoted to the avoidance of controversial issues, but to the management of them. In a Congress too variably divided for any individual to be called its leader, Madison had become, midway of his four-year service, its acknowledged spokesman whenever it used the voice of national authority or appeal. Of greater import, he was the skillful builder of majorities to that end, and the planner of strategy for those who fought against the dividers, the subverters, the exploiters, the defamers and the blunderers.

CHAPTER XIV

DEFENDING FRANKLIN

MADISON was assured of a lively time in 1782 by the three-fold task which he assumed: protecting the French alliance, defending honest public servants and upholding the dignity, honor and interests of his country against assault or error. The entrance into Congress of Arthur Lee and Ralph Izard, egocentric, provincial-minded enemies of France and Franklin, ballooned this into a full-time job.

Through most of that year, Madison engaged in a running fight with his colleagues, Lee and Bland, over Franklin's financial transactions. The issue arose when Luzerne gave notice that France no longer would meet the salaries and expenses of the American diplomatic corps in Europe, and wanted Congress to give Franklin power to settle the large open accounts between the two countries. This was painful news, the more so if, as the Chevalier reported to his court, everybody was "strongly disposed to consider the greater part of these advances as gifts."[1]

Madison was drafting a committee report on the subject when Morris transmitted a letter from Franklin, revealing an unexpected absorption of promised funds by old congressional drafts. "Every sou we can command during the year 1782 is already anticipated," was the financier's bitter comment. Without waiting for Madison's report, Bland leaped in with a motion for an inquiry into the authority under which European loans had been appropriated by Franklin. The Madison forces cut this to pieces with the familiar question, "Shall those words stand?" then ordered Morris to make a report on foreign loans.[2]

Congress a few days later adopted Madison's motion that foreign ministers be paid by the superintendent of finance. It accepted, likewise, his report directing Franklin to liquidate Franco-American accounts, and providing for a commissioner, under Morris, to settle the accounts of all public servants entrusted with expenditures in Europe. The Franklin inquiry was to be in friendly hands.[3]

This blissful state of affairs lasted for several weeks. Then the dilatory Commodore Gillon, after wasting nearly a year in Holland, Spain and tropical seas, arrived with some of John Laurens' Dutch purchases. He tried to throw the blame for mishandling on Laurens' other agent, Major William Jackson. The major, now assistant to the Secretary at War, spread a sensational and garbled account of Franklin's share in the matter. John Laurens, in addition to the specie he brought back from France, had sent a million and a half livres to Jackson to be carried by Gillon. Discovering this was taken out of the French subsidy to the United States—his own urgently needed funds—Franklin recalled it to meet overdue bills drawn on him by Congress.[4]

This was a grist pile indeed for Arthur Lee. "Absolute robbery," the work of a rapacious and irresponsible man—thus he described the step which Franklin took to save the credit of the United States from ruin. With accusations flying and Franklin's version unknown, his friends consented to new inquiries demanded by Lee, Izard, Witherspoon and others. Lee then resurrected the proposal to inquire into Franklin's handling of loans and also secured a reconsideration of Madison's resolve for appointment of a liquidator of foreign accounts. His aim was to take this away from Morris and let Franklin's enemies regulate his financial settlement.[5]

Lee was riding high now, for in every one of these moves he secured a committee hostile to Franklin and dominated by himself or his followers. Bland and Jonathan Jackson ruled the committee on goods and money in Holland. Lee and Izard controlled the investigation of European expenditures. Lee and John Morin Scott were to define the conditions under which Franklin would make his financial accounting. Third place on each committee went to a delegate impartial or friendly toward Franklin. Reports were spread that Franklin's spirit was broken, he was too intimate with the new British ministry, too susceptible to cajoleries and attentions. (That of the master cajoler of the century!) In dramatic contrast, private word came from Holland that John Adams had won national recognition and an alliance with the Dutch republic, opening visions of financial aid from a new source. Using a supersecret cipher,[6] Madison described the state of affairs to Randolph:

"The news from Holland has much emboldened the enemies of France. Doctor Lee declared that it might be considered as the epoch of our emancipation. Yesterday I was reminded by Izard that Franklin was interested in restoring the back lands to the crown. Soon after I was shown by Lee a proposition for reconsidering the commission and instructions for peace. The plan is to exclude F[rankli]n and J[a]y and to withdraw the others from the direction of France. The notes of Morris [governmental and personal notes issued to sustain an empty treasury] are also to be attacked. These and some other symptoms strongly portend a revival of party heats. I earnestly wish we had your aid in repressing them."[7]

Lee moved next day against the peace negotiators, and Madison took the floor in opposition. The objection, he pointed out, was to a single clause in the instructions, but the motion would unseat the ministers. Waiving that, he opposed the entire motion. Before the instructions were condemned, Congress should consider the critical situation when they were adopted, the threat of unfriendly mediation, the clash between John Adams and Vergennes, the rejection (at that time) of a motion to enlarge the commission. No harm, Madison said, could come from the instructions. Altering them might abate the zeal of France in the American cause. Others took the same view and Congress adjourned without a vote. "I have found means hitherto," Madison reported to Randolph, "of parrying the attack on the notes of Morris."[8]

Lee chafed in silence until, as Madison expressed it, a letter from Jay added "fresh leaven to the anti-Gallic ferment." Bills drawn on him by Congress for about £25,000 had gone to protest because neither Spain nor France would pay them. (France had just accepted four million livres of such unauthorized bills, drawn by Congress on Franklin in the face of French warnings.) Madison

saw a chance, by careful maneuvering, to revise the instructions to
Jay, in order to reassert the American claim to the Mississippi.
Warning that Lee's effort to combine the affairs of the two diplomats would create a suspicion of distrust of France as well as Spain,
he split off Jay's letter and secured control of it. The result was an
order to Jay to sign no treaty without submitting it first to Congress.[9]

Lee reoffered his motion against Franklin within a few days, but
Madison had a new defense. Lee could hope to attack Franklin
successfully only through an assault on the more vulnerable instructions. But Dr. Witherspoon, his ally against Franklin, was
the author of the particular instruction he was attacking. Though
Madison and Witherspoon were themselves at odds on the Virginia
land cession, Madison had been working for some months on his
old college president, trying to win him to a joint maneuver in
support of the Mississippi, the American claim to the West, and
fisheries. In June, Witherspoon introduced a motion which Madison drafted and seconded, but it was defeated by states inflamed by
jealousy of Virginia.[10]

Now, on August 8, Madison and Witherspoon heard Arthur
Lee declaim that the interest, honor and safety of the United States
demanded a revocation of the peace instructions. Never, perhaps,
had he been so eloquent along national lines. Here, agreed the two
wily Princetonians, was their chance. Madison granted—so Secretary Thomson recorded—that the instructions given "are a sacrifice
of national dignity. But it was a sacrifice of dignity to policy,"
made necessary by the circumstances of the time. Nor does it
weaken American security, for only if France lost confidence in the
United States would she oppose the enlarging of American boundaries. Nothing would tend more strongly to produce that jealousy
than a withdrawal of these instructions. As for the staining of
national dignity, would that be repaired by convincing Europe
that we are a people "governed wholly by circumstances, *abject
and profuse* of promises when in distress and difficulties," but so
ready to veer about that no reliance can be placed on their promises? He was impressed, however, by what had been said about the
objects of American interest. If any member believed that more

could be done to secure them, he would have no objection to that, provided the old instructions were left in full force. In fact, he would himself move to postpone Lee's motion in order to offer one of his own to that end. He then presented a paraphrase of the motion he had written for Witherspoon two months earlier: That a committee "report to Congress the most advisable means of securing to the United States the several objects claimed by them and not included in their ultimatum for peace of the 15th day of June, 1781."

Witherspoon seconded the motion and lulled the suspicions of anti-Virginians by explaining that he was not interested in continuing the war for the sake of boundless Western claims of contentious states. He was for the motion because commercial objects would come within its scope. Adopted almost unanimously, the proposition was put into the hands of Madison, Duane, Rutledge, Jackson and Witherspoon. Not only did Madison bury Lee's anti-Franklin, anti-French maneuver under the adverse majority of a committee headed by himself, but he achieved his own previously defeated objective in the process.[11]

One defeat was no deterrent to the doughty doctor from Virginia. If Franklin could not be ousted, Lee would see to it that the rapacious villain made a strict accounting of the vast sums he had expended in France. The hand of Chairman Scott, guided by the pathological mind of Lee, drafted a report for the committee on that subject. Knowing that Franklin, cut off from Congress for months at a time, had been forced again and again to make unauthorized expenditures, the report demanded "clear, minute and satisfactory proofs" not only of the money spent, "but also of the ground of authority" for each individual expenditure. All goods must be accounted for by vouchers sworn to by the original issuers, and carried down and proved by a record not only of the particular bales, chests, trunks and packages but also the particular invoices of each, the vessels in which shipped, etc. In the confusion of war, all the bookkeepers in the world could not have met these demands.[12]

Lee's requirements for the "dishonest and incapable" Franklin, as he called the minister, were the more striking because of the way his own diplomatic accounts had been settled. First relieving him

of responsibility for 66,853 livres of federal money which he had
diverted without authority to the use of Virginia, Congress in 1781
took Lee's word of honor (for he was unable to produce papers)
that the Treasury owed him $9,950 55-90ths. This was paid to him
in Continental loan certificates—interest-bearing paper money
whose value was maintained by the ingenious device of drawing
bills on France for the interest, without that country's prior consent. When France, getting tired of this, cut off the interest in
1782, Lee informed Congress that he had never been paid for his
diplomatic services, and by six months of steady bullying obtained
a repayment in bills of exchange on France. Lee, it seemed, trusted
French money more than he trusted France. And Franklin? For
the support of the war, he had put his entire fortune into American loan certificates and silently watched it vanish to nothing.[13]

Madison had his eyes on Scott and Lee. The former left for New
York on August 28, before the committee report was delivered.
Like a shot, Madison secured his own election to the committee.
He joined with Rutledge in throwing out the Scott-Lee report. The
two, overriding Lee, promptly submitted a new one, which Con-
gress adopted, merely giving the commissioner of accounts author-
ity to sue, appoint clerks and administer oaths. Another of Arthur
Lee's projects was on the rocks.[14]

What were two failures among so many openings? Heading the
committee to investigate Franklin's expenditures, Lee with Izard's
help would reveal how he had squandered his general diplomatic
funds. But Ralph Izard, though he hated Franklin, was an honest
man of good intentions. Embarrassed by the "perpetual chicanery"
of Lee (as Luzerne phrased it), Izard and third member Wharton
found that Franklin had drawn eight thousand livres less than his
own salary. Allowed four hundred thousand livres a year for the
entire diplomatic establishment in Europe, he had spent an average of 263,072 livres. The committee would say so. In that case,
Chairman Lee would say it—"affectation of candor" again. He
said also that hundreds of thousands of livres had been appropriated by Franklin for which the *Journals of Congress* revealed no
authority. Under the management of Duane and Madison, Congress killed that charge by postponing the report.[15]

Meeting with defeat after defeat, Lee began swinging wildly.

Congress ordered him to draft instructions for Franklin to negotiate a treaty with Sweden. That was bitter gall, for the king
seemed to want the treaty largely for the distinction of dealing
with Franklin. "Notwithstanding the particular desire of the
king of Sweden," Madison reported, "Lee, Izard and Bland, particularly the first and last, struggled violently to deprive the doctor
of the honor intended him. Their struggles and maneuvers however had no other effect than to display their extreme enmity."[16]

Of the entire campaign against Franklin nothing remained now
but Henchman Bland's inquiry into the detention of goods and
money in Holland. Here things were going swimmingly. Bland
presented a report which Madison described as "one of the most
signal monuments which party zeal has produced. By mutilating
and discoloring facts in the most shameless manner it loaded
Franklin with the whole guilt and proposed finally a severe repre-
hension of him. This unfair hostility did not meet with the expected countenance of Congress." Madison and Daniel Carroll
were added to the committee and quietly let the whole matter
die.[17]

Outside of all this, Lee attempted, according to Luzerne, to
revive the old animosities between Generals Washington and
Gates. "He has been no happier in this move." Refusing to force
the restoration of Gates to active command, Congress left his future
status to Washington's discretion. Lee sensed his failure in time to
make the recommendation himself, thus appearing on the public
records as Washington's champion.[18] Philadelphia was an unpleasant place after this 100 per cent record of total defeats, nearly
all of them personally administered by Madison. "Doctor Lee set
out the day before yesterday for Virginia," his quiet young colleague wrote on October 8 to Randolph. "He left this place I believe in not the best of humors. In Congress he has been frustrated in several favorite objects and from the press he has been
most rudely handled."

The newspaper assault on Lee was quite apart from congressional matters. Sticking his hand into the buzz saw of Pennsylvania politics, he was naïve enough to refer to his European career,
and sign himself "Virginius," in an anonymous article purporting

to be written by a Philadelphian attacking that city's depravity
and toryism. Lee's mastory of invective, great as it was, made him
but a tyro compared with the professional vituperators in the city
of brotherly love. Madison sent to Virginia "a mild sample of his
sufferings"—an article likening him to a stallion from whom all
other animals and "the very groom who fed him received his bites
and lashes." At his departure the *Independent Gazetteer* bade
farewell to the "principal scribe to the skunk Confederation." Randolph was shocked beyond measure by the article Madison sent
him. "Does the sacred liberty of the press justify such invectives
against men in high office?" he cried. Congressional immunity,
he seemed to think, covered anonymous assaults by a delegate
upon a hostess state.[19]

This was not the end of Lee's troubles. In his rage at the succession of defeats administered by Madison, he wrote so violent an
anti-French letter to Mann Page of Virginia that it led to a legislative hearing and motions of censure and recall. Summoning
Bland to Richmond to aid him, he tried to obtain a statement that
most of the members of Congress were under the influence of the
French minister. Bland went no farther than to disclaim such
influence over himself. Madison was so immune to this insinuation, his cousin James, of William and Mary, informed him, that
nobody even thought of him in connection with the singular
question. Saved by the absence of Patrick Henry (so Randolph
said), Lee escaped recall by a two-vote margin.

Arthur Lee's opinion of his fellow Virginian can be found in
his response to Thomas Lee Shippen's glowing praise of Madison's conversational gifts. Saying that both he and others agreed
with his nephew on that point, Lee continued: "It is his political
conduct which I condemn, that without being a public knave himself he has always been the supporter of public knaves, and never,
in any one instance has concurred to check, censure, or control
them—that he has had such vanity to suppose himself superior to
all other persons, conducting measures without consulting them
and intolerant of all advice or contradiction—that in consequence
he has been duped by the artful management of the rapacious
Morris and the intriguing Marbois. It is possible he may have

thought himself right in all this, but in acquitting his intention we hazard the credit of his understanding." Considering its source, that was hardly less than eulogy—the only instance, perhaps, in which Lee ever acquitted an opponent of active wickedness.[20]

The shrewdest appraisal ever made of Arthur Lee came from the Chevalier de la Luzerne during this embattled period. Believing at first that the Virginia doctor had some secret connection with the London court, he saw on long observation not the slightest evidence of it. "But Mr. Lee is an ambitious man who, having once been excluded from the Department of Foreign Affairs, sees no other road open to his ambition in the present state of affairs and consequently applies himself to stop all the motions of the administration. . . . He flatters himself that . . . it will be easier for him to achieve his goal in the midst of disorder, than if he allows the order now being introduced to be maintained. If he cannot achieve his aims, and peace brings independence in spite of his efforts, he will have prepared in good time the means of a personal connection with England, by capitalizing with that power the opposition he has shown against us in nearly all circumstances."[21]

The uncanny accuracy of this estimate is evident from Arthur Lee's soliloquy, after his recognition of defeat, upon a possible removal to his vacant lands in Kentucky:

"Ambition and avarice seem therefore to join in their invitation. But after the scenes through which I have passed such an ambition seems low; and the avarice without an incentive. . . . He who pursues ambition in that country must . . . first agitate its separation and independence, then control the various turbulent spirits who are gathered there. . . . A single man intent upon gratifying his taste, might accomplish this purpose with great certainty and at a moderate expense in London. . . . Could I be restored to the situation that I enjoyed [there] before the Revolution, unless the tumult of political commotion may have unparadised it, I might be happy."[22]

Madison had now clipped the wings of John Adams in Europe and drawn the fangs of Arthur Lee at home. While engaged in the latter task, he found himself confronted with a replica of the former one. Francis Dana, minister-designate to the Russian court, had been ordered to avail himself of the advice of Franklin and Vergennes and present his credentials only with the approval of French Ambassador Verac. He set off for St. Petersburg in defiance of Franklin's suggestion that he first find out whether he would be welcome, but with a reluctant promise to Vergennes that he would keep his commission secret unless overtures were made to him by the Russian ministry.[23]

Dana's promise evaporated during a stopover with John Adams in Holland. "America, my dear sir, has been too long silent in Europe," the exceedingly nonsilent Bostonian admonished his fellow townsman. Long-delayed letters streamed in from Dana in the spring of 1782, all revealing suspicion of France, distrust of Verac, fervent American nationalism and utter ignorance of Russian policy. His intention was to notify the court of his mission within a few days. The fact that Catherine had just denied the existence of the United States by refusing to admit "the revolting colonies" to mediation without England's consent made no impression on him whatever.[24]

Madison at once took a vigorous stand against Dana, though harmony-loving editors eliminated all trace of it from his published writings. Dana's "proposed rash step," he told Randolph, had probably been taken months before. Rash? Let not the American people know that one Founding Father spoke thus about another. A committee of Congress, Madison said, "animadverted on his precipitancy." What? An American statesman rebuked? That too was expurgated from his writings.[25]

Dana's friend and fellow Bay Stater, Samuel Osgood, put Madison at the head of a "systematical junto" which leveled "envenomed shafts" at the diplomat for the better part of a year. "Junto" was a word of the day—applied chiefly to the alliance of New England followers of Samuel Adams and the Virginia Lees, and therefore used by them about others. There was really no venom in Madison's shafts. He did not, for instance, call Dana "the little sore-eyed insignificant from Massachusetts," as another delegate did. But he distrusted Dana's judgment and sought to curb his actions.[26]

The report criticizing Dana, written by Scott, of New York,

was referred to Secretary Livingston with the expectation, as Madison understood it, that it would be sent "in his dress to Petersburg." The secretary, instead, asked for congressional approval of the letter which he based on the report. With only seven states present, Massachusetts alone could cut it to pieces with the "chaos clause." The instant this process began, Madison countered with a motion restraining Dana but not censuring him. Massachusetts joined in its adoption, and Congress then ordered "That the copy of the letter be returned to the Secretary for Foreign Affairs."[27]

This step, a technical approval, allowed Livingston to send the letter of rebuke to Dana, along with Madison's resolution. He promptly did so—"an unpardonable piece of cunning," Osgood declared when he heard of it months afterward, for "it was the sense of Congress that they [the committee report and the letter] should die." Osgood's own summary of the debate does not bear him out. Full of Madisonian phrases, it consisted of a defense of France against Dana's insinuations of impending treachery. Dana had written without ciphers, and missing sets of his letters were believed to have fallen into French hands. Livingston's letter of rebuke was written for effect on France. Throwing the Bay Staters off guard with his mildly worded resolution, Madison made it possible for Livingston to give Minister Luzerne a copy of his letter. In doing so, he did not override the will of Congress. He merely circumvented the "chaos clause," by which one state attempted to override six. A resolution by Madison on that same day, calling on absent states to send delegates at once, makes it plain that he was prepared to continue the fight if his strategy failed.[28]

Half a year later, Madison was moved to scoffing comments (all carefully suppressed by squeamish editors) about Russo-American trade proposals by Dana. In the spring of 1783 Congress was thrown into an uproar by letters from the diplomat telling of his plans to negotiate a commercial treaty, after he should be received, and then come home. Actually, he had about as much chance to win the Empress Catherine to a treaty as to marry her. The only notice she had taken of him was to rebuke the Russian ambassador in Holland for attempting to forward a portrait of George Washington to "one Dana," concerning whom, or any other American, "her majesty's ministry does not know who they are, nor why they are here." The congressional roar was due to a request from Dana for nine or ten thousand pounds with which to rub the palms of Catherine's ministers. Russian custom, he said, compelled this. Otherwise, no treaty.[29]

Madison at once challenged Dana's authority to negotiate a treaty of commerce, declaring that no powers or instructions had been given him for that purpose. Made chairman of a committee to revise previous general instructions as to commercial treaties, he brought in a report directing Dana to decline entering into such a treaty without further orders of Congress, unless he had already engaged the faith and honor of the United States. In that case he should limit it to fifteen years. He was "permitted to return" home as soon as propriety allowed—a virtual recall order. Without waiting for Congress to act on this report, Livingston wrote to Dana flatly denying his power to do anything more than "communicate" on the subject of a treaty. No money, therefore, would be needed for the treaty, nor did Congress wish to "buy one at this day."[30]

The uproar increased when Dana's friends learned of the letter and Madison admitted he was wrong as to Dana's powers.[31] Thomas Higginson, Boston merchant-delegate, described the development to Theodorick Bland in revealing retrospect—revealing, because of the evidence he furnishes of Madison's leadership of the anti-Dana forces, and the fine sample he provides of anti-Gallic suspicions:

"Congress, when Madison's report for calling him home was under consideration last spring, thoroughly attended to his commission and even Mr. Madison determined that his powers were plenary. This was done when the secretary was present, and Mr. Madison's report was rejected; but the junto had determined that Mr. Dana should come home, and that no treaty should be made with Russia, perhaps by the order of the Count de Vergennes, and the views of the junto must not be defeated; if Congress could not be brought to order him home, Mr. Secretary would do it himself."[32] Higginson, a leading member of the Essex Junto, hurled the word most readily where it did not apply, just as he charged Livingston most vehemently with offenses he did not commit.

Madison's report was defeated, according to its author, by a coalition of shipbuilding states and South Carolina, the former allured by Dana's promise of hemp and iron imports, the latter by his picture of a future market for rice. Hamilton and Madison then teamed up in a new move. Each one drew up a resolution, designed to check Dana without recalling him. Madison held his back and seconded Hamilton's after the latter had been modified to include some of Madison's proposals. One section forbade payment of the Russian bribe. Hamilton helped Rutledge (rice) and Holten (hemp and iron) knock this prohibition out of his own motion, whereupon Madison joined a North Carolina delegate in putting it back in milder form—no palm grease unless already promised. The whole resolution was then defeated by the "chaos clause," six states for it, rice and hemp and iron against.

On the following day (May 22, 1783) Madison offered his own held-back resolve. Beaten at first, its provisions were adopted piecemeal after restraints on Dana were dropped. He, poor man, getting Livingston's sharp rebuke, and receiving some final aid from Catherine's boots, shook the snows of Russia from his own.[33]

This conflict, of slight importance as far as Dana was concerned, was in fact one of the epochal events in American history. Currents were set in motion, policies were outlined, which ruled the political and economic relations of the United States with the rest of the world for the next hundred and fifty years The original impetus, in every instance, appears to have come from James Madison.

In his motions on commercial treaties, Madison was thinking not of Russia but of Great Britain. Secretary Livingston had just outlined an Anglo-American treaty of commerce. Its terms impressed him, Madison told Jefferson, as a scheme to give New England a carrying trade between the West Indies and the rest of the world. In exchange, British subjects were to gain equal privileges with American citizens, a concession which "will chiefly if not alone affect the southern states." These should at least retain the power to encourage their own merchant marine, "to prevent a relapse under Scotch monopoly, or to acquire maritime importance."[34]

Looking at it nationally, Madison declared himself generally opposed to commercial restrictions or preferences, but "a young and inexperienced nation" might take notice that Great Britain broke foreign monopolies by favors to her own subjects, and made this the basis of her existing maritime supremacy. At present, to encourage agriculture and obtain consumer goods, American ports should be opened wide. But "as our lands become settled, and spare hands for manufacture and navigation multiply, it *may* become our policy to favor those objects by peculiar privileges bestowed on our citizens." At any rate, each generation should be free to judge of its own needs and act accordingly.

To insure a foreign policy consistent with these ideas, Madison proposed two safeguards. Treaties of commerce should be limited to moderate periods. To guard against injury to individual states and resulting damage to the confederacy, all treaties of commerce, before being finally signed, should be submitted to Congress for approval, with full liberty in that body to accept or reject. Both of these propositions found a place in Madison's report on Dana, and were finally adopted as separate measures. Thus, in the closing period of the Revolution, Madison brought an end to treaty-making by ministers whose work Congress was pledged in advance to accept. This was the prelude to treaty ratification by the United States Senate. So, too, without favoring the policy of a protective tariff, he declared the possible future necessity of it and opened the way to its adoption.

A third and more dramatic feature of American foreign policy had its origin in Madison's moves against Dana. Here is found the first expression of the warning against entanglement in the politics of Europe which took lasting form in the Farewell Address of Washington and the first inaugural address of Thomas Jefferson. The issue arose over the question of American membership in the armed neutrality of Europe, to which, as a war measure, Francis Dana had been authorized to accede. Madison's position was foreshadowed in his attitude toward commercial treaties. Whereas it had previously been necessary for military reasons to court the influence of European nations, he remarked to Randolph, "the attainment of the object of the war has happily reversed our situation and we ought no longer to enslave ourselves to the policy of the moment."

The very day after he wrote this the broader question of national policy came to the fore. Hamilton's motion on Dana, seconded by Madison, rejected American membership in the armed neutrality. The rejection was not Hamilton's idea. The manuscript draft of his motion shows that he first declared Congress to be "desirous of acceding" to the European confederacy, then "willing to accede," finally "unwilling at this juncture." An amendment from the floor, italicized below, converted this into a general declaration of political isolation. Congress was "unwilling, at this juncture, to become a party to a confederacy *which may hereafter too far complicate the interests of the United States with the politics of Europe.*"[35]

That Madison was the author of this amendment seems evident from his prior declaration to Randolph and the events which followed. Although Congress approved the amendment, defeat of the whole resolution blocked its effective adoption. Two weeks later, Secretary Livingston proposed that the principles of the armed neutrality be written into the definitive treaty of peace. A resolve by Madison, unanimously adopted on June 12, 1783, repelled that suggestion and wrote these words into national policy:

"The true interest of these states requires that they should be as little as possible entangled in the politics and controversies of European nations."[36]

This doctrine of no entanglements was formally adopted as national policy thirteen years before the classic utterance of Washington on the subject, eighteen years before that of Jefferson. Madison reaffirmed his conviction in 1786, opposing a suggestion that Spain and the United States guarantee each other's territory. Such an American promise, he said, would be infamous if insincere, hazardous if genuine: "In either case we get farther into the lab-

ALEXANDER HAMILTON AND ROBERT MORRIS

MARQUIS DE LA FAYETTE

yrinth of *European politics* from which we ought religiously to keep ourselves as free as possible."[37]

A knowledge of these moves by Madison, immediately after American independence was insured, is essential to a fair appraisal of his part in the stormy controversies over peace terms and the French alliance, during the final year of the war. It absolves him completely of innuendoes that he was subservient to the French, for his "no entanglement" resolution was in effect a preliminary notice of the withering away of the French alliance after the American need for it had passed. The Count de Vergennes had no illusions on this score. "We have never based our policy in regard to the United States upon their gratitude," he wrote just after the adoption of Madison's 1783 resolution, but before he heard of it. "That sentiment is infinitely rare between sovereigns, and republics know it not. . . . I am convinced that their views and their affections will be very changeable and that we cannot count upon them if ever new disputes with England come upon us."[38]

The qualities Madison exhibited in this shaping of foreign policy go far to explain his leadership in Congress. His outlook was American and national. This made him a partisan of the French alliance, during the period of need for it, without being a partisan of France. He had a rare faculty for looking ahead, both to the near and distant future. His stand against foreign entanglements bore no resemblance to the provincialism of those who stood for isolation when European help was needed. His attitude was a thought-out response to America's changing status in a disorderly, predatory world. He sensed the moment at which participation in European politics ceased to be part of the chess game of independence, and became a snare for distant innocence. If (as Spain might think) the United States was not quite so innocent, that did not diminish the wisdom of the policy.

Madison saw America both as it was and as it would be. As it was—a raw agricultural country whose increasing population would be absorbed for some decades onto vacant fertile lands; a people, therefore, in need of unrestricted foreign trade to carry away farm surpluses and bring in manufactured goods. As it would be—a nation expanding quickly as far as the Mississippi, with a population too great for the farm lands, turning to manufacturing and commerce and thereby creating new economic and political problems.

Such thinking—American, national, foresighted and constructive—did not insure perfect judgment in the formulation of policy. Its certain effect was to make Madison a leader among those who were groping, with constructive desires and varying degrees of clarity, into the future of a new continent.

CHAPTER XV

Impost or Bankruptcy

To MEMBERS of the Continental Congress, the money troubles of the United States were just an enlarged replica of their own. The national Treasury was empty. So were the pocketbooks of the delegates. When Washington's unpaid soldiers grew too cold and hungry, they went home. So did the delegates when they could no longer pay the landlady. Congress put out vast quantities of Continental currency which lost its value through depreciation. Delegates took in state money which tobogganed downward faster and farther.

The impotence of Congress, due to lack of power to lay and collect taxes, was matched by the inability of the individual states to exercise the power they had. Madison had devoted friends in the Virginia state government who put his welfare ahead of their own. But what could they do when a Virginia courthouse was burned to destroy tax records, local officers were refusing to make collections and the people were rejecting state money? Imagine the difficulty of remitting in a currency whose official value in specie, as determined by the Virginia legislature at the end of 1781, ranged from seventy-five paper dollars for one of silver in January to 1,000 for one in December. In solid old Pennsylvania itself, the western counties refused to pay taxes at any time during the Revolution and the mere threat of collection was enough to start a secession movement.[1]

Madison collected not one penny of salary during his first three years in Congress. State law allowed him $20 per diem and reasonable expenses. As prices soared, the expense account went up, but not the per diem. By the end of 1781, $20 had the buying power of two cents. Kindhearted auditors held back his salary accounts until, in 1782, the legislature ordered a settlement of back pay at the rate of $8 per day in hard money.[2] During his first full year in

Congress, Madison received £39,000 in Virginia paper currency. Its specie value was £525.9.6. His total receipts up to the end of 1782 had a specie value of £547.16.3 and the state still owed him £865.8.3[3] Things were not so pleasant for the state treasurer either. He died of apoplexy in the spring of 1782, after the civil employees of the state had gone nine months without pay. His successor, Jaquelin Ambler, soon told Madison that the treasury had not received ten pounds in hard money since he took office, and that was more than the specie value of his own unpaid salary for three months.[4]

As the pinch came on, Madison arranged for moderate payments to him by his father, but there was difficulty in sending money from Orange. He had previously shipped sugar and coffee to Montpelier, when there was space on some traveler's wagon, also quinine for his mother's malaria and "a number of little books" for the library of sister Fanny. Books were his own desire too, and when Colonel Izaac Zane drove in from the Shenandoah Valley with a library of rare volumes for sale—part of the great William Byrd collection for which he had paid £2,000 in 1778— Madison could not resist a few purchases. He covered them with a draft for nineteen pounds on his father. So heavy were his obligations, he reported, that unless the legislature made a more liberal provision for the delegates, he would be "under the necessity of selling a negro." As for going home for a visit, as his father kept urging, the public trust forbade it at such a crisis (three of his Virginia colleagues were blithely absent at that moment); besides which, he could not leave without paying his debts and buying a carriage "and where the means for effecting either are to be found is totally without my comprehension."[5] To Randolph, who was belaboring the state government in his behalf, he wrote on August 27, 1782: "I cannot, in any way, make you more sensible of the importance of your kind attention to pecuniary remittances for me, than by informing you that I have for some time past been a pensioner on the favor of Haym Salomon, a Jew broker."

Salomon, a dealer in foreign exchange and purchaser of supplies for the Continental Army, plied his profession in a time and place where the prevailing estimate of Jewish moneylenders was that which came down from Shakespeare. This, however, is what Madison wrote to his Virginia colleague a month later:

"I am almost ashamed to reiterate my wants so incessantly to you, but they begin to be so urgent that it is impossible to suppress them. The kindness of our little friend in Front street, near the coffee-house, is a fund which will preserve me from extremities, but I never resort to it without great mortification, as he obstinately rejects all recompense. The price of money is so usurious, that he thinks it ought to be extorted from none but those who aim at profitable speculations. To a necessitous delegate he gratuitously spares a supply out of his private stock."[6]

Little Haym—he must have been little to be called so by five-foot-six Madison—was a war contractor but hardly a typical one. He used so much of his own money in the purchase of military supplies, and was so slow in exacting payment, that the government forgot it owed him anything. He died in 1784, leaving no other property than these unpaid claims, validated decades later by a committee of Congress but still unpaid. As for the delegates, blessed with a satchel of tax money from Sheriff Satchele of the Eastern Shore, a thousand-pound bill to Virginia payable in Philadelphia, and three hundred more which Ambler and Randolph dug up from other corners, they got out of debt early in 1783. By the time Madison left Congress near the year's end, the state (contrary to a common belief) owed him only £13.16.3. Unfortunately, there was no corresponding improvement in the financial condition of the country at large.[7]

The first real effort to give taxing power to the federal government was made on February 3, 1781, when the states were asked to "vest a power in Congress" to lay a five-per-cent duty on imports. Madison voted against this motion by Thomas Burke and helped to defeat a stiffer proposal by Witherspoon and Burke that Congress be "vested with a right of superintending the commercial regulations of every state."

What a paradox! Burke, the great champion of state rights, demanding that Congress be authorized to levy taxes and regulate commerce; Madison, the nationalist, against both proposals. There

was really no illogic in it. Burke was a strict constructionist, but
wanted a federal government capable of protecting seaportless
North Carolina against commercial oppression by Virginia. Madison thought it unwise to ask for powers which the states were
almost certain to refuse. He proposed that the states pass laws
laying the impost (thus retaining the primary taxing power) and
vest Congress with "full power to collect and to appropriate the
same" to the public debt. To reconcile the conflict over jurisdiction he proposed that the federal collectors receive their legal
powers from the states.[8]

Had Madison's plan gone into effect, any maritime state could
have destroyed the impost, nationally, by repealing its own law.
But he believed, it must be remembered, that Congress had an implied power to compel the states, by force, to meet the costs of
federal government. He may have reasoned that, with federal
collection making evasion impossible, the resulting invigoration
of Congress would balk any attempt at tax repeal.

Slight as his hope was for adoption of the plan which Congress
preferred to his own, Madison was impatient for action in Virginia.
"What a prodigious sum we are losing," he remarked to Pendleton
on May 29, "from the delay of the states to authorize the collection." In a year's time, all had ratified except Massachusetts, Rhode
Island, Maryland and enemy-held Georgia, but the proposal was
caught in forward currents and backwashes. Massachusetts protested that the proposed duties threw an extra burden on importing states. Congress replied that ultimate consumers in all states
paid the tax. How well that elemental fact was known in non-
maritime Connecticut and New Jersey; how hard it was to grasp
in seagoing Massachusetts and Rhode Island![9]

While the states faltered thus on granting the impost, they fell
down completely on the payment of requisitions. "Not a farthing
of money has been paid into the general treasury from any of
the states, excepting Pennsylvania, for more than a year," wrote
Delegates Mowry and Varnum of Rhode Island, vainly appealing
for ratification in the fall of 1781. Financier Morris submitted the
draft of a circular letter to the states. Writing with all the tact of a
wounded rhinoceros, he accused them of endangering the country

through dishonorable neglect of past calls, of concentrating on local affairs until the fate of the nation hung by a hair. "Now, sir," he thundered to each governor, "should the army disband, and should scenes of distress and horror be reiterated and accumulated, I again repeat that I am guiltless; the fault is in the states; they have been deaf to the calls of Congress, to the clamors of the public creditors, to the just demands of a suffering army, and even to the reproaches of the enemy, who scoffingly declare that the American army is fed, paid and clothed by France." That, Morris added, was a true charge, dishonorable as it was to America, but soon there would be something worse—an army unfed, unpaid, unclothed, which would subsist itself or disband itself.[10]

This proposed address shocked Congress as much by the truth it contained as by the danger of uttering it bluntly. The specter of an army looting the country, unless fed by France, lent fervor to the first business of the day, which was to inform Louis XVI: "We pray God, great, faithful and beloved friend and ally, always to keep you in his holy protection." The subject of the adjectival praise was a trifle ambiguous, but no harm could result if both addressees accepted it.[11]

Madison's desire was to secure a vigorous appeal to the states without antagonizing them. Moving for a different procedure by Morris, he was elected chairman of a committee of five to confer with the financier. On the evening of that same day, as Morris told of it in his diary, he "laid before these gentlemen a true picture of our present situation; but after much conversation they appeared to be disinclined to sending the circular letter." The superintendent then proposed that delegations be sent to the several states, to put the crisis before executives and legislatures. The result was an order of Congress, secretly dispatching Rutledge and Clymer to the South, Montgomery and Root to the East. All the money these journeys produced could have been carried in a snuffbox.[12]

Sharp alarm for the fate of the impost now supplanted Madison's brief optimism. He and Joseph Jones had decided, just before the latter went home in May of 1782, to propose a bit of coercion by Virginia—that their state's consent to the impost be conditioned upon an "honorable adjustment" of the terms of its land cession. Barely was Jones on his way south when Madison heard that Rhode Island delegates had been dropped because of their support of the impost. Chase of Maryland was inflexible against the tax. With these states and Massachusetts holding out against the impost, and all of them likewise opposed to Virginia's land title, coercion went glimmering. Madison sent hasty notice to Jones to drop the scheme.[13]

Massachusetts and Maryland both approved the impost in July 1782. With Georgia's government still unsettled, Rhode Island's consent alone might have been enough to bring the new revenue system into effect. A small obstacle, territorially, but not in a federal union where a titmouse equaled an elephant!

The vexing nature of the obstacle became evident when David Howell, whose demagogic vigor turned Rhode Island against the impost, brought that unpleasant quality with him to Congress. Howell was scornfully called a geometry teacher in politics. This underrated his abilities. Having graduated from Princeton ten years before Madison entered, he taught natural philosophy, mathematics, French, German and Hebrew on the two-man faculty of what is now Brown University, and used his spare time to become one of the leading lawyers of his state. In political geometry, he could fly off on a tangent at terrific speed, while his mathematical genius saved Rhode Island one hundred cents in every dollar of its dues to Congress, or would have done so except that the dollar of that day was divided into ninetieths.

"It is easy to see," Madison remarked after the July ratifications raised the total to eleven, "that the states whose jealousy and delays withhold this resource from the United States will soon be the object of the most bitter reproaches from the public creditors." That bothered Howell not at all. His first move was to seize upon Madison's coercion plan (of which he knew nothing) and use it in reverse. Rhode Island would not "part with all the benefits of its maritime situation"—that is, would not stop collecting duties on imports transshipped to Connecticut—unless the back lands were "considered as a continental acquisition" and devoted to paying off "a great part of the national debt." He exhorted his state not to destroy that noble system by which, after carefully scrutinizing the intended appropriations of Congress, "you are to grant your money like freemen, from time to time, bound only, as a sovereign and independent state, by your sentiments of justice, of virtue and by your sacred honor." In other words, go right on paying nothing at all.[14]

Madison's prediction of public clamor was more than fulfilled. As federal funds failed, unpaid soldiers and influential creditors turned upon their own state governments, demanding a settlement of their claims with money earmarked for federal use. In September New Jersey served notice that, other states having done the same, it could no longer resist the demand that it pay the soldiers of its own Continental line. The reply of Congress came from Madison's pen. If individual states undertook to dispense moneys requisitioned for the Union, "the federal constitution must be so far infringed" and plans for a uniform revenue system subverted. The chief value of the resolve is in the light it throws upon Madison's constitutional views. What does it leave of the effort to prove, by his disgusted comments on federal impotence, that he did not believe there was a federal constitution prior to 1789?[15]

Pennsylvania's threat to pay defaulted federal interest to her own citizens led to a federal-state conference in which Rutledge, Madison and Hamilton spoke for Congress. As Madison described the meeting, his group warned that if Pennsylvania violated the right of appropriation delegated to Congress by the federal articles, the action would be imitated and extended until the whole administrative system and bond of union would be dissolved. "The committee," Madison concluded, "appeared to be considerably impressed with these remarks, and the legislature suspended their plan."[16]

Acting for another congressional committee, Hamilton prepared a formal reply to the Pennsylvania memorial. Madison's account of this led to a violent attack upon him after his death by Hamilton's son and biographer, John Church Hamilton, who accused Madison of making a false record of the debate in order to discredit his famous antagonist. The charge was not only a false one, but was rendered absurd by the fact that Madison and Hamilton, in this first fortnight of their acquaintance, struck up a quick friendship and partnership in their common aim of strengthening the federal government. In Hamilton's report, Madison noted, it was observed that France appropriated her loans to the immediate use of the American army. "This clause was objected to as unnecessary, and as dishonorable to Congress. The fact also was controverted." Hamilton and Fitzsimons, he said, defended it as expedient, in order to justify the failure of Congress to pay the creditors, while Wilson and Madison sought to strike out the reference to France.[17]

That, declared John C. Hamilton, was "no less than a charge of stating an untruth, and justifying it on the score of expediency, on the part of two gentlemen whose probity never was suspected." It was completely disproved, he said, by the fact that *"no such clause can be found"* in the text of Hamilton's report, published in full in the *Journals* of January 30, 1783. Unfortunately for the impassioned scion, the report published on that date was not written by Hamilton. It was a revision, by Fitzsimons, of the recommitted report.[18]

No less absurd was John C. Hamilton's charge that Madison falsified the record, in this same period, to make it appear that Alexander Hamilton sought to sacrifice public faith in the redemption of Continental currency. Describing a grand committee meeting of December 7, 1782, Madison said that Hamilton voted to redeem Continental currency at one hundred for one, in settling with states which had taken up more than their share of old money under the forty-for-one devaluation plan. The biographer, finding that Hamilton voted to retain the forty-for-one rate in Congress a month later, accused Madison of transferring these proceedings from January 7 to December 7, and from Congress to a grand committee, for the purpose of deception. Hamilton, he asserted, was not even a member of the grand committee, whose personnel was given in the January 7 *Journals*. Quite convincing, until one notices that the published committee list does not include Madison. A careless clerk put in the original committee appointed six months earlier, after which Jackson, Lee and Duane went home and were succeeded by Osgood, Madison and Hamilton.[19] The

basic charge, that Madison was trying to convict Hamilton of sacrificing public faith, was nothing less than ludicrous. Since Madison wanted an even greater disparity—something above one hundred fifty for one—he could have seen no bad faith in Hamilton's
position without convicting himself of worse.[20]

Right here, however, was the living germ of the great controversy which broke out between the two men a decade later. Madison moved that states which had redeemed more than their share
of old money receive such credit "as equity might require." Hamilton urged a high rate because "it would multiply the advocates
for federal funds for discharging the public debts, and tend to
cement the Union." Madison protested that the states which had
redeemed a surplus had not done so within the period fixed by
Congress, "but in the last stages of depreciation, and in a great
degree, even after the money had ceased to circulate." Holders of
it should "receive the value at which it was current" when they
received it.[21] Here are the essence and almost the words of the
later conflict between Hamiltonian federalism and Jeffersonian
democracy—between Hamilton's desire to bind the country together through the self-interest of moneyed men, and Madison's
and Jefferson's hatred of gifts to speculators out of the public
treasury. Here too is proof that the Jeffersonian position originated
with Madison. It reduces to nonsense the partisan claim that ties
with Jefferson caused Madison to turn against Hamilton after
their period of early friendship. They were in thorough agreement, at the outset, on the need for a vigorous federal government.
They disagreed, from the outset, on social and economic matters.
This disagreement grew until it produced a change in Madison's
political and constitutional views, but there was no deviation from
the straight line he followed on economic and social issues.

Madison and Hamilon were brought into quick partnership by
Rhode Island's final and unanimous rejection of the impost, news
of which reached Congress in November 1782. That action, Madison declared, had "pretty thoroughly blasted" the hope for federal
revenues, and the indignation against "this perverse sister" was "increased by her shameful delinquency in the constitutional requisitions." As to a report that his own state was about to send two or

three thousand dollars to Congress: "If anything can add to the mortification which we feel at the receipt of nothing, it will be the receipt of so beggarly a sum."[22]

Affairs stood thus when Congress was thrown into commotion by a Rhode Island newspaper article designed to prove that the five-per-cent impost was unnecessary. It was an article, Madison said, "misrepresenting the state of our [foreign] loans, as well as betraying the secret proposal of the Swedish court to enter into a treaty with the United States." It was a fair guess that a member of Congress was the author and "unanimous suspicions were fixed on Mr. Howell." Delegates undertook to smoke him out. One moved an inquiry into a matter injurious to public finances and to "the national character of the United States and the honor of Congress." Another remarked that if self-respect did not induce any member present to admit authorship, it might be concluded that no member present was the author of it. Mr. Howell, Madison wrote, "was visibly perturbated but remained silent."

Williamson, Carroll and Madison were elected to conduct the inquiry. Hamilton followed with a motion, partly written by Madison, to send a delegation to Rhode Island to urge the absolute necessity of agreeing to the impost. Supported on a plea of justice to creditors and the need "to maintain our national character and credit abroad," it carried with only Rhode Island in opposition.[23]

In the report on the Rhode Island article Madison called for an inquiry into the violation of congressional secrecy, but at his request no action was taken on this pending an investigation—which Congress ordered—into the authorship of the article. Howell then admitted that he wrote it.[24]

Meanwhile, Hamilton, Madison and Fitzsimons were commissioned to draw the blood of federal revenues, if they could, from the Rhode Island turnip. Hamilton essayed the task, in the form of a letter replying to one from the state legislature. As a study of the taxation of commerce and an argument for financial support of the Union, the paper he produced was irrefutable. However, the compulsory nature of federal requisitions was set forth in so truculent a tone that it is surprising Madison joined him in presenting it to Congress. He could not disagree with Hamilton's argument, which nearly duplicated his own 1781 report on the implied powers of Congress. But the way Hamilton rammed the authority of Congress down the throats of the states was bound to defeat the purpose of the appeal.

Still more significant does the joint sponsorship of this letter become when one compares it specifically with Madison's earlier statement on implied powers. He asserted in 1781 that Congress possessed a general implied power to coerce the states into payment of funds requisitioned for federal use. Hamilton now wrote: "The measure in question [the five-per-cent impost] if not within the letter, is within the spirit of the Confederation. Congress by that are empowered to borrow money for the use of the United States, and by implication to concert the means necessary to accomplish the end." Hamilton himself left no doubt about the meaning of those significant words. "One thing only is now certain," he wrote to Governor Clinton, "that Congress having the discretionary power of determining the quantum of money to be paid into the general treasury towards defraying the common expenses, have in effect the constitutional power of general taxation."[25]

The agreement between the two men was further indicated when Madison, in debate, repeated Hamilton's most positive assertion of the binding force of federal law upon the states and added this even more positive one of his own: "A requisition of Congress on the states for money is as much a law to them as their revenue acts when passed are laws to their respective citizens." Here is added proof of the monstrous perversion of Madison's views by Professor Van Tyne, who converted the United States into thirteen separate nations by such statements as: "The whole system was what Madison defined as a league or a treaty," and resembled an international congress of "representatives who claimed no part of the sovereignty of the participating nations." Had Congress possessed the will and the strength to exercise the sovereign authority Madison and Hamilton saw in it, the Constitution of 1787 never would have been written.[26]

Delegate Howell was disturbed not at all by the verbal cannonading of Rhode Island, foreseeing, probably, that it would strengthen his own position at home, but fought furiously against a motion of censure against himself. His conduct was so offensive, Madison reported, that even those most inclined to spare his reputation turned against him. The effort of Congress to identify the author of an anonymous newspaper article was termed by Howell an infringement upon a delegate's right to report to his constituents and "a precedent dangerous to the freedom of the press, the palladium of liberty, civil and religious." Nay, it even violated the constitutional guaranty of freedom of speech and debate in Congress.

"The indecency of this paper, and the pertinacity of Mr. Howell in adhering to his assertions," Madison reported, excited "great and universal indignation and astonishment" among all delegates except its author and his colleague Arnold. He was repeatedly warned "of the certain ruin in which he would thereby involve his character and consequence." Congress would be forced to "expose and condemn him to all the world." As Howell's arrogant conduct was described to Minister Luzerne: "No scene so indecent has taken place in this assembly since it has existed."[27]

Unable to keep his own name out of the record, the Rhode Island delegate forced his denunciatory counterattack into the *Journals* by demanding the yeas and nays. Hamilton called for sharp action against Howell, but Madison, foreseeing that Rhode Island would "abet or not resent the misconduct of their representative," toned this down to a resolve that the state executive be furnished with the various resolutions on Howell and with a true account of foreign loans.[28]

One avenue of influence was left—the junket to Rhode Island by a trio of delegates to plead for the impost. Chosen from delegations which could spare a man, this committee[29] was a bit slow in both head and feet. After it had dawdled for eleven days, Hamilton and Madison pushed through a motion for speed. Madison felt a desperate need for affirmative action. Without it, other states would go on diverting federal requisitions to their own citizens. No need to trace the effect of that, he and Joseph Jones reported to their governor, "on the Union itself, on the common defense, on our national character and on the councils of the enemy." Urging once more that Virginia comply more fully with the impost,

Madison received a devastating cross-reply which he passed on to Abner Nash of the Rhode Island mission just as it was starting.[30]

The junketers had jolted for half a day, over frozen roads, when Nash casually mentioned what Madison had said. Virginia, hearing of Rhode Island's rejection of the impost, had repealed her own assent to it. That jolt stopped the coach. No use going to Rhode Island with a plea for unanimity, if this unofficial news proved true. In Congress, when the two-way travelers told their story, Howell and Arnold grinned with joy. Madison read the paragraph from Pendleton and promised to give any information he might receive from the post, now one day overdue. At that moment the delayed mail carrier galloped up. Madison tore open a letter from Randolph, and found the bad news confirmed. In his notes he wrote:

"The most intelligent members were deeply affected and prognosticated a failure of the impost scheme, and the most pernicious effects to the character, the duration and the interests of the Confederacy."

On that day, December 24, 1782, Congress in truth heard the tolling of the Confederation's death knell. Those who recognized it, however, did not give up. They determined, Madison wrote, "to persist in the attempt for permanent revenue." Hamilton, Madison and Fitzsimons, now the recognized leaders in finance, were named to report further measures upon the subject. Howell set out for Rhode Island, to use his mastery of demagogy against the impost and for his own political salvation.[31]

Virginia's sudden repeal of her impost act both dismayed and mystified Madison. If the Lees had done this as a stab at Robert Morris, he remarked to Randolph, it would hardly have been done so quietly. As for the future:

"Congress cannot abandon the plan as long as there is a spark of hope. Nay, other plans on a like principle must be added. Justice, gratitude, our reputation abroad and our tranquility at home require provisions for a debt of not less than $50,000,000. . . . If there are not revenue laws which operate at the same time through all the states, and are exempt from the control of each—the mutual jealousies which begin already to appear among them will assuredly defraud both our foreign and domestic creditors."[32]

A hint of the truth came from Governor Harrison, who remarked cryptically about the repeal: "A certain preamble will point out the cloven footed monster." Randolph's report verified Madison's first suspicion. The assembly had been shocked with fanciful fears but underneath was the opportunity "presented to the L[ee]s of piquing Morris. . . . The tenor of their daily language justifies the suspicion—their character for malice confirms it."[33]

In that preamble, Madison found the cloven hoofmarks cut in a blanket of words: "The permitting any power, other than the General Assembly of this Commonwealth, to levy duties or taxes upon the citizens of this state within the same, is injurious to its sovereignty." That was no mere handle to repeal. It was an instruction to the congressional delegates to oppose any proposal whatsoever for a taxing power in Congress.[34]

In Congress, pressure for further action boiled up from the unpaid, bitterly resentful army. On January 6, 1783, Major General McDougall and Colonels Ogden and Brooks sent in a memorial for overdue pay and other claims. This, according to Madison, breathed a proper spirit, but the unrest of the armed thousands behind it was so serious that a grand committee was appointed to meet the army deputation. Superintendent Morris said positively that nothing could be paid to the troops and asked Congress to name another committee with power to give him secret advice. This was looked on as an improper delegation of power, but Rutledge, Osgood and Madison were directed to confer with him and report.[35]

Morris told this trio that American resources in Europe had turned out to be three and a half million livres short of the bills already drawn against them. He was compelled to draw still more bills on France—without that country's knowledge or consent—or public service would stop. This must not become known, lest the danger of protest debase the bills. He was unwilling, therefore, to

COLONEL WILLIAM FLOYD AND HIS WIFE, HANNAH JONES FLOYD

Madison Jas

Philad.ª apl. 22. 1783

Dear Sir

Your favor of the 1ª inst: written on the Susquehanna with the several letters inclosed were safely delivered to me. I did not fail to present as you desired your particular compliments to ———

[several lines scratched out / enciphered]

The report on funds &c. passed Congress on Saturday last with the dissent of R. Island, and the division of N. York only. The latter vote was lost by the rigid adherence of Mr. Hamilton to a plan which he supposed more perfect. The clause providing for unauthorized expenditures, could not be reinstated, and consequently no attempts was made to link the all the parts of the act inseperably together. As it now stands it has I fear no bait for Virgª. which is not particularly interested either in the object or mode of the revenues recommended, nor in the territorial cessions, nor in the change of the constitutional rule of dividing the public burdens. A respect for justice, good faith & national honor is the only consideration which can obtain her compliance.

BURIED CIPHER, TELLING OF MADISON'S ROMANCE WITH CATHERINE FLOYD

This is what he scratched out: 885 164 36 1053 753 597 1080 824 658 921 278 421 461 2 694 9 273 312 922 520 243 444 525 287 957 146 380 332 758 427 1053 989 704 400 997 1046 181 834 36 1031 441 595 430 575 166 271 818 561 411 989 1060 268 380 830 449 410 1000 970 289 743 181 155 763 287 734 528 429 219 399 1072 1096 359 173 the 930 1069 430 721 1053 750 1015 654 868 162 359 1069 430 708 668 243 535 538 1007 23 831 862 42 170 The 708 513 315 36 1041 930 667 6 181 1080 636 47 1053 830 1052 977 843 83 23 1070 827 106 536 1069 824 430 777 420 50 181 315 243 232 1008 41.

disclose the facts to a full Congress, which spilled all secrets. The committee could not give the approval he asked for but it was ready to co-operate at the expense of France. In the previous September, Madison and Duane had put through a request for a $4,000,000 loan for 1783. France, he remarked then to Randolph, had just canceled all past and future interest on loans to America and this fresh demand would be thought an unfit return for such favors. But how could it be avoided? "The arrears to the army in January next will be upwards of six million dollars. Taxes cannot be relied on. Without money, there is some reason to surmise that it may be as difficult to disband as it has been to raise an army."[36]

The crisis was now at hand, and the still ungranted loan was their only hope. The committee and Morris agreed, said Madison, that there was little danger of the unauthorized bills being dishonored. With peace about to be signed, France would rather pay them than force the United States to borrow from the enemy! The result was a unanimous authorization to Morris to go on drawing bills up to the full amount of the $4,000,000. One delegate, Eliphalet Dyer of Connecticut, did indeed protest against it at first as "an unwarrantable and dishonorable presumption on the ability and disposition of France." But Dyer was "the most boring speaker of Congress"—though a great educator. It was he, Luzerne said, "whose harangues introduced the custom of reading newspapers in Congress."[37]

Over the week end, Madison and Richard Peters of Pennsylvania did some thinking about the army. If France could be tapped for the current pay of civil servants, why not for back pay of the military? This was a seductive idea and Congress passed their resolution, but Robert Morris turned thumbs down. He did not want his own levies on France jeopardized by additional ones.[38]

It was on the evening of this day (January 13, 1783) that the grand committee met with the army delegation. The meeting had been postponed from Friday till Monday because a snowstorm and General McDougall's rheumatism kept the army officers in the Indian Queen tavern, while the snowstorm and congressional dignity kept the grand committee from going there. The officers, as Madison described the evening, did most of the talking. They

told of the sufferings and services of the men, of "sequestered con-
sultations" of sergeants and "the most intelligent privates" (in that
day, it seems, intelligence raised a private to the sergeant's level
and spurred both to mutiny), of the lessened vigor of commissioned officers. They spoke indignantly of "the ease, not to say
affluence, with which the people at large lived" while Congress
was denied a general revenue. The army, McDougall said in summary, was "verging to that state which we are told will make a
wise man mad."

The delegates said little in reply, and Madison least of all. The
soldiers' claims are just, he wrote to Randolph, "but what can a
Virginia delegate say to them, whose constituents declare that they
are unable to make the necessary contributions and unwilling to
establish funds for obtaining them elsewhere?" Morris gave a new
turn to Madison's proposal that France pay the army, promising
the officers that part of the proceeds of the bills drawn on Franklin
would be applied to back pay. This, Minister Luzerne reported to
his government, "appeased for some time the clamors of the officers."[39]

As a result of the conference, Hamilton, Madison and Rutledge
were made a subcommittee to work with Morris and report a new
fiscal plan. Another grand committee was named on revision of
the eighth article of Confederation—never enforced—which required that congressional requisitions be based on land values in
the several states, instead of population. Congress took up once
more the promise that officers who served through the war would
receive half pay for life.

The original promise, dating from the black days of Valley
Forge when unpaid officers were threatening wholesale resig-
nations, was for seven years' half pay. Two years later Arnold's
treason caused a panicky Congress to extend it to life. Madison
supported the extension and treated the promise thereafter as a
binding obligation. When New England delegates attempted to
scuttle the measure in the summer of 1782, by authorizing individual states to settle with the officers of their respective lines, he denounced this as a violation of the Articles of Confederation, by
which all charges of war were "to be paid out of one treasury."

In December, a renewal of this proposal was thwarted by the addition of Hamilton and Madison to a committee of three, reversing its majority. The McDougall mission called on Congress to support its promise, but also offered a compromise. Half pay for life could be commuted into a gross sum to be paid in installments over a period of years.[40]

The subcommittee—Hamilton, Madison and Rutledge—gave the officers a choice between half pay for life and a commutation of it to full pay for six years—one half of their average expectation of life under Dr. Price's actuarial table. In Congress the New England economy bloc defeated even lesser figures and attacked the validity of the 1780 half-pay resolution, pointing out that it was adopted by fewer state votes than required by the later-ratified Articles of Confederation. Madison, anticipating notable decisions of the Supreme Court, replied that the act was valid "because it was decided according to the rule then in force."[41]

The New Englanders were beaten in a new effort to turn the matter over to the states, but returned to the attack, aided now by a freshman Virginia delegate, John Francis Mercer. He protested that the funding of public debt tended to establish and perpetuate a moneyed interest. This would gain ascendancy over the landed interest (the classic fear of philosophers from Aristotle to Hume) and by the example of its luxury and splendor, become dangerous to republican constitutions.

In his usual manner, using strong terms quietly, Madison dissected this and other speeches. Commutation was a compromise with those who found pensions obnoxious; now it too was stigmatized as a perpetuity. If payment of the public debts was suggested, it was said—and truly—to be impossible. If funding of them was proposed, "it was exclaimed against as establishing a dangerous moneyed interest, as corrupting the public manners, as administering poison to our republican constitutions." He was as much opposed to perpetuating public debts as anybody, but the way to get rid of them was by paying them. Although the sum involved was frightening—close to $500,000 a year plus interest—seven states now voted for a five-year commutation. Nine were needed for the actual appropriation of money. In a month's time, the menace of an army officer revolt produced the two additional votes.[42]

This fight over half pay was just a pin jab in the swordplay of finance. The Hamilton-Madison-Rutledge subcommittee brought that to the fore in a resolve, written by Hamilton, that Congress make every effort "to obtain from the respective states *general* and substantial funds adequate to the object of funding the whole debt of the United States." The word "general," underlined by Madison in his notes, was the crux of the matter, for it implied a tax applying throughout the country. However, it was stricken out as ambiguous, since it might apply to all objects of taxation rather than all states.[43]

Wilson resumed the subject after a Sunday layoff. Echoing Hamilton's argument that a funded public debt was a cement to the Confederacy, he offered a new motion. With a clarifying amendment, it declared that justice could not be done nor credit restored nor the war carried on "but by the establishment of permanent and adequate funds to operate generally throughout the United States, to be collected by Congress." Bland spearheaded the opposition with a demand that Congress put into effect the system provided for in the Articles of Confederation—requisitions upon the states, apportioned according to the value of land.[44]

This put a double decision up to Madison, to obey or disregard the instructions of the Virginia legislature on these two points. On land valuation the assembly's position was explicit. The delegates had been notified that it was inexpedient "to alter the mode appointed by the Confederation." On general revenues, the impost repeal act declared against any federal taxing power whatever.[45]

Madison had recorded his opinion of land valuation on January 8, when a Southern-dominated committee called for enforcement of the valuation system. Southern land being cheap and poorly developed, this would throw federal costs onto the North. Hamilton and Madison, so the latter wrote in his Notes of Debates, "were of opinion that the rule of the Confederation was a chimerical one." If the states made the valuation each one would be biased. (Let them all cheat equally, said Dyer.) Leave it to Congress and there would be delay, expense and uncertainty. Hamilton was free to take this position on its merits. Madison, to do so, had to ignore both his instructions and the selfish interest of his state. If there must be a land valuation, he proposed that it be made by Congress without the intervention of the states. Madison, Carroll and Wilson then were made a subcommittee to report a mode of valuation.[46]

The other decision—whether or not to be guided by the sweeping Virginia declaration against federal taxation—came up at a ticklish moment. Arthur Lee of the cloven foot returned to Congress on the day Wilson offered his motion for a general revenue. In a maneuver against that motion, Lee and Bland required their delegation to place the repeal act before Congress, together with a resolution of the Virginia Assembly declaring its inability to pay more than fifty thousand pounds toward the requisitions of Congress. Coupling these two things together, said Madison, defeated their purpose. They merely exposed Virginia to attack for refusing either to grant the impost or furnish funds outside of it.[47]

Madison had no choice now but to join Lee and Bland in support of the legislature's position, or fight them and it. He chose the latter course, believing, he wrote to Randolph, that without such federal funds, "the foundations of our independence will be laid in injustice and dishonor," and the federal compact will be of short duration.[48] Having chosen his course, Madison offered a new version of the Wilson motion, changing it from a negative to a positive form:

"That it is the opinion of Congress that the establishment of permanent and adequate funds to operate generally throughout the United States (to be collected under the authority of Congress) is indispensably necessary for doing complete justice to the creditors of the United States, for restoring public credit and for providing for the future exigencies of the war."[49]

The words shown here in parentheses were held back, to be introduced later, because the Wilson motion had been divided for voting purposes.

This action brought Arthur Lee to his feet, angry but devious. A general tax was repugnant to the Confederation. By placing the purse in the same hands with the sword, it subverted the fundamental principles of liberty. So great was Virginia's aversion to federal taxes that when the assembly voted to repeal its assent to the impost, he himself cast the only vote against the motion. At this astonishing statement, Madison and Jones looked at each other. What sort of maneuver had that been? A repetition, Jones thought, of Lee's tactics in organizing a campaign to have Edmund Randolph declared ineligible to re-election to Congress while Lee himself made a speech in defense of his eligibility.[50]

By the time he got thoroughly warmed up, Lee was declaiming against Madison's motion as if it proposed that Congress should proceed at once to lay taxes without getting prior authority from the states. Wilson corrected him on this point, but Hamilton played into the hands of the opposition by arguing that federal revenue collectors, interested in supporting the power of Congress, were needed to enable the federal government to pervade and unite the states. This argument, Madison commented, "was imprudent and injurious to the cause which it was meant to serve." All delegates who feared federal power smiled at the disclosure and Bland and Lee remarked that "Hamilton had let out the secret."

Madison undertook to repair the damage by less dangerous logic. It was needless to prove the necessity of paying the public debts. "The idea of erecting our national independence on the ruins of public faith and national honor must be horrid to every mind which retained either honesty or pride." All must agree to the motion before the house unless its objects could be attained by some other plan. What else was there? Requisitions? Nobody would regard them as adequate. Permanent state funds for federal purposes? Being under state control, they could be diverted to state objects and mutual distrust would lead to suspensions of remittances.

A general revenue superintended by Congress, Madison declared, would end all this jealousy and make diversion of funds impossible. It would give instantaneous confidence to creditors at

home and abroad. It would stop the appropriation by the states, to
their own citizens and troops, of money requisitioned by Congress.
If this irregular conduct was not stopped, what tie would hold the
states together? How would the army be subsisted and clothed?
"The patience of the army has been equal to their bravery, but
that patience must have its limits; and the results of despair cannot
be foreseen, nor ought to be risked."

Instead of ridiculing Lee's constitutional oratory, Madison answered his arguments soberly. Congress, he asserted, already was
invested with authority over the purse as well as the sword,
through the binding force of federal requisitions. He defended his
own violation of instructions. Members of Congress, in addition
to representing the states from which they came, "owed a fidelity
to the collective interests of the whole." They should be ready to
hazard personal consequences when clear conviction required it.
This issue entailed the preservation of the Confederacy, our reputation abroad and tranquillity at home.

Taking note of a suspicion that he and Wilson were scheming
to hold back objects of taxation until the principle of a federal revenue was irrevocable, Madison proposed that Congress broaden
the debate at once to take in sources of revenue. He would suggest,
in addition to the impost, a poll tax with Negroes rated lower than
whites and a land tax with values fixed by the inverse ratio of
acreage to population. Arthur Lee now revealed his real position.
Raising sword and purse aloft once more, for all to see "who had
ever opened a page or read a line on the subject of liberty," he declared that it was a waste of time to be forming resolutions on
revenue. The states were "jealous of the power of Congress," they
never would agree to its aggrandizement and he agreed with them.

So deep was the effect of Madison's speech that Congress resolved itself into a committee of the whole, approved his motion
for a general revenue (with minor amendments), and proceeded
to consider specific duties and other taxes. Finding that Southern
delegates were unwilling to consider a revenue plan which omitted land valuation, Madison called together his dormant subcommittee on that subject. They proposed that the states classify lands
as occupied or unoccupied, the lands so classified to be valued by

a traveling federal commission with one member from each state. The grand committee rejected this seven to six, in favor of the original Rutledge plan of valuation by the states, and was supported in committee of the whole.

Unwilling to accept defeat, Madison made a flank attack. The report, he observed, "lay in a great degree of confusion." He proposed taking the sense of Congress distinctively and successively on all points, the result to be referred to a special committee. This was rejected, but was reconsidered and adopted after the state valuation plan fell two votes short of the required seven.[51]

Madison asked nearly all of the questions (five out of seven) including the crucial one whether each state should make a valuation. He startled his hearers with the assertion that official valuations were fifty per cent higher in Virginia than in Pennsylvania, although the real value of land in Pennsylvania was admitted to be three times as high as in the former state. That knocked the bottom out of the state valuation plan, and led to a final decision (February 17, 1783) that a grand committee of Congress should make the valuation. Madison and Hamilton both opposed this plan as ineffectual, even though it set up the principle of federal control.[52]

The way was cleared now for action on general revenues. The Wilson-Madison motion had been formally adopted some days earlier, but the strong opposition convinced Madison that a compromise was necessary. Gorham warned of disaffection in Massachusetts. Lee found a vociferous ally in his former enemy Mercer, who, "from what motive God knows, [so wrote Madison] says that he will crawl to Richmond on his bare knees" to prevent readoption of Virginia's assent to federal revenue. "Having already changed his opinion on the subject he fears perhaps the charge of unsteadiness." Using once more the system of successive questions, Congress voted to limit the impost to twenty-five years. Hamilton's effort to knock out the time limit was supported by Rhode Island—sure evidence that it played into enemy hands—but Madison's opposition cut off a seventh state. Madison and Hamilton then united to beat down a scheme of appropriating the impost exclusively to the army. But when Hamilton moved to hold public sessions of Congress on financial matters, he got no support from his Virginia friend. Madison did not like one of the suspected motives—to influence Congress through "the presence of public creditors numerous and weighty in Philadelphia." The rich man's lobby, it seems, was struggling to be born.[53]

Leaders of the fight for federal funds gathered at the home of Thomas Fitzsimons on the evening of February 20. Hamilton and Peters, Madison recorded, turned in alarming reports on the army. Officers and men had secretly determined not to lay down their arms until provision was made for their pay, and were laying plans to subsist themselves (a fulfillment of Madison's September prediction). Washington's opposition to this was making him unpopular, and "many leading characters" were seeking to destroy the army's confidence in him. Their purpose was to displace him with General ———. Madison wrote and scratched out the name —a long one. Hamilton disclosed that he had written to Washington, urging that he make himself spokesman for the demands of the army, in order to control and moderate them. He did not reveal that he suggested just enough of a moderation to let the claims "operate on those weak minds which are influenced by their apprehensions more than by their judgments," thus causing the states to grant "measures which the exigencies of affairs demand." In other words, use army unrest to frighten local nitwits into granting federal revenues.[54]

Next day in Congress, Madison undertook to fortify the constitutional base of the revenue plan. Some delegates, he remarked, had termed Congress merely an executive body, wherefore the granting of a permanent revenue to it would be placing sword and purse in the same hands. This was an unsound opinion. Even the existing revenue powers of Congress were legislative as well as executive. Requisitions for money "were a law to the states" and "the federal constitution was as sacred and obligatory as the internal constitutions of the several states." Congress had power to borrow money indefinitely, emit bills of credit and bind the state legislatures to repayment. How could that be done by a purely executive body?

Having thus defended the fundamentals of federal power, he

made a conciliatory plea for a permanent revenue collected by Congress. Though wishing for more, he saw no chance to secure anything beyond duties on commerce. He particularly disclaimed the idea (Hamilton's and Wilson's) of perpetuating a public debt as a cement to the Confederacy.

To Lee and Mercer, the olive branch Madison waved looked like a thorn-apple club. Replying to his colleague's "specious arguments," Lee said he would "rather see Congress a rope of sand than a rod of iron," while, as for fulfilling public engagements, he did not want Virginia drained of money to pay public creditors living in Pennsylvania. Mercer was shocked by Madison's description of the constitutional powers of Congress. If the federal compact had such a meaning, he would "immediately withdraw from Congress and do everything in his power to destroy its existence." This brought a counterthreat from Gorham. If justice to public creditors could not be obtained through the general Confederacy, "the sooner it was known the better, that some states might be forming other confederacies adequate to the purpose." To Madison, this was not a threat but a symptom. Unless financial conflicts are straightened out, he told Randolph, "a dissolution of the Union will be inevitable." In that event the Southern states, "opulent and weak" at sea, would be an easy prey to the "powerful and rapacious" East. The weaker side and then the stronger would seek foreign alliances "and this country be made subject to the wars and politics of Europe."[55]

At the end of these oratorical crashes, Gorham, Hamilton, Madison, Fitzsimons and Rutledge were directed to frame the revenue plan called for by the Wilson-Madison resolution. This committee promptly called for a five-per-cent impost, plus specific duties, with collectors appointed by the states but removable by Congress. In the meanwhile, Hamilton sought to have costs of war abated to states which had been ravaged by the enemy. Arthur Lee at once pointed out that the Virginia legislature had taken a stand against that proposal. Madison once more disregarded his state's position. The Hamilton motion, he said, was conformable to justice. But instead of being taken up by itself, he suggested that a comprehensive plan be made, uniting equitable objects of interest of all the states, in order to gain the concurrence of all in the general revenue.

Though he had no thought of making a gift to posterity, Madison at that moment invented one of the most sacred, most effective and tenacious of American political institutions—the congressional system of logrolling. He brought it into being not to put bad measures through a willing Congress, but to put a good measure through unwilling state legislatures. His colleagues saw that the idea had possibilities and gave Madison the job of writing a new report. He had it ready in two days.[56]

Madison's plan opened with the federal import duties already approved by the committee or by Congress. To these was added a request to the states to furnish $1,500,000 from revenues of their own choosing. "A precarious basis for public credit," Madison called this, but some delegates wanted it so in it went. Then came various provisions which he described to Jefferson as "bait."[57]

Bait for Rhode Island, Maryland, New Jersey, Delaware, New York and Pennsylvania—a clause calling on the states to cede their Western lands to Congress, or revise and complete their compliances.

Bait for New York, Virginia, the Carolinas and Georgia—Hamilton's plan of abating war costs to ravaged states.

Bait for Massachusetts, New York, Virginia, the Carolinas and Georgia—a proposal that the United States take over and pay all war costs incurred by the states without the sanction of Congress.

This last proposition, the historic "federal assumption of state debts," became a basic article seven years later in Secretary of the Treasury Hamilton's fiscal policy—with Madison opposed to it. Be that as it might be, he was unquestionably its author. Not only is the draft in his handwriting, but he described it as "laid before the committee," and a full week earlier, outlining the objects he had in mind, he placed this item in his notes: "A transfer into the common mass of expenses of all the separate expenses incurred by the states in their particular defense." And what did Jefferson think of federal assumption at this time? Expressing fear that the inducements were not great enough to win Virginia's approval, he told Madison that the clause "which proposed the conversion of state into federal debts was one palatable ingredient at least in the pill *we* were to swallow."[58]

To complete his revenue plan, Madison proposed that land valuation, as a means of apportioning federal expenses, be stricken out of the Articles of Confederation. In its place he sought apportionment according to population, with a reduction in the count of those "who are bound to servitude for life." In phrasing this section he first wrote "who are deemed slaves," but struck it out, foreshadowing the more labored exclusion of the obnoxious word from the Constitution of 1787.

Finally, Madison bound his twelve-paragraph report together by a concluding proviso that none of the preceding provisions should take effect until all were acceded to by every state. The committee shifted this section to the middle of the plan, between the revenue provisions and the "bait." There it continued to bind the tax clauses together, but left everything after it open to separate acceptance or rejection. Either the committee did not understand the new art of logrolling, or it thought some parts of the log too knobby for easy rotation.

The Madison revenue plan came before Congress at a time of heightening crisis and shortening tempers. Since January 24, the resignation of Finance Superintendent Morris had been lying upon the table. It was a conditional resignation. He would sacrifice time, property and domestic bliss to complete "the last essential work of our glorious Revolution"—the funding of the public debt—but the end of May was the limit unless Congress by that time made provision for the public debts of every kind. This letter, Madison recorded, "made a deep and solemn impression on Congress." It was looked on "as producing a vacancy which no one knew how to fill, and which no fit man would venture to accept." Nevertheless, feeling that Congress could not "condescend to solicit Mr. Morris," Madison blocked a move to consider the letter. Disclosure of it would ruin credit and cheer the enemy, so it was decided to keep the matter secret and proceed with the revenue plan.[59]

Morris himself, at the end of February, gave the letter to the press. Its peremptory style and publication, Madison noted, furnished a handle to the financier's enemies both in and out of Congress. Arthur Lee declared that a man who "published to all the world such a picture of our national character" was unfit to hold office. Wilson and Hamilton poured praise on Morris, and Madison found himself on a committee to deal with the subject.[60]

On the heels of this came word of a threatened military insurrection. General Washington forwarded "two anonymous and inflammatory exhortations to the army" (the description is Madison's) to assemble for the purpose of seeking the justice their country denied them. The steps Washington took to avert the storm "excited the most affectionate sentiments toward him." So felt Madison and his colleagues, but it was otherwise with Major John Armstrong, Jr., close confidant of General Gates and author (though this remained unknown for years) of these Newburgh Addresses to the army. As the young cynic wrote to Gates, Washington was "the Illustrissimo of the age" if measured by illustrious foibles, Congress was "weak as water and impotent as old age," while as for the army officer (Colonel Brooks) who had been chosen to carry the plot onward, "the timid wretch . . . betrayed it to the Commander-in-Chief. . . . Such a villain!"[61]

From private letters, Madison reported, "there appeared good ground for suspecting that the civil creditors were intriguing in order to inflame the army into such desperation as would produce a general provision for the public debts." This accusation came from Washington to Joseph Jones and Hamilton, but the latter did not clarify the general's ensuing remark, directed squarely at himself, that members of Congress had encouraged this course. As for Madison, little did he think that he as President would one day name the author of the insurrectionary addresses to be his Secretary of War.[62]

That the army officers were inflamed was evident to everybody. "When they meet members of Congress," said Luzerne, "they attack them in unguarded talk, they reproach their mean conduct, they threaten loudly to procure satisfaction by force of arms." Intensifying the worry of Congress was the disclosure in dispatches from Paris of a rift between the American and French negotiators of peace.[63]

All of these converging elements of crisis, Madison commented, "gave peculiar awe and solemnity to the present moment, and oppressed the minds of Congress with an anxiety and distress which has been scarcely felt in any period of the Revolution." Yet even at that tense moment, the love of a jest which lurked beneath his sober manner moved him to a sardonic maneuver. Apparently at his instigation—for he alone records it and it runs true to his nature—a few members of Congress arranged to have Washington's letter and its inflammatory inclosures referred to Gilman, Dyer, Clark, Rutledge and Mercer. The purpose, Madison wrote in his notes, was "to saddle with this embarrassment the men who had opposed the measures necessary for satisfying the army."[64]

The report of this committee was a classic in futility. It directed Superintendent Morris to inform Congress how much the army could be paid out of present resources. This mental bankruptcy offered grim proof that the fate of the country, as far as Congress could determine it, rested with the little group—Madison, Hamilton, Wilson, Fitzsimons, Gorham, Carroll and a few others—who saw the issues clearly and put nation above state.

CHAPTER XVI

ADDRESS TO THE NATION

GENERAL conditions were so bad that legislative prospects seemed fairly good when Madison's "revenue and bait" plan came up for action in the third month of 1783. Two important converts to federal revenues—important because of their strategic positions—had been gained in Congress. Holten of Massachusetts came across, and so did Mercer, the Virginia jumping bean. The latter said some plan was essential and the opponents had none. His conversion reduced Lee and Bland to a minority in the Virginia delegation.[1]

The shift of honest, unbrilliant Holten likewise isolated Thomas Higginson, who was bitterly opposed to the impost. This new-rich privateersman-turned-merchant was part of the Samuel Adams political machine. To him, Madison was a leader of "the aristocratic junto," which appeared to signify Southern landowners as contrasted with Northern importers.[2] The fight over Madison's plan had been going on for several weeks when Higginson wrote to Theophilus Parsons:

"We are still hammering on a strange, though artful, plan of finance, in which are combined a heterogeneous mixture of imperceptible and visible, constitutional and unconstitutional taxes. It contains the impost, quotas [of state funds for federal purposes], and cessions of western lands, and no part of it is to be binding unless the whole is adopted by all the states. . . . The cessions are to serve as sweeteners to those who oppose the impost; the impost is intended to make the quotas more palatable to some states; and the receiving it in whole is made necessary to secure the adoption of the whole, by working on the fears of those states who wish to reject a part of it only. . . . The states will see, I trust, that Virginia and New York mean only to give them what is of no value, and not their property to dispose of [the Northwest], in order to secure to themselves a valuable territory [Kentucky and western New York] which they now have no good claim to, and oblige the continent hereafter to guarantee and defend it for them. Madison has clearly, I think, shown that such is their intention in this scheme; this he did in an unguarded moment."³

Higginson said nothing about the clause which would have transferred his own state's Penobscot expenses to the Union, presumably because he did not want to advertise this sweetener for Massachusetts. His statement about Madison was untrue, for the Virginian had been urging his state for months to cut all strings to her land cession except those restraining speculators. Two weeks after he wrote this letter, Higginson helped block a Virginia motion that the land cession be accepted without the territorial guaranty he accused Madison of seeking.⁴

Congress hammered at the Madison report for more than a month. Clark and Bland tried futilely to submit the impost by itself—good evidence that they thought it weaker standing alone. Adding numerous specific duties, Congress laid the groundwork for one of the great political issues of the next two centuries. It was governed, Madison reported, by "the general policy of encouraging necessary manufactures among ourselves." Hamilton sought to add a land tax, but was defeated by the increased acceptance of Madison's contention that "a *complete* general revenue was unattainable from the states." Even this represented optimism. In recording that the people no longer absolutely refused to pay taxes, Minister Luzerne remarked to his court that "the little that is obtained is not given; it is in some fashion wrung from them." Those were state taxes. As for Congress, it had asked the states for $8,000,000 in 1782, and received $430,031.⁵

To the president of Congress and a few delegates, Luzerne now passed along a secret communication from the Count de Vergennes. The French foreign minister (as Madison records his warning) "was alarmed at the extravagant demands of Doctor Franklin in behalf of the United States . . . surprised . . . that the inhabitants paid so little attention to doing something for themselves." With the king asking about repayment of the 10,000,000 livres borrowed in Holland for American use, Vergennes "hardly dared to report in favor of the United States to the king and council." He urged Congress to establish permanent revenues "for paying our debts and supporting a national character."

Luzerne made a clever maneuver of his own by adding that in the previous October, he had misinformed his court by saying that Congress had funded their debts. Vergennes replied rejoicing at the news, which had enabled him to secure a grant of 6,000,000 livres to the United States. Now, faced with the necessity of confessing his error, Luzerne begged Congress for action which "would enable him in his next dispatches to give some satisfactory account to his court on this head." That was a telling appeal, to save the poor minister from the effect of a blunder which rescued the American Treasury. But why did Vergennes chide the Americans thus if he had been told the debts were funded? Luzerne's plea of October 6 for a loan actually stated that financial arrangements were completely suspended by Rhode Island's obstinate rejection of the impost, and Vergennes in telling him of the six millions said it would certainly be the last because "The United States do not show themselves sufficiently disposed to create the means of meeting their debts." Still it was a useful story. Believing that the last loan had been granted on a false premise, Congress could have no hope whatever of getting another one unless the premise was made good.[6]

To Madison the prospect looked bad. With French aid for the year "unalterably limited to six million of livres," and most of that spent in advance, how could the army be kept together? How it had been kept together for the past three months was beyond his solution. Washington had eased the tension by calling his own meeting of army officers, in place of the scheduled rebellious gathering, yet Madison felt that this opened the way to still more dangerous events if the troops remained unpaid. Adequate and certain revenues were imperative, yet "I fear," he wrote to Randolph, "it calls for more liberality and greater mutual confidence than will be found in the American councils."[7]

On the first test things went well. Bland and Lee, trying to eliminate "a legislative idea" from the resolutions, moved to strike out "levy" and insert "collect." Only two delegates stood with them. They joined then with Clark, Rutledge and others in a campaign to drop the sweeteners from the Madison plan.

Facing a motion to strike out federal assumption of state war expenses, Madison appealed for full consideration of so important a step. Part of these expenses, he said, would have been approved by Congress if there had been time to put in a request. Others were incurred in winning control of territories which some of the states were being asked to cede to Congress. These states would not cede the lands if they had to bear the cost of winning them from the enemy; other states would not grant federal funds unless the lands were transferred. Thus the rejection of this clause would threaten the whole plan with failure.

Even Wilson wanted the word "necessary" written in—Congress to assume expenses occurred in a "necessary defense" of approved objects. Madison replied "that the term *necessary* left a discretion in the judge as well as the term *reasonable,*" which was already in the clause. Here Madison anticipated the broad meaning he gave to the power of the United States Congress to pass "necessary and proper" laws, when he wrote about it in No. 44 of *The Federalist,* contrasting with his narrow definition of it in later years. It is one more evidence of his broad approach to federal power before his conflict with Hamilton turned him into a narrow constructionist.

Agreeing that the paragraph on state debts was loosely written, Madison proposed that a board of thirteen commissioners be set up, any seven of whom would be empowered to "determine finally on the reasonableness of all claims for expenses incurred by particular states" and report those "supported by satisfactory proofs." The nature of the business, Madison told his colleagues, "was unfit for the decision of Congress, who brought with them the spirit of advocates rather than of judges." Here was the modern (and even now frightening) principle that facts determined by a quasi-judicial administrative body, and supported by evidence, shall not be subject to review. It certainly frightened the delegates. Congress reacted so violently that the entire proposal of federal assumption of state debts went by the board, Virginia alone supporting it.

Defeated also was Hamilton's abatement plan, which Madison tried to save by revising its wording.[8]

When the proposal to abolish land valuation came up, Bland's defense of that system was overwhelmed by Madison, Gorham, Wilson and others. Still ahead was the difficult question of the rating to be given slaves in a count of population for taxing purposes. Madison's proposal that two slaves be rated equal to one freeman touched off a strange debate. Delegates from the slaveholding South began to depreciate the value of forced labor. It took three slaves, said a South Carolinian, to equal one freeman. Four to one, affirmed a Marylander. Slaves, asserted Williamson of North Carolina, had no value at all. But he was against slavery in principle.

From New England opponents of involuntary servitude came a contrary line of talk. Slaves were but a shade less productive than their free brethren. Four to three, and no more, was the extent of the difference they would admit. The two sides even wrangled over the relative value of black and white child labor. The children of slaves, Madison recorded the Southerners as saying, "were not put to labor as young as the children of laboring families." That pulled down the ratio of production.

In seemingly hopeless deadlock, Congress put the subject aside, but Madison carried on in private talks. Before the day was over he offered the compromise which ultimately found a place in the United States Constitution: To prove his liberality, "he would propose that slaves should be rated as five to three." Rutledge came from one side, Wilson from the other, and seven states approved the new proposal. Bland and Lee then united the opposing extremists and knocked out the whole proposition by means of the "chaos clause." The return of Hamilton from New York, a few days later, furnished a seventh state and the opposition collapsed. But one vote was cast against a restoration of the constitutional amendment.[9]

Surveying the structure of his plan after five weeks of congressional mauling, Madison found it loose at the joints and lopsided. Gone was its symmetry of shape and purpose. No longer did assumption of state debts balance the allurement of Western cessions, one appealing to Virginia, the other to the landless states. The territorial clause now jeopardized Virginia's return to the impost, but Congress slapped down an effort by Bland, Rutledge and Madison to eliminate it. Westward of the Alleghenies, they were told in debate, Congress had a truer right to make cessions to the states than the states to Congress.

Stripped of all sweetening except to the land-hungry states, the Madison revenue plan was adopted on April 18, 1783. Rhode Island voted No, joined only by tax-allergic Higginson and—of all people—Alexander Hamilton, who divided New York's vote, Madison related, by his "rigid adherence . . . to a plan which he supposed more perfect." More perfect, yes, but unattainable. Even Bland voted with the Continentalists, led thereto (in the absence of Arthur Lee) by a correspondence with Washington which so tickled his vanity that he began rhapsodizing on "the necessity of stabilizing a national character" and subordinating local interests and prejudices "to a great and general good."[10]

Would that feeling extend to Virginia? Madison had his doubts. He and Hamilton made a vain effort, even after the final vote, to reinstate the clause on state debts. Its failure caused him to abandon the effort to link all parts of the plan together, instead of the revenue clauses alone. "As it now stands," he commented to Jefferson, "it has I fear no bait for Virginia. . . . A respect for justice, good faith and national honor is the only consideration which can obtain her compliance."[11]

The weakness of that incentive magnified the need to carry the battle to the states. Not in Virginia and Rhode Island alone. Bills repealing the impost had passed the lower houses in both Massachusetts and South Carolina. Relaying this information to Randolph, Madison renewed an entreaty to his friend to give up his salaried post as attorney general and lead the fight in the legislature. With federal measures "losing ground so fast in the temper of the states," there must be the utmost possible support of them. A few enlightened and disinterested members in each legislature could carry the day, but without them there was "room for nothing but despair." Randolph's heart was right, but poverty barred compliance. He had no resources, outside of his salary, except a "little fortune" left him by his uncle on his father's death, which his father's rapacious creditors would seek to swallow up if he resigned the attorney generalship and thus put himself in a position to be sued. But what was this news he heard from Philadelphia? Robert Morris had resigned to escape a financial sacrifice? Randolph could not believe it. "At such a season to quit his office, even if it were steeped to the lips in poverty and difficulty!"[12]

Adoption of the revenue plan brought the Morris resignation to the fore. The time was approaching when he would retire unless Congress took care of the public debt. Even Arthur Lee admitted, or rather charged, that his resignation was "a great shock to public credit"—a maneuver, he alleged, to enable Morris and his friends to realize immense wealth through purchases of depreciated loan office certificates. With the Treasury empty and the unpaid army in a tumult, Congress threw aside its dignity and delegated two enemies and three friends of the financier—Osgood, Bland, Madison, Hamilton, Peters—to solicit him to remain in office. The superintendent wanted to stay, if publicly asked to do so, until the army could be paid enough to permit its peaceable disbanding. Chairman Osgood's report sounded to him like permission to remain in office for no particular reason. He whaled Congress over the head with a peremptory refusal, whereupon that body doctored the *Journals* to implant his terms in the resolution as if they had been there from the first. Thus one part of the financial crisis was surmounted.[13]

Now came the task of presenting the revenue plan to the states. Madison, Hamilton and Ellsworth were assigned to prepare an address in support of it. Written by Madison without prior consultation with the committee (so Hamilton said a few years later), and unanimously approved by Congress on April 26, 1783, this address to the states ranks as one of the major papers of the Confederation.[14]

Madison opened with an exposition of the debt and revenue problem, all couched in terms of national obligation. The successful termination of the war, together with the crisis in public affairs, made it the duty of Congress to provide for gradual extinguishment of the debts left upon the United States. They must "look forward to the means of obviating dangers which may interrupt the harmony and tranquility of the Confederacy." Out of "mature and solemn deliberations on these great objects" had come the recommendations of April 18.

For the arguments in favor of the impost, Madison referred the state governments to Hamilton's letter of December 16, 1782, to the governor of Rhode Island. This he briefly summarized and also inserted as Appendix No. 2 to his address. There were eight of these appendices, running diversely from an estimate of the national debt ($42,000,375) to Washington's proclamations and correspondence on the threatened revolt.

Madison pointed to the twenty-five-year limitation upon the impost, the appointment of collectors by the several states—changes, he termed them, to remove earlier objections, but also relaxations from "the strict maxims of national credit." With total receipts from the impost estimated at $915,956, there remained a deficit of $1,500,000 in interest on the debt. This the states were asked to make up in any way they chose. "Here again," Madison observed, "the strict maxims of public credit gave way to the desire of Congress to conform to the sentiments of their constituents." (In other words, please furnish the million and a half, though we know you won't.)

The address continued with an explanation and defense of the clause binding the revenue provisions together into "one indivisible and irrevocable act." Without it, some states might adopt only one provision, some only the other, so that no revenue at all would be furnished. If the grants were revocable, "a single state out of the thirteen might at any time involve the nation in bankruptcy, the mere practicability of which would be a fatal bar to the establishment of national credit."

Turning to the public creditors, Madison said they were entitled in justice and good faith to immediate payment of their principal, but that was impossible. They would receive it, ultimately, through the natural increase of revenue from commerce, new requisitions, and sales of Western lands. In the meantime, interest on the debt should be so thoroughly secured as to enable the security holders to transfer their stock at full value. He urged the cession of the vacant Western territory to Congress and followed with a vigorous argument for abandoning land valuations—as yet unused but sure to be inaccurate, unjust and costly—in partitioning federal costs among the states.

The remainder of the address—a full third of it—was an eloquent plea to the states. Madison urged them to work for the happiness of the confederated republic and "render the fruits of the Revolution a full reward for the blood, the toils, the cares and the calamities which have purchased it." The national debt, though great, should be borne with cheerfulness and pride, especially when "compared with the burdens which wars of ambition and of vainglory have entailed on other nations." But great or small, it had been fairly contracted and justice and good faith demanded that it be fully discharged.

To whom, he asked, were these debts to be paid? To an ally who had added the exertions of his arms to the succors of his treasure. To foreign individuals "who were the first to give so precious a token of their confidence in our justice and of their friendship for our cause."

To the army, that "illustrious and patriotic band of fellow-citizens whose blood and whose bravery have defended the liberties of their country" and who should now be enabled "to retire from the field of victory and glory, into the bosom of peace and private citizenship."

Finally, to those fellow citizens who either lent their money to the public or manifested confidence in their country by receiving transfers from the lenders, and those whose property had been either advanced or assumed for the public service.

"To discriminate the merits of these several descriptions of creditors would be a task equally unnecessary and invidious. If the voice of humanity plead more loudly in favor of some than of others, the voice of policy, no less than of justice, pleads in favor of all. A wise nation will never permit those who relieve the wants of their country, or who rely most on its faith, its firmness and its resources, when either of them is distrusted, to suffer by the event."

The address concluded with a eulogium of the American people and a plea that the principles of the Revolution be lived up to in the conduct of their state governments:

"Let it be remembered finally, that it has ever been the pride and boast of America, that the rights for which she contended, were the rights of human nature. By the blessing of the author of these rights, on the means exerted for their defense, they have prevailed against all opposition, and form the basis of thirteen independent states. No instance has heretofore occurred, nor can any instance be expected hereafter to occur, in which the unadulterated forms of Republican government can pretend to so fair an opportunity of justifying themselves by their fruits. In this view the citizens of the United States are responsible for the greatest trust ever confided to a political society. If justice, good faith, honor, gratitude and all the other qualities which ennoble the character of a nation, and fulfill the ends of government, be the fruits of our establishments, the cause of liberty will acquire a dignity and luster which it has never yet enjoyed; and an example will be set which cannot but have the most favorable influence on the rights of mankind. If on the other side, our governments should be unfortunately blotted with the reverse of these cardinal and essential virtues, the great cause which we have engaged to vindicate will be dishonored and betrayed; the last and fairest experiment in favor of the rights of human nature will be turned against them, and their patrons and friends exposed to be insulted and silenced by the votaries of tyranny and usurpation."

This appeal well deserves its high place in the polemics of the Revolution—a passionate call to the people not to throw away what they had so dearly won. It carries also a solicitude for public security holders quite in contrast with Madison's attitude toward them when Hamilton sought to fund the public debt after the advent of the new government. In 1783, however, speculation in military certificates subject to funding had not yet become an orgy. Finally, this address furnishes a useful corrective to students of American dual sovereignty. In it, a reference to "thirteen independent states" follows the statement that "a single state out of the thirteen might at any time involve the nation in bankruptcy." Here is irrefutable evidence that a revolutionary statesman could talk of thirteen independent states and still regard the United States as a nation.

Congress ordered the Madison address published in pamphlet

form, along with its accompanying exhibits and the revenue plan of April 18. Distributed everywhere, it was praised or damned according to the views of those who read it. So great was the demand that private reprints were made in Massachusetts, Connecticut, New Jersey and Virginia, and also in England.[15] Sending it to his court, Luzerne called attention to the listing of the French debt "at the head of all." He translated Madison's praise of France and continued:

"This address, written with as much dignity as vigor, deserves to be read and it is greatly desired that it will make an impression upon the people. But after so many frustrated efforts and attempts one cannot flatter oneself with hope of more success now than in the past."[16]

Washington praised and supplemented Madison's appeal. Congress, he said in a circular of his own to the states, have stated the obligation "with so much dignity and energy that in my opinion, no real friend of the honor and independency of America can hesitate a single moment. . . . If their arguments do not produce conviction . . . a national bankruptcy, with all its deplorable consequences, will take place."[17]

How would the address be received in Virginia? Not as a product of Madison's pen, for he did not tell his own father that he wrote it, but as a stimulus to action? Even before the revenue plan reached Richmond, the fight over the impost had begun to shape up in the newly convened legislature—Richard Henry Lee opposed, John Tyler in favor, others trailing. So Madison heard from Jefferson and Randolph in early May. But what of the redoubtable Patrick Henry, maker and fanner of popular currents? "Henry as usual is involved in mystery," wrote his unworshipful compatriot of Monticello. "Should the popular tide run strongly in either direction he will fall in with it. Should it not, he will have a struggle between his enmity to the Lees, and his enmity to everything which may give influence to Congress." Randolph was not without hope, even though the oratorical Patrick, from his home in the Blue Ridge, was ominously proclaiming the inability of the people to pay taxes. The impost, commented the attorney general, "is supposed to fall heaviest upon men of opulence, for whose sakes the diminution of the taxes is by no means intended."

The tide in Virginia was actually running violently in both directions. The fear of an army revolt converted once vehement opponents, but fantastic terrors ran through Capitol and tavern. Congress would use the impost to maintain an army with which to seize Virginia's Western empire. Congress had tampered with Rhode Island by sending Tom Paine there to work for the impost ("a fiction of malice," Madison called that story.) Appeals based on peace and harmony in the Union were seen as the product of misdirected zeal or ill-founded fears. Saying that he had foreseen some of these topics which Randolph reported, Madison replied: "I dread their effect from the eloquent mouths which will probably enforce them. But I do not despair." All who love justice and aim at the public good must be advocates for the congressional plan, provided they draw their arguments "from a general survey of the federal system, and not from the interior policy of the states singly."[18]

When Patrick Henry arrived in Richmond, he found Richard Henry Lee holding up the opposition banner, not whipping in a clear hard breeze, but dangling in the false calm of the conflicting currents. That was enough for him. Without even waiting for the contents of the federal plan, he jumped in as a strenuous supporter of the impost. The glorious news came to Madison from his two confidants. "This will insure it," cried the jubilant Jefferson. Now, rejoiced Randolph, "little need be apprehended from the *Lee*ward quarter."

Henry threw himself into the battle. Not knowing that Madison had excluded federal collection from the new plan, he leveled sarcasm at those who shivered at it. If there was danger from such agents of Congress, let their teeth be drawn and their nails cut. He brought out his own incongruous plan of tax relief, a moratorium on all payments until December, that the people might have a holiday in which to rejoice on the glorious termination of the war. When Lee took the lead against this sure-to-win proposal, arguing

with logic but doubtful sincerity that state taxes must be collected
for Congress because the impost was sure to be delayed, Henry was
really in clover. Delay is inevitable, he cried, because the people
cannot pay. So speed the impost and let it "supply Congress from
the pockets of the wealthy consumer."[19]

So matters stood when Joseph Jones and Arthur Lee came in
from Philadelphia on May 20 and 24, the former bearing the new
revenue plan and Madison's address, the latter bringing all the
adverse arguments his brother might have overlooked and a
greater genius for using them. Legislators friendly to federal revenues read the address and applauded. Instantly probing its
anonymity, Randolph sent word that he would repeat the praise
it was receiving, "did I not perceive the marks which it bears of
your pen." Richard Henry Lee read it and wept for America. To
him, its "plausible arguments" represented "too early and too
strong an attempt to overleap those fences established by the Confederation to secure the liberties of the respective states." Possession of power creating a thirst for more, the excellent plan of the
Confederation "is to be gradually sapped and the all-important
power of the purse vested (under arguments, some only of which
are plausible) in an aristocratic assembly. For, given the purse, and
the sword will follow . . . and that liberty which we love and now
deserve will become an empty name." Let us be cautious, he continued with Leevian logic, how we "furnish the most distant pre-
text for foreign troops to interpose in favor of government against
the people, as hath lately happened in Geneva." What did he
think, that France was more likely to intervene if debts to her
were made secure, than if they were defaulted?[20]

The real damage, according to Joseph Jones, was wrought by
Appendix No. 2, Hamilton's letter to Rhode Island. Assemblymen
shuddered at its assertion that the federal government already
possessed "an absolute discretion" in determining the amount of
national expenditures, with the states limited to the mode of compliance, and that a government so constituted ought to have the
means to answer the end of its institution. Such a doctrine was
"alarming and of dangerous tendency," the more so because of the
challenging, almost scornful tone of the letter, very different from

the soothing seductiveness of Madison's address. These sentiments, Jones affirmed, "operated so powerfully on people's minds here that nothing could induce them to adopt the manner recommended by Congress for obtaining revenue."[21]

It is easy to contrast the writings of Hamilton and Madison and blame the former for this revulsion of feeling in Virginia. But Madison was one of a committee of three which reported the Hamilton letter to Congress; he himself used similar language in that body and he incorporated the Hamilton letter into his own appeal to the states with no apparent premonition of harm from it. At bottom, it was not the manner of the appeal for federal funds, either by Madison or Hamilton, that created opposition to them. The most conciliatory argument could be given a hobgoblin face by the fears and prejudices of those who felt such emotions. Nobody saw this more clearly than the Chevalier de la Luzerne. When the freemen of Fairfax County (home of Washington and George Mason) sent a protesting memorial to the Virginia legislature, he forwarded it to his government with an analysis of the forces behind the opposition not only there but throughout the country:

"They begin by saying 'that they do not like the style of the last address of Congress to the different states.' All fairminded persons agree however that it is a composition as admirable for the energy of the exhortations made to the states that they provide for payment of their debts, as for the equity and wisdom of the means to bring it about. But there are some classes of men to whom this matter is odious, and who, as soon as one speaks of satisfying the army, of reimbursing France and the American or foreign creditors of the states, raise loud outcries and say, like the freemen of Fairfax County, that Congress is aiming at absolute power, that it should not have even the shadow of the power to raise taxes, that if the scepter and the purse are in the same hands, that is the end of liberty. . . . The necessity of taxes . . . although recognized by all who are capable of feelings of gratitude and justice, is the object of terrors, real or feigned, of all those who wish to make themselves popular in their states. They see despotism or tyranny hidden under the least imposition."[22]

On top of the "purse and sword" revulsion against the congressional appeal, a new line of false reasoning was reported by Randolph. "It is now a cant phrase on the tongues of the disaffected," he told Madison, "that we cannot rate our ability to pay by our consumption, as the other states fairly may." Virginians, it was said, spent an undue proportion of income on goods of foreign origin. Therefore they should insist that their state receive credit for all import duties collected in excess of its quota of the national debt. A nice arrangement, especially for their North Carolina neighbors, who, drawing their imports through Virginia ports, would be compelled to pay Virginia's share of the national debt instead of their own.[23]

Patrick Henry now found himself in the situation he most abhorred—going the wrong way in a tail wind. He had secured a resounding victory over the Lees, winning a state tax moratorium until November, which meant an empty treasury until the following March.[24] But what was that compared with the ignominy of being defeated by underlings on the federal impost? There was but one way out and Henry took it. He reversed himself on the impost and snatched the opposition leadership from Richard Henry Lee.

It would have been humiliating to duplicate the Lees' position completely, so Henry whipped up the terror over Virginia's alleged excess of foreign consumption and moved that the impost be granted only if credited to the state's quota of federal expenses and collected by the state. Jealousy of Congress, and an unsupported assertion that the United States owed Virginia a million pounds, sent the new proposal sweeping through the assembly without even a recorded vote. "You cannot well conceive the deranged state of affairs in this country," was the comment of Joseph Jones to Madison.[25]

A mild recovery from panic was under way when help came in the form of Washington's circular to the states. Written to reinforce the Madison address, it struck like a new version of Thomas Paine's call to independence. Now was the time of choice, said America's greatest leader, whether the United States of America was to be "respectable and prosperous or contemptible and miserable, as a nation." This was the time of their political probation, this "the moment to establish or ruin their national character forever." By giving tone to the federal government or by making this "the ill-fated moment for relaxing the powers of the Union," the states would decide "whether the Revolution must ultimately be considered as a blessing or a curse." Under the impact of this powerful message, the reviving friends of the impost, led by Tazewell, secured a postponement of the whole subject to the October session. Had they not been within a day or two of adjournment, Joseph Jones believed, a satisfactory bill would have been passed without delay.[26]

The postponement hit Madison hard. Virginia's example, he had been telling his friends, would have "great and perhaps decisive influence" on the fate of the federal plan. Not even Rhode Island, deluded by the belief that it could keep on taxing its neighbors, would take "the odium and the consequences" of holding out against hearty unity in the other twelve states. Now all hope of early pressure was dashed and the future dimmed. "The interval preceding the next session," he warned Randolph, "will give full scope to malignant insinuations."[27]

This evil turn to the drive for revenues gives point to a little-noted fact in American history. The dividing line between continental and provincial views in the Revolution was not a vertical one. Only a handful of men were antifederal on military issues. Few were so on diplomatic matters to the conscious detriment of general security. But shortage of hard money, dislike of taxes and jealousy of neighboring or distant states could win innumerable recruits in the economic field.

So prosperous was this tax-resisting America, so promising its future, that when some of the last French regulars were ordered home they had to be enticed on shipboard by trickery and held there by force, to prevent wholesale desertion into American citizenship. So the French minister reported to his government. Not that these Frenchmen had been thoroughly Americanized. In nine months, Madison was told by his reverend cousin, Rochambeau's army did less mischief than one company of militia would have done in a week. When that army marched north through

Philadelphia, one year to the very week after its gala passage southward, Madison heard a repetition of "the praises bestowed on their
discipline and sobriety in Virginia." He also heard and strenu-
ously opposed Arthur Lee's suggestion that French cavalry retake
federal goods seized by the state of Pennsylvania—if French soldiers would not embroil the allies by misconduct, let Congress create the embroilment. The same men who railed at France were
pulling the Union toward impotence and disruption.[28]

All of this was part of the transition from war to peace. Or was
it? The American army was disintegrating for lack of food and
pay while enemy troops still held New York. France had suffered
a naval disaster in the West Indies and showed no signs of recovering from it. The financial debility of Congress, reflected in the
collapse of international credit, jeopardized the peace treaty and
invited the contempt and aggression of European powers.

To Continentalists like Madison, Hamilton, Washington, Jefferson, these truths were clear as ocean water. To others no less patriotic at heart they were as opaque as stone. Madison's address to the
states, like the letter of George Washington supporting it, like
Hamilton's appeal to Rhode Island, was an attempt to guide the
transition to peace along the way of national honor and stability.
Narrow vision, a narrower self-interest or local bias, not malevolence or disloyalty, ruled the opposition, but produced the consequences of malevolence. Always, to the men of vision, the visible
dangers at home were swollen into a more fearful aspect by the
looming shadows of European militarism and imperial ambition.
Ever in their thoughts, distorted by the uncertainties of time and
distance, but paramount to all that was going on in America, was
the negotiation of peace at Versailles. There the nation's right to
exist was being determined, its form and sinews were taking shape.

CHAPTER XVII

WAR OVER PEACE

FEW and far between were the diplomatic pouches that came through the British naval blockade of the United States in 1782. New York's enemy-controlled press was full of news, but was it truth or treacherous propaganda?

Beyond this curtain of obscurity, events were moving forward in London and Paris at a pace that would have dismayed a fairly lively snail. Stubborn King George, on hearing of the Yorktown defeat, wanted to keep right on losing the colonial war, but Lord North toned him down to retention of occupied territory. In Parliament, the ministerial majority kept shrinking and the friends of America found their vocal powers enlarged. On March 20 Lord North resigned. The moderate Lord Rockingham took over and chose Lord Shelburne and Charles Fox for his secretaries of state. Pro-American thunderers and interlocutors filled the new cabinet—Burke, Cavendish, Camden, Grantham, General Conway, Colonel Barré, the Dukes of Richmond and Grafton—but some of them wanted to come to terms with the United States so as to isolate and weaken France.

Which of the secretaries of state should negotiate with the American commissioners? 'Tis my job, said Shelburne, because my department includes colonial affairs. 'Tis mine, said Fox, for I am foreign secretary and the United States are no longer colonies. Rockingham, in ill health, did not settle the issue.

Right at this moment—after the North ministry fell but before the news reached Paris—Benjamin Franklin felt an impulse to write to his old friend, the Earl of Shelburne. It was a letter of no importance, just to reaffirm "my ancient respect for your talents and virtues," offer congratulations on the prospects for a general peace, and tell him of the pleasure Madame Helvetius had derived from Shelburne's gift of some gooseberry bushes. It was, in short,

254

a shrewd preparation for the earl's return to the ministry. Shelburne responded by sending the old slave trader, Richard Oswald, "an honest . . . pacifical man," to discuss peace terms with Franklin. Secretary Fox promptly sent young, clever, ambitious George Grenville to do likewise, and to tell Franklin that Oswald had no authority. Thus the negotiations opened.[1]

Congress heard of these developments from the new British commanders in America, Sir Guy Carleton and Admiral Digby. In August, Carleton sent word that Grenville had been instructed to propose the independence of America ahead of a general peace treaty—information, Madison cautiously observed, which "clearly calls for our watchfulness at the same time that it flatters our expectations." In the wake of this, again through enemy-held New York, came upsetting news. Rockingham was dead. Shelburne had become prime minister. Fox and Burke, the champions of America, were out. It was now September, and not one letter of later date than March had been received from France.

"We are still left by our ministers in the most painful suspense," wrote Madison on the tenth. "The new revolution in the British cabinet in favor of the Shelburne party has a sinister aspect on peace. Unless however this party be reinforced out of the late administration it must be too feeble to resist the popular champions whom they have exiled from office." The uncertainty did not deter him from offering, that day, a resolution which Congress instantly adopted, directing Livingston to send the peace negotiators an authentic statement of the slaves and other property carried off or destroyed in the course of the war. This was to offset the claims of Loyalists for restoration of confiscated property.[2]

The next day things seemed worse. Holland dispatches said the mail from England "breathes war." A New York paper gave Shelburne's defense of his failure to follow the policies of Fox. He "speaks out his antipathy" to American independence without being able to deny its necessity, was Madison's interpretation of his speech. From Franklin, a week later, came meager word that negotiations had opened in June, with prospects of planned delay. John Jay, arriving in Paris from Spain, sent word that Fox (still in office when he wrote) leaned toward independence but Shelburne wanted a royal compact with America like that between Britain and Ireland.[3]

The alarm increased when Vergennes, who dealt only with Fox's man Grenville, reported through Luzerne that he had encountered "tergiversations on the part of the British negotiator," while the rival Shelburne "had no other aim than to deceive all parties, and above all to incite the Americans to acts of perfidy." A tale from Lafayette now capped the climax of suspicion. After telling Vergennes that King George agreed to unconditional acknowledgment of American independence, Grenville refused to put his signature to the declaration when the foreign secretary wrote it down. He would only say that the king was "disposed" to grant it. This, Madison commented, "illustrates the *shade* of difference between Shelburne and Fox."[4]

All of this bad news was referred to Duane, Rutledge, Montgomery, Madison and Carroll. They would have felt less agitated, perhaps, if they had known that certain things were wrong with the murky picture. Shelburne, it was true, called American independence the setting of England's sun. But he termed the recognition of it a "fatal necessity," and indorsed a statement that such action was "the first great principle" of the new administration. What was it that launched the mighty word "tergiversation" against young Grenville? Vergennes was not referring to him at all, but to the delay in passage of a parliamentary bill to authorize peace negotiations. And Grenville's refusal to sign what he had said orally? Just a garbled account of his valid protest that his word *"disposé"* had become *"resolu"* in the French reply. The committee of Congress knew nothing of this. It had only the alarming rumors to go on.[5]

Madison had some feeling other than alarm, for he seized this opportunity to reassert the American claims to the fisheries, Western territories and navigation of the Mississippi, toward which he had been working all year. The emphasis, however, was upon solidarity with France, whose minister urged the committee to destroy "all hope that the enemy could form of a special negotiation to bring about a separate peace." Written by Duane, the resolutions of October 3 and 4 pledged inviolable adherence to the alliance, denounced separate peace maneuvers and called for the arrest of enemy emissaries and spies sent to divide the Allies. "We all know that this poison requires no antidote here," Madison commented, but it might be useful in Europe. Included in both sets of resolutions was the wording of Madison's resolve of the previous May 31, which thus was written into law three times. "Resolved, unanimously," the final version read, "That Congress will not enter into the discussion of any overtures for pacification, but in confidence and in concert with his most Christian Majesty." Even those valiant anti-Gallicans, Arthur Lee, Izard and Bland, joined in this reknotting of French apron strings. Self-reliance was a noble virtue, except when danger threatened.[6]

Meanwhile, what had been going on beyond the silent Atlantic? Seventy-six-year-old Franklin talked one day with Oswald, the next day with Grenville, and weighed their merits. Old Oswald was intent on doing good, young Grenville on making good. He preferred Oswald. But Grenville had elbowed Oswald out of the picture by displaying a commission to negotiate the peace—the natural result of Fox's independence proposal, which shifted the matter from colonial to foreign affairs. Shelburne, refusing to accept defeat, came back with a confidential memorandum to Oswald, offering him any commission that might be agreeable to him and Franklin.

The American diplomat had to choose, not only between Grenville and Oswald, but between Fox and Shelburne—Fox the avowed champion of American independence, Shelburne its reputed opponent and now in apparent eclipse. To test the feeling of the men he was dealing with, Franklin proposed to Oswald (who indorsed it heartily) that Britain *voluntarily* cede Canada to the United States as a fourteenth state. Serving as reparations for damages inflicted by Indians, Franklin contended, this would conciliate American feeling and eliminate a long, disorderly, dangerous boundary line. Besides showing Franklin's informal memo to Shelburne, Oswald carried the suggestion to Rockingham and Fox as an idea of his own. Shelburne and Rockingham, he reported to Franklin, did not seem "very averse" to the cession but Fox "appeared to be startled at the proposition."[7]

On the one side, then, Franklin had brilliant, ambitious Grenville, representing a Fox who was too easily startled. Oswald impressed him as honest, plain and sincere, and Shelburne's failure to cut the string of his Canada kite foretold a yielding attitude on Western territories. The American minister addressed a note to Oswald, for Shelburne's benefit. Praising the emissary's "candor, probity and good understanding," Franklin expressed the hope that the old Scotchman would be made plenipotentiary to negotiate the peace, or at least be given equal standing with Grenville.[8]

Five days later Rockingham died. Shelburne became prime minister. Fox left the government. Grenville resigned. Oswald was given the commission Franklin asked for him. For a second time, the American commissioner had notified Shelburne of striking confidence in him, just before his sudden promotion. This time, in addition, he had nominated the British peace negotiator.

Franklin judged men by character and conduct, but had his avoidance of "popular champion" Charles Fox been known in Philadelphia, it might have furnished final proof of the rumor then in circulation that his mind had failed. How could he have proved the contrary? He did not know that Fox had told the king his independence proposal was directed more to detaching allies from France than "to the object of success in the present treaty." He did not know that Fox had instructed Grenville to bring the treaty to a point where the demands of both sides could be placed before the pro-British King of Prussia, so that "we could have his approbation for breaking it off," with affairs so managed that America would blame France if the war continued. He did not know of Fox's plan to destroy Shelburne on the issue of Canadian annexation. These were some of the hazards Franklin avoided by his judgment of men and measures. In Philadelphia, Arthur Lee was writing about him: "The wickedness of that old man is beyond example; and his good fortune in escaping the punishment due to his crimes, is as extraordinary."[9]

For three months, from September until mid-December, no more was heard of the American negotiations. Madison gave vent to his impatience in a resolution calling on the ministers in Europe to "transmit full and frequent communications." It would have been more to the point to order ships to travel faster and more safely. At this time, too, he succeeded in a cherished design to bring Thomas Jefferson back into public life. Madison had been willing to "lament it in silence" when his friend retired from the Virginia governorship in 1781. He rejoiced at Jefferson's "honorable acquittal" of legislative charges—the product of hysteria and malice—against his by-no-means impressive war record in that office. But when the refusal of a seat in Congress and of a place on the peace commission were added to this, Madison saw in it "a fixed disinclination to all public appointments." Then came that "stupor of mind," as Jefferson himself called it, resulting from the long illness and death of his wife. Waiting for six months, till Jefferson's sensibility might "bear a subject of such a nature," Madison moved on November 12, 1782, that the retired statesman be renamed to his old place on the peace commission. The motion was adopted "unanimously and without a single adverse remark."[10]

This action had a surprising immediate result. Livingston came to Madison and said he intended to resign the foreign secretaryship because his living expenses were $3,000 a year greater than his salary. Did he think Jefferson would prefer this office to the overseas appointment? "I answered him in the negative." Would Jefferson take Jay's post at Madrid if the latter were made foreign secretary? Madison did not know but doubted that Congress would take Jay off the peace commission. So sure was he of Jefferson's lack of interest that he wrote to Randolph suggesting that he "feel the pulse of our friend McClurg" with respect to the prospective vacancy. That too is proof conclusive that he did not want the place himself. McClurg did, and straightway laid out a course of study in foreign affairs, but dropped it when he heard about the $3,000 entry in red ink, which Madison at first forgot to mention.[11]

Livingston was a great entertainer, whose pride, according to Luzerne, would not allow him to live without éclat. Madison had no sympathy with that approach to diplomacy. He was at this time trying to cut down the salaries of overseas diplomats, urging the poverty of the United States, the wants of the army, and "the simplicity of republican government." Éclat was one thing, dignity was another, and Madison stood on it (not his own but the nation's) when a committee cited Livingston's preference for the chancellorship of New York as a reason for his retirement. To publish such a preference for state office, Madison argued, tended to degrade the United States. The wording was changed to "satisfactory reasons"—meaning, of course, unsatisfactory ones. So unsatisfactory, indeed, that when a hint came of the secretary's willingness to linger awhile longer, Madison gladly persuaded him to do so. Within the week Jefferson arrived in Philadelphia, took up his residence in the House-Trist establishment, and, aided by Madison and Livingston, began "industriously arming himself for the field of negotiation."[12]

News was coming in now from Europe, but only, Madison said, in obscure fragments. The murkiness extended to Delaware Bay, where the French frigate *Danaë* ran aground and was dismasted in a driving snowstorm. Its bulging diplomatic pouch, brought overland to Philadelphia on December 23, was opened by eager hands. Straightway a new kind of obscurity developed—that caused by the brightness of conflicting lights.

It was remarked (Madison noted) that our ministers "although on a supposed intimacy and joined in the same commission . . . wrote *separately* and breathed opposite sentiments as to the views of France." Franklin told of a commission empowering Oswald to treat with the thirteen American "colonies or plantations." This being objected to, a new commission directed him to treat with the commissioners of "the thirteen United States of America." After two months' delay from this cause, it took but eleven days for Franklin, Jay and Oswald to agree on a treaty and send it to London—a treaty recognizing American independence, accepting the boundaries demanded by Congress, upholding American fishing rights off Newfoundland. Oswald thought the treaty would be accepted: Franklin had doubts. The court and people of England were very changeable. He would count on a treaty when it was signed.[13]

Jay's letters were a breathing mass of apprehension and distrust of France. Vergennes (whose advice was supposed to be binding) had urged acceptance of Oswald's first commission. Jay positively refused. "Had I not violated the instructions of Congress," he wrote, "their dignity would have been in the dust. . . . I told the minister that we neither could nor would treat with any nation in the world on any other than an equal footing." The purpose of France, the diplomat firmly believed, was "to postpone an acknowledgment of our independence by Britain to the conclusion of a general peace in order to keep us under their direction." That would make it possible to achieve not only French aims but those of Spain. Both courts "will dispute our extension to the Mississippi."[14]

To support his suspicions Jay enclosed the translation of an intercepted letter from Marbois to Vergennes, presumably given him by a British agent. It advised the undermining of American claims to the Newfoundland fisheries by an intimation to Congress that they conflicted with those of France. This should be done before the British evacuated New York, so as to weaken those who "fly out at the idea of giving up the fisheries and western territories for the sake of peace." Franklin, Jay added, disagreed with him on these matters, believing that the French mean nothing "but what is friendly, fair and honorable."[15]

Madison saw "great jealousy of the French government" in Jay's attitude, but even he was jolted by what he read. France, he feared, was using artifice instead of "direct and generous means" of winning American gratitude. The purpose must be to leave the country exposed to the cruelties of her enemies in order to gain the credit of relieving her. The French position was delicate, in regard to Spain, yet, Madison concluded: "If France acts wisely, she will in this dilemma prefer the friendship of America to that of Spain. If America acts wisely she will see that she is, with respect to her great interests, more in danger of being seduced by Britain than sacrificed by France."

No such balanced judgment swayed the mass of congressional delegates. Indignation against Marbois swept through them. Strong jealousies, Madison recorded, were excited by the policy of keeping America tractable by leaving the British in possession of her ports. It might even lead to a complete reversal of the American attitude toward France, "as the closest friends on a rupture are apt to become the bitterest foes."[16]

The friends of France soon recovered their equanimity, aided by certain facts which Secretary Livingston pointed out in a mild reprimand of Jay. If Vergennes was seeking to postpone acknowledgment of American independence, he should have accepted Grenville's proposal that the subject be dealt with in the Anglo-French negotiations. Instead, he denied the power of France to speak for America, and steered the Anglo-American treaty into a separate channel. As for Marbois, he had always argued in this fashion. But France had taken no steps in consequence of his advice.[17]

All this had no tempering effect on the anti-Gallic heat. Once again, two days before the year ended, a motion was made to revise the peace instructions and strike out the clause binding the American negotiators to follow the advice of France. Once again, and this time under a terrific handicap, Madison came to its support. He explained at length the original reasons for its adoption—explained it to a Congress which had no firsthand knowledge. For of all those who voted for the clause, only Joseph Jones, Daniel Carroll and Madison himself were still present. Telling of the conditions which led to the instruction—the dark military outlook, the collapse of continental money, France's distrust of John Adams—Madison contended that the action was at worst only "a sacrifice of our pride to our interest." His explanation impressed nobody except himself, Jones and Carroll.

Madison now swung onto a new tack. What good would be served by revoking the order? If Great Britain was disposed to grant what America claimed, France could not prevent it. If Britain struggled against those claims, France alone could secure them, and "to withdraw our confidence would lessen the chance and degree of this aid." This made sense and Congress wavered. Livingston aided with a promise from Luzerne. The French navy would break the Atlantic blockade. Rochambeau's army would return in case of need. A wave of feeling for France supplanted the resentment. The revocation motion was postponed without a vote, thus keeping all trace of it out of the *Journals*. Nothing was to be said to the French about the Marbois letter, which many (Madison said) now regarded as "adulterated if not forged."[18]

This secrecy, of course, only magnified the letter's importance.

Confidence in France became tied to the assumption of forgery. After four months, as Madison tells it, Marbois heard of the matter in a report from Boston. Bringing up the subject in "our family" (the House-Trist circle) but in Madison's absence, he "signified that he was no stranger to the letter transmitted to Congress which he roundly averred to be spurious." Years later he admitted it to be genuine. Had the question been put straight up to Marbois and Luzerne in December, they would have needed only to reveal Vergennes' reaction to the letter—a complete rejection of the advice it contained. France would not prolong the war to force England to sacrifice her fisheries, but, aside from this, would "render willingly to the United States any service upon this subject that they consider appropriate."[19]

Not knowing this, Congress had nothing with which to discredit Jay's suspicions. Nor could it measure the actual folly of his course. When he objected to the word "colonies," Franklin and Vergennes pointed out that British acceptance of the Americans' strongly worded credentials would constitute national recognition and avert dangerous delay and uncertainty. Jay held up the treaty for two months, while in England resentment was rising and Charles Fox and Lord North were coming together in a sinister political alliance. The making of the peace was a race against Shelburne's coming downfall, and in the midst of it Jay paralyzed all progress on an empty point of pride.

That was not half of it. In September, Vergennes sent his secretary Rayneval to London to form an estimate of Shelburne. Just before he left, at Jay's request and with Vergennes' approval, Rayneval wrote out a memoir on American territorial claims. Its effect was to support Britain's right to the American Northwest and Spain's to the Southwest. Coupled with the Marbois letter, this convinced Jay that Rayneval was being sent to London to delay recognition of American independence until the fisheries could be divided between France and England and the Western territories between England and Spain. Saying nothing to Franklin, he sent a secret note to Lord Shelburne asking him to "delay taking any measures with M. Rayneval," and followed this with an oral statement delivered by British Agent Vaughan. France, Jay

said, desired to suspend American independence until after the
war, in order to force the United States to stay in it to the end,
hence it was to the British interest "to cut the cords which tied us
to France." He warned Shelburne not to "think of dividing the
fishery with France and excluding us," nor to oppose the United
States on Western boundaries and navigation of the Mississippi.
To do so would sow the seeds of future war.[20]

Shelburne received this amazing communication at the very
time that Rayneval, among other things, was "expressing a strong
opinion against the American claims to the Newfoundland fishery." With each of these expressions to reinforce the other, the
British prime minister could not question their validity. Assuming
that Rayneval spoke for Vergennes (though in fact he violated
his instructions and put in a false report on his return) and that
Jay voiced the American position, Shelburne added nought to zero
and got two for an answer. The Franco-American alliance was on
the rocks and breaking up fast. He could choose peace with France
at the expense of America, or peace with America at the expense of
France. He chose the latter, gave Oswald his second commission,
and speeded the negotiation of a liberal American treaty while
terms with France dragged.[21]

Measured by actual results, Jay's second indiscretion canceled
the effect of his first, but either of them would have been fatal if
Shelburne and Vergennes had been the kind of men he believed
them to be. Not twice in all history, probably, has the safety of a
victorious nation been made so dependent upon the integrity and
good will of the head of an enemy government, and seldom have
men held power who would have responded as the Earl of Shelburne did.

Another long period of silence followed the December deluge.
Madison took notice of lesser features of the treaty negotiation—a
provision for reciprocal British and American trade rights; also
the British desire, which Franklin rejected as outside the powers
of Congress, for restoration of Loyalists' property confiscated by
the states. Urging additional instructions on the commercial
clause, Madison found himself chairman of the committee to draft
them. Congress unanimously adopted his resolve, submitted next

day, that the American negotiators seek "a direct commerce to all parts of the British dominions and possessions" in exchange for British trade rights in "all parts of the United States." At the very least they should hold out for trade in the British Isles and the West Indies. That was the beginning of the American open-door policy in relation to colonial trade.[22]

South Carolina, Rutledge of that state reported with alarm, was moving toward a repeal of her confiscation law because of a belief that restoration of property would be required by treaty. Madison called on Congress, "without inquiring into the expediency of confiscations," to do all it could "to prevent the repeal and even the attempt of a repeal of the confiscation law of one of the states." Otherwise Great Britain would think the United States lacked firmness on this point, and the negotiations would be impeded. New England delegates blocked the effort to secure action—some delegates, Madison said, failing to distinguish between confiscation of property and repudiation of debts.[23]

Encountering a movement by Fitzsimons and Hamilton to suspend the long-pending consular agreement with France, Madison protested against thoughtless abandonment, by a new congressional membership, of obligations entered into by their predecessors. The object they desired—a continuance of the right of American consuls to engage in private trade—should be sought by negotiation, not repudiation. Some earnest conversation "by the old members with the most judicious of the new" abated the zeal for innovations and the proposal was postponed.[24]

Past decisions seemed less binding a couple of weeks later, when Madison was made chairman of a committee to pass on the treaty of amity and commerce with Holland negotiated by John Adams in October 1782. He reported that Adams had exceeded his instructions by introducing an article which "seems more cautiously to exclude" alien ownership of real estate than Congress had intended. On the whole, however, "the treaty ought to be immediately and fully accepted and ratified." What Madison did not mention was that he himself, seven months earlier, had protested against a guaranty of alien land ownership in the proposed treaty and Congress had overwhelmingly voted down his motion to direct Adams to exclude any such right. Now Adams had omitted it and Madison tapped him with a feather.

In one respect, however, the treaty with Holland aroused his ire. "The language of the American column is obscure," he protested, "abounding in foreign idioms and new coined words, with bad grammar and misspellings." Indeed it was a queer paper. Ships were subject to "visitation at land." A bond against misconduct became a "caution for malversation." And who but a philologist could regulate "the affair of refraction"? He thought it would be improper to suspend the treaty, but would not object to an instruction to Adams "to substitute with the consent of the other party a more correct counterpart in the American language." During the Revolution, the English language was something used in England.[25]

While waiting for peace news, Madison gained and threw new light on the foibles of diplomats. Jefferson left for Baltimore at the end of January, to sail for France. Frozen waters and British cruisers barred the way, so, after his small boat had perilously followed an ice-breaking sloop twelve miles down the river, he found himself on a French frigate with nothing to do for several weeks but write letters. In one of them he relayed what has become a widely quoted anecdote concerning "Mr. Z" in Paris—a story which Jefferson's amanuensis, Major Franks, heard "from Dr. Franklin himself." Mr. Z, it appears, sought to barge in on Franklin's negotiations with the French court, and was decently rebuffed. At length Franklin "received from Mr. Z a very intemperate letter. He folded it up and put it in a pigeon hole." Four or five more letters followed. Then came Mr. Z himself "and gave a loose to all the warmth of which he is susceptible. The Doctor replied, 'I can no more answer this conversation of yours than the several impatient letters you have written me (taking them down from the pigeon hole). Call on me when you are cool and goodly humored and I will justify myself to you.' They never saw each other afterwards."

The story, Madison replied, was new to him, but it was enough, "if there were no other key," to decipher "the implacability of the party triumphed over." Historians have commonly identified Mr.

Z as Arthur Lee, although one editor of Jefferson's letters thought it was John Adams. Who could it be, however, but Ralph Izard? The letter "Z" was shallow concealment to men who knew that the alphabet ran "from A to Izzard." For confirmation, one need but read the string of letters Izard wrote to Franklin in 1778. The last of them, four thousand words long, accused the minister of employing "every artifice to evade giving any written explanation" of his refusal to admit Izard to the secrets of Franco-American treaty-making, with which the Carolinian had nothing whatever to do.[26]

Madison went on to tell of letters received the day before from John Adams in Holland. They were "not remarkable for anything unless it be a display of his vanity, his prejudice against the French court, and his venom against Doctor Franklin." Could this be true? Prejudice, yes; venom, yes; but vanity? John Adams did not believe in vanity. A full year earlier he had expressed his opinion of it to Secretary Livingston: "Vanity, sir, is a passion capable of inspiring illusions which astonish all other men." As for himself—why, in the letters Madison was telling about, he merely repeated the encomiums heaped upon him by his diplomatic brethren at The Hague: "Sir, you have struck the greatest blow of all Europe ... the greatest blow that has been struck in the American cause. . . . It is you who have filled this nation with enthusiasm; it is you who have turned all their heads." Vanity? Tush, tush. These tributes were not offered in flattery. They, said the modest, blushing Adams (this time to his friend Dana) were "confession *arrachées*"—torn from the unwilling through "the triumph of stubborn independence" and the "more delicious" on that account.

Adams' vanity, Jefferson responded, was "a lineament in his character which had entirely escaped me. His want of taste I had observed. Notwithstanding all this he has a sound head on substantial points, and I think he has integrity." His dislike of all parties and all men might put his prejudices in balance and "give the same fair play to his reason as would a general benevolence of temper. At any rate honesty may be extracted even from poisonous weeds." It was a remark not so different from Franklin's appraisal of his unfriendly and envious colleague, of whom he wrote, concerning his violent attacks on France in the presence of British ministers: "I am persuaded, however, that he means well for his country, is always an honest man, often a wise one, but sometimes and in some things absolutely out of his senses."[27]

Shortly after this, as peace prospects opened new diplomatic vistas, Madison found fresh material for his pen. "Congress," he reported to Jefferson, "have received a long and curious epistle from Mr. Adams. . . . He animadverts on the revocation of his commission for a treaty of commerce with Great Britain, presses the appointment of a minister to that court with such a commission, draws the picture of a fit character in which his own likeness is ridiculously and palpably studied, finally praising and recommending Mr. Jay for the appointment provided injustice must be done to an older servant." When Gilpin came to publish Madison's letter in 1840, he was uncertain of the best way to conceal the fact that one national hero had written thus scornfully about another national hero. He first marked out Adams' name, then restored it and omitted the offending passage. Between the statesmen of the Revolution all must be sweetness and light, or be covered by the concealing darkness of expurgation. James Madison never rose to a popular prominence that would win him the services of a Parson Weems, but blue-penciling editors have done quite well in robbing him of everything but a disembodied brain.[28]

Peace rumors rolled in from the West Indies during the early part of February. Naturally skeptical of them, Madison wrote to his father that these were given weight by a "material fall in the price of imported goods," a circumstance by no means to be despised "considering the sagacity and good intelligence of merchants." The very next day their sagacity and his was rewarded by the arrival of New York papers carrying George III's address of December 5 to Parliament. Going to the full length of the powers vested in him, he had offered to declare the colonies free and independent states. "Provisional articles are agreed upon," the king announced, "to take effect whenever terms of peace shall be finally settled with the court of France."[29]

"I heartily congratulate you on the dawn of peace," wrote Madison to Randolph on that most excellent February 13 (Thursday). Great joy was produced by this news, he remarked in his congressional notes, "except among the merchants who had great quantities of merchandise in store, the price of which immediately and materially fell." The Virginia delegation rushed an express southward to forestall speculation in tobacco, whose price was certain to shoot upward. Madison notified the marooned Jefferson that Congress ordered him to suspend his voyage until their further instruction, and added his own hope that his friend would return to Philadelphia. The mission was not canceled. Never having lost his apprehensions "that some tricks would be tried by the British Court notwithstanding their exterior fairness of late," Madison was "peculiarly solicitous that your mission should be pursued as long as a possibility remained of your sharing in the object of it."[30]

More weeks went by, and doubts merged with hopes. "The length of the negotiation may be explained," Madison commented to Randolph on March 11, "but the delay of all parties to notify its progress is really astonishing. Our last official information is nearly five months old and that derived from the royal speech upwards of three months."

Even as Madison wrote, the American packet *Washington* was sailing up Delaware Bay under the first passport ever signed by a British king for a vessel of the United States of America. On the following day, March 12, 1783, the provisional treaty and the letters of the American ministers were laid before Congress. It was a glorious treaty with everything in it—independence, the Western territories, the fisheries—everything that counted. "On the whole extremely liberal," said Madison, with his microscopic eye on one little flyspeck, or it might even be a fly, in the creamy ointment. Congress was to recommend to the states a restitution of confiscated property. This "had the appearance of sacrificing the dignity of Congress to the pride of the British king," although "it could scarcely be understood that the states would comply." It was perplexing, also, to find at the end of the treaty a separate article, separately signed, defining the boundary with West Florida, this article to come into effect if Great Britain retook that territory from Spain.

Madison and his fellows spent four days reading the accompanying letters, and as they read they gasped. Writing jointly, Adams, Franklin, Jay and Laurens disclosed the manner in which they had obeyed their instructions to act "in confidence and in concert" with the French court, and to be finally bound by its advice:

"As we had reason to imagine that the articles respecting the boundaries, the refugees, and fisheries did not correspond with the policy of this court, we did not communicate the preliminaries to the minister until after they were signed, and not even then the *separate article*. We hope that these considerations will excuse our having so far deviated from the spirit of our instructions. The Count de Vergennes, on perusing the articles, appeared surprised, but not displeased, at their being so favorable to us."[31]

Franklin, writing separately, offered no explanations. John Adams wrote several letters—or rather, each of the two John Adamses put his hand to the quill. The wise and honest Adams gave a well-reasoned argument against rigid adherence to the instructions of Congress, when changing scenes compelled immediate action which could not be submitted to a distant government. From the Adams "absolutely out of his senses" came a charge that France tried to dupe the United States on virtually every item of the peace treaty. He revealed that following his arrival in Paris on October 26, he did not so much as pay a courtesy call on Vergennes for two weeks, and then did so only because Lafayette and Franklin told him the foreign minister felt hurt at having no knowledge of his presence but through the returns of the police. Franklin was described by Adams as one whom the French "puffed up to the top of Jacob's ladder in the clouds" because he was "submission itself" on the peace issues, leaving "every other man depressed to the bottom of it in the dust."[32]

Whatever happened to his breeches, no dust could cling to John Adams' silken ego. In his journal of the negotiations, sent to Congress, he allowed the French guests at a little dinner party to describe his diplomatic prowess. From them came *"le compliment le plus sublime possible,"* which he refused to sully by translation: *"Monsieur, vous êtes le* Washington *de la négociation."* The compliment appeared so well-deserved that he recorded it twice, adding the comments, "This is the finishing stroke, 'tis impossible to exceed this," and again, "A few of these compliments would kill Franklin, if they should come to his ears." If laughter could kill, Old Ben might not have outlasted the evening. For he was present at this dinner, and the French hosts and guests, whom Adams named, consisted without exception of Franklin's most intimate friends in Paris.[33]

John Jay's letters also contained suggestions of a split personality. He testified to the "perfect unanimity" which had prevailed from the start among the American commissioners and praised the firmness, acuteness and spirit of Franklin. Separately, in a long and detailed account of his activities from June to mid-November, he told the full story of his suspicions of Vergennes and Rayneval, his secret communications to Lord Shelburne, and his continuing belief that France would support England in the peace negotiations in order to keep the United States weak and dependent.[34]

In Congress, according to Madison, various delegates reacted very differently to the secrecy of the American ministers toward France and their confidential manner toward the British ministers: "Many of the most judicious members thought they had all been in some measure ensnared by the dexterity of the British minister; and particularly disapproved of the conduct of Mr. Jay in submitting to the enemy his jealousy of the French without even the knowledge of Dr. Franklin." The separate article on West Florida "was most offensive, being considered as obtained by Great Britain, not for the sake of the territory ceded to her, but as a means of disuniting the United States and France, as inconsistent with the spirit of the alliance, and a dishonorable departure from the candor, rectitude and plain dealing professed by Congress."

The separate article put Congress in a dilemma. If, said Madison, they told all to the French minister, they would totally destroy French confidence in the American ministers, and might engage the ministers "in dangerous factions against Congress"—dangerous because the treaty terms they had secured "were popular in their nature." If Congress should conceal everything, and the French court learn the truth from the enemy or otherwise, "all confidence would be at an end between the allies; the enemy might be encouraged by it to make fresh experiments, and the public safety as well as the national honor be endangered."

Upon the whole it was thought that the American ministers, particularly Jay, had joined with the enemy to increase France's perplexity with regard to Spain, "and that they had made the safety of their country depend on the sincerity of Lord Shelburne, which was suspected by all the world besides, and even by most of themselves." In this business, Madison remarked to Randolph, "Jay has taken the lead and proceeded to a length of which you can form little idea. Adams has followed with cordiality. Franklin has been dragged into it. . . . The torment of this dilemma cannot be justly conveyed without a fuller recital of facts than is permitted. I wish you not to hazard even an interlined decipherment of those which I have deposited in your confidence." (Not being used to reading his letters backward, Randolph did the interlining, then came to the request that he omit it.)[35]

As if all this were not enough, Minister Luzerne added to the dismay by revealing to sundry delegates (as Madison recorded it) "the displeasure of the French court at the neglect of our ministers to maintain a confidential intercourse and particularly to communicate the preliminary articles before they were signed." But a few days before the signing, they had deceived Vergennes by saying that agreement was distant. The king had "expressed great indignation . . . he did not think he had such allies to deal with." Vergennes' final comment, though indignant, was not harsh. "I accuse nobody," he wrote. "I do not even blame Mr. Franklin. He yields perhaps too easily to the suggestions of his colleagues, who do not pretend to know anything of courtesy. All their attentions are devoted to the English whom they have met in Paris. If we may judge the future by what I have just seen, we shall be badly paid for all we have done for the United States of America and for securing them that title."

The delegates felt better when they learned that the foreign minister under later date had countermanded his order for a formal protest because Franklin "had given some explanations that had been accepted." The senior American minister did a noble job of explaining. Not only did he persuade Vergennes (in the latter's words) to "let the misunderstanding be well buried in silence and forgetfulness," but clinched a new 6,000,000-livre loan in the process.[36]

The diplomatic crisis was not over in Congress, for Madison saw no evidence that either Vergennes or Luzerne was aware of the separate article. However, Franklin had eased the tension, and his standing with the delegates rose sharply. It rose, that is, except among the anti-Gallic faction. Not twenty-four hours before the peace news came, Arthur Lee was accusing Franklin of deliberately keeping Congress in the dark, whence would ensue a grievous continuance of the war. Now, as he sat at the Virginia table while dispatches were being decoded, new glooms and furies swept over him. Robert Morris, he wrote, was holding back the deciphering "for the sole purpose of speculation" through which he had already "become as rich as a Jew." Interrupted, at that precise moment, by the bringing in of swiftly decoded letters, he swung back to his first nonlove with a denunciation of "the treachery of old Franklin. . . . There never I think existed a man more meanly envious and selfish than Dr. Franklin."[37]

Far different was Madison's appraisal of "the judgment, acuteness and patriotism" displayed by the veteran minister. "Franklin's correspondence on this occasion denotes a vigor of intellect, which is astonishing at his age," he wrote to Randolph. "A letter to the British minister on the case of the Tories in particular is remarkable for strength of reasoning, of sentiment and of expression. He concludes his letter to Congress with observing that he is now entering his seventy-eighth year, fifty of which have been spent in the public service, and that having lived to see like Simeon of old the salvation of his country his prayer is that he may be permitted to retire from public life." To which Randolph replied: "The contrast which your eulogium on Franklin presented was truly grateful to my mind, being a complete antidote to the insinuation of Mr. Lee."[38]

It might be used also to counteract the artful implications of John Adams' statement, which gullible historians have swallowed whole, that on his arrival in Paris he gave Franklin his opinion of the "wisdom and firmness with which Mr. Jay had conducted the negotiation in his sickness and my absence." Franklin's illness was an attack of gout and gravel in late August and early September. Thus a comment which, carelessly read, appears to deny Franklin credit as a negotiator of peace, actually refers to the period during which Jay stalled the treaty and jeopardized the alliance by objecting to Oswald's commission and informing the British government of his distrust of France. Jay himself, laid up with influenza throughout July, was still suffering its aftereffects in November.[39]

Madison had good reason for liking Franklin's letter to Oswald about the Tories. The core of it was his own resolution of September 10, 1782, setting up the value of slaves carried off by the British, and other property destruction, as an offset to confiscations by the Americans. Received by Franklin at a moment of final crisis, it was used by the old diplomat with dramatic effect to repair a blunder by John Adams and secure British signatures to the provisional treaty. It was not Vergennes alone whom Adams shunned on arriving in Paris. Waiting three days before calling on Franklin, he and Jay conferred before that with the British negotiators, Oswald and Undersecretary Strachey. Adams promptly agreed to their proposal that the treaty validate British debts in America. His action made a good impression, he wrote in his journal, Strachey "smiling in every line of his face."[40]

All that this did to Franklin was wipe out his entire stock of trading material. He had been holding the debt clause in reserve to avoid or tone down the British demands on confiscated property. Not until he sought to use it did he discover that his weapon was gone. Two weeks later, with British insistence on restitution of Loyalist property as the only bar to agreement, Adams made another blunder. He proposed that the British delegation return to London for new instructions. This was so dangerous, with Parliament reconvening in anger against Shelburne, the British cabinet opposing his peace terms and national spirit lifted by a victory at Gibraltar, that even the enemy negotiators warned against it as they began to accede. Franklin then played his final card. Saying that he would give them something to take to London, he drew out of his pocket a letter to Oswald. In it, quoting

Madison's resolution as a basis for the claim, he set forth a bill of particulars which included the burning of Falmouth, Norfolk, New London and Fairfield, devastation of farms, scalping and butchering by Indian allies—all adding up to a huge bill of reparations. This threat carried the day. Final compromises were made. The treaty was signed. Nothing remained but for lesser men to whittle away at the credit due to Franklin, who had won the confidence of Shelburne, gained Oswald's support for every major provision of the treaty, counteracted the blunders of his associates, soothed the sensibilities of France and clinched the victory by his skill at the finish.[41]

Jay and Adams were upright, forceful, patriotic ministers who, like Franklin, gave strong and intelligent support to the territorial and fisheries demands. Without Franklin's guidance or offsetting influence, which they resented, they would have wrecked both the treaty and the French alliance. With all their carping at Vergennes, the record shows not the lifting of his little finger to retard American peace aims or enforce the authority given him by Congress over the American negotiations. To bring Spain into the war, Vergennes had given that country a free hand to conquer the American West from England. He regarded the American claim to it as extravagant and unattainable, especially when based on the "delirium" (as he called it) of South Sea charters.[42] But he did nothing to give Spain by negotiation what she failed to gain by conquest. Vergennes himself insisted on the separate negotiations which gave a free hand to the American negotiators, holding with absolute faithfulness to the course he defined to Franklin when Grenville sought to consolidate the negotiations:

"They want to treat with us for you, but this the king will not agree to. He thinks it not consistent with the dignity of your state. You will treat for yourselves, and every one of the powers at war with England will make its own treaty. All that is necessary for our common security is that the treaties go hand in hand and are signed all on the same day."[43]

What would Jay, Adams and the congressional anti-Gallicans have said if Vergennes had been the one to sign a separate and secret treaty, leaving the United States, instead of France, to encounter stiffened British peace terms? There was selfish warrant for the American action, but not in the distrust which motivated two of the commissioners. Jay and Adams have won plaudits through the years for their "manful upholding of national dignity" against the orders of a submissive Congress. Yet they did little more than add discourtesy and suspicion to the course Franklin had been pursuing, first by himself and later with Jay. Franklin said not a word to Vergennes about his proposal for the annexation of Canada. He and Jay kept totally quiet about the treaty draft approved by them and Oswald on October 8. Six days later, before Adams reached Paris, before the recorded decision for secrecy was taken,[44] Vergennes wrote to Luzerne: "Messrs. Jay and Franklin maintain the most absolute reserve in respect to me. They have not yet even sent me a copy of Mr. Oswald's commission." On October 24, questioned by Rayneval about the negotiation, Franklin and Jay merely said they were having difficulty over boundaries. They did not tell him that all was settled except the Maine frontier. On November 23, one week before the third and final treaty draft was signed, Vergennes wrote that he did not know whether the Americans and British had yet begun to discuss the subject of fisheries.[45]

Left to himself, Franklin would have told the French no more than he felt it safe to tell, but whatever was concealed would have been cloaked in gracious friendship and the convincing assurance of American loyalty with which he rewon the confidence of Vergennes. Franklin later gave his own reasons for secrecy, widely different from those of his fellows: The instructions did not bar the commissioners from using their own judgment. The treaty contained nothing inimical to France, and could come into force only through the signing by France of her own treaty. The French court, though willing to have the United States gain all it could, feared that excessive American demands would prolong the war.[46]

"The British buy the peace more than they make it," was Vergennes' first comment. This took no account of a fact little recognized even today—that Prime Minister Shelburne, once he was forced to concede the loss of the American colonies, deliberately sought to remove sources of future conflict by giving the United States limitless room for westward expansion. Years afterward, congratulating an American friend on Britain's final surrender of the Western forts, he explained the long delay. Ministries after his own did not realize that the boundary line was drawn by choice, not necessity.[47]

The liberality of these peace terms saved the American ministers from censure, though not from criticism, when Congress on March 19 took up the treaty. The first need, Madison reported in his notes, was to put an end to the popular belief that the war was over. The impetus for this came from Minister Luzerne, who, encountering Theodorick Bland at the home of President Boudinot, found him harboring a project of declaring the Anglo-American treaty in effect as soon as France and Britain agreed on terms, without waiting for peace with Spain. Luzerne believed that Bland, "a weak and poorly informed man but a vain and obstinate arguer," was being used by Arthur Lee to put forward ideas he dared not offer himself. This particular one, it appeared, spread to "the Quakers and the women" and was combatted by "divers articles calculated to enlighten the people," which the French minister caused to be inserted in the public press.[48]

A motion in Congress, designed to spread the enlightenment, led to an immediate counterattack by Lee. Accusing France of a desire to sacrifice American interests, he asserted that the true cause of the clash at Versailles was the instruction binding the Americans to follow French advice—"the greatest opprobrium and stain to this country which it had ever exposed itself to." Bland echoed the accusation.

Madison knew that these shafts were directed straight at him and Joseph Jones—the only men present who had voted for the 1781 resolutions. Taking the floor, he expressed his surprise at the attempt to fix all blame on this instruction, "when it appeared that no use had been made of the power given by it to the Court of France, that our ministers had construed it in such a way as to leave them at full liberty; and that no one in Congress pretended to blame them on that account." He believed that the construction made by the ministers was just. They were required to follow the advice of France only in relation to concessions to Great Britain "necessary and proper for obtaining peace and an acknowledgment of independence." This did not cover concessions for other purposes or for the benefit of other powers.

Many who were loudest in disclaiming this article, Madison suspected, would have been foremost to adopt it in the circumstances of 1781. But in any event it had not been violated. The instructions which the ministers had violated, and whose violation caused the present dilemma, "were those which required them to act in concert and in confidence with our ally." Lee and Bland must have squirmed when he said this, for instead of citing the original direction that the ministers "undertake nothing" without French concurrence, he quoted his own thrice-adopted pledge which both of his Virginia antagonists had voted for.

These instructions, Madison went on, "had been repeatedly confirmed in every stage of the Revolution by unanimous votes of Congress." He then specified the support given them by "several of the gentlemen present" (naming Lee, Bland and Rutledge in a footnote) and added that one of them (Rutledge) had himself penned two of the acts.

"National honor and national security," Madison asserted, required that the secret article be communicated to France. Otherwise the United States would "be considered by all nations as devoid of all constancy and good faith." Only absolute necessity or "some perfidy on the part of France" could justify a breach of these assurances. As for perfidy, that charge had nothing behind it but "suspicions and equivocal circumstances," with the ministers themselves divided. Admitting every fact alleged by them to be true, he argued, French opposition to our claims showed no design except to reconcile them with those of Spain. Furthermore, we had derived substantial advantages from Spanish participation in the war, and had made professions corresponding to our obligations. The hostile aspect of the separate article, and its concealment, "would be regarded by the impartial world as a dishonorable alliance with our enemies against the interests of our friends."

Nobody could question the fact, Madison declared, that concealment of the separate article would endanger our national safety. What would our situation be, in a still possible renewal of the war, if France and Spain had no confidence in us? His words were wasted. The ministers had done such a fine job that few cared how they did it. Stormy resistance met the demand to disclose the secret article to France and Congress adjourned for the week end without a vote.[49]

Sunday was not solely a day of religious contemplation. To President Boudinot, Madison and a few others, the French minister read confidential extracts from the latest letters of Vergennes. The patient godfather of the Revolution had been treated "with great indelicacy" by the American commissioners, but Franklin had "prevailed on him to bury it in oblivion." English commissioners were trying to incite Spain against the United States. However, the King of France had told the Spanish monarch that he would leave the whole territorial affair to America and England and not interfere except as he might be asked for advice.[50]

That was good news but better followed. Darkness had fallen, on that Sunday evening, when tumultuous shouting called delegates and townspeople into the streets. "Peace!" ran the cry. "Peace in Europe, peace in America! The war is over." An express rider, galloping five miles up the Delaware, had brought verbal messages from Commander Duquesne of the cutter *Triomphe,* thirty-seven days out of Cádiz. A general peace was signed, with hostilities to cease in America on March 20. That was three days past. Madison sent word of the happy event to his father and friends in Virginia. "Happy it may be indeed called," he wrote, "whether we consider the immediate blessings which it confers, or the cruel distresses and embarrassments from which it saves us."[51]

In the emphasis upon happiness, delegates concluded next day that the French king's statement to his Spanish cousin "happily released" the United States from the obligations to France contained in the 1781 instructions. However, the ministers had violated the orders and pledges of Congress. The whole day was spent in harsh discussion of a proposal to disapprove their action in "the softest terms that could be devised." Madison recorded this inquest over a dead horse, but took no part. When it was buried, the dispute over the separate article went with it. The Anglo-Spanish peace treaty, transferring West Florida to Spain, rendered the subject moot.[52]

Peace brought new perplexities. Hostilities were ended, but the British in New York had no official word of it. Congress called in American privateers, and, instead of merely notifying the British of this action (as Madison wanted them to do), sent a request to Carleton and Digby to suspend hostilities at sea. The result was a snub which left Congress "exceedingly at a loss" (Madison said) how to warn American citizens of the continuance of naval hazards and yet not "publish to the world the affront they had received." They decided to let the correspondence leak to the press. The snubbing, however, was not all on one side. When the enemy commanders sent formal word of peace in early April, a grand ball celebrated the joyous event but Philadelphia girls refused to dance with the young British officer who brought the news. He would have been totally neglected, if Luzerne had not taken care of him. The hate, distrust and jealousy between these two nations, commented the minister, cannot be ended by the signing of a treaty.[53]

Problem number three: When did the war really end? The day after the young Redcoat got his tardy partner for the minuet, a ship came in with supplemental papers on the peace. Hostilities in America were to end, not on March 20 as reported, but "at the terms and epochs" agreed on in the French and Spanish treaties. Alas, the two treaties did not coincide—a circumstance, Madison recorded, which greatly perplexed merchants, lawyers and Congress. The genius of Secretary Livingston, however, was equal to the occasion. Using his wording, Congress proclaimed April 3, also April 9, as the date of the official termination of fighting. One thing was certain. Since the proclamation was adopted on April 11, the hostilities were over, except among the lawyers.

But what were these fearful words in the proclamation? "We do further require all governors and others, the executive powers of these United States respectively, to cause this our proclamation to be made public." Could Congress talk that way to the governors of sovereign states? Not in the region where "no sir" was pronounced "no suh." Only one delegate, the emphatic Mr. Mercer of Virginia, cast his vote against what Madison termed the "absurdities and improprieties" of the proclamation, but down in Richmond, he learned from Randolph, the words of Congress "excited a jealousy of their *high powers* and pointed out the propriety of wresting from them some of their constitutional authority." Madison sought to soothe the clamor by assurance that "the offensive passages were adverted to by some," and only escaped correction because of the general eagerness for action.[54]

Does this mean that Madison regarded the proclamation as unlawful? By no means. The "absurdities and improprieties" were several and separate, and he listed two. The absurdity was the double date for ending the war. The impropriety was the "authoritative style of enjoining an observance." Not lack of power, but the roughness of an ungloved fist, was what he objected to. Madison himself wrote the next proclamation of a treaty (the one with Sweden) and he went far beyond Livingston in serving notice of its binding force upon state governments and upon the people. These were his words, written in a day when "officers of the United States" included state officials:

"Now therefore, to the end that the said treaty may . . . be performed and observed on the part of these states, all the citizens and inhabitants thereof, and more especially all officers and others in the service of the United States, are hereby enjoined and required to govern themselves strictly in all things according to the stipulations above recited."[55]

Problem number four: Was it necessary to ratify the provisional treaty? Problem number five, related to it: When should prisoners of war be released?

Madison, Peters and Hamilton were ordered to report on the puzzling facts and no less perplexing policy. By the time they had gone through all of the agreements they could agree on nothing except that Cornwallis had surrendered. The provisional treaty was to be incorporated in, and thereupon was to constitute, the treaty of peace, which was not to be concluded until France and Britain agreed on terms. But the Anglo-American declaratory act said that the provisional treaty was to take effect when Anglo-French peace was established. That already had happened. Hostilities were to cease, and all prisoners be released and British-held posts be evacuated, upon ratification of the treaty. But hostilities were to cease, also, when the provisional treaty came into effect.

Madison reached the conclusion—Peters agreeing with him—
that the treaty to be ratified was "distinct—future—and even contingent." The provisional treaty ought not to be ratified because
that might make it a definitive treaty and force the United States
to a one-sided, premature and inadvisable discharge of prisoners.
Hamilton, dissenting, contended that Congress was bound to
ratify the provisional articles at once and execute its stipulations,
particularly as to the discharge of prisoners. Economy-minded
New Englanders, anxious to stop the cost of feeding captive
mouths, swept to Hamilton's support. Madison's report was laid
aside in favor of a proposal by Hamilton that the provisional
treaty be ratified and the commander in chief make necessary arrangements for enforcement of article 7, on prisoners, etc. Congress converted this into a more specific order for liberation of
prisoners and then proceeded to a unanimous ratification of the
treaty.

By this time Hamilton was alarmed at the product of his own
reasoning. Acknowledging (as Madison recorded it) "that he
began to view the *obligation* of the provisional treaty in a different
light," he undertook to have the previous action reconsidered in
order to limit Washington's course to "preparatory arrangements."
That would allow step-by-step enforcement of the treaty by both
sides. Madison supported him, as did the entire South, but the
opposition of the economy bloc left them two votes short of the
needed seven. The result was just what Madison feared—a premature release of prisoners and consequent loss of coercive power.[56]

Part of the original difference of opinion between the two men
was due to the manner in which they reached their conclusions.
Madison used a rigid view of the treaty wording to force the
adoption of a common-sense policy on prisoners. Hamilton adopted
a common-sense view of the wording, which led him into a rigid
and dangerous policy. Had they come together at the start as they
did at the finish, in acceptance of ratification (Hamilton's idea)
and step-by-step enforcement (Madison's policy), their unity
might have produced a congressional majority. In that event,
Detroit almost certainly would have passed into American hands
in 1783 instead of 1797.[57]

CHAPTER XVIII

ROMANCE

THE *Journals of Congress* for November 27, 1782, open with this entry: "Mr. W. Floyd, a delegate for New York, attended and took his seat." After an absence dating from the middle of May, the Floyd family had returned to Philadelphia and taken up its residence once more under the House-Trist roof. The older daughter was being ardently wooed by a young army officer. But what had happened to little Kitty, who was barely past her fifteenth birthday when she went back to Long Island in the spring? In six months she had blossomed, or at least budded, into young womanhood, and Bachelor James Madison, aged thirty-one, fell in love with her.

The same overwhelming shyness which kept Madison so long out of congressional debates deprived him of ease and grace in the company of attractive women. Mrs. Bland testified to his stiff, unsocial ways in the presence of a dancing butterfly like herself. It was easier to talk with a fifteen-year-old girl than with a society sophisticate—easier to be in love with her. In the household the romance was quickly noted and aided with everything from whimsical banter to outright urgings. Catherine had been back but a month when Thomas Jefferson took up his intermittent residence with Madison and became at once an energetic matchmaker. During his journey home in the following April he wrote back in cipher:

"Be pleased to make my compliments affectionately to the ladies and gentlemen. I desire them to Miss Kitty particularly. Do you know that the raillery sometime experienced from our family [the House-Trist group] strengthened by my own observation, gave me hopes there was some foundation for it. I wished it to be so as it would give me a neighbor whose worth I rate high, and as I know it will render you happier than you can possibly be in a single state. I often made it the subject of conversation, more exhortation, with her and was able to convince myself that she possessed every sentiment in your favor which you could wish. But of this no more without your leave."[1]

Madison replied in the same numerical cipher, but what he wrote lay buried under still heavier secrecy for more than a century. Following Jefferson's death, when Madison was nearly eighty years old, this letter of April 22, 1783, came back into his hands. His action reveals the deepness of a wound inflicted nearly fifty years before. He scratched out the ciphered passage, of which there was no interlined decipherment, until scarcely a trace of the numbers could be seen. Then he wrote along the side of the page, "undecipherable."

It was not so deeply buried as he thought. In the course of a hundred fifty years, the original ink has faded into brown, causing traces of the numbers to be distinguishable from the overmarking. Digits are easier to identify than letters, and this entire cipher can be read from the fragments of numbers that are visible. So it is possible to present Madison's own confirmation of his engagement and plans for an early wedding:

"I did not fail to present as you desired your particular compliments to Miss K. Your inference on that subject was not groundless. Before you left us I had sufficiently ascertained her sentiments. Since your departure the affair has been pursued. Most preliminary arrangements, although definitive, will be postponed until the end of the year in Congress. At some period of the interval I shall probably make a visit to Virginia. The interest which your friendship takes on this occasion in my happiness is a pleasing proof that the dispositions which I feel are reciprocated."[2]

Jefferson responded in a cipher which Madison also scratched out, but less thoroughly:

"I rejoice at the information that Miss K. and yourself concur in sentiment. I rejoice as it will render you happier and give to me a neighbor on whom I shall set high value."[3]

Madison had been planning to spend the winter of 1783-84 in Philadelphia, engaged in a course of reading and the enjoyment of "agreeable and even instructive society."[4] With marriage in prospect, the agreeable society could be taken along. Definitive arrangements postponed to "the end of the year in Congress" indicated a wedding in November; after that, home and companionship in Virginia.

Colonel Floyd and his family left for New York on April 29—five days after Kitty became sixteen. Madison rode with them sixty miles to Brunswick, New Jersey, through Trenton and the familiar town of Princeton. It was the first time he had been away from Philadelphia since March 18, 1780—three years and six weeks of continuous attendance, a record unapproached by any other man in the history of the Continental Congress. At the end of two days' travel, James Madison and Catherine Floyd said their farewells, with plans laid for their future. They never met again.

At his next writing to Jefferson, Madison inclosed "two letters for Miss Patsy, one from Mrs. Trist, the other from Miss Floyd with the copy of a song." Patsy (Martha) Jefferson came right back with a letter to Kitty, for the safe delivery of which, her father wrote to Madison, "she trusts to your goodness." Frail indeed was the Madison-Floyd romance, in which a thirty-two-year-old congressman found himself forwarding the correspondence of his sixteen-year-old fiancée and her eleven-year-old friend.[5]

No hint of uncertainty, however, clouded Madison's planning for the immediate future. Informed that the Virginia legislature wished him to remain in office until March of 1784, when his three-year limit under the Articles of Confederation would expire, he told his friends that such an idea "does not coincide with the plans which I have in view after November next." Only Jefferson knew that the refusal was based upon matrimonial plans. It was a wasted sacrifice, though some good came of it. His friends joined in a resolve that no person ineligible to a full year should be re-elected—and thus got rid of Bland.[6]

It was Madison's intention to leave Congress by midsummer. On July 17, he acknowledged a "letter for Miss Floyd" along with an original version of the Declaration of Independence which Jefferson sent him. The rift in his domestic hopes became visible eleven days later, when he wrote to Randolph that he would be detained in Philadelphia for several weeks "by a disappointment in some circumstances which must precede my setting out for Virginia." A fortnight later all was over. His letter of August 11 to Jefferson, though not in cipher, was so carefully guarded in language that no inquisitive postman could have guessed its subject. Yet so thoroughly did Madison mutilate it, a half century later, that only occasional words and phrases can be made out.

"At the date of my letter in April," he wrote in a part which remains untouched, "I expected to have had the pleasure by this time of being with you in Virginia. My disappointment has proceeded from several dilatory circumstances on which I had not calculated." Inked out, after this, are thirteen lines which appear to say, in part: "One of them was the uncertain state into which the object I was then pursuing has been brought by one of those incidents to which such affairs are liable. This (?) has rendered the time of my return to Virginia less material as the necessity of my visiting the state of New York no longer exists." It would be improper, he went on, to relate the details here (i.e. without cipher) "and perhaps needless to trouble you with them at any time." Little more can be made out, except for the significant words, "a profession of indifference at what has happened," and a closing reference to a more propitious turn of fate.[7]

Jefferson did what he could to comfort his friend. He wrote:

"I sincerely lament the misadventure which has happened, from whatever cause it may have happened. Should it be final, however, the world presents the same and many other resources of happiness, and you possess many within yourself. Firmness of mind and unremitting occupations will not long leave you in pain. No event has been more contrary to my expectations, and these were founded on what I thought a good knowledge of the ground. But of all machines ours is the most complicated and inexplicable."[8]

It is customary to emphasize the difference in age between Madison and Miss Floyd as if his sixteen extra years made him altogether

My dear Sir   Philad.ᵃ Aug. 11ᵗʰ 1783.

At the date of my letter in April I expected to have had
the pleasure by this time of being with you in Virginia. My disappointment has proceeded from several dilatory circumstances on which I had
not calculated ~~[several heavily struck-out lines]~~

~~[struck-out lines]~~

~~[struck-out lines]~~

~~[struck-out lines]~~

~~[struck-out lines]~~

~~[struck-out lines]~~

My journey to Virg.ᵃ is still somewhat contingent in point of tim
cannot now be very long postponed. I need not I trust renew m
assurances that it will not finally stop on this side of Monticello.

The reserve of our foreign Ministers still leaves us the sport
of misinformations concerning the Def: Treaty. We all thought a little
time ago that it had certainly arrived at N. York. This opinion
however has become extinct, and we are thrown back on the newspaper evidence which as usual is full of contradictions. The probability
seems to be that the delay arises from the discussions with the Dutch.
Mr. Dana has been sorely disappointed in the event of his announcing
himself to the Court of Russia. His written communications obtain verbal
answers only & these hold up the mediation to which the Empress with
the Emperor of G——y have been invited as a bar to any overt transaction
with the U. S. and even suggest the necessity of new powers from the latter.

MADISON'S DISCLOSURE OF HIS BROKEN ENGAGEMENT

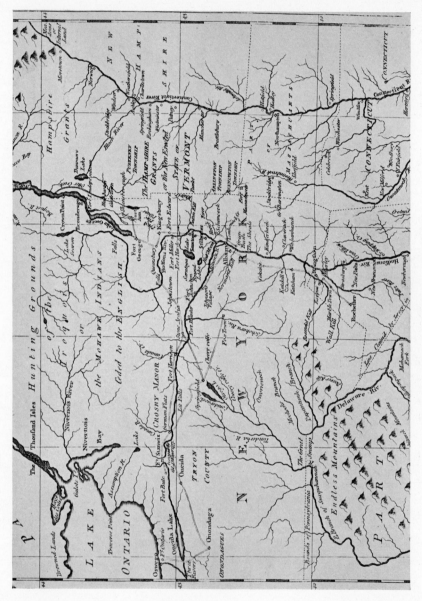

THE MOHAWK COUNTRY, A 1780 MAP

too old for Catherine (Dolly Madison was twenty years his junior)
while his studious ways, as Sydney H. Gay put it, caused him to
seem "a much older man than he really was." On the contrary,
he seemed younger. It was only two years before this that Thomas
Rodney called him "just from the college" and filled with "the
impertinence of youth." In 1783, Madison was the third youngest
member of Congress, eleven years younger than the average of a
body remarkable for its youthfulness.[9] The trouble was, he had
a rival in whom youth was glamorous and love impassioned.

As the tradition came down, not quite accurately, in the Floyd
family and was related to Gay, Catherine discarded her statesman-
wooer in favor of a young clergyman who "hung round her at the
harpsichord," and was encouraged to be on with the new love "by
a friend somewhat older than herself." Gaillard Hunt added the
guessed-at detail that the friend "belonged to the young parson's
party, in the little boarding-house world where she and Madison
lived." Nineteen-year-old William Clarkson, medical student at
the College of Philadelphia, and son of a prominent physician of
that city, no doubt did plenty of hanging over the harpsichord,
but Jefferson's letters make it plain that the boarding-house verdict
went the other way. The rift in Madison's lute developed after
Kitty arrived at Mastic, Long Island, and whatever advice she may
have had from an older friend, the choice was her own. Away
from both wooers, she knew which one she yearned for. A curious
feature of the Floyd tradition, that Catherine sealed her letter of
dismissal with rye dough, may have some relationship to Madison's
hurt remark about her "professions of indifference." Young Dr.
Clarkson, whom she married upon his graduation in 1785,
practiced medicine in Philadelphia for nine years, then (as the
aftermath of serious illness) turned to the Presbyterian ministry.
Catherine became a widow four years after Madison's election as
President.[10]

CHAPTER XIX

PREPARING FOR PEACE

THE RUPTURE of his engagement to marry intensified Madison's desire to spend a period of time in concentrated study, the only question being whether this should be done in Philadelphia or at Montpelier. Only a few days before Kitty Floyd brought her disturbing presence to Philadelphia, he had undertaken to secure the establishment of a Library of Congress. Working, as usual, partly through others, he secured his appointment "to report a list of books proper for the use of Congress," and he submitted an array of titles which was enough to frighten that learned body out of its senses.[1]

In preparing his list, Madison had the use of what is now called the "1783 catalogue" of Jefferson's library—called so because of the erroneous assumption that the date on the title page, March 6, 1783, marks the time at which he began its compilation. In reality, on that day, Jefferson was staying with Madison at the home of Mrs. House in Philadelphia, and had been away from his library for months.[2] The title page refers to 2,640 volumes, of which, Jefferson noted, "the books I have" bear check marks while "those unchecked I mean to procure." Thus it was not an actual record of the books at Monticello, but was largely a purchasing list which Jefferson intended to take with him to Paris, the book-buying center of the world. Thus enlarged, it covered every field of knowledge, and was the more useful to Madison on that account.

His use of it is evident in the great number of books which follow one another consecutively in both papers, and even in some of the deviations. Jefferson listed Burnett's *History of his Own Times* under British history. Madison put it in general history. There it appears as an interlining in the manuscript, indicating a transferred entry due to disagreement with Jefferson's classification.[3] More than sixty of Madison's authors, including some of the most radical, are not in the Jefferson list. Presumably they came from the catalogues of booksellers such as Boinaud.

In presenting his list to Congress Madison and those supporting him urged it as indispensable "that Congress should have at all times at command such authors on the law of nations, treaties, negotiations, etc., as would render their proceedings in such cases conformable to propriety." Lack of such information had damaged several important acts. Also, "no time ought to be lost in collecting every book and tract which related to American antiquities and the affairs of the U.S."—not only as materials for a history but to combat the future pretensions of Spain or other powers to American territory.[4]

Perhaps it was a good thing for Madison that he presented this list as a member of Congress rather than a civil employee, and in 1783 rather than after the establishment of a Committee on Un-American Activities. It contained standard works on international law, treaties, politics, geography, law, war, languages, general history, eighteen classifications of national history, and Americana. More notable, however, was the way it leaned toward the works of European heretics, freethinkers, antimonarchists and Catholic skeptics. Leading the whole list was that precursor of the French Revolution, the *Encyclopédie Méthodique* based on Diderot. This was followed by such names as Bayle (skeptic and social revolutionist), Voltaire, Gentili (who fled from the Inquisition), Barbeyrac (who defied the church by contending that marriage was a civil contract), D'Ossat (anti-Jesuit cardinal and diplomat), Jeannin (who tried to prevent the St. Bartholomew massacre), Mably (Catholic ex-priest turned Communist), Vertot (historian of revolutions and Premonstratense Jesuit who fell in love with Madame du Staël), Le Clerc (accused of Socinianism), Velly (ex-Jesuit), Hutcheson (tried for heresy by Scotch Presbyterians), Priestley (afterward mobbed by Anglicans because of sympathy for the French Revolution). Hobbes and Selden were present, with their defense of monarchy and war, but overshadowed by those who tore them to pieces—Cudworth, Cumberland, Hutcheson, Hume, Pufendorf, Bynkershoek. A Congress gorged on such pabulum would either start a new revolution or call out the militia to prevent one.

Congress, however, adopted an equine attitude. Madison could lead it to the water of knowledge but could not make it drink. At such a crisis, it was objected, not even a few hundred pounds could be spared for such a purpose. Defeated, Wilson and Madison moved to purchase "the most essential part of the books. This also was negatived." It was a quarter of a century before President Jefferson and more willing legislators brought the Library of Congress into being. When it was burned, in President Madison's administration, he secured its restoration by the purchase of Jefferson's library, by this time swollen to more than six thousand volumes. Thus, although the 1783 attempt resulted in failure, Madison planted the idea where it was bound to grow, and even took most of the seed from what became in time the catalogue of the congressional library. At this time, too, Madison read and made copious extracts from Jefferson's to-be-famous "Notes on Virginia," just written in response to a set of questions by Marbois. In his turn, Jefferson made a study of Madison's Notes of Debates in Congress, and later sought a copy of them.[5]

The spring of 1783, with its emphasis on finance, marked the summit of Madison's congressional career. Following his return from New Jersey, he took a diminishing part in general lawmaking, though an active one in the transition from war to peace. The subject of a peace establishment was referred on April 4 to Hamilton (the congressional military expert), Madison, Ellsworth, Wilson and Osgood—four men of action and a Massachusetts economizer. The purpose as outlined by Madison was to "provide a system for foreign affairs, for Indian affairs, for military and naval establishments; and also to carry into execution the regulation of weights and measures and other articles of the Confederation not attended to during the war."[6]

Army reorganization was the big question, but while waiting for General Washington's report on that, the committee dipped into the white man's side of the red-man problem. It reported favorably on Pennsylvania's desire to be allowed to acquire lands from the Indians in a "dignified, humane, expeditious and economical mode"—that is, to buy their lands with a keg of rum instead of murdering the owners after the fashion of the Virginia Big Knife or Pennsylvania's "Paxton boys." Blocked by suspicious New Englanders, the report finally became a part of the proceedings which led to the Western territorial plan of 1784 and the Ordinance of 1787.[7]

As the spring advanced, soldiers shouted for pay and discharge —but no discharge without pay. Americans had thrilled with pride when the veterans of Yorktown marched north to rejoin their fellows on the Hudson. "You will be charmed to see our countrymen well dressed, since you used to admire them even in their natural beauties," wrote Livingston to Lafayette—a remark so shocking to early nineteenth-century modesty that Editor Jared Sparks changed "beauties" to "rags."[8] But uniforms implied pockets, and these were empty. The army was speeding toward dissolution. The economy advocates had no thought but to get rid of it, paid or unpaid, and cut off future expense. Madison wanted it held together until all enemy troops had left the United States. As a compromise, he and Hamilton helped produce a decision that enlistments for the war were binding until the definitive treaty was signed, but which also authorized the commander in chief to grant furloughs or discharges.

This angered the troops and failed to satisfy the economizers. Hamilton, convinced that the war was over, joined the latter group and undertook to order the immediate discharge of all troops enlisted for the duration. Madison took the lead in opposition, but his motion to recommit was beaten by the "chaos clause." He then joined in an effort to change the order to immediate furlough, so that the country might "be not wholly unprepared" for a resumption of fighting. Beaten on this, his Southern bloc defeated Hamilton's report, after which the two sides came together and put over the compromise—immediate furlough—unanimously.[9]

For the committee on a peace establishment, Hamilton reported the plans of Washington and the ordnance expert, General du Portail,[10] for a small regular army and a uniform state militia. The basic question, however, was whether Congress had constitutional power to maintain any sort of military force in peacetime. Extreme state righters, zealous economizers and fearers of standing armies said No. Inside the committee only one man took this view— Holten, who replaced Osgood. He represented what Madison called the "penurious spirit [of Massachusetts] which if indulged will be fatal to every establishment that requires expense."[11] Upholding the power were four outstanding constitutional authorities —Madison, Hamilton and future Supreme Court justices Wilson and Ellsworth—but when did the bar of reason ever pry open a mind tied with purse strings?

The Articles of Confederation empowered Congress to build a navy, agree upon the number of land forces, requisition them from the states and limit the number of state troops in peacetime. The no-army delegates contended that the reference to peacetime, in connection with state troops, implied that everything else was limited to wartime. Hamilton's report challenged this. The power to Congress was granted "generally and without mention of peace or war." If military authority belonged to the states in peace and the Union in war, the United States would have to *begin to create* an army at the very time they had to *employ* it. So grave was the danger from such a construction, the committee advised, that if Congress had any doubt as to the true meaning, it should leave the general power in full force unless all the states or a majority of them declared a different interpretation.

Madison explained this moderate advice, for which he probably was responsible. If Congress should construe the power favorably to itself or even ask the states to sanction it, "the present paroxysm of jealousy may not only disappoint them, but may exert itself with more fatal effect on the revenue propositions." On the other side, to renounce the power would not only render the plan of defense defective, but might later, when the tide of prejudice flowed the other way, expose Congress "to the reproach of unnecessarily [throwing] away a power necessary for the good of the Union, and leaving the whole at the mercy of a single state."[12] This was sound reasoning, much more in line with the caution of Madison than the aggressiveness of Hamilton. The advice it refers to bears even more clearly the stamp of Madison's mind, for it contains the germ of his greatest constitutional fallacy—the theory, set forth in his Virginia Resolutions of 1798, that the individual states, acting in concert, have power to interpose against acts of Congress which they regard as unconstitutional. That doctrine, which others ultimately twisted into a right of nullification and secession, originated not in denial of the powers of Congress, but in their defense.

Unable to secure action on a peacetime army, Madison looked into a future "pregnant with difficulties." On the arrival of the definitive treaty Congress must "suffer the whole military establishment to be dissolved, every garrisoned post to be evacuated, and every stronghold to be dismantled." Other troubles were due for a quicker birth. "The troops in the barracks at this place," he reported on this same June 17, "emboldened by the arrival of a furloughed regiment returning to Maryland, sent in a very mutinous remonstrance to Congress, signed by the noncommissioned officers in behalf of the whole. It painted the hardships which they had suffered in defense of their country and the duty of their country to reward them, demanding a satisfactory answer the afternoon on which it was sent in, with a threat of otherwise taking such measures as would right themselves." Prudent and soothing actions by their commanders had obviated the danger, Madison believed, but he might not have thought so had he been a frequenter of taverns. Soldiers ordered home by platoons were refusing to go, the French minister wrote to his court next day. They "talk loudly in the cabarets of plundering the bank, of doing violence to Congress, and of bringing the city to a contribution."[13]

On the nineteenth an express rider from Lancaster brought word that seventy or eighty armed soldiers, led by sergeants, were marching on Philadelphia, gaining recruits en route. The Pennsylvania council, appealed to, sent word that the state militia could not be relied on.

Madison recorded these events with seeming unconcern, and continued his matter-of-fact recital next day: "The soldiers from Lancaster came into the city under the guidance of sergeants. They professed to have no other object than to obtain a settlement of accounts, which they supposed they had a better chance for at Philadelphia than at Lancaster." And on June 21: "The mutinous soldiers presented themselves, drawn up in the street before the

State House, where Congress had assembled." One turns to the Philadelphia newspapers for a more vivid account—and keeps on turning. Some suppressed the story entirely, but not the *Pennsylvania Packet*. Standing boldly on the rights of a free press, it reported: "Several corps of continental troops have arrived in town, from different parts, previous to their being discharged in consequence of the peace."[14]

It was left to Minister Luzerne to give a pictorial view of the scene. He was living downtown now, after the destruction of the French legation by lightning, and from his house he could see about three hundred men approach the hall of Congress. They marched up "in good order, led by their sergeants, drums beating, bayonets on their muskets. . . . Arrived before the State House, a detachment crossed to establish itself in the courtyard and the main body formed in a circular line around the house with the intent of not letting anyone leave." Madison continued the story from inside the building:

"The soldiers remained in their position, without offering any violence, individuals only occasionally uttering offensive words, and wantonly pointed their muskets to the windows of the hall of Congress. No danger from premeditated violence was apprehended, but it was observed that spirituous drink from the tippling houses adjoining began to be liberally served out to the soldiers, and might lead to hasty excesses. None were committed, however, and about three o'clock, the usual hour, Congress adjourned; the soldiers, though in some instances offering a mock obstruction, permitting the members to pass through their ranks."[15]

What was Congress to do? Hamilton, Madison said, demanded that General St. Clair and the Pennsylvania executive council "take order for terminating the mutiny." St. Clair made a fruitless speech to the soldiers. The Pennsylvania president threw up his hands. Congress held a night meeting and listened to the conflicting reports brought from the barracks. "At one moment," Madison recorded, "the mutineers were penitent and preparing submissions; the next they were meditating more violent measures. Sometimes the bank was their object; then the seizure of the members of Congress with whom they imagined an indemnity for their offense might be stipulated." Convinced that the Pennsylvania council was making a bid for soldiers' votes in the October election, Congress notified that body that it had been "grossly insulted" by disorderly troops, and authorized its own removal from Philadelphia.[16]

As Major John Armstrong, secret provoker of the mutiny, described this move to General Gates, would-be supplanter of Washington: "The grand Sanhedrim of the nation, with all their solemnity and emptiness have removed to Princeton, and left a state, where their wisdom has been long questioned, their virtue suspected, and their dignity a jest." Madison went to Princeton, but came back three days later on private business and made what was to prove a final entry in his journal of congressional debates: "After the departure of Congress the mutineers submitted, and most of them accepted furloughs under the resolution of Congress on that subject. At the time of submission they betrayed their leaders, the chief of whom proved to be a Mr. Carberry, a deranged [retired] officer, and a Mr. Sullivan, a lieutenant of horse; both of whom made their escape. Some of the most active of the sergeants also ran off."[17]

Captain Carberry wrote from a ship rounding Cape Henlopen that he was feeling "gay as the soaring lark" at the prospect of visiting his companion's "rich and wealthy father" in Ireland. Lieutenant Sullivan bubbled over to his former commander, Colonel Moylan: "We are now wafted along by a gentle and generous gale, and possess the most perfect tranquility of mind. Conscious of no unworthy action, all we regret is failing in a noble attempt. 'And more true joy Marcellus exiled feels, Than Caesar with a Senate at his heels.'" Three years later they rashly tempted fate by returning to America, and paid the penalty which is usually meted out to army officers for such grave offenses. Carberry was sentenced to draw his commuted half pay for life. Sullivan, his half-pay application blocked by a technicality (he had left the country without leave *before* being deranged) "remained publicly and without disguise in Philadelphia, unquestioned by public authority." The sergeants were condemned to death by an army court-martial, but Congress pardoned them. No marble temple or shining obelisk is likely to be raised to the memory of these valiant forerunners of the "march on Washington," but at least Christian Nagle, John Morrison, gunner Tilly, drummer Horn, Thomas Flowers and William Carman can be rescued from an undeserved anonymity.[18]

Madison remained in Philadelphia to do some writing for which he needed access to his papers. This held him all summer, save for an occasional quick trip to Princeton behind the hard-driven horses of the Flying Machine, whose winged wheels flew from Philadelphia to New York in a single day.[19]

Delegates drifted in and out of Philadelphia. Alexander Hamilton came over, and penned a note to Madison (a second note, in fact, the first being left in Princeton) asking him to testify to Hamilton's views on the removal of Congress, which he was being accused of inspiring for the purpose of taking that body to New York. By some mischance, the letter was not delivered to Madison until October. He then replied that Hamilton "was opposed to the removal of Congress except in the last necessity," and yielded only to "the peremptory expostulations of others." Was it because of their friendship at that time, or because of the weight of Madison's word, or both, that he was singled out for the inquiry when two dozen others were more readily available?[20]

Mercer went through, en route to the New Jersey seashore because of illness, and borrowed $200 when he came back. Arthur Lee paid a visit on his way to Princeton, from which place Mercer soon sent a call of distress: Come and stop the doings of Lee and Bland. The doings were small stuff—tricky defeat of a return of Congress to Philadelphia—nothing to call for pell-mell departure though sufficient to make Madison use the words "national dignity and welfare." So, when Joseph Jones ambled in from Fredericksburg, enabled to re-enter Congress by the cropping up of a 1,200-pound bill, he and Madison spent ten days together there before resuming their seats.[21]

Madison had two objects in going to Princeton: to bring about final acceptance by Congress of the Virginia land cession, and to work for the establishment of a permanent national capital at

Georgetown, on the Potomac. The first proved fairly easy—much easier than to obtain the cession of a bedroom in the crowded environs of his beloved Alma Mater. "Mr. Jones and myself," he wrote to Randolph on August 20, "are at length put into one bed in a room not more than ten feet square." The longer he stayed in the room the smaller it grew. "Scarcely ten feet square," he told his father. "Not ten feet square" was the word to Jefferson three weeks later, and he was "obliged to write in a position that scarcely admits the use of any of my limbs." Unless an effective vote could be taken on removal, Congress must spend the winter "in this village," this "obscure village," where members could not be "decently provided for, nor those connected with Congress provided for at all."[22]

That furnished a gloomy prospect for "Long Tom" Jefferson, who, expecting to enter Congress late in October, had asked short Jemmy Madison to find living quarters for him. Beating around a rambling bush to avoid direct reference to the Madison-Floyd romance, Jefferson wanted to know whether his friend's project of leisurely study in Philadelphia was now as it originally had been. If so, he hoped that Madison's visit to Virginia would come early enough to allow them to return together.

The plan for a winter of close reading, Madison replied, was not entirely given up until Congress left the city and refused to return. The added prospect of Jefferson's society "would have confirmed my intention after the abortive issue of another plan, had not the solicitude of a tender and infirm parent exacted a visit to Virginia and an uncertainty of returning been thereby incurred. Even at present if Congress should make Philadelphia their seat this winter and I can decline a visit to Virginia or speedily get away from it, my anxiety on the subject will be renewed." As it seemed likely that their paths would cross, might they not plan a rendezvous at the Alexandria races?[23]

For Jefferson's benefit, Madison summarized the state of government in this first fall month of 1783. There had been no decision "on any of the great branches of the peace establishment." The military question was "without any prospect of a hasty issue." Election of a foreign secretary to succeed Livingston had been the

order of the day for months, with nothing done. Inaction in the
Marine Department was unimportant, as nearly all naval vessels
had been sold. The Finance Department "is an object of almost
daily attack and will be reduced to its crisis on the final resignation of Mr. M[orris] . . . in a few months."

These attacks, of course, came from Arthur Lee, who, charging
that the entire press of Philadelphia was in Morris' pay, cried out
to a Boston friend: "Thus while fallacious reports on this man's
conduct are published in all the papers . . . the public money is
lavished away, the soldiery defrauded and the public plundered."
This was occasioned by the financier's proposal that clothing material received from Europe after the end of the war should be sold,
and the proceeds given as a bonus to veterans, instead of being
made up into uniforms to be handed to them as they were being
demobilized.[24]

Madison himself was trying to uphold the claims of the soldiers
by enforcing a national policy based on sound national credit.
Maryland had recently revoked the appropriation of a particular
tax to the support of Congress, and ordered its proceeds used to
give Maryland Continentals five months' pay. Reporting on this
as committee chairman, Madison approved a protest already sent
by Morris and termed Maryland's action one "to subvert the foundations of public credit." To this young Hawkins of North Carolina added that if essential and valid acts of Congress may be defeated by the interference of individual legislatures, "vain must be
every attempt to maintain a national character or national credit."
Congress must have thought so too, for it did exactly nothing.[25]

Madison found himself also (September 18, 1783) chairman of
a committee to work out a final overnight solution of a half-pay
tangle. Replying to his April address to the states, the Massachusetts legislature in July called the commutation to five years' full
pay for officers "more than an adequate reward for their services"
(all they had done was secure the country's independence) and
"calculated to raise and exalt some citizens in wealth and gran-
deur, to the injury and oppression of others." Also, civil officers
were paid much too high salaries. A committee headed by Duane
thereupon defended the original half-pay measure and upheld the
commutation as an act to which the national faith was pledged.

However, engaging in what Madison termed "almost a general anarchy," Eastern delegates aided by Lee and Bland secured a re-committal to three New Englanders. They recommended that the separate states settle with their officers and that everybody in the War, Marine and Foreign departments be discharged except the heads of them. These would be given small sums ($3,000 for the War Department) to hire assistants or clerks. This economy fare was too birdlike even to peck at, and was put aside without a vote. The officers' pay proposal was then knocked out, four to five, and the original Duane report was referred to Madison, Mercer and Duane.[26]

Madison had no light feelings on the subject of army half pay or the spirit of the Massachusetts memorial, which he described to Jefferson as "pregnant with the most penurious ideas not only on that subject but on several others which concern the national honor and dignity." New England army officers came to him in Phila-delphia with their tales of woe. "I pity from my heart the officers of the Eastern line who are threatened by these prospects with dis-appointments which the Southern officers have no idea of," he commented. Without a Continental provision, they not only would "be docked of their halfpay," but would be likely to lose much of their other pay on the pretense that their states had paid more than their share of war costs.[27]

With the subject placed in his hands, Madison amplified Duane's arguments for Continental action. He then gave warning that should so important a state as Massachusetts "withhold her solid support to constitutional measures of the Confederacy, the result must be a dissolution of the Union; and then she must hold herself as alone responsible for the anarchy and domestic confusion that may succeed."[28] That was more than rhetorical appeal. It testifies to the impressive place which the idea of a permanent union held in the language of the times. The threat of anarchy and confusion could be used as effectively in Massachusetts as elsewhere, since the difference was not in concepts of nationhood, but in the rela-tive affection felt for army officers and money. In this instance, the Duane-Madison way of thinking prevailed by a vote of seven to two.[29]

The question of a national capital had two aspects—location and jurisdiction. A committee to which Madison was added during a July visit to Princeton favored exclusive jurisdiction by Congress over a district from three to six miles square. Madison objected to the exclusion of the local inhabitants. His proposal was that the district "be entirely exempted from the authority of the state ceding the same; and the organization and administration of the powers of government within the said district concerted between Congress and the inhabitants thereof." A decision was put off while North, South and center wrangled over location.[30]

Wanting Georgetown, Madison studied the way to get it. Congress was now between Philadelphia and New York, and thoroughly uncomfortable. If it went temporarily to New York, the jump to Georgetown would be too great. From Philadelphia it would be easy. For a permanent site, he concluded, "the best chance both for Maryland and Virginia will be to unite in offering a double jurisdiction on the Potomac." The only dangerous rival in that case would be "a like offer from New Jersey and Pennsylvania on the Delaware."[31]

It was October before this strategy was put to the test. Eastern delegates, Madison said, *appeared* to favor the Potomac, but when the vote came they lined up with Pennsylvania and its neighbors for Trenton, New Jersey. There was still a chance to change the decision, Madison believed, if Congress went temporarily to Philadelphia. Arthur Lee disagreed. He was one of those to whom (as Madison expressed it) that city "will ever be obnoxious while it contains and respects *an obnoxious character*"—Robert Morris. Make Annapolis the temporary seat, Lee argued, and then take the easy hop to Georgetown. Dangerous advice, Madison replied, for the change was to take effect some weeks in the future. At any moment a second New Hampshire delegate might arrive and upset the decision, carrying Congress direct to Trenton. On the motion for Annapolis, Madison and Mercer outvoted Lee and cut off a seventh state.[32]

On the main issue of a permanent site, the Potomac must win New England support. Putting their heads together, the Southerners worked out a plan. Seven states, they remarked to all within hearing, could fix the seat of government at Trenton, but nine were required to vote money for buildings and they would not approve a penny for that purpose. They went then to the New Englanders and proposed two permanent seats of government, at Trenton and Georgetown, to be occupied alternately, with the temporary seat divided between Trenton and Annapolis. Besides being bait for Maryland, this appealed to the anti-Morris New Englanders as a way of knocking Philadelphia completely out of the picture, thus, as Gerry put it, avoiding the danger that men of wealth would "subject us to an oligarchy or aristocracy." The penny-pinching Bay Staters were even persuaded that the double set of government buildings would cost nothing—they would be paid for by the increase of real estate values at the two locations. In short, the Southerners "maneuvered in such a manner as to take in the Eastern members . . . completely," or so it seemed to President Boudinot, a Jerseyite. The measure was passed by "the most heterogeneous coalition that was in the power of Congress to form."[33]

There was no expectation among the triumphant Virginians that the United States would actually have two capitals, one on the Potomac, the other on the Delaware. As Thomas Jefferson summarized it after a talk with Madison in Philadelphia, the decision for Trenton had been unhinged, "leaving the whole matter open for discussion at some future day. It was in fact a rally, and making a drawn battle of what had at first appeared to be decided against us."[34] The final decision a decade later was the fulfillment of Madison's original plan.

October 25, 1783, was James Madison's last day in Congress. His fourth yearly term was to come to an end on November 2. He entered that body an unknown, hardly noticed youth, too shy for public speech. He left it the acknowledged leader in every activity that bulwarked independence and pointed toward a strong, firm national union of the states. He was the champion of American nationhood against divisive provincialism, of republican government against monarchy or aristocracy, of the general welfare against the selfish policies of individual states, and of the common run of humanity against speculators and profiteers. But so quietly did he work, with so little desire for personal credit, that it is only through a persistent search of the records that his creative and strategic leadership can be uncovered. Hamilton wrote at this time that "the road to popularity in each state is to inspire jealousies of the power of Congress." Madison, like Hamilton, courted no such popularity. He stood against the policies of his own state, when they conflicted with the basic law or vital necessities of the Union, as readily as against the weakest and most distant member of the Confederacy.

The articles to which Madison devoted a good part of the summer came into print in the final weeks of his congressional service, under the title of "The North American" No. 1 and No. 2. Published anonymously by his friends the Bradfords in the *Pennsylvania Journal* of September 13 and October 8,[35] they form a veritable epitome of his congressional career, revealing not only his predominant concern with the consolidation of nationhood but the gravity of the obstacles to be faced and overcome. "At an era so awful and so critical," he wrote in the first of them, "it is the design of this address deliberately to investigate and to expose with freedom the real situation of these states, and in anticipating evil and misfortune to suggest their remedy." He never publicly acknowledged the articles. To do so, with their scornful disparagement of state political systems and state sovereignty, would have been embarrassing in Virginia then and in the nation later. Only Jefferson was allowed to know that he wrote them.[36] Their style ranges from the typical complexity of some of his state papers to the poetic fervor of his early days in the American Whig Society.

Here, set forth one after another, are the great subjects to which Madison devoted himself for nearly four years in Congress—international relations, the supremacy of the Union, the transfer of Western lands to the nation, justice to the army and other creditors, the establishment of federal revenues, the menace of interstate commercial conflicts—set forth not in boastful or complacent terms of accomplishment, but of grave shortcomings and overshadowing perils.

Why was it that the civil institutions of America were "cursed with the impotence of old age, when they should enjoy the vigor of youth"? Why did "the horrors of anarchy and domestic confusion" threaten to succeed the dissolution of the British bond? Am-

Dictionnaire de Trevoux. 5. vol. fol. @ 5 f/r — — — — — — — — — 28 - 0 - 0
La Conquista di Mexico. De Solis. fol. 7 f10. reliure 7 f — ———— 14 - 10
Traité de morale et de bonheur. 8vo. 2. v. in 1. - - - - - - - 2 - 8
Wiequefort de l'Ambassadeur. 2. v. 4to - - - - - - - 7 - 4
Burlamaqui. Principes du droit Politique 4to 3 f12. reliure 2 fs. - - 5 - 17
Conquista de la China por el Tartaro por Palafox. 12mo - - - - - 3 -
Code de l'humanité de Felice. 13. v. 4to . - - - - - 104 - 0
12. first livraisons of the Encyclopédie 8v. vols 4to (being 28 f lf5 : subscription) 348 - 0
14th. livraison of do. 4. v. 4to . . . - - - - - - 24 - 0
Personel - - - - - - - - - - - 2 - 0
Bibliothèque physico-oeconomique . 4. v. 12mo 10 f4. rel. 3 f - - - 13 - 4
Cultivateur Americain. 2. v. 8vo 7 f17. rel. 2 f10 - - - 10 - 7
Mirabeau sur l'ordre des Cincinnati: 10 f13. rel. 1 f5 (prohibited) 11 - 15
Coutumes Anglo-Normands de Houard. 4. v. 4to 40 f rel. 10 f . 50 - 0
Memoires sur l'Amerique 4. v. 4to - - - - - - 24 - 0
Tott sur les Turcs. 4. v. in 2. 8vo 10 f. rel. 2 f10 - - - 12 - 10
Necker sur l'Administration des Finances de France. 3. v. 12mo 7 f10 rel. 2 f5 9 - 15
le bon-sens. 12mo 6 f rel. 15s - (prohibited) - - - 6 - 15
Mably. Principes de morale. 1 vo 12mo 2 - 12
          etude de l'histoire 1. - - - 2 - 10
          maniere d'ecrire l'histoire 1. 2 - 8
          constitution d'Amerique 1 - - 1 - 16 reliure de
          sur l'histoire de France. 2. v. - 6.   11 vols 4to 8 f5 41 - 1
          principes de la legislation - - 12
          droit de l'Europe 3. v - - - 7 - 10
          ordres des societés - - - - 2 -
          principes des negotiations - - 2 - 10
          entretiens de Phocion - - - 2
          des Romains - - - - - 2 - 10
                                    32 - 16

wanting to complete Mably's works which I have not
not been able to procure
    les principes de legislation
       sur les Grecs
       sur la Pologne   2460

                                    718 - 6

PART OF LIST OF THE TWO TRUNKFULS OF BOOKS BOUGHT IN PARIS BY
JEFFERSON FOR MADISON

Brought over - - - - - - - - - - 716 - 6⁶

Chronologie des empires anciennes de la Combe . 1.v.8ᵛᵒ . — . — — — 5 - 0 - 0

de l'histoire universelle de Hornst . 1.v.8ᵛᵒ . 4f₁₀ 6 - 0 - 0

de l'histoire universelle de Berlié . 1.v.8ᵛᵒ . 2f₁₀ rel.1f₅ 3 - 15

des empereurs Romains par Richon . 2.v.8ᵛᵒ . 8f rel.2f₁₀ 13 - 10

des Juifs . . 1.v.8ᵛᵒ . 3f₁₀. rel.1f₅ 4 - 15

de l'histoire universelle par Du Fresnoy . 2.v.8ᵛᵒ . 13f rel.2f₁₀ 15 - 10

de l'histoire du Nord. par la Combe . 2.v.8ᵛᵒ . 10f. rel.2f₁₀ 12 - 10

de France. par Hénault . - - - 3.v.8ᵛᵒ . 12f rel.3f₁₅ 15 - 15

Memoires de Voltaire. 2.v.in 1. 2f₁₀. rel.15ˢ . - - - - 3 - 5 - 0

Linnaei Philosophia Botanica. 1.v.8ᵛᵒ . 7f rel.1f₅ 8 - 5

Genera plantarum 1.v.8ᵛᵒ 8f rel.1f₅ 9 - 5

Species plantarum. 4.v.8ᵛᵒ 32f rel.6f 37. 0

Systema naturae - 2.v.8ᵛᵒ 26f rel.5f 31 - 0

Clayton Flora Virginica. 4ᵗᵒ 12f rel.2f₁₀ 14 - 10

D'Albon sur l'interet de plusieurs nations. 4.v.12ᵐᵒ 12f. rel.3f 15 - 0

Systeme de la nature de Diderot. 3.v.8ᵛᵒ 25f (prohibited) 21 - 0

Croustin. histoire Romaine. 2.v.in 6.12ᵐᵒ

de Constantinople 8.v.in 10 ⎫

de l'empire de l'Occident 2.v ⎬ 16. vols.12ᵐᵒ 36 - 0 - 0

de l'eglise. 3.v.in 2. ⎭

Droit de la Nature. par Wolff. 6.v.12ᵐᵒ 15f rel.4f₁₀ 19 - 10

Voyage de Papet 8ᵛᵒ. 3.v.in 2 - - - - - 9

Mirabeau. Ami des hommes 5.v.12ᵐᵒ ⎫ - - 12

Theorie de l'imp.t 2.v.in 1.12ᵐᵒ ⎬ - - 8

Buffon. Supplement 11.12. Oiseaux 17.18. Mineraux 1.2.3.4. 24.

Lettres de Pascal. 12ᵐᵒ 2f. rel.15ˢ - - 2 - 15

Le sage à la cour et le roi voiageur (prohibited) - - 10 - 15

Principes de legislation universelle 2.v.8ᵛᵒ 12 - 0

Ordonnances de la Marine par Valin. 2.v.4ᵗᵒ. - 22

Diderot sur les sourds & muets 12ᵐᵒ. 3f₁₂ - sur les aveugles 3f ⎫

sur la nature 3f sur la morale 3f₁₅ - ⎬ 4.v.12ᵐᵒ 13 - 7

Mariana. histor. of Spain 11.v.12ᵗᵒ - - - - - 21 - 0

2 trunks & packing paper - - - - - 43 - 0

1154 - 13

2461

CONTINUATION OF THE LIST OF BOOKS BOUGHT BY JEFFERSON

bition, and the desire to exalt communities, he declared, were the cause of this perversion. "Unhappily then for America, the separate sovereignties of our respective states have left these principles to act with a force but feebly restrained by the weak barrier of a nominal *union*. An undeviating adherence to state interests, state prejudices, state aggrandizement, (or, to comprehend the evil in a term, to state politics) is the sad prognostic of that discord, confusion and never ceasing war, which has been the invariable lot of separate sovereignties and neighboring states."

Owing to a *"partial* view of continental affairs," the requisitions of Congress were ignored, state accounts were unliquidated. The honor of Congress, with that of the nation, hung on the fate of a general revenue plan. There *was* an American army in the *late* war, but it had become unpopular to mention it or the unpaid claims of soldiers. "The eye of him whose hand now writes these lines has often traced their route, on the cold snow, with the blood of their bare feet." At present, "the unavailing complaints of individuals rend the hearts of the honest man, the man of feeling and sentiment—but they touch not the callous multitude." Once let individual states, by paying their soldiers, become possessed of their claims, "the style will be instantly changed. It will be then, 'do us justice, or we will pay ourselves' "—out of the rich commerce, perhaps, of the weak Southern states, "who would necessarily seek the protection of foreign nations. What a prospect does this idea present for America?"

Writing anonymously, Madison was able to reveal his inner sentiments about the Western lands, which he had been forced to defend as Virginia's property even while managing the transfer of them to the nation. In this article published on the very day his state's cession was accepted, he used the phrases of Maryland, so hated in Virginia, to warn against a denial of justice to the landless states: "Will they not with an united voice, and the voice of truth allege, that these lands were wrested from the crown of England, for whose emolument, and not for the benefit of any class of citizens of these United States would they have been sold, but for that revolution which has been effected by their joint expense of blood and treasure." Of the same sort was the choice between commercial duties levied by Congress for the benefit of all, or by individual states to gain advantages over their neighbors. All the refinements of sophistry could not draw a distinction between a national policy on commerce and on Western lands, yet Rhode Island, "enveloped in the mist of state prejudices," opposed the one while contending with heated anxiety for the other.

"North American No. 2" was to unfold the situation of the author's countrymen "in the character they have assumed, as one of the nations of the earth." In Europe, "we have seen in our day the great inland powers dividing the fairest of all regions"—Poland—after discord and anarchy rent asunder the bonds of empire. So would it be with America "if ever civil dissension should loosen that Gordian knot, which binds these states together, and leave them resting on their individual impotence and insignificance." Great Britain's late discrimination against American commerce "sprang confessedly from an early conviction, that we could not act as a nation."[37] Lack of a general legislative power for regulating commerce made it possible thus to sow the seeds of disunion, restrict trade and cut off "a rising Navy of America," the whole policy constituting an "insult on our national character."

Happily in America, said Madison, no one class of citizens can think or act for the people at large. But they, in turn, must be "superior to the machinations of intrigue, and the snares of treachery. Let them then be taught as the first step to political wisdom, to discard a flattering delusion of their unsuspicious minds." They think that all the powers of the world are their friends, when they really but share a common hostility to a common enemy. "Be too wise," he adjured, "to believe that thy vindication of the rights of mankind can be pleasing to despots, on whose government it is a satire—or that the haughty monarchs of Europe are in haste to prostrate their dignity at the feet of untitled citizens, whom education and habit have taught them to contemn."

Not even France, whose ruler had proved himself "the *Friend* of mankind," should be relied on. Too long America had leaned on that supporting arm. Support and protection, protection and dependence, join each other so imperceptibly "that it is hard to say where one begins, or the other ends—therefore to be truly *free,* we must depend *only* on ourselves."

Ahead lay a gloomy and solemn prospect of domestic confusion and foreign war, "but still there is a light, although it glimmers at a distance"—not like a blazing meteor that vanishes in endless night, but fixed as a constellation—the light of liberty. "Liberty! thou emanation from the all-beauteous and celestial mind! To Americans thou hast committed the guardianship of the darling rights of mankind. . . . The band of patriots who are here thy votaries . . . will instill this holy truth into the infant minds of their children, and teach them to hold it sacred, even as the divine aphorisms of religion, that the SAFETY of AMERICA will be found in her UNION."

On this note James Madison concluded his four years in the Continental Congress. He journeyed with Jefferson[38] to Annapolis in the last week of November, and went on from there to his native Virginia and long unseen Montpelier.

CHAPTER XX

CONTINENTALIST IN RICHMOND

LEAVING Annapolis hurriedly to take advantage of fine autumnal weather, Madison ran into such a sequence of rains and floods that he did not reach Montpelier for nine days. A night with George Mason at Gunston Hall provided a good roof and better conversation. After that it was one flooded waterway after another—Occoquan, Quantico, Aquia creeks, the Rappahannock River and its southerly branches—while on the rolling hills between them, sodden November leaves were carried deep into December mud by the wheels of the two-horse chaise. There was a bottom, however, to the ever-reddening clay of the Piedmont, and clouds and rain could not wholly blot out the nearing shoulder of the Southwest Mountains. At last, through bare woods and fallow fields sweeping down to the Rapidan, the great white mansion came in sight. Along the line of Negro cabins a cry was heard and heard again: "Massa Jemmy's come."[1]

Colonel James Madison, Sr., ex-county lieutenant, justice of the peace, vestryman, wartime organizer, leading landowner and most substantial citizen of Orange County, was now sixty years old. Nelly Conway Madison, the "tender and infirm parent" whose solicitude brought Madison home, was fifty-one. Chronically ill with malaria and generally enfeebled, she had but forty-six more years to live. Sharing the management of the huge estate, and owner by gift of 350 acres, was third son Ambrose, lately a captain of Virginia troops. All of Madison's brothers (Francis, Ambrose and William) were married now and lived on the paternal acres with their wives, born Bell, Lee and Throckmorton. Jefferson's departure had interrupted young Willey's plan of studying law in his Charlottesville office. Sister Nelly, bride of Isaac Hite, was still of the Montpelier circle. Sarah was just emerging from her 'teens and little Frances had not yet entered them.[2]

306

The elder Madison, at the close of the war, was rich in lands, rich in slaves (about 120, practically all born on the place) but money-poor. Like many another big plantation owner in the lean war years, he had been forced to borrow heavily while poorer men were in debt to him. The sale of close to 700 acres in five years eased the strain, but his overdue notes were held by kindly Judge Dandridge, whom he silently stalled off, and flinthearted Tobacco Buyer S. Jones, by whom he was not only threatened "but very ungenteelly treated."[3]

News of Madison's arrival started a general saddling of horses in Orange County. His plan to plunge at once into a course of reading gave way, for the time, before a procession of uncles, aunts, cousins and friendly neighbors—the Taylors, the Barbours, the Taylors, the Cowherds, the Taylors, the Burnleys—who wanted all the news about everything in the world and his immediate presence at their own dinner tables. The Madison table, on almost any midday, warranted such an entry as Cousin Francis Taylor made in his diary[4] when he began keeping it immediately after this period:

"Went with G. Taylor to Col. Madison's to dinner. James Coleman of Halifax, Uncle E. Taylor, Hardin Burnley, Mr. Shepherd, Major Lee, A. Madison and William Madison dined there. Mr. Shepherd and Major Lee went home, as did A. and W. Madison, the rest stayed. Miss Jane Taylor was there. Weather good."

Next day:

"We stayed to dinner. Col. Burnley and W. Madison were there. Cloudy morning. Snow. Rain (and hail in evening). My father, Uncle Taylor, C. Taylor and myself came home."

And ten days later: "There was a dance at Col. Madison's this evening."

Every guest who wanted to remain overnight at Montpelier was welcome, and the next night too. If one of them complained to Diarist Taylor (who didn't sleep much himself) that he lay awake all night because sent to bed in winter between cotton sheets, that

was a reflection of the Madisonian standard of civilization or hardi-
hood, not a godspeed signal. However, as the winter of 1783-84
advanced, Madison's fear of social intrusions on his studies was
buried under a severer cold and snowfall than anybody could remember. "On the other hand," he told Jefferson in February, "it
has deprived me entirely of the philosophical books which I had
allotted for incidental reading." He was in truth isolated between two libraries. All his trunks from Philadelphia, containing
Buffon's fifty-six volumes of natural history and other anticipated
pleasures, were snowbound at Fredericksburg. Jefferson offered
him everything at Monticello, but a first call by one of his brothers
found the caretaker gone to Richmond and bad weather prevented
a renewal of the effort. For his main purpose, a study of law, he
had Coke on Littleton "and a few others from the same shelf."
Also, for whatever it might be worth, he had part of the confiscated library of British Governor Dunmore, which he bought just
as he was leaving the executive council in 1779 and had not seen
since.[5]

While waiting for philosophical and historical fare, Madison
relaxed by converting a conversation with Jefferson on the oblate
form of the earth into written calculations ("the difference then of
the semidiameters is 44.9 E. miles, that is 1/87.94 of the mean semi-
diameter") but the earth really took on a new shape when melting
snows brought the scientific and speculative animal lore of Buffon
within his ken. Never content to be merely a reader, he was soon
and for several years making measurements and descriptions of his
own, in order to compare American mammals with their European counterparts in Buffon. Servants brought in an injured woodchuck, a mother opossum with seven young; dead weasels, moles
and other animals. Madison made thirty-three measurements of
the weasel, inside and out, going straight through it from the
length of the ear to the hair at the end of the tail, and listed it all in
a comparative table with Buffon's measurements of the belette and
hermine. It was the careful amateur work of a statesman who
could have been a scientist, but there was more lasting value in the
fact that he called the woodchuck a monax, which was the educated man's word for what the hillbillies called a moonack after
the Delaware Indians told them it was a monachgen.

In the spring of 1784, Madison began keeping records of wind, rain, sunshine and clouds, to which he added temperatures as soon as he was able to secure a thermometer. Lack of one kept him from joining Jefferson and Madison of the College in a threeway comparison of heat and cold at Annapolis, Williamsburg and Orange. Jefferson proposed this to verify his shrewd guess (in a day of nonexistent weather records) that in cities no farther apart than these, altitude was more important than distance north and south.[6]

For the next six years, first at Annapolis and then in Paris, Jefferson acted as Madison's buyer of everything he wanted and Virginia lacked. A neat credit was at hand to begin with. The unsuspecting Jefferson entered Congress under a delusion that he would draw his pay and expenses as the law said he should. He gave Madison an I.O.U. for $333 1/3 at Annapolis, "exclusive of what I had borrowed in Philadelphia," and a few months later had his horses "turned out of the livery stable for want of money." Madison did not want his whole loan repaid at any time, nor any of it at that time, but he did want a pair of good spectacles for his mother. So would Jefferson please ask the reliable Dudley of Philadelphia to send "one of his best pebble and double jointed pair, for the age of fifty-five or thereabouts—with a good case"—an order so well executed that two pairs arrived. Jefferson deposited $333 1/3 to Madison's credit in the Philadelphia bank, leaving the remainder of his debt, about $200, to fulfill a request for "the occasional purchase of rare and valuable books."[7]

In particular, Madison wanted "whatever may throw light on the general constitution and droit public of the several confederacies which have existed. I observe in Boinaud's catalogue several pieces on the Dutch, the German and the Helvetic. The operations of our own must render all such lights of consequence. Books on the Law of N[ature] and N[ations] fall within a similar remark." He approved Jefferson's proposed purchase for him of a set of Bynkershoek, adding, "Is not Wolfius also worth having?" This was like saying: "While posting myself on freedom of the seas and of commerce, shall I not also find meat in the exaltation of philosophic reason over kingly law?"

From all this it is plain that while Madison was studying the private law of the lawyer (Co: Litt:) his thoughts were on the affairs of government. He wanted to study confederacies throughout the world and through all time. This is enough to explode the belittling implications of a statement made three years later by Stephen Higginson to Henry Knox:

"As early as '83, while I was at Congress, I pressed upon Mr. Madison and others the idea of a special convention, for the purpose of revising the confederation, and increasing the powers of the Union; the obtaining of which we all agreed to be essential to our national dignity and happiness. But they were as much opposed to this idea as I was to the measures they were then pursuing."[8]

Of course Madison was opposed to it in 1783, when its only effect would be to kill the five-per-cent impost, which he was supporting and Higginson was fighting. But he did more than look ahead to it with favor when the time should be ripe. He began to prepare, through years of careful study, for his own major role in the work of such a convention.

As affairs stood when Madison left Congress, the first national task lay in the several states, and he took up his part of the work as soon as the Potomac River lay behind him. His stop with George Mason was a planned one. "I found him much less opposed to the general impost than I had expected," he wrote back to Jefferson. The gouty Mason seemed "sound and ripe" for a revisal of the Virginia Constitution (his own baby, which Jefferson and Madison both thought a brat), and was not averse to the territorial cession. "His heterodoxy lay chiefly in being too little impressed with either the necessity or the proper means of preserving the confederacy." This mild federal swing was quickly reflected in the state legislature, which approved both the federal impost and the land cession before the year was out. It was needless for Madison to go to Richmond to lend his influence in their behalf, as he had been thinking of doing.[9]

Another problem, however, was looming up—the evil effect of Virginia's dependence upon Philadelphia and Baltimore importers. The commercial situation, he told Jefferson, was even more deplorable than he had conceived. A comparison of prices with those in Europe indicated that Virginia paid a tribute of thirty or forty per cent to the importing merchants and their governments, "a tribute which if paid into the treasury of the state would yield a surplus above all its wants." Regulations were needed to build up Virginia ports of entry, but that raised a puzzling question.

Maryland's boundary was the *southern shore* of the Potomac, in which Virginia retained only the right of "free navigation and use." Might not that language, Madison asked, be construed as a total relinquishment of jurisdiction, fatal to port regulations? He had been told, while traveling along the Potomac, of flagrant evasions of Virginia law, "practiced with impunity and success, by foreign vessels which had loaded at Alexandria." How should the boundary error be repaired? By extending Virginia's law upon the river? Or by appointing commissioners from both states to negotiate a harmonious settlement? "The last mode squares best with my present ideas," he concluded, and suggested that Jefferson, taking advantage of Maryland's good humor over the Western land cession, bring up the subject at Annapolis. Jefferson promptly arranged for joint sponsorship of the scheme by himself and Delegate Thomas Stone, with nothing said about Madison's prior proposal lest Maryland react unfavorably to a proposition of Virginian origin.[10]

With projects like this in his mind, and with melting snows letting in a stream of visitors, Madison was in no shape to resist their demand that he go back to his old place in the Virginia legislature. That would be "most noxious to my project" of reading in the law, he remarked to Randolph, though it would have the advantage of bringing him into contact with a living legal oracle—the attorney general himself.

This oracle had just asked Madison's opinion of the right of the governor of South Carolina to demand the extradition of one George Hancock, who fled to his home in Virginia after hospitalizing Jonas Beard, "a valuable good man" (as Madison described him) and member of the South Carolina legislature. Randolph thought everything depended on whether it was in reality a "high

misdemeanor" (the term used in the extradition clause of the
Articles of Confederation) to beat up a legislator with fists and a
switch. Or was it just an ordinary misdemeanor (as it would have
been, no doubt, if the "valuable good man" had beaten up the
roughneck)? Madison put it on a different basis. "The respect
due to the chief magistracy of a confederate state, enforced as it is
by the Articles of Union, requires an admission of the fact as it has
been represented." If the governor of South Carolina said it was a
high misdemeanor, it was. Beyond this, however, Madison believed there were reasons in the American system of government
why practically all extradition requests should be granted, even for
less serious offenses.

"By the express terms of the Union," he observed to Randolph,
"the citizens of every state are naturalized within all the others,
and being entitled to the same privileges, may with the more
justice be subjected to the same penalties. This circumstance materially distinguishes the citizens of the United States from the
subjects of other nations not so incorporated." The bond was tightened, in his opinion, by similarity of state laws and the universal
requirement of trial by jury, also by the common interest of the
states in preventing a criminal from escaping all punishment by a
few hours' travel. "In a word," Madison concluded, "experience
will show if I mistake not that the relative situation of the U. S.
calls for a 'droit public' much more minute than that comprised in
the federal articles, and which presupposes much greater mutual
confidence and amity among the societies which are to obey it,
than the law which has grown out of the transactions and intercourse of jealous and hostile nations."[11]

In this analysis, Madison knocked down in advance the superfi-
cial analogies of twentieth-century writers who try to interpret the
doings of the thirteen states, before 1789, in terms of international
action by separately independent nations.[12] Extradition took its
rise in international law and still carries the flavor of it into the
mutual relations of the states of the Union. Yet Madison saw this
obligation, in 1784, as something modified, strengthened, and set
into contrast with the relations among foreign nations, by the
fact of a common American citizenship. This established a closer

bond than was to be found even in the written requirements of the act of national union.

No free drinks of whisky were needed to induce Orange County freeholders to send Madison to Richmond this year. He was elected along with Charles Porter, whose gurgling demijohns had defeated him in 1777. In fresh-leaved late April, along a road bright with dogwood and redbud and loud with mockingbirds, Brother William drove him to the capital in a two-wheeled chaise.[13] The assembly, dilatory as usual, failed to produce a quorum until May 12. This gave Madison time to look after the sale of his father's tobacco, and enabled him, by holding back for a time, to get forty shillings a hundred instead of thirty-eight. He also received and sent his father, along with the tobacco money, a draft for £200 on Captain S. Jones, which was to be credited to "Mr. Anderson's" bond to the senior Madison and to the senior Madison's bond to Captain Jones. Very simple, except that Madison's letter crossed one from his father saying that the county tax collector, wanting a quick and safe way of forwarding £144 to the state treasury, had given it to Madison, Sr., who had sent it to S. Jones at Fredericksburg, as a payment on that same debt. Wherefore Madison, Jr., was asked to take £170 out of the tobacco money (by this time en route to Montpelier) and turn it over to the treasurer, the extra £26 being what Madison, Sr., still owed on his own taxes. Whoever lost, S. Jones didn't.[14]

As others saw it, Madison had a strong strategic position in the new assembly. Chronically split in two by the great rivals, Patrick Henry and Richard Henry Lee, it had divided three ways in 1783. Speaker John Tyler's third faction was "but a temporary bubble" in Randolph's opinion, but now, in 1784, many new members had come in, including "some children of the Revolution," who disdained the old factions but needed a strategist if they were to make headway. "This renders it probable," the attorney general wrote to Jefferson in mid-May, "that our friend of Orange will step earlier into the heat of battle, than his modesty would otherwise permit. For he is already resorted to, as a general of whom much has been preconceived to his advantage."[15]

Madison himself was trying to probe the purposes of the still

absent Henry. From Philip Mazzei, who visited both Red Hill
and Montpelier in April, he heard that the Voice was very friendly
toward the Confederacy, cautiously favorable to amendment of the
state constitution, inclined toward the payment of British debts and
possessed of a scheme for a general assessment for the support of
religion. Only the last was natural to him. Talking with Henry
immediately after his arrival in Richmond, Madison found him
"strenuous for invigorating the federal government though without any precise plan," but he could get "no explanations from him
as to our internal government. The general train of his thoughts
seemed to suggest favorable expectations." The real trouble, probably, was that Richard Henry Lee had not arrived, and Patrick
could not run the risk of inadvertently getting on the same side
with him.[16]

Richmond at the opening of a legislative session awoke suddenly
to tumultuous gaiety and disorder. The German traveler Schoepf
saw it in this same year of 1784, during the earlier winter session.
"One could almost fancy it was an Arabian village," he wrote, "the
whole day long, saddled horses at every turn, and a swarming of
riders in the few and muddy streets, for a horse must be mounted
if only to fetch a prise of snuff from across the way." At the open
door of the small assembly house "stands a doorkeeper, who is
almost incessantly and with a loud voice calling out for one member after another. In the ante-room there is a tumult quite as constant; here they amuse themselves zealously with talk of horse
races, runaway negroes, yesterday's play, politics, or it may be, with
trafficking."

Madison was familiar with scenes like this from his membership
in the convention of 1776 and the governor's council, but, unlike
the early days in Williamsburg, he had no cousin's house to offer
a shelter from the nightly turmoil. At the tavern kept by the
Neapolitan Mr. Formicola, two enormous rooms on each of two
floors threw everybody together for eating, drinking and sleeping.
"Every evening," reported Schoepf, "our inn was full. Generals,
colonels, captains, senators, assemblymen, judges, doctors, clerks
and crowds of gentlemen, of every weight and caliber and every
hue of dress, sat all together about the fire, drinking, smoking,

singing, and talking ribaldry. . . . The indelicate custom of having so many beds together in one room is the more surprising since elsewhere in America there is much store set by decorum and neatness."[17]

In the organization of the House of Delegates, Madison obtained the chairmanship of the Committee on Commerce. He was a member also of the committees on Religion, Privileges and Elections, Propositions and Grievances, and Justice. These were vast, unwieldy bodies, swollen by the good democratic principle that everybody from tidewater to Kentucky, no matter how incompetent, should be able to reel off a string of committee assignments to his goggle-eyed constituents.[18]

From the vantage point of his chairmanship, Madison launched his campaign to build up one or two great seaports to rival Baltimore and Philadelphia. He first planned to make Norfolk the only port of entry and clearance. This concentration, he told his fellows, would give the state adequate import and export facilities, check smuggling and develop commercial and financial houses strong enough for the needs of commerce. Also, by keeping British ship captains and supercargoes out of little ports and riverside warehouses, it would prevent the recurrence of the old "Scotch monopoly" based on initial favors to planters culminating in an inescapable burden of debt. It was one thing to plan a system like this, something else to put it over in the face of local rivalries, jealousies and hidden oversea ties. The bill went through, but not till the one great seaport had become squalling quintuplets.

"We made a warm struggle for the establishment of Norfolk and Alexandria [that addition was to win the North] as our only ports," Madison reported to Jefferson, "but were obliged to add York, Tappahannock and Bermuda Hundred, in order to gain anything." Secret advocates of British monopoly joined with merchants attached to the *status quo* and with planters who wanted ships at their own wharves. All these, he said, "are busy in decoying the people into a belief that trade ought in all cases to be left to regulate itself," and that its concentration in one place would mean higher prices. So intense was the opposition, and so plausible the unsound argument, that he feared the bill would be rescinded before it took effect. If not, it would be because of the undeniable fact that goods were much dearer in Virginia than in states where trade was drawn to a central mart, and that scarce a vessel from Continental Europe ever came into Virginia waters. They even went to other states when in quest of the Virginia staple, tobacco.[19]

Madison's chief purpose in entering the legislature, he said afterward, was to promote "new grants of power to Congress" in order to bring about "a rescue of the Union and the blessings of liberty staked on it from an impending catastrophe." Here the question was a simple one: would Patrick Henry help or hinder? At first all went smoothly. On Madison's motion, the legislature approved his amendment to the Articles of Confederation, to base financial quotas on population instead of land valuation. It declared for faithful compliance with federal requisitions. It instructed Virginia's delegates in Congress to speed up a settlement of federal-state accounts and declared that balances due to the United States ought to be forcibly collected by "distress on the property of the defaulting states or of their citizens." Here was close teamwork between Madison and Henry, for this followed Madison's 1781 doctrine of coercion, but Henry was taunted with its authorship after he started declaiming against the Constitution of 1787. "I am sure that the gentleman recognizes his own child," George Nicholas said to him in the ratifying convention, and Henry made no reply. He could have replied, probably, that he merely introduced what Madison wrote, also that he expected the coercion to be applied against other states for Virginia's benefit. For did not everybody know that Virginia had paid more than its share of the cost of the Revolution?[20]

For a state which believed that a million dollars was owing to it, Virginia had a strange reluctance to get down to figures. Ordered by the legislature to inquire into the progress toward a settlement, Madison reported that a federal commissioner had been in Richmond for eight months, prepared to receive both the debits and demands of the state and its citizens, but neither had been presented to him. On his motion, the state's solicitor was instructed to get into action. Likewise on his initiative, a commissioner was appointed to represent Virginia in securing reimbursement of the cost of conquering the Northwest Territory, as provided for in the state's land cession to the United States. With no more difficulty, he put through a resolution to grant Congress power, for fifteen years, to retaliate in kind against Great Britain's exclusion of American vessels from the West Indies.[21]

As long as they cost Virginia nothing, Madison's federal policies slipped through like oysters in a funnel. The instant they began to hit the state's pocketbook, they were snagged. When that happened, ease and Patrick Henry's aid vanished together. Two readings were secured of a declaration that the state should pay, in 1784, three quarters of what it owed Congress for 1781. Madison was named to a committee of five to recommend revenues for making up deficits and paying unfunded debts. Then Patrick Henry rose up and moved to postpone the 1784 collection of taxes until the next year.

This motion, besides jeopardizing the state's solvency, made a joke of the Henry-backed pledge to fulfill federal obligations. It was made in a year when, according to Madison, the high price of tobacco "brought more specie into the country than it ever before contained at one time." He and Speaker Tyler joined Richard Henry Lee in fighting the moratorium. They won by thirty votes in committee of the whole. In the final debate in the House, Patrick Henry turned loose all the power of his oratory. Who could resist when the most persuasive voice in America told simple legislators that they—the people—could not afford to pay taxes? Henry reversed the verdict with a like majority for the moratorium. "We shall make a strange figure," Madison wrote to his father, "after our declarations with regard to Congress and the Continental debt, if we wholly omit the means of fulfilling them."[22]

Beyond the serious effect of this blow to the federal Treasury was the deadly influence of the example upon other states. A year before, Madison had reported how Virginia's repeal of the impost "very much emboldened" the backward states. With little time left, and working against odds, he managed now to shorten the suspension of the land tax from January to October, and secured its allocation to Congress. Also passed was a measure which Randolph, naming Madison as its author, called "a stamp act under a less offensive name." It levied duties on law proceedings, deeds, probates, etc., to the extent of £15,000 or £20,000.[23]

Madison's disgust at the refusal to collect taxes was matched by his opinion of the way money was handled. "Nothing can exceed the confusion which reigns throughout our revenue department," he asserted to Jefferson. "We attempted but in vain to ascertain the amount of our debts, and of our resources, as a basis for something like a system. . . . This confusion indeed runs through all our public affairs, and must continue as long as the present mode of legislating continues."

No waster of money, Madison was disgusted with the assembly's penuriousness. Taking up the neglected three-year work of Jefferson, George Wythe and Edmund Pendleton—their great revision and codification of the laws of Virginia—he was able to secure an appropriation of £500 apiece for the unpaid revisers and an order that the revisal, rotting in pigeonholes, should be printed for public study. "A frivolous economy restrained the number of copies to five hundred," he reported to Jefferson. As for the salary warrants, they were worthless, being issued against "unappropriated money" in a treasury which contained none. The assembly, he averred, would not even employ accurate penmen for extending resolutions into bills, whose faulty drawing "must soon bring our laws and our legislature into contempt."[24]

The basic remedy was a revised constitution. Devoted as he was to this, Madison was determined to silence by "the adverse temper of the house and particularly of Mr. Henry." But Richard Henry Lee arriving with favorable sentiments, "we thought it not amiss to stir the matter." Unluckily Lee became ill the day before the motion came up and Henry "showed a more violent opposition than we expected." The result was not merely a defeat but a declaration that the assembly had no power to call a convention until directed to do so by "a majority of all the free people." To make this the more ridiculous, it followed a speech in which Madison pointed out that the Constitution of 1776 was drafted without authorization by the people and was never ratified.[25]

All that was needed, now, was for Madison and Patrick Henry to clash on the British debt clause of the peace treaty. They did.

With Madison, John Marshall and other young men demanding observance of the treaty and Speaker Tyler opposing it, Henry looked for a means of seizing leadership. Just as a compliance motion was about to be offered, the orator secured his own appointment to investigate British infractions of the treaty. The inquiry was a quick one. Henry merely asked Delegate Walke of Princess Anne County about the trip he made to New York, seeking a return of his slaves from General Carleton. Walke himself agreed with Madison that one treaty violation did not justify another. But the story he told of a positive rejection, and of the shipment of 300 Negroes to Nova Scotia and freedom, gave reluctant debtors a firm feeling that they should not pay what they owed to Glasgow merchants. Henry, Tyler and their aids thereupon bowed to the federal constitution before kicking it. The power of making treaties with foreign nations was "wisely vested in Congress," their motion read, and the assembly had no inclination to interfere with it, but the repeal of laws interfering with collection of British debts must wait until Congress should act on a remonstrance against Britain's violation of the slave clause.

In place of this, Madison asked for adoption of his own report asserting "the duty and determination of this Commonwealth, with a becoming reverence for the faith of treaties," to give effect to the article on debts, duly ratified and proclaimed by Congress. To chip away the opposition, he proposed that the debts be paid in four installments and that Congress be asked to take peremptory measures to secure the return of "sundry negroes the property of citizens." (Even in his home state, he would not use the word "slave.") Twice Madison sought to substitute his wording for Henry's. Twice he was voted under, thirty-three to fifty and worse, after which the antitreaty resolution was passed without a roll call.[26]

On one other proposition Madison and Patrick Henry stood together. Washington wrote to both of them proposing that Virginia follow the example of New York and present a farm to the author of Common Sense. "Can nothing be done in our assembly for poor Paine?" he inquired of Madison. "Must the merits and services of 'Common Sense' continue to glide down the stream of

time, unrewarded by this country? . . . He is poor! he is cha-
grined! and almost if not altogether in despair of relief. . . . A decent independency is I believe all he aims at. Should he not obtain
it? If you think so I am sure you will not only move the matter,
but give it your support."[27]

Madison reported the result to Washington. A bill was offered,
giving Paine one-half of the "Secretary's land," a public tract of
500 acres on the Eastern Shore. The cordial reception of this bill
caused the amount to be doubled. The revised bill sailed through
two readings, then was suddenly thrown out "on considerations of
economy and suggestions unfavorable to Mr. Paine." Next it was
proposed that the land be sold and £2,000 allotted to Paine. "This
was lost by a single vote." Madison's recital conceals not only his
own share in this, but his superior judgment. The original bill,
drafted by Henry, gave Paine the whole tract. Madison cut this,
before introduction, to one-half. Henry's overconfident restoration
of the full acreage opened the way to defeat. Madison wrote the
second bill, but the poison had sunk too deep. And what was the
poison? Madison gave its formula in a footnote. The reversal was
"produced by prejudice against Mr. Paine thrown into circulation
by Mr. Arthur Lee." Here was gratitude indeed! Thomas Paine
was thrown out of public office and reduced to poverty because of
a letter he had written in 1779 supporting Arthur Lee in his controversy with Silas Deane. But the author of *Common Sense* and
The Crisis, the prophet of American independence, also had written *Public Good,* opposing Virginia's title to the Western territories. Thumbs down on such a fellow![28]

The Virginia Assembly was more willing to thank Washington
for his services to the Revolution than to reward Paine. A committee for this purpose, including Madison, combed the dictionaries
for three weeks to find adequate words. The committee of the
whole then tried its hand, and finally a joint committee of House
and Senate. The following and a few unimportant connectives
were finally put together: congratulating, felicities, affection, gratitude, patriotic, felicities (again), powerful, admiration, wisdom,
councils, arduous, firmness, dignity, trials, fortune, moderation,
equanimity, triumph, exemplary, respect, exalted, fame, country,
grateful, affectionate, fervently, rewarded, blessing, happiness.

Stone being more enduring than nouns and adjectives, the assembly decided also to procure a statue of General Washington— a statue to "be made of the finest marble and best workmanship with the following inscription on its pedestal, viz." This final requirement made it compulsory, under the law, that the famous Houdon statue of Washington, when it became a reality a few years later, should bear the following tribute from the pen of Madison:

"The general assembly of the commonwealth of Virginia have caused this statue to be erected as a monument of affection and gratitude to George Washington, who, uniting to the endowments of the hero the virtues of the patriot and exerting both in establishing the liberties of his country, has rendered his name dear to his fellow-citizens and given to the world an immortal example of true glory: done in the   year of Christ and in the   year of the commonwealth."[29]

Houdon did not like this inscription. It was too long for the available space. He probably told Madison so, without knowing of his authorship, for they were together at Mt. Vernon in the fall of 1785. Returning to France, the sculptor complained to Jefferson. The latter relayed the protest to Madison along with a proposed substitute, the best of several suggested in Paris. This one he said might be translated as follows: "Behold, Reader, the form of George Washington. For his worth, ask History; that will tell it, when this stone shall have yielded to the decays of time. His country erects this monument: Houdon makes it."[30]

Madison's idolator, Rives, was mystified by Jefferson's preference for this "singularly jejune and pompous" composition with its bathetic, almost ludicrous ending. How could he place it above a masterpiece which was "worthy to go down, with the spotless marble and the shining fame of its immortal subject, to the latest generations of mankind?" The preference was no mystery to Madison. He knew well enough that the proposed substitute was of Jefferson's own authorship. "His country erects," as a substitute for credit to the General Assembly, was straight Virginia-ese. It came from no Frenchman, but from a man to whom state and nation were both "my country." Careful not to wound his friend,

Madison replied with characteristic self-depreciation: "The inscription for the statue is liable to Houdon's criticism, and is in every respect inferior to the substitute which you have copied into your letter. I am apprehensive notwithstanding that no change can be effected. The assembly will want some proper ground for resuming the matter." Good or bad, Madison's wording was required by law. Of the two inscriptions, neither one is so good or so bad as extremist critics thought it. The flamboyancy of Jefferson's wording would disappear in Latin. "Fecit Houdon" has no bathos in it. Madison's inscription is robbed of grace by its one-sentence form, but the separate clauses have simplicity and nobility. They are from the heart.[31]

Just as the Virginia Assembly was approaching its July 1 adjournment, two subjects came up which cast long shadows into the future. One was Madison's project of joint control of the Potomac River by Virginia and Maryland. On his motion, the legislature appointed commissioners to meet with those of the northerly neighbor and "frame such liberal and equitable regulations concerning the said river as may be mutually advantageous to the two states." Four names filled the blank which he left for them: George Mason, Edmund Randolph, James Madison, Jr., Alexander Henderson.[32]

The other shadow, a dark and ominous one as Madison saw it, spread over Virginia from clouds silhouetted with Patrick Henry's profile. These were bills backed by the Protestant Episcopal church, seeking to restore, by indirection, the links between state and church which Madison pried open in the 1776 Bill of Rights and Jefferson severed with the abolition of the tithe system. One sought to levy a general tax assessment for the support of religion, the other to incorporate the Protestant Episcopal clergy. The assessment scheme was launched through petitions from various county groups, setting forth "the present neglected state of religion and morality," the usefulness of taxes "to restore and propagate the holy Christian religion," etc. Patrick Henry gave it private support, but wasn't sure enough of a following to be willing to lead. "The friends of the measure," Madison was able to report, "did not choose to try their strength in the house."[33]

The purpose of Episcopalian incorporation, as the church stated it, was to put an end to state regulation of its spiritual concerns and relieve it of various handicaps in existing laws. The purpose as Madison detected it was to give Episcopal clergymen life tenure by making it impossible for the lay vestries to remove them. It was not an incorporation of the church, but of the clergy. In fighting it, Madison had powerful support from the Reverend John B. Smith, a Witherspoon disciple and Presbyterian head of Hampden-Sidney College. Rallying dissenters, Smith wrote him that the exclusion of the laity was "an indefensible remain of the Star-Chamber tyranny," while the granting of authority to regulate spiritual concerns was "an express attempt to draw the state into an illicit connection and commerce with them." The measure did not pass, but it was not defeated. "Extraordinary as such a project was," wrote Madison to the absent and much-needed Jefferson, "it was preserved from a dishonorable death by the talents of Mr. Henry. It lies over for another session."[34]

CHAPTER XXI

Mohawk Interlude

AT HOME in Montpelier in the summer of 1784, Madison considered his future. He was devoting his time to study, but the ninety-mile arc of the Blue Ridge, visible from his father's house, carried his thoughts away from the plantation. Jefferson wanted him to buy a little tract of land near Monticello, as James Monroe and William Short were doing. "What would I not give [if] you could fall into the circle," he urged. "With such a society I could once more venture home and lay myself up for the residue of life, quitting all its contentions which grow daily more and more insupportable." Jefferson even had a place picked out—140 acres of old but good land, "with a small indifferent house on it," no more than two miles from his own, where one might conduct "a farm of experiment and support a little table and household."

Madison was pleased with the "affectionate invitation" and knew not how to answer. "I cannot altogether renounce the prospect," he replied. "Still less can I as yet embrace it. . . . A few years more may prepare me for giving such a destiny to my future life." What did that mean? Escape, obviously, from the binding ties of a great plantation. Yet those ties were about to be tightened. In August, Madison's father made a gift to him of 560 Montpelier acres. It was as a farmer in his own right, now, that he studied the ravages of an insect, later identified by him as the chinch bug, which made the wheat crop scanty and was attacking the corn. Tobacco, he thought, should be grown intensively as long as the price kept up, but with an expectation that the market would be lost in a few years because of "the richness of soil and fitness of climate on the western waters."[1]

This landlordism had no confining effect. On the contrary, coming into some ready cash by a land sale to Jonathan Cowherd, Madison was to be found a fortnight later writing to Jefferson from the familiar quarters of Mrs. House in Philadelphia: "Some business, the need of exercise after a very sedentary period, and the view of extending my ramble into the eastern states which I have long had a curiosity to see, have brought me to this place."

The letter was addressed to Jefferson in Paris, where he was soon to succeed Franklin as American minister. The House-Trist circle was a broken one when Madison wrote thus on September 7. Mrs. Trist had set off in the previous spring on a lonely journey down the Ohio and Mississippi, to join her husband in Louisiana. Late in May, Madison received a letter from her written at Fort Pitt, just as she was about to enter the "very snug cabin" fitted up for her on a flatboat. With it came one from her brother Samuel House, telling of an event unknown to her. At the end of her journey she would find her husband dead. Madison resumed the tale to Jefferson in September:

"We hear nothing of Mrs. Trist since her arrival at the falls of Ohio, on her way to New Orleans. There is no doubt that she proceeded down the river thence, unapprized of her loss. When and how she will be able to get back, since the Spaniards have shut all their ports against the United States, is uncertain and gives much anxiety to her friends." Shortly after this he was able to report that Mrs. House had "received a letter from poor Mrs. Trist, every syllable of which is the language of affliction itself. She had arrived safe at the habitation of her deceased husband, but will not be able to leave that country till the spring at the nearest. The only happiness she says she is capable of there is to receive proofs that her friends have not forgotten her." Two letters which Madison wrote to her from Philadelphia were the first ones, except from her family, that she received on the "Acadian Coast." Telling Jefferson about them, she said that she "experienced joy in the extreme" at this evidence that she was wrong in thinking her friends no longer remembered her.[2]

Madison's decision to extend his trip to the northward was due to a chance encounter with the Marquis de Lafayette in Baltimore. The young Frenchman, revisiting America, had just spent ten days with George Washington. Now he and his aide, the Chevalier de Caraman, were on their way to Fort Stanwix, at what is now

Rome, New York, to attend a treaty with the Six Nations. As they pushed their horses toward Philadelphia, Lafayette urged Madison to make the trip with them, but the latter left the decision to be made in New York. The ride from Baltimore was a gala affair. "Wherever he passes," Madison said of the marquis, "he receives the most flattering tokens of sincere affection from all ranks." Between the huzzaing and handshaking, Madison found time for more serious matters which he reported in cipher to Jefferson:

"The relation in which the Marquis stands to France and Amerca has induced me to enter into a free conversation with him on the subject of the Mississippi. I have endeavored emphatically to impress on him that the ideas of America and of Spain irreconcilably clash; that unless the mediation of France be effectually exerted, an actual rupture is near at hand."

In that event, the American enemies of France would have a weapon with which to forge an Anglo-American front against both France and Spain. America, he told the young Frenchman, "cannot possibly be diverted from her object, and therefore France is bound to set every engine at work to divert Spain from hers," the more so because of a French interest in American trade through the Mississippi. "He admitted the force of everything I said; told me he would write . . . to the Count de Vergennes . . . and let me see his letter at New York before he sends it."[3]

A moment later, as Madison continued to write, Lafayette stepped into his room, saw the cipher spread out, and was able to infer, Madison thought, "that the Mississippi is most in my thoughts." He would have thought so indeed had he seen another letter which Madison wrote to Jefferson at Montpelier and brought with him thus far on its way to Paris. In it, on the legal side, he upheld the right of all inland nations to have access to the sea—the United States through the Mississippi, European nations through the Rhine, the Maas, the Scheldt, the Elbe, the Oder, the Dardanelles. In it too one finds the first expression of a principle which was to guide Madison in the work of framing an American constitution.

The permanent security of Spain, he asserted, lay not in trying to hold back an irresistible tide of Western settlement, or to close the Mississippi against the overwhelming pressure of commerce. Republics "have like passions with other governments," and the United States would soon have power in addition to passion. Spain, therefore, must look for security "in the complexity of our federal government and the diversity of interests among the members of it." Extended to domestic affairs, where it was counted on to protect property rights and the freedom of minorities, Madison made that the justification for republican federal government, on a democratic basis, over a continental area.

Lafayette fulfilled the promise to write to Vergennes, and showed Madison the letter. Five months later, Madison was alarmed to receive a long-delayed letter from the marquis, written on the eve of his embarkation for France, which showed that he had been unsettled by Washington's fear that immediate opening of the Mississippi would block the development of waterways through the Appalachian Divide. "I fancy it has not changed your opinion but beg you will write me on the subject," Lafayette requested. Madison did so, rejecting the "very narrow and very delusive foundations" of the belief in a conflict of interest between seaboard and interior. Upon navigation of the Mississippi, he asserted, "depends essentially the value of that vast field of territory which is to be sold for the benefit of the common treasury," and by its settlement, reduce the burden of war debt upon the older states. The people who do the settling will be "bone of our bones and flesh of our flesh." What is sought for them is a right which Nature has given "as she gave to the United States their independence. . . . If the United States were to become parties to the occlusion of the Mississippi they would be guilty of treason against the very laws under which they obtained and hold their national existence."[4]

There was little need to argue thus to Lafayette, who at that very time was pressing for a transfer of New Orleans to the United States.[5] However, the intensity of Madison's feeling made it plain that he was steeled against all contrary influences. That fact put him in an ideal position to fight for ratification of the Constitution of 1787, against the insinuation of Patrick Henry that the new government would surrender the Mississippi to Spain. Had Madison wavered on that subject, had his record been equivocal, there can be little doubt that Virginia would have rejected the Constitution, with an ensuing likelihood that the United States would have been split into two nations.

Madison's northward trip with Lafayette was entirely too enjoyable to be cut off at New York. In that city the marquis received "a continuation of those marks of cordial esteem" which his companion had noted before, and with them a welcome manifestation of continuing American affection for France. It was a gayer scene than in Philadelphia, especially among the feminine admirers of martial prowess and a French title. No modest Quaker girls here, demurely tapering from base to crown, but young ladies of fashion with "tremendous crap'd heads [of] two feet diameter and bell hoop tail of four"; inferior, however, to their Philadelphia sisters in beauty, comeliness, gait, complexion and physiognomy, and so alike in appearance "that it is impossible to determine rank or fortune." So, at any rate, they were described at this time by an American soldier (ever the world's best judge of pulchritude) who was likewise on his way to the Indian treaty.[6]

Madison's record of the journey to Albany is found in one meager sentence of a September 15 letter to Jefferson: "We shall set off this afternoon in a barge up the North River." Lafayette did a little better. Detained six days by adverse winds, he recorded, they did not reach Albany until the twenty-third.[7] What was it like, beating up the Hudson River in a sailing barge against the wind? One need not speculate on it. The young soldier, Griffith Evans, so attentive to billowing skirts in New York, had a weather eye likewise on clouds and water, and his boat trailed Madison's by only a few miles clear to Albany. After catching the turn of the tide at four o'clock that Wednesday afternoon, they sailed far into the night, past "beautiful seats near town," past ruined Forts Washington and Lee, past the craggy eminence of Stony Point with its leveled fortifications. Forty-six miles were covered by Evans' boat, a little more by Madison's, before the ebbing of the tide brought them to anchor. Next day, becalmed, the boats floated ten miles on the rising tide, as far as West Point, on a narrow river winding between green bluffs.

Then the weather changed. Rain and contrary winds held them virtually motionless all day. Below them a sloop capsized and lost its cargo. The eighteenth was "a dreadful morning, a heavy storm of rain and wind, a furious sea"; in the afternoon, calm; at midnight a hurricane. Sunday was beautiful, but wind and tide held them at anchor. After that, a boisterous day, sudden and violent flaws of wind; above Newburgh, a smart and fair breeze, then a high wind, a calm, another hurricane; another calm, a fog, and finally a fair wind and the dangerous sand bars of Albany.

That was the way Madison traveled up the Hudson, saying nothing about it, and, to judge from a later comment, probably seasick. At Albany his party was overtaken by François de Marbois, French chargé d'affaires. Having started from Philadelphia on his wedding trip with the former Elizabeth Moore, daughter of a recent president of Pennsylvania, he had left his bride of three months at New York, loaded his honeymoon phaeton and horses onto a swift sloop, and sailed to Albany in three days. Marbois accepted an invitation to travel with Madison and Lafayette and sent a long and vivid account of their trip to his former fiancée in France. (She, it may be added, soon mended a broken heart by a secret marriage to the Chevalier de la Luzerne, and broke his by her death a few months after the announcement of it.)[8]

The four travelers set out by carriage and on horseback, with their servants, and stopped on Sunday at the Shaker village of Niskayuna. Melancholy music came from the wooden hall in which a hundred worshipers were gathered, the men on one side, the women on the other. A speaker declaimed against marriage, citing the example of a Saviour who "never had any carnal connection with a woman," and made use, in his discourse, "of expressions which even the least chaste writer" would avoid repeating. Shakers were having convulsions and continued to have them while talking with the visitors, the men in ecstacy and pain, the women pale and weeping, yet all able to engage in serious and rational conversation. Lafayette, intensely interested in Mesmer's new art of animal magnetism, proceeded to try it out on a Shaker.

He "hypnotized him with all his force" and called for his life history. This was promptly given, but the facts of it convey no suggestion of having been dragged from subliminal depths.

As the travelers moved up the once-rich Mohawk Valley, burned villages, ruined farmhouses and unplanted fields testified to the ruthless raids of Indians, Tories and British. Now new settlers were pouring in (mostly Hollanders) with ten or twelve children in a single bed. Butter was plentiful, and if milk was asked for it was brought in huge wooden pails. The four men made a division of duties. Madison directed the march, which lasted four days. Lafayette took charge of the horses. Caraman looked after the lodging and Marbois supervised the cooking. His soup, he modestly confessed, was so marvelous that they often found themselves feeding their hosts instead of being fed. With them they carried a great bag of cornmeal, tea and chocolate, to ward off any threat of hunger when they should come to the red man's country.

Higher up the river, Indians became more and more numerous. Scattered farmhouses were surrounded by stockades. The forest became heavier, the road worse and worse. The clumsy phaeton was abandoned at German Flats, fifty miles from Fort Stanwix. They camped in the forest now. Madison, Caraman and Marbois rolled up in cloaks and rugs against the sharp September frosts. Lafayette, immune to cold, wore no wrap except a marvelous gummed taffeta raincoat which he had just received from France. Marvelous indeed, for it had been sent wrapped in newspapers, which stuck to the gum, and he had no time to clean it. So, depending on the angle at which they approached him, his friends could read the *Journal de Paris,* the *Courier de l'Europe* or some other gazette cemented to the taffeta.

Indians prowled around their camp. They came in: Indians with meat and chickens; Indian boys eager to build fires, to act as living candlesticks or fire screens, to turn the spitted meat. But woe to the lad who came second to a spit and reversed the rotation. He got a good thumping and hair pulling for such ignorance, since everybody knew, or at least the first boy did, that if the spit was turned backward the chicken would be unroasted.

On the last night out, nine miles from Stanwix, they reached the home of Judge White, who gave his name to Whitestown and Whitesboro.[9] They marked the wonderful soil—rich loam twelve feet deep, as shown by the channels cut by creeks in freshets. Here, Madison thought, was one of the coming centers of prosperous American agriculture.

At last they were at the fort—old Fort Stanwix, officially re-named Fort Schuyler in 1776, but still known by the title made famous through Indian treaties. Here was something to impress the gathering Indians with the might and majesty of the United States—a fort consisting of two cabins, one filled with cheap gifts for them, the other an unchinked barracks of earth and wood hardly better than the open shelters the Indians were throwing up. The unfilled one was destined for the three American treaty commissioners but was occupied now by Missionary Kirkland, the Indian agent. The commissioners had not arrived (Madison saw one of them at Albany, waiting for the two others), so Kirkland took the party in for the night. Next morning, while willing Indians began to build a bark cabin for them, they set off to visit the Oneida Nation, eighteen miles away. Marbois described the ride:

"We had to make our way on horseback through the woods, fol-lowing as best we could a footpath that was easy enough for the savages, who always go on foot. The brooks create a continuous miry marsh, into which we sank at every step. Huge trees fall of old age in all parts of the forest. They obstruct the path for horse-men, though nothing prevents the savages from climbing over them. We traveled in gloomy, rainy weather, and once went astray, but our guides soon recovered the road. The trees served them as a compass, and they recognized the north by the bark, which is brown and more covered with moss on that side than on the south. After having traversed this extensive forest, sometimes on foot, sometimes on horseback, now fording the streams, now swimming our horses, we arrived, very wet and very tired, at the main village of the Oneidas."

Madison and the Frenchmen took with them five "breasts of milk" (small kegs of brandy) each carried by an Indian. Or so they thought until one of the carriers identified himself, in excellent French, as Nicholas Jordan, born near Amiens. Captured by Indians in the Seven Years' War and stripped naked for a cannibal feast, he had been saved from death by a chief's daughter, who, admiring his appearance as he was about to be tossed into the kettle, said she would like to marry him. It was a rich match, the former soldier assured them. The princess' dowry included 700 pins and needles, a gun, a house and garden, a cow and twelve scalps—against which, to be sure, he had to record that she was drunk from morning to night and was "not so beautiful as a woman from Picardy." Thus the story was recorded when Marbois sent it to his ex-fiancée, but in the duplicate furnished to the French government, the left-handed allusion to Picardy women was discreetly eliminated. M. Jordan's wife was "fort laide"—very ugly.

Later, Madison and his French companions evened things up by hammering (verbally) at an Indian squaw, who pretended not to understand English, until she admitted that she was a white woman—a New York farm servant who had escaped beatings and hunger by fleeing to the Indians. Among them she had no master and was the equal of any woman in the tribe. She could marry if she wished and be unmarried again whenever she wished. Where was there such independence in the white man's society?

At the Oneida village, Madison renewed his acquaintance with the great Chief Grasshopper, who visited Congress in 1781. The chief received his guests in a Bavarian court hunting costume which the Chevalier de la Luzerne, one-time ambassador to the King of Bavaria, had received as a gift at that court and passed along to aboriginal American royalty. In the evening, young warriors began a masked dance, interrupted only by side trips to the brandy kegs. Under this potent stimulus, they announced their intention of dancing all night. To four men exhausted by an eighteen-mile struggle through forest and swamp, this was an appalling prospect. Etiquette forbade them to leave before the dancers did. Grasshopper was appealed to: he had no right to stop them. Lafayette saved the day, or rather the night, by appealing to one of the dancers who had been his servant during the war. The young brave ended the dance with an oration. So all retired, the white men's servants going off with temporary wives who gave up on the masters when the likeliest of them, the youthful Caraman, refused to be seduced. In the morning the strayed horses were brought down from the hills, goods left unguarded in tents were assembled without loss, servants said farewell to squaws bright with wedding ribbons, and the arduous return was made to Stanwix. The new cabin there was welcome, for the thermometer dropped three degrees below freezing.

Lafayette, according to Madison, was the hit of the conclave. The Iroquois were pro-French anyway, and they knew the figure cut by Kayewla (as they called him) in the Revolution. But chiefly they were impressed by the fulfillment of his predictions to the Indians that those who joined the British would find themselves on the losing side. At Albany the chief American commissioner, General Wolcott, had suggested "either in compliment or sincerity" (the words are Madison's) that Lafayette might be of service in the negotiations. Kirkland called his aid essential. The attachment of the Indians to his person—an attachment, said Madison, "verified by their caresses"—would make it possible for him to frustrate the Tory followers of Joseph Brant, who were telling the Whig Indians that the Franco-American alliance was insincere and transitory.[10]

Unluckily, the commissioners were not at hand to sanction a speech, Lafayette and his friends were to stay but a few days, and the Oneidas must be called in at once or it would be too late. Appealed to in this dilemma, Madison advised that the Indians be summoned, with an invitation so worded that there could be either a public address or private entertainment. The arriving Oneidas took care of that. They brought with them such an idea of Lafayette's importance, Madison reported, that no private reception would have been adequate. To make things no easier, Commissioners Arthur Lee and Richard Butler arrived ahead of Chairman Wolcott, who was taken ill on the road.[11] Lafayette sent them a letter and received a chilly half-acceptance from Lee. A personal visit added to his embarrassment but finally (all three commissioners being present) "they changed their plan and concurred explicitly in his making a speech in form."

The result, Madison said, exceeded all expectations. Not only in the speechmaking, but "even during the whole stay of the Marquis, he was the only conspicuous figure. The commissioners were eclipsed. All of them probably felt it. Lee complained to me of the immoderate stress laid on the influence of the Marquis, and evidently promoted his departure." Lafayette sensed this jealousy, but was consoled by the probable service of his Indian speech to the United States—also, Madison thought, by the fact that it would "form a bright column in the gazettes of Europe," as in fact it did.

Madison expected little from the treaty. In the great gathering he could see nothing to "impress a high idea of our power or opulence," nothing to offset British refusal to give up the Western forts. A similar impression was made on Marbois—skimpy, belated presents, the bad housing of the commissioners, the straggling in, one or two at a time, of a hundred soldiers "as badly clothed as in wartime." To make it worse, the Indians were angered and alarmed at an attempt by New York to buy their lands in total disregard of the approaching national conclave—an attempt, Madison said, which might be constitutional but "violated both duty and decorum." He was greatly surprised, therefore, when he learned that after his and Lafayette's departure, the sachems and warriors of the Six Nations relinquished their claim to all territory from Buffalo to the Mississippi, in exchange for a (worthless) guaranty of their lands to the east and north.[12]

Madison, Lafayette, Marbois and Caraman left Fort Stanwix on October 6, eight days after their arrival. The chargé d'affaires described the easy return to civilization: "We chartered a little boat in which there was room for just eleven persons, including five rowers, and descended the River Mohawk in the most beautiful weather in the world." Only the half-mile portage at Little Falls, by horse and chariot, broke the two-day voyage. At Schenectady they found their waiting horses and rode on through the rose and orange of oaks and maples, the scarlet sumac and the yellow hickories. From Albany, Lafayette, Caraman and an Indian boy set off across the Berkshires to Boston, Madison and Marbois turned down the Hudson, the latter to rejoin his bride, the former to take his seat, after paying a fine for unexcused absence, in the October session of the Virginia legislature. Stopping briefly at Philadelphia, Madison sent Jefferson an appraisal of the twenty-seven-year-old Frenchman who would soon be with him in Paris:

"The time I have lately passed with the Marquis has given me a thorough insight into his character. With great natural frankness of temper he unites much address and very considerable talents. In his politics, he says, his three hobbyhorses are the alliance between France and the U. S., the union of the latter and the manumission of the slaves. The two former are the dearer to him, as they are connected with his personal glory. The last does him real honor, as it is a proof of his humanity. In a word, I take him to be as amiable a man as can be imagined and as sincere an American as any Frenchman can be; one whose past services gratitude compels us to acknowledge and whose future friendship prudence requires us to cultivate."[13]

Madison encountered Lafayette's Indian protégé in New York after some years. Just back from Paris, he was "instructed in dancing, fencing and everything that was thought necessary to form what was called a gentleman's education . . . a complete *petit maitre,*" Gotham society exclaimed. Madison followed up the boy's history and narrated it years afterward to British Minister Augustus J. Foster: "In a fortnight after his return to his tribe he had cast off his whole French wardrobe and its appurtenances and resumed his former habits, becoming to all appearances an Indian hunter that had never stirred out of his native forest."[14]

Madison and Lafayette were quickly thrown together again in 1784. The frigate *La Nymphe* brought the marquis up the James River on November 18, four days after Washington arrived to visit the legislature. In addition to serving on the reception committee and (to judge by the wording) writing the official message of praise and greeting, Madison took note of the fact that the governor had never executed the assembly's 1781 order that a marble bust of Lafayette be made in Paris. He and Joseph Jones secured a unanimous renewal of the command—a renewal so worded, Madison stated, as both to change and conceal the original instruction that the bust be given to the marquis himself. Now there were to be two statues, one given to the City of Paris, one to be set up in Virginia in the same spot with the new statue of Washington. Out of this came the two Houdon marbles of Lafayette, the one which a Jacobean mob destroyed in the French Revolution, the other still in the Richmond State House.

Lafayette's reply, when he received these resolutions from Madison, revealed the high esteem in which he held the Virginian. "The warm expressions of regard which it contains are extremely flattering to me," Madison wrote in acknowledgment, "and the more so as they so entirely correspond with my own wishes for everything which may enter into your happiness." Finding, in this legislative adulation, a further opportunity of penetrating Lafayette's character, Madison sent a new estimate of him to Jefferson:

"Though his foibles did not disappear all the favorable traits presented themselves in a stronger light on closer inspection. He certainly possesses talents which might figure in any line. If he is ambitious it is rather of the praise which virtue dedicates to merit than of the homage which fear renders to power. His disposition is naturally warm and affectionate, and his attachment to the U. S. unquestionable. Unless I am grossly deceived, you will find his zeal sincere and useful, wherever it can be employed in behalf of the U. S. with[out] opposition to the essential interests of France."

Not long after this, Lafayette was naturalized by the Virginia Assembly (following Maryland's example), thus giving official sanction to the American citizenship which he had previously claimed for himself as a major general in the Continental Army.[15]

Madison could not get the Mohawk Valley out of his mind. Soil, he told Jefferson, perhaps scarcely inferior to Kentucky's, safely distant from every frontier, watered by a navigable branch of the Hudson, bordered within twenty miles by populous settlements. The ramble inflamed rather than extinguished his desire to see the North and Northwest, and he hoped to resume his travels in the summer of 1785.[16]

This was no fleeting thought, and later considerations gave it added force. Pursuing his study of law, Madison spent two winter weeks in the office of Attorney General Randolph, gaining "insight into the juridical course of practice." If he had been thinking of becoming a member of the bar, this apparently put an end to the thought. The spring was spent chiefly in reading, "and the chief of my reading, on law," but desires and purposes were taking shape which caused him to write in this wise to Randolph on the twenty-sixth of July:

"I keep up my attention as far as I can command my time, to the course of reading which I have of late pursued and shall continue to do so. I am however far from being determined ever to make a professional use of it. My wish is if possible to provide a decent and independent subsistence, without encountering the difficulties which I foresee in that line. Another of my wishes is to depend as little as possible on the labor of slaves. The difficulty of reconciling these views has brought into my thoughts several projects from which advantage seemed attainable. I have in concert with a friend here one at present on the anvil which we think cannot fail to yield a decent reward for our trouble. Should we persist in it, it will cost me a ride to Philadelphia, after which it will go on without my being ostensibly concerned."[17]

The desire for escape, and the obstacles to it, were likewise evidenced when Jefferson repeated his appeal to Madison to establish himself near Monticello—an action which would make his friend "believe that life still had some happiness in store" for him. Coupled with this was an invitation to spend half a year in Paris, at no cost except 200 guineas for passage money, clothes and theaters. The latter suggestion was disposed of by Madison's fear "that crossing the sea would be unfriendly to a singular disease of my constitution." Not that he still suffered from the epileptoid hysteria of his youth—he had just told Lafayette that he enjoyed "a satisfactory share of health"—but the tossing deck of that barge on the storm-lashed Hudson must have produced unpleasant suggestions of a return of the falling sickness. "The other part of your invitation," Madison continued, "has the strongest bias of my mind on its side, but my situation is as yet too dependent on circumstances to permit my embracing it absolutely."[18]

Again, in this same period, his college friend Caleb Wallace heard a belated report of Madison's matrimonial engagement and invited him to move to Kentucky, though "perhaps you smile at the idea of being politically buried in this wilderness." Answered Madison: "I do not smile at the idea of transplanting myself into your wilderness." Such a change was "not indeed probable, yet I have no local particularities which can keep me from any place which promises the greatest real advantages."[19]

Here was Madison's quandary: He could not accept an easy living on his father's plantation without feeling the guilt of condoning slavery. He was mentally equipped for the law, but not for "the difficulties which I foresee in that line"—its courtroom oratory, the rough-and-tumble of its practice. He wanted leisure for continued studies and for public life. How could this be attained? The project then "on the anvil" apparently did not develop, but the nature of it is suggested by later ones which did. In this same month of July 1785, James Monroe, with whom a close friendship was developing, wrote to him from New York, the new temporary seat of Congress: "What say you to a trip to the Indian treaty to be held on the Ohio—some time in August or September—I have thoughts of it and should be happy in your company." Or, he went on, "perhaps you have thoughts of a trip this way," to Boston and Lake George. Mistaking this for "an option of rambles" with Monroe, and deciding on the northerly one, Madison set out for Philadelphia at the end of August. There he found that Monroe had passed through a few days before on his way to the Wabash. The widowed Mrs. Trist, saddened "by the scenes of adversity through which fortune had led her," and robbed of nearly everything in the sale of her husband's Spanish property, had just reached home from Louisiana by way of Havana. Her small-merchant brother, Samuel House, was made Madison's tobacco buyer—a move to gain the higher price prevailing in Philadelphia. With this attended to, he went on to New York, where Congress by "constantly standing at the pump" was managing to keep the federal ship afloat.[20]

With Monroe's company unavailable, Madison gave up the northern journey and returned to Virginia, stopping for two days at George Washington's "well resorted tavern," as the general

called it when persuading his mother not to move in with him.
Mt. Vernon was a busy and messy place on October 12 and 13, with
Houdon and three French assistants casting a preliminary model
of the Virginia statue in "plaister of Paris." An all-day rain added
to the intimacy, and gave ample time for discussion of a subject on
which Madison's thoughts were concentrating. What did Washington think of the Mohawk Valley as a spot for real estate speculation? The response was emphatic. The general intimated that
"if he had the money to spare and was disposed to deal in land,
this is the very spot which his fancy had selected of all the U. S."
He must have meant it, for he had just given New York's Governor
Clinton his note for $2,500, to cover his half of a Mohawk purchase
financed by the governor.[21]

Three months later, at Madison's request, Monroe was talking
with "young Mr. Scott" in New York about the terms on which
he would sell Madison a portion of 8,000 acres on the Mohawk.
The latter unluckily had no cash but his desires were strong. "My
private opinion," he told Monroe, "is that the vacant land in that
part of America opens the surest field of speculation of any in the
U. S." Did Monroe have any thought of turning his own speculations that way? He did, most decidedly he did. For Monroe had
traveled as far as the Mississippi, following his pipe smoking with
the Western Indians, and came back thoroughly disgusted with
the "miserably poor" country he went through—extensive plains
which apparently had not had and would not have a bush on them
for ages. These barren lands (western Ohio, Indiana, Michigan
and Illinois) would in all likelihood never support enough inhabitants to entitle them to statehood. But the Mohawk Valley! Monroe had seen that paradise of forest greenery and flowing streams,
and shared Madison's enthusiasm for it. He knew, moreover, of a
better bargain than young Scott's—a thousand acres belonging to
one Taylor, and if Madison didn't want to go it alone, Monroe
would take a half interest and make the entire first payment. Indeed, why limit it to a thousand acres?[22]

Monroe, an impecunious lawyer, wrote this on his wedding day
(February 16, 1786) when emotions and thoughts of future need
were both running strong. Congress in fact was bursting with

connubial impulses just then—Monroe, King, Gerry, all being married, besides which, another Virginia delegate informed Madison, "Many more maneuvers are going forward among the members of Congress which seem to portend a conjunction copulative. In short I think we have got into Calypso's Island. I heartily wish you were here, as I have a great desire to see you figure in the character of a married man."[23]

Having less comprehensive motives for desiring wealth, Madison postponed the enlargement of the venture till they should have a sight of the land and know what they were buying, but "I join you cheerfully," he wrote to Monroe, in the purchase immediately proposed. The deal was made: 900 acres at a dollar and a half an acre, one half paid down, the balance due in 1787. Madison had a half interest in Lot 2 of the Sedachqueda Patent, stretching north from the Mohawk River near the mouths of Oriskany and Nine Mile Creeks, that many miles from Fort Stanwix. He owed Monroe $337½ in Spanish specie.[24]

No real estate boom could swell a $675 investment into a fortune, and Madison knew it. He had an idea, however, which he was eager to discuss with Monroe, and waited impatiently through a capricious half year of 1786 weather—almost no winter, deep snow in March, four inches of hail on April Fool's Day, drought until May 19, incessant torrents of rain till June 4, then three weeks of drought and heat that baked the earth "as hard and dry as a brick." Wheat and rye were blasted, fruits damaged. Tobacco prices followed the barrels down the "rolling road." Hard money vanished. Planters once more were plunged into debt to merchants. Things really were tough in Virginia, and Madison found them bad in Philadelphia too. The bank had gone out of business. Samuel House could not collect from his customers, therefore could pay but a fraction of what he owed under the Madison contracts. Charged with extensive purchases for the family, and chagrined over his inability to pay Monroe, Madison wrote to his brother Ambrose that he had chosen the lesser evil "of leaving you still longer to parry your creditors."[25]

Cash or no cash, Monroe was eager to enlarge their purchase, but Madison held back—both through caution against buying unseen and from mortification over his lack of money. Now for the big plan. With Monroe's approval he wrote to Jefferson, suggesting that the minister use his credit privately "for borrowing say four or five thousand louis more or less [$16,000 to $20,000] on the obligation of Monroe and myself . . . for our triple emolument." With occupied lands in the Mohawk Valley selling at eight or ten pounds to the acre, and vacant lands a little higher up only a dollar and a half, the lower price was bound to overtake the higher and produce a profit far above the six per cent on the money. Jefferson replied that there was no incentive for Frenchmen to make loans in the United States when the French government not only offered them six per cent on their money, but paid it.[26]

Staying long in Philadelphia in these efforts to raise money, Madison so perplexed his friends in Congress that one of them, General Lighthorse Harry Lee, reported a current belief that he was "in full gallop to the blessed yoke." Thereby was created the myth of a mysterious romance with "some lady whose identity has been lost."[27] Madison did manage to raise $100 for Monroe, and took over, on assignment, a worthless bond for £790 which Samuel House had received from a merchant in Westmoreland County, Virginia. The two friends, with Mrs. Monroe, then rode back to Virginia, Madison to renew his legislative work and help in the management of the great Montpelier plantation, Monroe to hang out his shingle as a lawyer in Fredericksburg, both of them to wait for Mohawk Valley real estate to come out of the nationwide depression of the late 1780's.[28]

Madison discharged the balance of his debt by paying for the furniture for Monroe's new home. Four years later, the second half of the Mohawk purchase price was three years overdue, and the extremely patient Mr. Taylor needed his money. It was Lawyer Monroe, now, who had none. Would Madison care to take over the whole contract? He was willing, but offered to carry Monroe's share for him and split the profits. When that was declined, he bought out his partner and fixed the terms—full repayment of Monroe's investment at seven-per-cent interest, with $150 thrown in as a conjectural profit. Madison then held the property for six more years, selling it in 1796 for $5.83 1/3 per acre.[29]

The buyers, two urban New Yorkers, pointed out to Madison at the last moment that although the deed was for 900 acres, the surveyor's plot showed far less. Madison believed that the map was in error. For one who had figured out the dimensional variations produced by the oblate form of the earth, it was no trick at all to jot down five possible variations of the survey. The results ranged from 722 acres to a possible maximum of 953. He thereupon agreed to a resurvey, at their joint expense, with the price adjusted to the quantity of land. After the signing it was discovered that a plot of the adjoining lot, owned by Madison's ex-prospective father-in-law, Colonel Floyd, indicated that the tract would run to the maximum figure. Alarmed at what they had started, the New Yorkers went up the Mohawk for a look at the land, declined a resurvey and paid for 900 acres.[30]

Often cited as evidence of Madison's lack of business judgment, this modest real estate speculation bears a different aspect when carried through from purchase to sale. Paying $1,350 for the land, with interest charges of $438.48 and a $150 gift to Monroe, he sold it for $5,250—a profit of $3,311.52. This was much less than he expected in a region filling up with settlers. But, as his adviser in Whitestown, New York, remarked, "All that a man brings in the country with him is his wife and six or eight children." On credit, these farmers would buy without asking the price, but four dollars an acre was their limit in cash.[31] Madison got half as much again from New Yorkers who, relatively at least, were more proficient at raising cash than children. He also demonstrated, at all stages of the enterprise, his honesty, fairness and generosity. Lack of capital, not faulty judgment, was what defeated Madison's hope for "a decent and independent subsistence" free from reliance on the labor of slaves. For better or worse, he was yoked to the Virginia plantation for the rest of his life.

CHAPTER XXII

Freedom of Religion

RELIGIOUS freedom hung in the balance when Madison resumed his legislative duties in the fall of 1784. Half a month late, technically, he came in from his northern journey only two days after a quorum was secured, and two days before the start of a deluge of church petitions asking for the support of religion by taxation. In the first of these, inhabitants of Isle of Wight County lamented that there was not "the smallest coercion" upon people to support religion in spite of "a principle old as society itself that whatever is to conduce equally to the advantage of all should be borne equally by all." In reality, the old principle had been that the minority must be forced to conform to whatever religion the majority believed in. Deprived of that compulsion by Madison's "freedom of conscience" article in the Virginia Declaration of Rights, the dominant Episcopalians turned with plausible sophistry to the doctrine of the general welfare.[1]

No longer doubting that the state was behind him, Patrick Henry offered and pressed a resolution that the people "pay a moderate tax or contribution annually for the support of the Christian religion or of some Christian church, denomination or communion of Christians or of some form of Christian worship." Madison faced heavy odds as he took the lead against this motion. Not a single opposing petition had been received. The Presbyterian clergy, seduced by the prospect of state support, joined the Anglicans in favor of it. With usual political lines broken, Henry had the support of such powerful men as Joseph Jones, Philip Barbour, the two Carter Harrisons, John Marshall, Joseph Prentis, William Norvell (chairman of the Committee on Religion), Henry Tazewell. Back of Madison were Wilson Cary Nicholas, George Nicholas, Zachariah Johnston (a fighting Presbyterian from the Shenandoah Valley), Archibald Stuart, French Strother, Spencer

Roane—some of them allied with Henry on nonreligious matters. Luckily Richard Henry Lee, who strongly favored the measure, was in Congress.[2]

Patrick Henry's speech in favor of religious assessments has not been handed down to posterity. Madison wrote almost half a century afterward that the measure was "supported by all his eloquence," but a plea to unite state and church is not of the sort on which libertarian fame is built. The nature of his argument is revealed only in the notes of Madison's reply to it, jotted down in microscopic writing on the back of a letter.[3] Henry told of the nations which had fallen after religion decayed, cited precedents for the assessment in other American states, and pictured the alarming decline of morals in Virginia—due, in his opinion, to the low estate of the Christian religion resulting from the repeal of the tithe law in 1777.

Madison began and ended his reply with the broad assertion that the assembly had no power to enact such a law. Religion was not within the purview of civil authority. The bill violated the Virginia Declaration of Rights. He then launched into the evils of state support. Even if Christianity in general was established, the tendency was first toward uniformity, then to penal laws for supporting it. The true question was not, "Is religion necessary?" but "Are religious establishments necessary for religion?" No, answered Madison, for religion is corrupted when established by law. The "downfall of states mentioned by Mr. H[enry] happened when there was establishment." What were the flourishing eras in the Christian religion? They were periods of growth in conflict with prevailing laws, as in primitive Christianity, in the Reformation, in the former status of Dissenters.

Turning to the affairs of Virginia, Madison rejected the inference that moral decay called for a religious establishment. War and bad laws were the true causes of the conditions complained of. The same complaints were heard in New England, where there was an established church. Laws to cherish virtue, a better administration of justice, personal example, the education of youth—these were the true remedies for declining morals and religion. He warned of the double blow a religious assessment would strike in a critically important matter—emigration from the state to escape taxes. By taking away liberty, it would both drive present inhabitants away and deter others from coming in for asylum.

Drawing upon the study of religion which he made after leaving college, Madison analyzed the defects of Henry's proposal in the face of theological conflicts. The courts must decide what is Christianity. By what edition would the Scriptures be tested: Hebrew, Septuagint or Vulgate? What books were canonical, what apocryphal? Were the Scriptures inspired in every word or in essential parts only? Is salvation by faith alone or by works also, by free grace or by will? These questions must be answered, he told his colleagues, because if some doctrines are essential to Christianity, those who reject them do not form a Christian society, hence are ineligible to support by taxation.

Madison concluded his discussion of Christianity with what is set down in his notes as "Panegyric on it, on our side." Or, as the pious Rives paraphrased this too objective fervency: "He concluded with vindicating its holy character."[4]

As the debate developed, Madison was disconcerted to find that his powerful argument did not produce the effect he expected. Instead of turning delegates against the assessment, it led to a move to include all religions—Mohammedan, Hindu or what have you—in order to relieve judges of the need to define Christianity. Patrick Henry rode to triumph, forty-seven to thirty-two, in committee of the whole, and was made chairman of a solidly factional committee of ten to write the bill. Cheered by this, he turned to his other religious project, and secured a declaration, sixty-two to twenty-three, that bills should pass for the incorporation of all Christian societies that desired it. This leverage enabled a committee to bring in a bill to incorporate the Episcopal Church, with the Presbyterians (who also sought a state charter) left out in the cold.[5]

What could be done in a legislature ruled by Patrick Henry, with a personal following built on oratory, and reinforced now by powerful Anglican conservatives? Obviously, nothing, except get him out. But how? Thomas Jefferson was penning his views on that subject to Madison almost at this moment: "What we have to do, I think, is devotedly to pray for his death." Madison had a

surer though less final solution: Work on his love of distinction
and elect him governor. Benjamin Harrison was ineligible to re-
election. If there was still talk of Madison for the place, as Jefferson had reported a year earlier, he gave it no encouragement. "It
is in the option of Mr. H[enry]," he wrote to Monroe three days
before the election, "and I fancy he will not decline the service."
With Henry's friends supporting him because he craved the position, and others doing so to get him out of the legislature, he was
elected "without competition or opposition."⁶

It was with real pleasure that Madison served on the committee
which notified Henry of his elevation to the weakest gubernatorial
office in the United States. Ten days remained, however, before he
would be compelled to step out of the assembly. Could he push the
assessment measure through? The answer came instantly: "Mr.
Henry the father of the scheme is gone up to his seat for his family
and will no more sit in the House of Delegates, a circumstance
very inauspicious to his offspring." Thus Madison wrote to Monroe, adding, a few days later, that the bill had been reported but
"Its friends are much disheartened at the loss of Mr. Henry. Its
fate is I think very uncertain."⁷

By this time the advocates of religious freedom were beginning
to be heard from. From Rockbridge County, in the Shenandoah
Valley, came a protest that this or any other "interference of the
legislature in aid of religion" was "unequal, impolitic and beyond
its power."⁸ It was heart-warming to Madison to see how broad
and firm an interpretation the foes of a religious establishment
gave to his 1776 declaration of the rights of conscience.

Sensing the repugnance to support of churches, the new leaders
of the assessment began to camouflage it as an educational measure. No longer defining the scheme as a levy upon taxpayers for
support of "some Christian church, denomination or communion,"
the official title called it "A bill establishing a provision for teachers of the Christian religion." The money was to be devoted to
"instructing such citizens, as from their circumstances and want of
education, cannot otherwise attain such [Christian] knowledge."
To emphasize the educational aspect still further, one clause provided that money not designated for any particular sect by the tax-

payers should be disposed of "for the encouragement of seminaries of learning within the counties whence such sums shall arise." This was chiefly a gloss over the basic purpose to support the dominant church, but it also reflected the mixing of secular and religious education in Virginia. Except in rich families, the schooling of young children was in the hands of the clergy. Every church or glebe house had its weekday gatherings of boys and girls, whose tuition supplemented the pastor's salary. Inability or failure of parents to support the parish schools was one of the reasons for desiring the assessment.[9]

In the background of this phase of the controversy was the impending conflict, ideological as well as financial, over public versus parochial schools. Jefferson's 1779 general education bill proposed a free public school system. "The principal foundations of future order will be laid here," Jefferson wrote of this bill in his "Notes on Virginia." "Instead, therefore, of putting the Bible and Testament into the hands of the children at an age when their judgments are not sufficiently matured for religious inquiries, their memories may be stored here with the most useful facts from Grecian, Roman, European and American history. The first elements of morality too may be instilled into their minds."[10] Madison's agreement with Jefferson's position was evident not only in his later efforts to secure passage of the public school bill, but in his speech against the religious assessment. There he put forward the education of youth as one of the answers to the decline of morals, yet did so as an argument against the use of state funds to support the clergy who had charge of schooling.

As the fight over the assessment went on, Madison saw that time was needed, to let the will of the people be impressed on the assembly. To gain this objective, he reluctantly withdrew his opposition to the Episcopal incorporation bill—now revised, under pressure from the laity of that church, to include both clergy and vestries. Passage of this measure, he believed, would cool "its warmest votaries," but its defeat "would have doubled the eagerness and the pretexts for a much greater evil." Following its adoption, forty-seven to thirty-eight, the assessment bill was taken up. Here Madison's first speech bore belated fruit in a vote to strike out the word "Christian" and insert "religious," but (he reported) "the pathetic zeal of the late Governor Harrison" re-established the discrimination against alien deities. Over-all support of the bill was weakening. A motion to give it a third reading barely squeaked through and was followed next day by a forty-five to thirty-eight decision to postpone that reading until the following November— eleven months away. Madison's strategy was justified by the event, for nine supporters of incorporation voted against the assessment and eight did not vote.[11]

In this interval between legislative sessions, Madison was inclined to keep silent and leave the matter to the spontaneous verdict of the people. "Some fermentation below the mountains, and a violent one beyond them," were evident to him in April. The Episcopal clergy and laity were for the measure, with some of them cooling, and the laity of all other sects unitedly opposed. "So are all the clergy," he reported to Monroe, "except the Presbyterian who seem as ready to set up an establishment which is to take them in as they were to pull down that which shut them out. I do not know a more shameful contrast than might be found between their memorials on the latter and former occasion."

Madison's chief lieutenants did not share his optimism. George Nicholas warned him that silence "would be construed into an assent." A majority of the counties were in favor of the measure, a great majority of the people against it, "but if this majority should not appear by petition the fact will be denied." Identical language in all the petitions would help deter the assembly. "All my expectations," Nicholas went on, "are from their fears, and not their justice. I have been through a considerable part of the country and am well assured that it would be impossible to carry such laws into execution and that the attempt would bring about a revolution." He urged Madison, if he agreed that an address was proper, to commit it to paper. "I risk this because ... you are most capable of doing it properly and because it will be most likely to be generally adopted."[12]

The April elections sustained Madison's confidence, numerous supporters of the religious assessment being ousted, its opponents returned. The Presbyterian clergy began to sing another tune, "either compelled by the laity" or fearful of what else the legislature might do. Finally, the Anglican incorporation act contained a blunder in wording (if it was a blunder) by which church affairs were to be controlled by an equal number of clergy and laymen in the state convention, instead of two laymen to each preacher. The practical effect was to give every rector a lifetime job, unless he added felony to the gambling and other complaints leveled against the profession. This started a movement within the Episcopal laity for repeal of the incorporation act, while Madison reported and indorsed the spread of resistance to a religious assessment, among the people of the middle and back counties. "They do not scruple to declare it an alarming usurpation on their fundamental rights," he wrote to Monroe in June, "and that though the General Assembly should give it the form, they will not give it the validity of a law. If there be any limitation to the power of the legislature, particularly if this limitation is to be sought in our Declaration of Rights or form of government, I own the bill appears to me to warrant this language of the people."[13]

Madison gave no more heed to the Episcopal incorporation act, except, perhaps, to aid the repeal movement (successful in 1787) by drafting a short petition.[14] His general battle with that church, however, led to a misunderstanding, generations later, of his own relationship with it. From Edmund Randolph, a revolting member of its state convention, he received a sample of the clergy's defensive propaganda and with it this facetious remark: "I dedicate to you as the patron of the Protestant Episcopal church, the enclosed journal. . . . We have squeezed out a little liberality from them, but at a future day they will be harder than adamant." Gaillard Hunt, failing to pierce the sarcasm in this, saw it as conclusive evidence that the recipient was an Episcopalian.[15] Staying out of personal polemics, Madison refused to answer a question submitted to him by the belligerent president of Hampden-Sidney, whether Carter H. Harrison (who now denied it) had not said in the presence of both of them that "the greatest curse which heaven sent at any time into this country was sending Dissenters into it." He begged to be excused from acting as witness or judge in any case where the characters of gentlemen were concerned.[16]

The Nicholas brothers were delighted with the memorial and remonstrance which Madison sent them at the end of June. No change could be made in it without injury, George Nicholas reported to him. "One hundred and fifty of our most respectable freeholders signed it in a day." Longhand copies were sent at once to the Scotch Presbyterian counties of the Shenandoah Valley. With George Mason's help, it was printed as a broadside by the Phoenix Press of Alexandria, with a space for signatures at the end, and distributed throughout the state.[17]

The political effect of this remonstrance was staggering. By the time the legislature convened the flow of petitions had become a tidal wave. Without naming himself as author, Madison recorded that the signatures to the remonstrance "displayed such an overwhelming opposition of the people, that the plan of a general assessment was crushed under it."[18] There was not even a vote on the bill. So far-reaching were the results of this victory, not only as an immediate blow to church establishment but in its effect upon American laws and constitutions, that more than 150 years elapsed before any important attempt was made to re-establish the system of state support for religion or religious schools.

Madison's "Memorial and Remonstrance Against Religious Assessments"[19] consists of an introductory protest against this "dangerous abuse of power" and fifteen numbered reasons for the protest. First of these is the right of every man, guaranteed by the Virginia Declaration of Rights, to exercise religion as his own conviction and conscience may dictate. This right is by nature unalienable because the opinions of men cannot follow the dictates of other men; "unalienable also, because what is here a right towards men, is a duty towards the Creator"—a duty older and deeper than the claims of civil society. "We maintain therefore that in matters of religion, no man's right is abridged by the institution of civil society, and that religion is wholly exempt from its cognizance." If exempt from the authority of society at large, still less can it be subject to that of the legislative body.

"The preservation of a free government," Madison declared, forbids any branch of it "to overleap the great barrier which defends the rights of the people. The rulers who are guilty of such an encroachment ... are tyrants. The people who submit to it ... are slaves."

That was strong language, coming after he had been told that enforcement of such a law would lead to overthrow of the government. If not incitement, it was a threat by way of warning.

"Because it is proper to take alarm at the first experiment on our liberties. We hold this prudent jealousy to be the first duty of citizens, and one of the noblest characteristics of the late Revolution. The freemen of America did not wait till usurped power had strengthened itself by exercise, and entangled the question in precedents. They saw all the consequences in the principle, and they avoided the consequences by denying the principle. We revere this lesson too much, soon to forget it. Who does not see that ... the same authority which can force a citizen to contribute three pence only of his property for the support of any one establishment, may force him to conform to any other establishment in all cases whatsoever?"

Here Madison was not referring to the size of the religious assessment, which was undetermined, but to the three-penny tax on tea which precipitated the American Revolution.[20] This was indeed his great contribution to the cause of religious liberty— that he looked beyond a seemingly trivial levy in aid of religious teachers, and saw its ultimate consequence in the denial of liberty and imposition of clerical control upon the state.

As in his first speech opposing the assessment, Madison attacked it as unnecessary for the support of the Christian religion, an incentive to emigration from the state, a source of animosities and jealousies, a corrupter of churches, a handicap to the diffusion of the light of Christianity. His heavy emphasis, however, was on the opening given to the evils of a church establishment, and the violation of the natural and constitutional rights of the people.

What role had religious establishments played in human society? "They have been seen to erect a spiritual tyranny ... seen upholding the thrones of political tyranny; in no instance have they been seen the guardians of the liberties of the people." The foreign sufferer must view this bill "as a beacon on our coast, warning him to seek some other haven. . . . Distant as it may be in its present form from the Inquisition, it differs from it only in degree."

Reverting once more to the Declaration of Rights, Madison asserted that the right of religious freedom it gave to the citizen was held by the same tenure with all our other rights—enumerated with equal solemnity, or rather with studied emphasis.

"Either then, we must say, that the . . . legislature . . . may sweep away all our fundamental rights; or, that they are bound to leave this particular right untouched and sacred: Either we must say, that they may control the freedom of the press, may abolish the trial by jury, may swallow up the executive and judiciary powers of the state; nay that they may despoil us of our very right of suffrage, and erect themselves into an independent and hereditary assembly: or we must say, that they have no authority to enact into a law the bill under consideration. We the subscribers say, that the General Assembly of this Commonwealth have no such authority."

Madison's comparison of a religious assessment with the Inquisition did not represent anti-Catholicism. It came from one who had described the emancipation of Irish Catholics from "the shackles on their religious rights" as one of the current "proofs of the progress of light and freedom."[21] Neither was he fighting the Episcopal church, as a church, but only its efforts to link itself with the state and secure support from public revenues.

This remonstrance against religious assessments continues to stand, not merely through the years but through the centuries, as the most powerful defense of religious liberty ever written in America. It did its work so well that at last even the memory of the actual issue passed out of the consciousness of the people. With tithe laws forgotten, "establishment of religion" became a phrase from the pages of history, suggesting only its culminating feature, the creation of an official state church. Not so to Madison and others who faced the living controversy. Observe the words with which he opens one paragraph after another of his remonstrance: "The establishment proposed by the bill," "ecclesiastical establish-

ments," "the establishment in question," "the proposed establishment." Sending the assessment measure to Monroe, he called it
"the bill for establishing the Christian religion in this state."[22] He
had no need to argue the point, nor even to think about it. No
supporter of the bill would have denied that it was an establishment of religion. Its very title identified it as a bill *establishing* a
provision for teachers.

The lasting significance of this lies in its bearing upon the guaranty of religious liberty in the First Amendment to the United
States Constitution, written by Madison five years later. The federal aspect of the matter was impressed upon him while the assessment fight in Virginia was still undecided. A committee of Congress, reporting a plan of government for Western territories, included a clause which set aside one section in each township for
the support of public schools, and one section for the support of
religion. Congress struck out the religious portion. Rejoicing at
this, Madison wrote in May of 1785: "How a regulation so unjust
in itself, so foreign to the authority of Congress, so hurtful to the
sale of public land, and smelling so strongly of an antiquated bigotry, could have received the countenance of a committee is truly
matter of astonishment."[23]

With this and the assessment fight fresh in his mind when he
came to draft the federal Bill of Rights, Madison went beyond the
generalities of the Virginia Declaration of Rights and produced
this positive and all-inclusive injunction: "Congress shall make no
law respecting the establishment of religion, or prohibiting the free
exercise thereof." The Fourteenth Amendment afterward made
that commandment binding upon the states. Madison himself confirmed the fact that in phrasing it, his aim was to strike down
financial aid to religious institutions out of the public purse.
"Strongly guarded as is the separation between religion and government in the Constitution of the United States," he wrote in his
essay on monopolies, "the danger of encroachment by ecclesiastical
bodies may be illustrated by precedents already furnished in their
short history. . . . The most notable attempt was that in Virginia
to establish a general assessment for the support of all Christian
sects." Not by the most microscopic concession would he deviate

from absolute separation between "the authority of human laws and the natural rights of man." Only in an iron rule against "giving to Caesar what belongs to God, or joining together what God has put asunder," could he discover a true standard of religious liberty.

That standard, however, could be and was presented in affirmative legislation. Under the momentum of victory against the assessment, Madison and his lieutenants brushed the dust off Jefferson's 1779 bill for religious liberty, and pushed it to passage by an overwhelming vote. Thus heresy was wiped out as a crime and religious tests for civil office were abolished—guaranties Madison had vainly sought to plant in the 1776 Declaration of Rights. The churchly opponents made every effort to weaken the Jefferson bill. They moved to change the word "Lord," in the preamble, to "Lord Jesus Christ," thus creating an implication that its assurance of liberty was confined to Christians. All that this netted them, said Madison, was a rebuke for profanation of a holy name, by using it "as a means of abridging the natural and equal rights of all men." Not a word was altered in the bill itself, not even the concluding assertion that if any future legislature were to repeal this law or narrow its operation, "such act will be an infringement of natural right."

Starting from the premise that "Almighty God hath created the mind free," the Bill for Religious Liberty laid down the principle "that to compel a man to furnish contributions of money for the propagation of opinions which he disbelieves, is sinful and tyrannical." Neither should he be compelled "to support this or that teacher of his own religious persuasion." These principles were given the force of law by provisions that "no man shall be compelled to frequent or support any religious worship, place, or ministry whatsoever," nor shall he suffer any disabilities for failure to do so. "I flatter myself," Madison wrote to the author of the bill, that its provisions, by their unaltered adoption, "have in this country extinguished forever the ambitious hope of making laws for the human mind."[24]

Jefferson's bill was Madison's and Virginia's answer, in behalf of the people of that state, to the attempt to establish religion by opening the public treasury to the teachers of it. The First Amendment to the United States Constitution was Madison's further answer, in behalf of all the American people, to every attempt, no matter how small or innocent it might seem to be, to establish religion by financial or any other means. In this principle of total separation between government and religion, he wrote twoscore years later, is found "the great barrier against usurpations on the rights of conscience. As long as it is respected and no longer, these will be safe. Every provision for them short of this principle will be found to leave crevices at least through which bigotry may introduce persecution; a monster that, feeding and thriving on its own venom, gradually swells to a size and strength overwhelming all laws divine and human."[25]

CHAPTER XXIII

Rocky Rivers, Rocky Justice

To REFORM the laws and courts of Virginia, it was necessary to fight the lawyers and judges. Madison's campaign for adoption of the Jefferson-Wythe-Pendleton revisal was made harder by the fact that it was more than a codification of existing laws. Jefferson drove toward political and social goals, the conservative Pendleton toward reform of legal procedure. Their revisal had lain without action for five years, and the lawyers would have made it five hundred.

The court system was so bad, litigation so costly, slow and uncertain that most people would suffer bitter loss rather than hazard the legal remedy. The root of the evil was the inefficient county court, made up of justices of the peace in each county. At the top there was too great concentration—criminal appeals to one General Court, civil cases to the Court of Appeals, both tribunals far behind in their dockets. Virginia was a litigants' hell, a lawyers' paradise, but a paradise in which the lawyers almost died of exhaustion struggling through the jungle.[1]

Madison's first move, after becoming chairman of the Committee on Courts of Justice in the fall of 1784, was to work for circuit Courts of Assize to decentralize the General Court. In spite of "much secret repugnance," this old Pendleton proposal went swiftly through. "It luckily happened," Madison reported to Jefferson, "that the latent opposition wanted both a mouth and a head." Patrick Henry, over whose living body no progressive bill could pass, was out. In order to rally public support for the financial outlay, commencement of the plan was postponed for one year.[2]

The rally occurred, but it was a rallying of courthouse lawyers and J.P.'s. Jumping into elections all over the state, they piled up such a majority in the 1785 legislature that Madison's supplementary bill went under, sixty-five to forty-nine. "A wretched combination of uninformed members," wrote Joseph Jones, "proved too powerful for reason and eloquence." Offering a fake reform—five J.P.'s to do the work of a Court of Assize—the courthouse crowd let even that trail down to a mere instruction to county judges to go through the docket quarterly. The law already required them to do it monthly! Madison hung onto the reform, by his teeth, for two years. He lost by only one vote, in 1786, in an effort to establish district instead of circuit courts. Another fake bill went through but was blocked in the Senate. The experience verified what Madison wrote in the wake of his initial victory: "The greatest danger is to be feared from those who mask a secret aversion to any reform under a zeal for such a one as they know will be rejected."[3]

The revisal of laws, delayed a year by the penurious and belated distribution of copies, started off with an unexpected flourish. In response to an order by the House, Madison presented 117 bills of the revised code. All had to be readopted as if new. A month later (December 9, 1785) he reported to Washington that they were through a great part of the revisal, and might have been at the end of it had they spent as much time passing bills as in debating whether there was time to pass them. Right at that moment things went wrong. The erratic John Francis Mercer came into the assembly and united with Speaker Harrison and Charles Thruston in a sidelong attack. The bill on crimes and punishment came up. "Here the adversaries of the code exerted their whole force," Madison wrote to Jefferson, and secured a year's postponement.[4]

There was real objection to that bill. Wythe and Pendleton had retained in it, over Jefferson's protest, a revolting provision for retaliation as a punishment for mayhem. Madison's committee struck that out before resubmitting the bill in the fall of 1786. Then the real animus of the opposition came out. They objected to its restriction of capital punishment to murder and treason. "The rage against horse stealers," Madison said, led to the bill's defeat by a single vote. "Our old bloody code is by this event fully restored." On two readings, by narrow margins, the House voted for Jefferson's bill for a free public school system, but protests based on economy and sparseness of population deterred Madison from asking for a final vote. Never, as the revisal progressed, was he "without opponents who contest at least every innovation inch by inch."[5]

The situation became critical when Patrick Henry refused a third term as governor. His return to the legislature was sure as fate and surer than taxes. The work already done, Madison concluded, must be put out of reach lest it be "left in a mutilated state" or lost entirely. Accordingly, he secured passage of an act putting the approved portions into effect. It was a wise precaution. "The revised code will not be resumed," he notified Jefferson a year later. "Mr. Henry is the inveterate enemy of it." Madison felt the pangs of partial failure as he considered his three-year effort, but Jefferson had a better opinion of it. The revisal languished until after the general peace, he wrote in his *Autobiography*, "when by the unwearied exertions of Mr. Madison, in opposition to the endless quibbles, chicaneries, vexations and delays of lawyers and demi-lawyers, most of the bills were passed by the legislature with little alteration."[6]

In the gala period following Patrick Henry's election to the governorship in 1784, Madison and Joseph Jones decided to try for a reversal of the resolve resisting payment of British debts. In addition to the fact that "Mr. Henry was out of the way," Madison saw a general improvement in sentiment following ratification of the definitive treaty of peace. A bill presented by Jones, Madison and six others went through the House easily. An attempt in the Senate to extend the benefits to Loyalists—possibly "a side blow at the bill"—was parried in conference. Both houses accepted a compromise on January 5, 1785, the day before final adjournment.[7]

On that night, as Madison tells the story, a number of legislators crossed the river to Manchester "with an intention it is to be presumed of returning the next morning. The severity of the night" prevented it. "Without them there was no house." Next day it was the same. The eight marooned legislators sent a canoe through the floating ice, but would they come too? Not even in a barge. For three days the assembly waited, then, said Madison, "patience could hold out no longer" and the House adjourned.

Here was the problem: the bill had passed both houses, but had not been enrolled, examined or signed. Was or was it not a law? It was not.

No study has ever been made of the British debts owed by the stormbound delegates. However, Madison recorded that a companion bill to allow deficiency judgments on such debts paid in depreciated paper was "laid asleep by the refusal of the interested members to vote in the question, and the want of a quorum without them." He did put through a bill against further confiscation of British property. It cost nothing to refrain from theft.[8]

In the fall of 1785 Madison drafted a new British-debt measure. This one—"extremely grating" he called it—required debtors to give security if they chose to pay in installments. The House not only struck out his security clause but turned the whole into "a scene of mockery" by refusing to exempt these debts from the statute of limitations. Feeling that passage of the emasculated bill would both "dishonor us and embarrass Congress," he let it die without a vote. A year later, with the country sunk in cyclical depression, nobody even brought the subject up.[9]

Not until 1787, after Madison left the legislature, did he learn from Foreign Secretary Jay that the first infractions of the peace treaty were by Americans, preceding even the British refusal to return Negroes, and that the American violations were "most numerous and important." This disclosure aided in the repeal, in that year, of the Virginia laws barring recovery of British debts, but with a vitiating proviso by Patrick Henry that it should not take effect until the British evacuated Western posts. That led to a demand that the United States pay reparations for losses sustained by British merchants and helped to delay the evacuation for ten years more. All this might perhaps have been avoided, including the national humiliation in the final settlement, if Madison's initial measure had not been defeated by Patrick Henry and John Tyler, or if there had been no ice in the James River in the first week in January, 1785.[10]

Better luck attended another international measure Madison sponsored in the fall of 1784, empowering Congress to surrender Virginia citizens to foreign countries to answer for crimes com-

mitted there. The chief purpose, he said, was to prevent embroilment of the United States with Spain "by the licentious and predatory spirit of some of our western people." In this instance, Patrick
Henry was a warm supporter (because of his friendliness toward
Indians) and his departure left the bill to squeeze through by one
vote. In drafting this law, Madison took care to plant Virginia's
action inside the authority of Congress. An accused person was to
be surrendered on demand of that body, for any crime which it
found to require extradition. The declared purpose was to show
reverence for the law of nations, cultivate amity and peace "between the United States and foreign powers, and to support the
dignity and energy of the Federal Constitution." In this extradition act—the first of its kind in America—the Virginia government was carefully excluded from any international contact.[11]

This regard for the prerogatives of Congress was evident in another act which Madison drafted, without enthusiasm, as chairman
of the committee on justice. It was occasioned "by the arrival of
two or three Algerines here, who, having no apparent object, were
suspected of an unfriendly one." Governor Henry and council
haled the Barbary Pirates before them, found themselves powerless
to do anything and asked the assembly for an exclusion law. Madison drafted one empowering the executive, after receiving notice
from Congress that the United States was at war or threatened
with war, to examine all suspicious aliens and hold or expel enemy
subjects. Thus he twisted Henry's antiforeignism into a recognition of the primary jurisdiction of Congress over aliens, and gave
them implied immunity from molestation in the absence of congressional action.[12]

Madison and those who thought with him had a far stiffer job
on their hands in 1785 when Carter H. Harrison undertook to
repeal the act of 1782 permitting slaves to be set free by their owners. Along with his belief that Dissenters were the worst curse
Heaven had visited upon Virginia, Churchman Harrison appeared
to believe that slavery was its greatest blessing. A petition for the
freeing of all slaves started the trouble. This was rejected without
dissent, but not, Madison said, until there had been "an avowed
patronage of its principle by sundry respectable members." A

motion to "throw it under the table" was "treated with as much indignation on one side as the petition itself was on the other." Harrison's report for repeal of manumission carried by one vote—the speaker breaking a tie—but Madison hoped for a better result on the bill itself. Otherwise, he wrote to Ambrose Madison, this retrograde step would "not only dishonor us extremely but hasten the event which is dreaded"—the freeing of all slaves. The House beat the bill thirty-five to fifty-two.[13]

This contest over manumission was economic, not racial. If slaves were set free, creditors of the owner might lose. On the social side, the prevailing attitude was shown when the legislature, giving effect to the last will and testament of Walter Robertson of Halifax County, passed an act vesting all of his property, real and personal, in "a negro woman named Anne Rose . . . for the use and benefit of the said Anne and her daughter Margaret," both of whom were declared to be free, and entitled to "all such rights, privileges and immunities as free negroes or mulattoes by the laws of this country do or may enjoy." The bill, written by Joseph Jones, came from a committee of which Madison was a member. If a Virginia planter thought so well of the services of a Negro slave that he wished all his property to descend to her and her mulatto daughter, that, in the opinion of the state legislature, was his business and no threat to society.[14]

British debts, slavery and things like that touched only the fringes of the main economic struggle in which, broadly speaking, Madison stood for taxation and state solvency, Patrick Henry and his followers for tax moratoriums and unbacked paper money. In the fall of 1784, Madison saw a prospect that a few years of plentiful crops, with tobacco high and the government steady, would "put our credit on a decent footing." His hopes were rudely dashed when tobacco prices dropped fifty per cent in the next year. Henry was gone, but that did not stop the remission movement. Madison found himself fighting ultraconservative Carter Braxton, who, seeking election to the governor's council, blossomed out as the savior of the people. To prevent outright cancellation, the Madison forces were driven not only to a new postponement of taxes, but to allow payment of them in tobacco and other goods. "The wisdom of seven sessions will be unable to re-pair the damage of this single act," he protested. The future looked even worse. An "itch for paper money discovered itself" and was likely to increase in 1786 because specie, no longer needed for taxes, would be carried overseas by the unfavorable balance of trade.[15]

Specie did vanish, and to increase the distress, the crash in to-bacco prices was followed by a similar collapse in corn. A cry to emit currency, Madison predicted in June, "will be rung in our ears by the very men whose past measures have plunged us into our difficulties." It is not surprising, therefore, to find among his papers the notes of a speech against paper money, delivered on the first day of November, 1786. Paper money without taxes to back it, he asserted, was unconstitutional—a device for confiscation of property by partial payment for it. It was antifederal, infringing upon the right of Congress to regulate the value of coin. It was unnecessary: enough paper money was afloat in tobacco notes and public securities. It was pernicious, fostering luxury, cutting off funds for Congress, destroying confidence between individuals, discouraging commerce, enriching sharpers, vitiating morals. It reversed the end of government by punishing the best and reward-ing the worst of citizens. If Virginia joined the paper money states of that day—Pennsylvania, New York, Rhode Island, North and South Carolina, with Maryland clamoring for it—she would be conspiring "to disgrace republican government in the eyes of man-kind."[16]

One day's debate decided the issue. In a resolution filled with echoes from Madison's speech, and by a top-heavy vote of eighty-five to seventeen, the House declared paper money to be "unjust, impolitic, destructive of public and private confidence, and of that virtue which is the basis of republican government." This would be a lasting victory—lasting until Patrick Henry re-entered the legislature. "If Mr. Henry should erect the standard he will cer-tainly be joined by sufficient force to accomplish it," Madison ob-served. "Remorse and shame are but too feeble restraints on interested indivduals against unjust measures, and are rarely felt at all by interested multitudes." He might as well have written then what he did a few months later: "The appetite for paper money grows stronger every day. Mr. Henry is an avowed patron of the scheme."[17]

In taking his stand against fiat money, tax postponements and remissions, Madison was not serving his immediate economic interests. He and his father and brother Ambrose were all in debt and pinched for money. They owned virtually no public securities, save for a few federal loan certificates which the senior Madison had taken for supplies and services to the Continental Army— repairing wagons, etc. They bought "indents," if any were available, to pay their taxes, thus cutting them by two-thirds. The buying of them is conclusive evidence that they lacked public securities producing such interest warrants. Even while benefiting from the law which made "indents" a legal tender for taxes, Madison opposed the system. "The advantage it gives to sharpers and collectors can scarcely be described," he remarked to Monroe. When he joined in making tobacco receivable for taxes, Washington protested that this would enrich speculators. "My acquiescence in the measure," Madison replied, "was against every general principle which I have embraced, and was extorted by a fear that some greater evil under the name of relief to the people would be substituted."[18]

Apart from his dislike of sharp practices, Madison's hostility to worthless money and tax postponements was due to the resulting threat to state and federal solvency. Finally he discovered that paper money was beginning to shake the Confederacy. "It is producing the same warfare and retaliation among the states," he wrote in 1786, "as were produced by the state regulations of commerce." The linking of these two subjects carried him a long way on the road to the new federal constitution.[19]

Madison's approach to commerce was not wholly controversial. When George Washington found himself free from army duties, he turned to the new Virginia legislator to promote the plans which had been in his mind for a dozen years, of uniting the seaboard and the Western country by an inland waterway system. Their first talk on the subject, apparently, was at Princeton in 1783, just after Washington returned from an inspection of military supply routes—Lake George and Lake Champlain, the Mohawk-Ontario and Susquehanna-Ohio portages. "Prompted by these actual observations," the general wrote then to the Chevalier de Chastellux, "I could not help taking a more contemplative and extensive view of the vast inland navigation of these United States. . . . I shall not rest contented 'till I have explored the western country and traversed those lines (or great part of them) which have given bounds to a new empire."[20]

Washington had tried vainly, in the 1770's, to secure public development of the rivers of Virginia, then turned to the formation of a private company. It was this that he discussed with Madison, for the latter remarked at the end of his first legislative session in Virginia that he "found no opportunity of broaching a scheme for opening the navigation of the Potomac under the auspices of General Washington." Jefferson, to whom he wrote this, had likewise pressed this course upon him, saying that a link between the Potomac and the Ohio would give Virginia "almost a monopoly of the western and Indian trade." Carrying coals to Newcastle, Jefferson also urged Washington's leadership in the development, and thereby eased the latter's conscience regarding the 30,000 acres he had just offered for lease on the Great Kanawha River. "I am not so disinterested in this matter as you are," the general responded, "but I am made very happy to find that a man of discernment and liberality (who has no particular interest in the plan) thinks as I do who have lands in that country."[21]

In the early fall of 1784, equipped with "a marquee, some camp utensils and a few stores," Washington set off by boat down the upper tributaries of the Ohio. With him went his friend and physician, Dr. Craik, fittingly supplied with "a few medicines, and hooks and lines," not all of them, presumably, intended for the same mouths. Indian troubles stopped them at Fort Pitt, but the result was a report to the governor of Virginia that the Western settlers "stand as it were upon a pivot; the touch of a feather would turn them any way"—down the Mississippi with their produce, or eastward to the ocean. All the produce of Fort Pitt, Washington said, could be brought to Alexandria by water, except for a thirty-one-mile land passage between the Yohoghaney and the Potomac,

or twenty miles by land between the Monongahela-Cheat and
Potomac. No greater barrier separated the James from a branch
of the New River "which yields a fine navigation."[22]

To people of a later day, there is a mystifying sound to this talk
of rivers navigable to their mountain sources. Washington lived
when the whole commerce of the West was carried by canoe or
flat batteau. "What is the face of the country," he asked Indian
Commissioner Richard Butler, at "the sources or canoe navigation
of the Cayahoga"? By connecting that stream and Big Beaver
Creek, he told Robert Morris, it would be possible "to bring all the
fur and peltry of the lakes, even from that of the Wood [Lake of
the Woods] to tidewater." Washington classed the tiny Monocacy
River as navigable. So too (unless its Indian name fell into it) was
"the Kiskeminetas Moghulbughkitum or Tobey's Creek," from
which a mountain portage led to the Susquehanna. Almost any
creek that would float a tricorn hat was fit for commerce, or could
be made so by pulling rocks out of its bed. This scheme actually
was to be applied to all falls and rapids of the Potomac above
Great Falls. As Madison described it, the plan was "to slope the
fall by opening the bed of the river . . . and by means of ropes fastened to the rocks, to pull up and ease down the boats where the
current is most rapid." These batteaux, sixty feet long and carrying up to ten tons, drew only eight to twelve inches of water. The
same principle was to be applied to canoe navigation in mountain
creeks—a fact utterly lost sight of, a century later, in Supreme
Court battles over the navigability of small streams.[23]

It was during this rising ferment over river navigation, for the
dual purpose of consolidating the American empire and channel-
ing Western commerce through Virginia and Maryland, that Madison took charge of the program in the 1784 General Assembly.
Washington discussed the matter with him at length, during his
November visit to Richmond, but a model bill for the Potomac
which he intended to deliver had been sent to Baltimore, to be
copied for the Maryland legislature. This he sent later to Madison
("or in his absence Joseph Jones") along with a joint petition of
Virginia and Maryland residents praying for a charter from the
two states. "Your own judgments in this business will be the best

guide," the general remarked, adding that his preference was for a corporate company to develop the waterway unless the public would take it up with efficient funds and without a limping conduct.[24]

The Virginia Assembly "lent a ready ear to the project," Madison reported, but protests were made against the height of the tolls proposed. To obtain a joint revision with Maryland, Washington was sent to Annapolis (as he described it) "with my bosom friend General G-tes, who being at Richmond contrived to edge himself into the commission." That interpretation may have come to him from Madison, whose letter of December 11 has been lost, but who wrote to Jefferson that Gates "happened to be in the way."[25]

Gates fell ill as soon as he saw Washington—a circumstance which threw more work than worry on the latter. By writing at midnight "with an aching head," Washington rushed the Annapolis results to Madison. The rate revision apparently had saved the charter in Maryland, overcoming what Madison expected to be one of the chief obstacles—the hostility of Baltimore to development of the rival Potomac route.[26] This was offset by winning the favor of western Maryland through low rates on bulky articles, and by cutting certain tolls to stimulate manufactures. The victory also reflected the great political power of former Governor Johnson, Washington's chief Potomac partner and Maryland's biggest speculator. Opponents said, and Washington seemed to agree with them, that the state "has been surprised into it."[27]

It was easier to deal with sectional jealousy in Virginia. Just add the James River to the program. Madison drew the bill for this purpose, and stirred up trouble of another sort by providing for ultimate government ownership of the canals and other works. Subscriptions were to be regarded as a trust fund lent to the state, at ten-per-cent interest, with the tolls "inviolably pledged for both principal and interest." Title would shift to the state when the subscribers had received twice their principal. This, Madison thought, represented an "exuberant harvest," but the prospective stockholders looked on it as confiscation. They demanded a virtual duplicate of the Potomac charter. Forced to concede this, Madison shifted to a new basis of public ownership. He kept the word

F. M. In Virga. Legislature previous to convining
Govt. . . . way whether the object be to

1. counteract foreign . . . laws
2. encourage Ships & seamen
3. — — manufactures
4. Revenue
5. frugality — particles of luxury most easily run from State to State
6. Embargo & in war — Case of Delaware in late war

necessary to prevent contention among States
   1. case of French provinces, Neckar says 23.000
      patrols employd. agt. internal contraband
   2. case of Mass.ts & Cont.
   3. case of N.Y. & N.J.
   4. Do & Delaware
   5. Wm. & Mary. late regulation
   6. Irish propositions

Necessary to Justice & policy
   1. Cont. & N. Hamps:
   2. N.J.
   3. N.C.
   4. Western Country.   U.S.

necessary. as a system convenient & intelligible to foreigners trading to
Necessary as within reason of federal constitution, the
   regulation of trade being as inseparable by States
   as. peace. war. amt. &c.

   Treaties of Commerce ineffectual without it

Safe with regd. to the liberties of the States.
   1. Congs. may be trusted with trade as well as war &c
   2. power of Treaties involve the danger if any —
   3. Controul of States over Congs.
   4. example of amphyctionic league. Acheon do.
      Switzerl? Holland, Germany —
   5. peculiar situation of U.S. increase the
      repellent power of the States

essential to preserve fedl. constitution
   1. declension of fedl. Govt.
   2. inadequacy to end, must lead States to substitute
      some other policy. no constitution remaining long when
      it ceases to be useful. &c .
   3. policy of G.B. to weaken union
magnitude of dissolution of confederacy; 1. appeal to sword in
internal squabble — 2 standing armies beginning with weak & jealous States
perpetual taxes — 4 sport of foreign politics — 5. last glory of Revolution

NOTES OF MADISON'S SPEECH ON FEDERAL REGULATION OF COMMERCE, 1785
(Enlarged one-third)

agst. Paper money. Novr. 1785 Virg. Assy.

unequal to specie. 1. being redeemable at future day and not bearing interest. 2. illustrated by —— of Bank notes – Stock in funds – paper of Spain Sp[r]ed during late war see Hacker ——— navy bills – tallies. 3. being of less ——— than specie which answers externally —— as well as internally – must be of less —— it depends on the uses

unjust. 1. to Creditors if a legal tender. 2 to debtors if not legal tender, by increasing difficulty of get-ting specie. This it does by increasing extravagance & unfavoreble balance of trade – & by destroying that confidence between man & man, by which resources of one may be comanded by another – 3 illustrated 1. by raising denomination of coin 2. increasing alloy of dr. brass made as silver by the Romans according to Sallust. 3 by changing weights & measures. 4. by case of Creditors within who are debtors without the State.

unconsti-tutional 1. affects Rights of property as much as taking away equal value in land, illustrd. by case of land fa. for down & to be conveyd. in future, & of a law spec-ialting conveyance to be satisfied by conveying a part only – or other land of inferior quality – 2. affects property without trial by Jury.

Antifederal. Right of regulating coin given to Congs. for two rea-sons. 1. for sake of uniformity. 2. to prevent fraud in States towards each other or foreigners. both these reasons hold equally as to paper money.

unnecessary. 1. produce of Country will bring in specie, if not laid out in superfluities. 2. paper, if necessary, one already in Tobo. notes, & public securities – 3. the true mode of giving value to these, and bringing in specie is to enforce Justice & taxes.

pernicious 1. by fostering luxury, extends instead of curing scarcity of specie – 2. by disabling compliance with requisition of Congs. 3. fomenting dissentions between States. 4. destroyg. confidence between individuals. 5. discouraging comerce – 6 enriching collectors & sharpers – 7. vitiating morals – 8 revers-ing end of Govt. which is to reward best & punish worst 9. conspiring with the examples of other States to dis-grace Republican Govt. in the eyes of mankind.

Objection. paper money good before the war.

Answr. 1. not true in N. Engd. agro in Vr. where exchange rose to 60 perCt. nay in Mary[d]. see Franklyn on paper money 2. confidence then not good – 3. principles of paper ed-debute then understood – Such as. not then nor now suc-ceed in Great Britain &c.

NOTES OF MADISON'S SPEECH AGAINST PAPER MONEY, 1786
(Enlarged one-third)

"perpetual" out, and inserted a provision giving the state a first right to buy stock, at whatever price "the proprietor shall really and bona fide sell." With fast work at the finish both charters swept through the legislature on the last day a quorum was present—the day of the famous canoe trip across the James. Under Madison's provision Virginia bought the James River system in 1820 and held it for many years of successful operation.[28]

In forming the Virginia-Maryland partnership, it had been overlooked that Pennsylvania's co-operation would be needed. Madison remedied the oversight with an instruction to the commission on Potomac tidewater navigation, of which he was a member, to join with Maryland in an appeal to the third state. Pennsylvania would be asked to extend a road "to the waters running into the Ohio; and to render these waters navigable as far as may be necessary and proper." The Potomac bill provided for a similar road from that river to the Cheat. Madison drafted a bill also for a general road survey in Virginia, to open highways between market towns and straighten the principal routes before rising land prices increased the cost. Support was so slight that he did not introduce it.

As an order was going through that the James River be surveyed, Madison broadened it to include a survey for a canal between Elizabeth River and North Carolina waters—across the Great Dismal Swamp. Besides the inflow of trade from the South, he predicted, this would double the value of the Virginia lands watered by the Roanoke. When Washington heard that this long-mired-down project of his had been put in motion along with everything else, his enthusiasm knew no bounds. Complete them all, he told Governor Henry, and "it will open channels of convenience and wealth to the citizens of this state that the imagination can hardly extend to and render this the most favored country in the universe."[29]

One feature of the Potomac and James River bills gave Madison an inspiration. They provided for purchase by the state of fifty $440 shares in the former company, one hundred $200 shares in the latter, amounting to ten and twenty per cent of the total. Why not give these to Washington as a token of gratitude for his services to the Revolution? This manner of reward, he thought, was less "injurious to his delicacy" and less dangerous as a precedent, than the pension some were talking about. Appointed, on the next to the last day of the session, a committee of one to prepare a bill to this end, he pulled it out of his pocket and it went through both houses in two days. Writing to Jefferson about Washington's sponsorship of river navigation, Madison revealed his own opinion of it as well as his estimate of the country's foremost citizen:

"The earnestness with which he espouses the undertaking is hardly to be described, and shows that a mind like his, capable of great views and which has long been occupied with them, cannot bear a vacancy; and surely he could not have chosen an occupation more worthy of succeeding to that of establishing the political rights of his country than the patronage of works for the extensive and lasting improvement of its natural advantages; works which will double the value of half the lands within the Commonwealth, will extend its commerce, link with its interests those of the western states, and lessen the emigration of its citizens by enhancing the profitableness of situations which they now desert in search of better."

The national aspect of this attempt to unite the seaboard with the interior was reflected in a declaration adopted by Congress on the initiative of Grayson of Virginia: "Resolved, that the navigable waters leading into the Mississippi and St. Lawrence and the carrying places between the same be, and are hereby declared to be common highways, and be forever free."[30]

Washington was both pleased and embarrassed by the gift of canal stock, with its dedicatory wish, written by Madison, that these public works which "will be durable monuments of his glory, may be made monuments also of the gratitude of his country." This action, he wrote to a friend, is "very flattering and honorable for me, not more so for the magnitude of the gift, than the avowed gratitude, and delicacy of its expression, in the recital of it. . . . But it is not my intention to accept of it." Fearing that outright rejection would seem disrespectful, or be imputed to ostentatious pride, he decided to hold the shares in trust for the benefit of the public—a course suggested indirectly by Madison and by others.[31]

The two men discussed the matter further at Mount Vernon in September (1785) and concluded that new legislation was necessary. Accordingly, Madison drew up a form of address, of which, Washington said in acknowledgment, "I now avail myself in a letter to the Governor, for the General Assembly. Your delicate sensibility," he went on, "deserves my particular acknowledgments: both your requests are complied with, the first, by congeniality of sentiment; the second because I would fulfill your desire." He asked Madison to inform him of the result, and, if it was favorable, to suggest objects to which the gift could be applied. "From what may be said upon the occasion, you will learn what would be most pleasing, and of the greatest utility to the public."[32]

The new bill, of course, went through easily, and Madison proposed to Washington "a partition of the fund between some institution which would please the philosophical world, and some other which may be of a popular cast." Washington's intention at the time had been to establish two charity schools, one on each of the two rivers. He changed his plan to one more in line with Madison's suggestion. The Potomac shares were dedicated to establishment of a university in the District of Columbia. The James River stock endowed Liberty Hall Academy, which became Washington and Lee University at Lexington, Virginia.[33]

Closely connected with Potomac development, in the minds of both Washington and Madison, was a mysterious invention by an artisan and hotelkeeper living at Bath in Berkeley County. James Rumsey presented a memorial to the legislature in the spring of 1784, representing, as Madison wrote about it, that he had invented a mechanism for running a boat twenty-five to forty miles a day against a ten-mile-an-hour current. He wanted the public to buy it. "The apparent extravagance of his pretensions brought a ridicule upon them." Things took a different turn after Washington saw a model of Rumsey's boat during his September trip to the Ohio. The general furnished a certificate which, Madison said, opened the ears of the assembly. They quickly passed Madison's bill giving Rumsey a ten-year monopoly which the state could abolish at any time by paying the inventor £10,000.[34]

So little did Madison know about the mechanical boat, even after patenting it, that he wondered whether its principle could be applied to balloons. At Mount Vernon, in the fall of 1785, he learned that Rumsey had built a full-sized boat which was destroyed by fire before he could demonstrate it. After that, the Bath mechanic turned to the invention of a steamboat, causing historians to jump to the conclusion that this was his original idea. Instead, the first was a pole boat, which was to move upstream when a paddle wheel, turned by the current, pushed rows of setting poles against the bottom of the river—hardly a satisfactory device for balloons. The swifter the current, the faster the boat would go against it—until something smashed.[35]

Madison was caught just in the edge of the bitter steamboat rivalry between Rumsey and John Fitch. The latter came to him at Richmond in the fall of 1785, presumably sent by Madison's college friend, the Reverend Nathaniel Irwin of Neshaming, Pennsylvania, in whose library Fitch studied steam. Madison presented the Fitch memorial to the legislature and was made chairman of a committee to deal with it, but was ordered to drop the matter three days later. Parsimony and skepticism apparently caused this, but Rumsey and Fitch flared into hostilities, the former seeking to stretch his 1784 patent to cover the steamboat, the latter securing a Virginia monopoly in 1787 and denying (for the rest of his life) that Rumsey ever attempted the use of steam until Fitch made his application. In reality, Rumsey completed a jet-propelled steamboat which moved against the current of the Potomac on March 14, 1786. The conflict between the two men, the apathy of Congress and legislatures, and Rumsey's early death in England, set back steam navigation for many years. One can only wonder what the result would have been if Madison's willingness to help both of them had been translated into a partnership of the two inventors, backed by the state.[36]

Throughout his life, Madison regarded the Rumsey patent act as a model in its protection of the public against the evils of monopoly. In the Continental Congress, following an appeal by Joel

Barlow, he had helped draft a recommendation for state copyrights, limited to fourteen years and a like renewal. A year later Noah Webster, who wanted to copyright his *Grammatical Institute of the English Language,* drew on their past acquaintance to request that he secure a copyright law in Virginia. He did so in the 1785 session—a bill defined as one to give authors exclusive rights "for a limited time." Here is the origin of those same words used by Madison in the patents and copyrights clause of the Constitution. Perpetual monopolies of every sort, he wrote years afterward, "are forbidden not only by the genius of free governments, but by the imperfections of human foresight." Every patent and copyright law should not only limit the duration of benefits but give the state "a right to extinguish the monopoly by paying a specified and reasonable sum.["][37]

Madison's attitude toward roads, rivers and canals reflected his broad nationalism. He talked of linking Virginia's interests with "those of the western states" when there were no Western states. He helped put through a penal law to frustrate Arthur Campbell's forcible effort to set up the state of Franklin in counties "we mean to retain." But if Kentucky sought, by legislative action, to be "handed over to Congress for admission into the Confederacy," that was another matter. "If they pursue their object through this channel," Madison remarked in 1785, "they will not only accomplish it without difficulty, but set a useful example to other western settlements which may choose to be lopped off from other states."[38]

At the request of his Princeton friend Caleb Wallace, Madison outlined his views on a form of government for Kentucky, putting emphasis on the need for a senate so constituted as to check the impulsiveness of the house, correct want of fidelity and give wisdom and steadiness to legislation. In other words, to take care of any future Patrick Henry. To achieve this, he would extend the right of suffrage in the lower house and narrow it in the upper—a principle he modified three years later. It was better, he then told another Kentuckian, to sacrifice the safety of property by giving too much power to the people than to diminish human rights by giving too much power to men of property.[39]

When Kentucky's petition for independence reached the assembly, citing "a mountainous desert of two hundred miles" as a bar to republican connection with Virginia, Madison was made chairman of a committee of ten upon it. They agreed that a Kentucky convention should vote on separation and readily settled most other points. The committee was apathetic, however, to Madison's plea that the partition act should not take effect until the new state had been admitted into the Union. Declining to present the report, he turned that duty over to Mann Page and sought an amendment on the floor.

No interval whatever, Madison urged, should be allowed between the release of Virginia's hold on that country and its assumption of federal obligations. Should it be made a separate state without this precaution, it might be tempted to remain so, "as well with regard to the United States as to Virginia." What would be its motive? To evade its share of the general debt, and, by an offer of exemption from taxes, to allure "the citizens of states groaning under them." He was aided by reports reaching him from Congress—the opinion was beginning to prevail "that a state has no right to dismember itself without the previous consent of the U. S." The amendment was adopted with hardly a dissenting vote. An Indian war preventing Kentucky from acting, Madison drafted a new act a year later. Two more Virginia laws, and nine Kentucky conventions, were needed before the state was admitted, along with Vermont, in 1792. During all that time, the restive region was held within state and national boundaries by Madison's requirement of joint action. It stood as an insurmountable bar to the treacherous disunion schemes of General Wilkinson.[40]

Madison had his first sight of the works of the Potomac in the summer of 1786, when, called to Winchester by the needs of a relative, he went on to Philadelphia by way of Harper's Ferry. The region itself moved him to this account to Jefferson:

"I had an opportunity of viewing the magnificent scene which nature here presents. I viewed it however under great disadvantages. The air was so thick that distant objects were not visible at all, and near ones not distinctly so. We ascended the mountain also at a wrong place, fatigued ourselves much in traversing it before we gained the right position, were threatened during the whole time by a thunder storm, and finally overtaken by it. Had the weather been favorable the prospect would have appeared to peculiar advantage, being enriched with the harvest in its full maturity, which filled every vale as far as the eye could reach."

Fifty men were at work clearing the sloping channel in the river bed, and had finished the most difficult part of the work. At Great Falls, he was told, three times as many were employed, with so much reliance on the rock-and-rope method of hauling boats that less than a mile of canal would be needed.[41]

Great Falls, before long, commanded Madison's attention for another reason. In 1788, convinced that this region would become a great center of manufacturing and commerce, his friend Light-horse Harry Lee paid £4,000 for 500 acres through which the canal was to be built. He at once offered Madison a third of it, proposing that they sell another third to Robert Morris and other men of wealth. The money thus received would take care of some arrearages in ground rent which must be paid to George William Fairfax before they could take possession. Properly handled, it "would ensure to both of us a very independent future."[42]

That kind of future was just what Madison needed. Trusting Lee's affectionate motives but skeptical of his fervency, he asked Washington what he thought about Great Falls. That was like asking the Pope what he thought of the Catholic Church. Lee, the general replied, had grabbed the land right out of the hands of Governor Johnson of Maryland, who had a scheme for developing millsites at the falls. Taking account, in addition, of the vast traffic of the upper river and western waters "it opens a field almost too extensive for imagination."[43]

Unluckily, or luckily, Madison's small resources were tied up in his Mohawk venture. But when he told Lee that he could not enter unless his share was paid for out of the profits of the bargain itself, the enthusiastic cavalryman swept both Madison and the canalsite into his embrace. "You shall be part owner of the lands," he replied, and proceeded at once to tell others of the partnership. There is no indication that Madison formally entered the speculation. His sole apparent contribution was a panegyric on it, written at Lee's request, for publication in monthly magazines. Two years later, with the hardhearted Fairfax demanding his pound of flesh (equal to £3,000 of Virginia currency), Lee began sending desperate appeals to Madison to borrow money to save the enterprise. Work two days for yourself as you do for the public and you will have the cash, he entreated. "Hamilton could and would get it for you."[44]

American history might have been different if Madison had acted on that lead. Instead he told Lee that poverty forbade him to retain an interest which should be transferred to someone with resources to support it. Thus, besides failure to acquire riches in the Mohawk Valley, Madison failed to have them thrust upon him at the Great Falls of the Potomac, where the bordering forests are as green today as they were in the 1780's. In each instance, it should be noted, his interest was directed to something unaffected by his current political activities. The true profit, to him, of the Potomac development, was the same as in the James, the same as in the service to Kentucky—the promotion of American development and the solidarity of the Union.

CHAPTER XXIV

ANNAPOLIS CONVENTION

ALMOST a year elapsed, after Madison secured the appointment of a commission on navigation of the lower Potomac, before it met with a like body from Maryland. Then, in March 1785, a conference was held suddenly, with Mason and Henderson present for Virginia, and (as Joseph Jones described it) "without the attendance or call for attendance of the other commissioners"—Madison and Randolph. Madison took this with his customary lack of vanity. What with spring mud, slow mails and the lack of a good tom-tom system, anything could fail to happen in Virginia. He understood, so he told Jefferson, that the most amicable spirit governed the negotiation. Not until July did he learn that Governor Henry had forgotten to notify the Virginia commissioners of a date set by Maryland.[1]

From George Mason, after he recovered from a long illness, came explanation and apology. Mason did not even know of his original appointment until two of the Maryland commissioners asked his company to Alexandria. They waited several days for Madison and Randolph, then accepted Washington's invitation to Mount Vernon and proceeded to business. "Nothing but absolute necessity should have induced me to enter upon [this] without you," Mason assured him, "but the Maryland gentlemen would have been much disgusted with a disappointment, after attending at such a distance in very bad weather." It was perhaps lucky, he commented, that they did not have a copy of the resolution appointing them, for Virginia won concessions in the Potomac by granting others in Chesapeake Bay, which was not included in the act at all.[2]

Madison headed a committee of six which dealt with the Mason-Henderson compact in the ensuing assembly meeting. It granted mutual use of harbors without tolls, exempted domestic produce from duty and prorated tonnage charges on foreign cargoes destined for both states. The Potomac was declared to be a common highway to all American citizens and friendly foreigners. Shore control and fishing were regulated, lighthouse costs divided, joint criminal jurisdiction established. In the ratification, Madison ignored the exceeding of authority and covered up the defect in attendance (the law required three to be present) by naming Mason and Henderson as the commissioners appointed by Virginia.[3]

Coupled with the compact was a suggestion that annual conferences be held on commerce. Knowing that this advice was to be given, Madison saw a chance to gain larger objectives. Why not, he asked Washington, during his rained-in October visit, use it as a handle for a general attack on the ills of the Confederation? Accordingly, keeping in the background because of his too-bright Continental label, he joined with John Tyler in a move to vest Congress with a general and permanent power to regulate the commerce of the United States. This was the precipitating step toward the drafting of the new Constitution.[4]

Madison saw earlier than Tyler did that commercial regulations must be nationwide. In 1784, he opposed and defeated Tyler's proposal that the federal impost be made effective in twelve states. That, he pointed out, would merely open a channel for smuggling through Rhode Island. He strongly approved a move by Monroe, early in 1785, to have Congress ask for a power over commerce, and sent him a summary of the situation in Virginia. Boston and Philadelphia merchants, at that time, were reviving tea-party methods to break a threatened British trade monopoly. If these discontents reached Virginia, Madison said, the protests would come from the planters, not the merchants. "Our trade," he told Monroe, "was never more completely monopolized by Great Britain when it was under the direction of the British Parliament." But as nearly all Virginia merchants were connected with Britain, and the state had neither ships nor seamen, no mercantile complaints were heard.[5]

Trying to convert Richard Henry Lee (now president of Congress) Madison asserted that the state's situation "precisely verifies the doctrine held out in Deane's intercepted letters. The Revolution has robbed us of our trade with the West Indies, the only one which yielded us a favorable balance, without opening any other channels to compensate for it." To make the monopoly more mortifying, both merchants and private planters who shipped tobacco "have received accounts of sales this season which carry the most visible and shameful frauds in every article."

Madison's effort to cope with this by limiting the ports of entry was under heavy attack. Arthur Lee, he was told, gained election to the assembly by promising to overset the port bill. With all of these difficulties at home, and Rhode Island vexing the whole country, Madison easily reached the conclusion he expressed to Monroe:

"If it be necessary to regulate trade at all, it surely is necessary to lodge the power where trade can be regulated with effect; and experience has confirmed what reason foresaw, that it can never be so regulated by the states acting in their separate capacities. They can no more exercise this power separately than they could separately carry on war, or separately form treaties of alliance or commerce."[6]

The opposing argument was voiced by Richard Henry Lee, who wrote to Madison that a congressional power over trade "would be dangerous in the extreme to the five southern or staple states, whose want of ships and seamen would expose their freightage and their produce to a most pernicious and destructive monopoly." Already familiar with this fear of New England, Madison refuted the argument four days before Lee penned it. "Will the present system of Great Britain ever give the southern states bottoms?" he asked Monroe. If not, "I should suppose it no mark either of folly or incivility to give our custom to our brethren, rather than to those who have not yet entitled themselves to the name of friends." As to the general objection to federal power over trade, drawn from the diversity of interests of the states, if that had been listened to there would have been no confederation. Furthermore, the commercial interests of the states harmonized in more points than they differed.

These sentiments, Madison conceded, would not be relished in the public councils of Virginia. The only hope he saw for a grant of power to Congress lay in the fact that it would be directed against Great Britain, therefore would be favored "by the animosities which still prevail in a strong degree against her." His preference was for perfect freedom of trade, but for that, the United States must be out of debt and unoppressed by foreign discriminations.[7]

Madison was further impressed with the need for action when he visited New York in September, 1785. Massachusetts and Pennsylvania were levying duties on foreign goods and tonnage—duties which were sure to be evaded by smuggling through neighboring states. The only result of such partial efforts would be "to drive their trade into other channels, and to kindle heart-burnings on all sides." At this time, a year and a half before the Constitutional Convention, his thoughts were still on coercion of the states. "A single frigate under the orders of Congress could make it the interest of any one of the Atlantic states to pay its just quota," he observed to Jefferson. Settle the state war accounts, apportion the national debt, recognize the authority of Congress to force the states to pay their quotas, grant Congress an adequate power over commerce (including an impost for revenue)—these were the chief necessities. On this last point, "The middle states favor the measure, the eastern are zealous for it, the southern are divided." Much would depend on Virginia.[8]

Such was the background of the Madison-Tyler move for federal regulation of commerce. Madison's estimate of the anti-British bias was confirmed by a flock of county petitions denouncing the prohibition of trade to the West Indies and praying for reprisals. Good fortune attended him when Arthur Lee was ousted from the assembly (though Madison voted for him) on the ground that his election to a post in the federal Treasury conflicted with a new law excluding members of Congress from the state legislature.[9]

Madison's argument for federal regulation is known through his customary microscopic notes.[10] He cited the injuries to Connecticut and New Hampshire, forced to pay tribute on goods imported through Rhode Island, New York and Massachusetts; New Jersey, at the mercy of New York and Pennsylvania; North Carolina, paying duties to Virginia; the Western country, victimized by all the maritime states. Federal control was the only system intelligible to foreigners. It was as necessary as national action in war. It presented no danger to the liberties of the states.

On this last point Madison's argument revealed a broad approach to federal power. Treaties of commerce, he contended, were ineffectual without general commercial regulations, wherefore the "Power of treaties involves the danger if any." In other words, national regulations of commerce could be established, and state regulations overridden, by exercise of the treaty power, even without a commerce clause in the Constitution. Thomas Jefferson expressed the same opinion to Monroe in that same year: "The moment these treaties are concluded the jurisdiction of Congress over the commerce of the states springs into existence, and that of the particular states is superseded so far as the articles of the treaty may have taken up the subject."[11]

Thus both Madison and Jefferson, on the eve of the writing of the Constitution, were thinking of the treaty power in the same broad terms with which the Supreme Court, over the violent protests of state righters, has interpreted it for more than a century and a half. This was not, of course, an effective means of action in a government declining into impotence. Power over commerce, Madison warned in his speech, was essential to preserve the federal Constitution. Without it there would be a dissolution of the Confederacy, an appeal to the sword in every petty squabble, standing armies and perpetual taxes for them in every state. The states would be the sport of foreign politics. The glory of the Revolution would be blasted.

The Madison-Tyler forces carried their resolution by a wide margin and Madison proceeded to draft the authorized bill. Rives credited him only with the preamble, which echoed his speech, pointing out that the rest of it fell short of his known views. However, Madison's original draft is among his papers, wrongly placed and unidentified. It contains not only the four resolves of the final measure but two others which represented his real thinking—a declaration that a power over foreign trade "would add energy and dignity to the federal government," and a resolve "that the unrestrained exercise of the powers possessed by each state over its own commerce may be productive of discord among the parties to the Union, and that Congress ought to be vested with authority to regulate the same in certain cases."[12]

These hard-hitting sentences, which would have been blown up as frightful bogeys by the Harrison-Braxton party, were dropped in favor of a mellifluous preamble on the need for commercial uniformity. Following the grant of federal power came a shrewdly worded paragraph which forbade the states to levy duties on imports from other states, but authorized them "altogether [to] prohibit the importation from any other state" of goods whose importation "is at the same time prohibited from all other places whatsoever." On the surface, that was a retention of the right to tax foreign goods, and to shut out foreign goods or all goods. In reality, it allowed only a total embargo of specific items. Short of that, American goods could not be banned, and how could foreign goods be taxed or banned when they could be brought in duty-free from other states? A final section placed a time limit on federal regulatory acts, but none on the basic power of Congress to regulate.

The purpose here was to grant more power than met the eye. As Madison put it, the bill was written to give Congress "such direct power only as would not alarm" and "indirectly require a conformity" of the states to federal regulations. So thoroughly was this purpose concealed that the issue never arose during a struggle in which other features of the bill were torn to pieces. A three-way coalition, Madison revealed, was formed against it—delegates holding illiberal animosities against the North, others frightened at a perpetual grant of power, and men flattered with a hope that a temporary grant might be renewed—the most visionary hope, he cried to Washington, that perhaps ever deluded men of sense. In their present temper, the states would not even renew "those sacrifices of sovereignty on which the federal government now rests."[13]

Bitter and illiberal beyond example (Madison said) against Congress and the Northern states, Speaker Harrison and his cohorts beat down the bill by emasculating amendments. They cut the perpetual grant to twenty-five years, then to thirteen, so completely destroying its value that its friends abandoned it and sought a new approach.[14] Returning to his original thought based on the Virginia-Maryland commercial conference, Madison now drafted and Tyler introduced a resolution which, the former believed, would have fewer enemies. Their strategy was to hold it back until some futile alternatives were voted on. The result was that they came to the last day of the session with no action on anything. The distress of merchants made some step imperative. So, crossing up the opponents who were alert against the old bill granting power to Congress, the Madison-Tyler forces called up their new measure and put it through almost without opposition. It was the resolution which led to the famous Annapolis Convention, fore-runner of the one which produced the Constitution. With names filled in, it read:

"Resolved, That Edmund Randolph, James Madison Jr., Walter Jones, St. George Tucker, Meriwether Smith, esquires be appointed commissioners, who, or any three of whom shall meet such commissioners as may be appointed by the other states in the Union at a time and place to be agreed on, to take into consideration the trade of the United States; to examine the relative situations and trade of the said states; to consider how far a uniform system in their commercial regulations may be necessary to their common interest and their permanent harmony; and to report to the several states such an act relative to this great object as when unanimously ratified by them will enable the United States in Congress effectually to provide for the same."[15]

At first only Randolph, Madison and Senator Walter Jones were to have been on the commission. Tucker, described by Madison as "sensible, federal and skilled in commerce," was added; then antifederal Smith; then William Ronald, who declined. The purpose of "this multitude of associates," Madison suspected, was to "stifle the thing at its birth," but he felt that much had been gained. The resolution was elastic as to new powers, and whatever came from the convention would "be of a permanent not a temporary nature, which I think will be a great point."[16]

Because Madison called the motion "that of Mr. Tyler," the

authorship of this historic paper has been claimed for the latter. John C. Hamilton and L. G. Tyler were strenuous in that assertion, even in the face of George Tucker's statement, "on the authority of Mr. Madison himself," that because of antifederal feeling in Virginia he "did not venture to offer his own resolution, but prevailed upon Mr. Tyler . . . to offer it." Madison made a similar but less positive comment in his unfinished sketch of events leading to the writing of the Constitution. Also responding to an inquiry from Noah Webster, he wrote: "In 1785 I made a proposition with success" for a meeting of commissioners at Annapolis—a statement not made to claim credit, but to correct Webster's belief that this was a first proposal of the new Constitution. Madison's authorship was supported, by implication, by President Tyler. Appealed to by John C. Hamilton for a statement that Judge Tyler wrote it, he replied that his father offered it in the House and it "was by adoption as thoroughly and completely his own as if he had penned it himself."[17]

Thinking it prudent to avoid Congress and large commercial towns, the Virginia deputies proposed Annapolis for the place and the first Monday in September, 1786, as the time for the convention. Should it fail, said Madison, all the world would know "that we are not to be respected nor apprehended as a nation in matters of commerce." Conditions grew worse as the year advanced. New regulations by the states only "set them by the ears." Connecticut, New Jersey and Delaware, by declaring their ports free, upset the acts of Massachusetts, New York and Pennsylvania. With no revenue from imposts, federal finance was drying up—only $400,-000 received in the previous year, Madison reported, and nearly all of that from Virginia "which will not supply a single shilling the present year." Commercial anarchy would reduce exports and drain more specie out of the country, thus furnishing "pretexts for the pernicious substitution of paper money, for indulgences to debtors, for postponement of taxes." He saw a chain of cause and effect, from commercial to political, from political to moral evils. With no action possible unless all the states concurred, he had meager hope, but "if the present crisis cannot effect unanimity, from what future concurrence of circumstances is it to be expected?"[18]

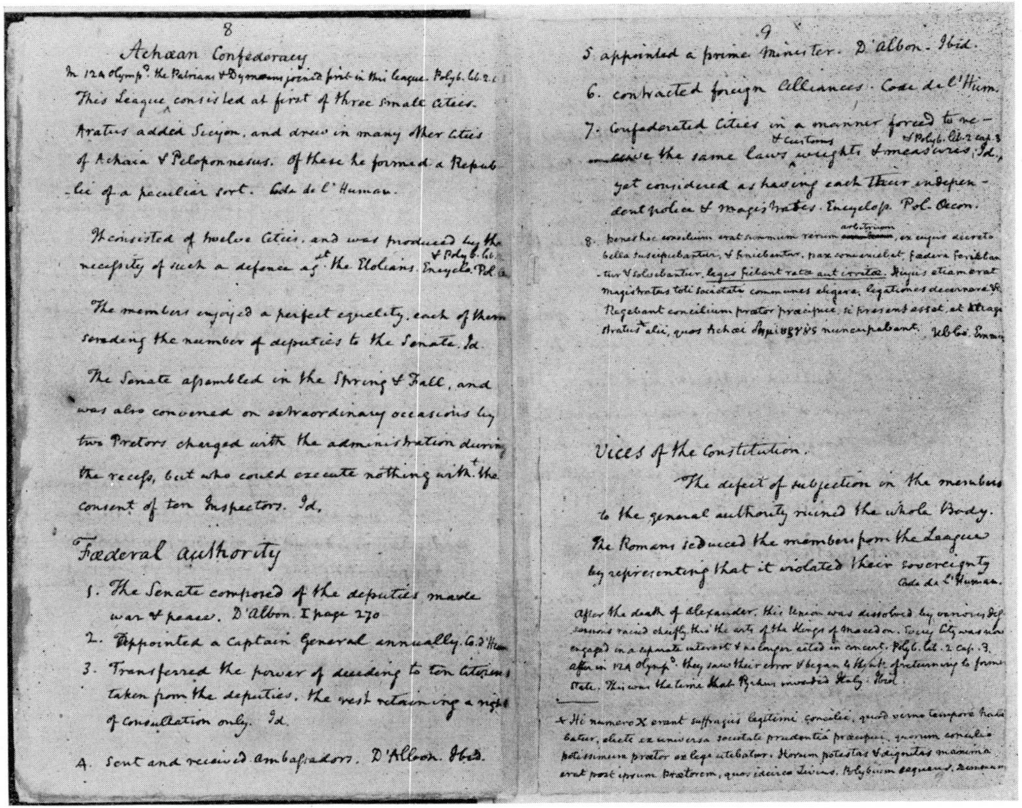

8

Achæan Confederacy

In 124 Olymp^d. the Patrians & Dymæans joined first in this League. Polyb. Lib. 2.

This League consisted at first of three small cities.

Aratus added Sicyon, and drew in many other cities of Achaia & Peloponnesus. Of these he formed a Republic of a peculiar sort. Code de l'Human.

It consisted of twelve Cities, and was produced by the necessity of such a defence ag^st the Etolians. Encyclo. Pol. & Polyb. Lib.

The members enjoyed a perfect equality, each of them sending the number of deputies to the Senate. Id.

The Senate assembled in the Spring & Fall, and was also convened on extraordinary occasions by two Pretors charged with the administration during the recess, but who could execute nothing with^t the consent of ten Inspectors. Id.

Fœderal authority

1. The Senate composed of the deputies made war & peace. D'Albon. I page 270
2. Appointed a Captain General annually. Co. d'Hum.
3. Transferred the power of deciding to ten citizens taken from the deputies, the rest retaining a right of consultation only. Id.
4. Sent and received Ambassadors. D'Albon. Ibid.

9

5. appointed a prime Minister. D'Albon. Ibid.
6. contracted foreign alliances. Code de l'Hum.
7. Confederated Cities in a manner forced to receive the same laws & customs weights & measures; Id, & Polyb. Lib. 2 cap. 3 yet considered as having each their independent police & magistrates. Encyclop. Pol. Oecon.
8. Penes hoc concilium erat summum rerum arbitrium, ex cujus decreto bella suscipiebantur, & finiebantur, pax conveniebat, fœdera feriebantur & solvebantur, leges fiebant ratæ aut irritæ. Hujus etiam erat magistratus toti societati communes eligere, legationes decernere &c. Regebant concilium prætor præcipue, si presens esset, et Magistratus^x alii, quos Achæi δημιουργούς nuncupabant. Ubbo. Emm.

Vices of the Constitution.

The defect of subjection in the members to the general authority ruined the whole Body. The Romans seduced the members from the League by representing that it violated their sovereignty. Code de l'Human.

After the death of Alexander, this Union was dissolved by various dissensions raised chiefly thro' the arts of the Kings of Macedon. Every City was now engaged in a separate interest & no longer acted in concert. Polyb. Lib. 2 Cap. 3. After in 124 Olymp^d. they saw their error & began to think of returning to former State. This was the time that Pyrrhus invaded Italy. Ibid.

x Hi numero X erant suffragiis legitimi concilii, quod verno tempore habebatur, electi ex universa societate prudentia præcipui, quorum consilio potissimum prætor ex lege utebatur. Horum potestas & dignitas maxima erat post ipsum Prætorem, quos idcirco Livius, Polybium sequens, Demiurgos...

Madison's Study of Confederacies

THE POTOMAC AT HARPER'S FERRY

Cheering news came in April, that Rhode Island had approved the impost, but in the same month New York killed it with a treacherous half acceptance. This was more ominous in its implications than in effect, for the impost, if adopted, would fall far short of the power Congress ought to have. "It leaves the door unshut against a commercial warfare among the states," Madison remarked, "our trade exposed to foreign machinations, and the distresses of an unfavorable balance very little checked." Such was the state of affairs when the Virginian and his servant mounted their horses and set off, through midsummer storms followed by days of exhausting heat, on a circuitous journey through Winchester, Harper's Ferry, Philadelphia and New York, to Annapolis.[19]

"Mr. Madison of Virginia has been here for some time past," wrote Rufus King from New York on September 3. "He will attend the convention. He does not discover or propose any other plan than that of investing Congress with full powers for the regulation of commerce foreign and domestic. But this power will run deep into the authorities of the individual states, and can never be well exercised without a federal judiciary. The reform must necessarily be extensive."[20]

What he saw, not what he desired, held Madison to this limited objective. Nothing, he wrote to his brother Ambrose from the seat of Congress, "can bear a worse aspect than our federal affairs as viewed from this position. No money comes into the public treasury, trade is on a wretched footing, and the states are running mad after paper money." Many in and out of Congress, he found, were talking of a plenipotentiary convention to amend the Articles of Confederation. "Though my wishes are in favor of such an event," he observed to Jefferson, "yet I despair so much of its accomplishment at the present crisis that I do not extend my views beyond a commercial reform. To speak the truth I almost despair even of this." Piecemeal reform was preferable, he had remarked a little earlier because "we have both ignorance and iniquity to combat," and it was necessary to humor the prejudices of the ignorant in order to defeat the iniquitous.[21]

Madison summarized the attendance prospect. Deputies had been appointed by New Hampshire, Massachusetts, Rhode Island,

New York, New Jersey, Pennsylvania, Delaware and Virginia. And the others? Connecticut disliked all conventions, not the object of this one. The Maryland Senate feared that the Annapolis meeting would derogate from the authority of Congress. (That from the state most often cited to prove that Congress had none!) The North Carolina legislature had not met. (Actually, the governor named delegates.) South Carolina concurred indirectly. "Of the affairs of Georgia I know as little as of those of Kamskatska."[22]

This was not so bad, since no state had shown hostility, but when Madison reached Annapolis on September 4 he found only two commissioners present. So he settled down to wait in George Mann's inn, where lodging was a shilling a night and sixpence for his servant. Others had arrived by the eighth but he saw no "prospect of a sufficient number to make the meeting respectable." The delay gave a chance, anyway, for fatigue to wear off—with a corresponding shift in the Madison expense account from wine, punch and porter to a steady entry of tea. Three days later, Delaware, New Jersey and Virginia alone had quorums, with two deputies just in from New York and one present from Pennsylvania. Unless more came soon, it was proposed to break up the meeting—first, however, choosing another place and date and advising an extension of the plan to other defects of the Confederation. The absence of Massachusetts was a particular blow, but what could one expect with men like Stephen Higginson named as delegates? This Boston merchant strongly suspected that the object of the Annapolis meeting was political rather than commercial. "The measure," he advised John Adams, "appears to have originated in Virginia and with Mr. Madison. The men I have mentioned are all of them esteemed great aristocrats. . . . Few of them have been in the commercial line, nor is it probable they know or care much about commercial objects." Higginson apparently divided the world into aristocrats and tax-allergic importers.[23]

At any rate, opponents of federal power stayed at home, so the twelve present were very much of one mind. Alexander Hamilton had called for revision of the Constitution as early as 1780. With him from New York was Egbert Benson, who promoted the

Hartford Convention's request that Congress use the army to collect delinquent state quotas. Tench Coxe of Pennsylvania held federal ideas too strong to be disclosed except to men of a philosophic turn of mind—meaning, when he said it, Madison. Delaware's delegation was headed by George Read, who said of the states that "a national government must soon of necessity swallow all of them up."[24] His colleague, Convention Chairman John Dickinson, wanted a strong federal judiciary to curb the states. Two of Madison's close friends, William C. Houston and Abraham Clark, led the four Jerseyites. Opposed to a consolidated government, they were eager to rescue their small state from New York's commercial tyranny.

Following a general discussion, Attorney General Randolph was made head of a committee to report "measures fit to be taken" by so few delegates. He plunged into a study of credentials granting various degrees of authority, while Madison and Tucker spent the recess trying to persuade Tench Coxe that they had no power to discuss Virginia's trade relations with Pennsylvania. Coxe found this hard to believe, since he had been given that duty pursuant to a request of the Virginia Assembly. What happened? Why, antifederalists called for two-state conferences as a maneuver against federal power over trade, then forgot to have commissioners named. Not to be cheated out of proving Pennsylvania's virtue, Coxe informed the Virginians, by letter, that his state admitted all American trade on a basis of perfect equality, then met with unfair discriminations in sister states.[25]

Randolph apparently expected to write a statement of convention policy, for a manuscript in his hand refers to "the report and resolutions following," then breaks off in the middle of a sentence about credentials. It was at this point, evidently, that the deputies decided to call for a convention with greater powers. The more nationalistic Hamilton, not a member of the Randolph committee, took over the writing job. Madison agreed completely with the shift of tactics. The experiment of a partial cure had been attempted and was failing. The time had come for radical action. Almost all of the delegates felt that way, he recalled later, each one being reinforced by the attitude of the others.[26]

Writing eighteen years after the event, Madison could not remember who first proposed the second convention. "I have an indistinct impression that it received its first formal suggestion from Mr. Abraham Clark of New Jersey," he replied to Noah Webster's inquiry. "Mr. Hamilton was certainly the member who drafted the address." The word "formal" is the key to what took place. New Jersey was the only state which had specifically authorized its delegates to act on other matters than trade. Only a New Jersey delegate could make a motion for a constitutional convention without being charged with taking the lead in a usurpation of authority. Clark's action, therefore, does not reduce the probability that Hamilton initiated the plan.

With the New Yorker writing the address to Congress and the states, it was sure to frighten the reluctant as much as it inspired the willing. In fact, the first to shiver was the chairman of the drafting committee. As Hamilton's biographer Morse relates the story, the address as first framed "set forth very elaborately and undisguisedly the grave condition of the country and the imperative necessity for a powerful government. But Governor Edmund Randolph objected to it as too strong; whereupon Madison said to Hamilton: 'You had better yield to this man, for otherwise all Virginia will be against you.' " This was no reflection of Madison's own inclinations. He remembered how Hamilton's cogent and powerful letter to Rhode Island had frightened Virginia into rejection of the impost. He was thoroughly acquainted, also, with the peculiar quirk which made Randolph take fright at concrete measures to attain less than he indorsed in the abstract. A mild pamphlet on American government, by Dr. Price of England, proposing much less than Madison did, was thought by Randolph to go "perhaps too far even for those among us who entertain sentiments the most federal." Madison knew also that in addition to having influence, the attorney general was a Virginia touchstone: the state by instinct would go no farther in the federal direction than he would.[27]

In its final form, Hamilton's Annapolis address led by gentle degrees to its mildly worded but crucial conclusion. A convention to follow this one was requested, not for the terrifying purpose of revising the constitution, but "for the same and such other purposes" as public affairs require. Larger powers were sought for the deputies, not directly, but by terming New Jersey's expansion of them an improvement which deserved inclusion in the new plan. Also, to make the commerce power effective and remove doubts about its nature and limits, other parts of the federal system might need adjustment. That is, let people think of a federal judiciary as a restraint upon federal power as well as a bulwark of it. There was an upward tilt, but nothing alarming, in the remark "that the defects, upon a closer examination, may be found greater and more numerous" than had been thought. They did not argue for a new convention. The "national circumstances" calling for a stronger government were so well known that it would be useless to point them out.

No less thickly and softly gloved was the final recommendation, offered "with the utmost deference," that all the states appoint commissioners to meet at Philadelphia on the second Monday in May next. There they were "to devise such further provisions as shall appear to them necessary to render the constitution of the federal government adequate to the exigencies of the Union; and to report such an act for that purpose to the United States in Congress assembled, as, when agreed to by them, and afterwards confirmed by the legislatures of every state, will effectually provide for the same."[28]

Written with all of Alexander Hamilton's grace and lucidity, the address was so thoroughly un-Hamiltonian in content—thanks to Randolph's alarm and Madison's warning—that nobody could find anything in it to attack except the proposition itself.

CHAPTER XXV

High Road to Philadelphia

WITH a constitutional convention in the offing, Virginia must be brought to its support. An extra month in Philadelphia, whittling down his debt to Monroe, forced Madison to go direct to Richmond. This meant a six months' absence from Montpelier, so he wrote home en route asking that servants be sent down with winter clothing and a supply of food. They arrived (John Tucker and Joe) four days after Madison did, but John had forgotten the bacon. No matter, the tavern had plenty, but "fresh butter would continue to be very acceptable." Richmond was beginning to look more like a capital. The courthouse could still be described by a traveler as "the shabbiest I ever saw," the governor's house was as poor as ever, and when one did not sink to his knees in mud he was blinded by dust. But the new capitol building (whose construction Madison had promoted) was casting an ever larger shadow, and not all of the spindly farm horses that brought in produce were harnessed with straw yokes and traces of twisted bark.[1]

No less acceptable than butter was the fact that Patrick Henry, though retiring as governor at the end of November, would rusticate for a year at Red Hill. It was jam on the bread when Edmund Randolph was elected to succeed him after an abortive boom for Richard Henry Lee.

By the time Madison was ready to seek action, the question of federal power had been complicated by two far-reaching developments. In the spring of 1786, after a year of futile negotiations with Spanish Minister Gardoqui, Foreign Secretary Jay reversed his strong position in defense of the Mississippi and asked Congress to abandon the right of navigation for a period of twenty-five years. Part of the motive, it was generally believed, was to turn Western commerce down the Hudson River, but the principal support came from New England fishing interests. "Our fish, and every article we sell in Spain," said Rufus King, "is sold upon the footing of . . . favor, and not right. Should we embarrass ourselves in the attempts of imprudent men to navigate the Mississippi below the northern boundary of Florida, we can expect no favors from the Spanish government."[2]

Madison's reaction was one of shocked surprise that such a move should be made after the crisis of war had passed. "The measure in question," he asserted to Monroe, "would be a voluntary barter in time of profound peace of the rights of one part of the empire to the interests of another part. What would Massachusetts say to a proposition for ceding to Britain her right of fishery as the price of some stipulations in favor of tobacco?" Passing through Princeton, he stirred up Dr. Witherspoon against the proposal, then, in Philadelphia, vainly solicited Delegate Wilson (who appeared to agree with him) to go to Congress and turn the tide in the wavering Pennsylvania delegation.[3]

"Figure to yourself," Madison wrote to Jefferson in the wake of these talks, "the effect of such a stipulation on the Assembly of Virginia, already jealous of northern politics," with many members attached to the West by interest and many others who "will zealously play off the disgust of its friends against federal measures." Figure its effect on the Western people themselves. Feeling sold by their Atlantic brethren, will they not be likely to "consider themselves absolved from every federal tie and court some [foreign] protection for their betrayed rights"? He saw no likelihood of nine states assenting to Jay's projected treaty, "but an unsuccessful attempt by six or seven will favor the views of Spain and be fatal I fear to an augmentation of the federal authority, if not to the little now existing."[4]

The situation became more acute when Congress pushed to reality an earlier threat to revoke the Mississippi instruction by a vote of seven states. Studying the history of the nine-state requirement at the time he took away John Adams' authority, Madison concluded that seven states could revoke a commission (as they did in that instance) but that nine were required for any positive step in treaty making. Instructions to a minister had the full solemnity of the treaty itself, because of the sovereign's promise to ratify what the minister signed. Repeal of an instruction, though negative in form, was positive in effect.[5]

Now Congress had taken an action which added "the insult of trick to the injury of the thing itself." It was particularly mortifying to Madison because ever since he came out of Congress he had worked to inspire confidence in that body as equally attentive "to the rights and interests of every part of the republic." He had argued to Western members of the legislature that if the Mississippi was to be defended, Congress must be made respectable by new powers. What could he say now? His position was undermined and the interests of the country jeopardized—nay, the durability of the Union threatened—by a course of conduct which placed "temporary and partial interests" ahead of the boasted maxims of just policy.

One maxim, he was certain, had been disproved—"the current one that the interest of the majority is the political standard of right and wrong." Taking interest to mean ultimate happiness, the proposition no doubt was true, but "taking it in the popular sense, as referring to immediate augmentation of property and wealth, nothing can be more false. In the latter sense it would be the interest of the majority in every community to despoil and enslave the minority of individuals, and in a federal community to make a similar sacrifice of the minority of component states." Congress was re-establishing force as the measure of right "and in this light the western settlements will infallibly view it."[6]

There was of course self-interest on both sides. Occlusion of the Mississippi, said Virginia's Grayson in Congress, "would destroy the hopes of the principal men in the southern states in establishing the future fortunes of their families," but would help New York settle her wasteland.[7] Madison's stand was in conflict with his economic interest. He was opposing a policy whose effect would be to channel Western commerce right through his lands on the Mohawk River, advocating one which would give Western tobacco growers a competitive advantage over the cash staple of Montpelier. Considerations of national welfare, not his own, determined his position.

"I find with pleasure," Madison wrote on reaching Richmond, "that the navigation of the Mississippi will be defended with as much zeal as could be wished." His pleasure was dimmed within a day by the violence of resentment against the federal councils. Even though Jay's surrender should be frustrated, he told Washington, "the effects already produced will be a great bar to an amendment of the confederacy, which I consider as essential to its continuance." The views of Congress, he assured the agitated Kentucky members, were likely to be changed, and it would be rash to let this one action interfere with the building up of the government. The report from Annapolis lay on the table, and it was his hope to secure action on it before the business of the Mississippi began to ferment.[8]

It was at this time that Madison received, from Henry Lee, his first detailed account of that other crucial event of the period—the armed uprising of Massachusetts war veterans and farmers against high interest rates, mortgage foreclosures, imprisonment for debt and the high cost of injustice in the courts. Shays' Rebellion was not, to be sure, presented to or by him in just that light. "Great commotions are prevailing in Massachusetts," he wrote to the elder Madison. "An appeal to the sword is exceedingly dreaded. The discontented it is said are as numerous as the friends of government and more decided in their measures." They professed to aim only at reform of abuses "but an abolition of debts public and private, and a new division of property, are strongly suspected to be in contemplation." Washington relayed the similar account which came from War Secretary Knox—12,000 to 15,000 unprincipled men determined to annihilate all debts by means of unfunded paper money, and dedicated to a creed: "That the property of the United States has been protected from confiscation of Britain by the joint exertions of *all,* and therefore ought to be the *common property* of all."

"Let us look to our national character, and to things beyond the present period," admonished Washington, as he called on Madison to secure Virginia's attention to that "great and most important of all objects, the federal government." As for the threat to order in Massachusetts:

"Will not the wise and good strive hard to avert this evil? Or will their supineness suffer . . . disaffected and desperate characters to involve this rising empire in wretchedness and contempt? . . . To you, I am sure I need not add aught on this subject. . . . Thirteen sovereignties pulling against each other . . . will soon bring ruin on the whole, whereas a liberal and energetic Constitution, well guarded and closely watched, to prevent encroachments, might restore us to that degree of respectability and consequence to which we had a fair claim, and the brightest prospect of attaining."[9]

Madison saw these gloomy events in the same light. If they failed to impress the American public, it would be a proof that the case was desperate. Having just taken part in one, the Virginian was not terrified at the idea of political uprisings. Revolt for social and economic ends was something else, and he knew nothing of the real grievances of these new embattled farmers of Massachusetts. He knew more, in fact, about conditions in France. Jefferson had recently described to him the misery of "the poor who cannot find work," resulting from property and revenues being "absolutely concentered in a very few hands." Legislators, the founder-to-be of Jeffersonian democracy remarked, "cannot invent too many devices for subdividing property," the one he suggested being "to exempt all from taxation below a certain point, and to tax the higher portions of property in geometrical progression as they rise."[10]

There was more actual revolution in that one idea—the genesis of the graduated income tax—than in all the muskets and pitchforks surrounding Daniel Shays, but it did not terrify Madison. "Your reflections on the idle poor of Europe form a valuable lesson to the legislators of every country, and particularly of a new one," he responded to the American minister. "I have no doubt but that the misery of the lower classes will be found to abate wherever the government assumes a freer aspect, and laws favor the subdivision of property, yet I suspect that the difference will not fully account for the comparative comfort of the mass of people in the United States." He then launched into a discussion of the effect of overpopulation upon human welfare—twelve years before Malthus dealt with that subject in his famous *Essay on the Principle of Population.*

"A certain degree of misery," Madison observed, "seems insepa-rable from a high degree of populousness. If the lands in Europe which are now dedicated to the amusement of the idle rich were parcelled out among the idle poor, I readily conceive the happy revolution which would be experienced by a certain proportion of the latter. But still would there not remain a great proportion unrelieved?" Let the lands be shared and labor divided ever so wisely, too much food, clothing and other comforts would still be produced by too few people, and what would be done with the rest of them? In the past they had become manufacturers of super-fluities, idle landowners, domestics, soldiers, merchants, mariners, but most of these classes would be reduced by the very virtues associated with an equal division of property—simplicity of man-ners, a juster government. He left the problem unsettled.[11]

Madison saw France as the scene of misery, America as a place where all classes lived in comfort. General Knox did not tell Washington, nor Washington relay the word to Madison, that Massachusetts veterans of the Revolution were rebelling against farm interest rates of twenty-five to forty per cent per year; that their $200 average taxes exceeded the cash income of the average family; that in one county (Worcester) a single year's lawsuits, mostly for debt, involved as many litigants as there were families in the county; that twenty times as many men were in jail for debt, in that same county, as for all other offenses combined; that the mere cost of being sued (seven pound court costs on a four pound debt) was enough to rob a poor man of land and liberty; that every particle of property a person owned—homestead, tools, furniture, bedding, "the last potato in his cellar and the only cow or pig in his barn"—could be and was sold for debt at a fifth of its value and the debtor clapped into jail for the deficiency. All this lay behind the forcible closing of the courts by Massachusetts farmers, and the assumption of leadership by the "desperate and unprincipled" Daniel Shays, who learned how to carry a gun at Lexington, Bunker Hill, Ticonderoga, Saratoga and Stony Point.[12]

Madison held no brief for men of wealth. He hated speculators,

monopolizers and usurers and despised their political allies. Had
he been acquainted with the realities of farm life in Massachusetts, he would have looked with more tolerant understanding
upon the rebels, but with no acceptance either of their violence or
their remedies. An armed uprising struck at the basis of public
order on which the welfare of all depended. Escape from debt by
a tender of worthless currency was both dishonest and ruinous to
trust between man and man. Forcible closing of the courts was
an evidence of disease, not a cure of it. Thus, whether presented
in its true light or through the frightened optics of "the wise, the
rich, the good" who did the moneylending and ran the government in Massachusetts, Shays' Rebellion was something to inspire
a feeling of insecurity among all who believed in order under law.
The surest and deepest effect of it was to promote the movement
to strengthen the federal government.

Virginia showed no signs of catching the Shays contagion. On
the contrary, the first word of it came just in time to increase the
revulsion against paper money, and that in turn was accompanied
by a strong upswing of federal sentiment. This offset the bitterness over Jay's effort to give up the Mississippi, and, to Madison's
pleased surprise, led to *unanimous* adoption of a resolution approving the recommendations of the Annapolis Convention. Acting for a committee of seven, he drafted a bill to put the decision
into effect, then addressed himself to Washington:

"It has been thought advisable, to give this subject a very solemn
dress, and all the weight that could be derived from a single state.
This idea will be pursued in the selection of characters to represent
Virginia in the federal convention. You will infer our earnestness on this point from the liberty which will be taken of placing
your name at the head of them."[13]

Fearing an immediate rejection, Madison suggested that Washington's decision wait until it had to be made. In the meantime,
the naming of him would "assist powerfully in marking the zeal
of our legislature, and its opinion of the magnitude of the occasion." The very solemn dress consisted of a single piece of cloth—

one sentence—six hundred words long, which by some miracle gained cumulative force throughout. It explained the by-passing of Congress not as a recognition of that body's unpopularity, but fear that its ordinary work would interrupt the revision. The new modeling of federal government was not termed a plan to coerce the states and check their follies. It was to reap the just fruits of independence and a Union cemented with blood, and "secure the great objects for which that government was instituted, and to render the United States as happy in peace as they have been glorious in war."[14]

Madison withheld his motion to elect deputies until he should hear from Washington, who, failing to send to Alexandria for his mail, was rather slow in replying. Pleased as he was to hear that the assembly was following "the sure paths that lead to national happiness," it was out of his power to share in it consistently. For a combination of reasons—private affairs, a wish for retirement, and rheumatic pains—he had just declined to attend the triennial convention of the Society of the Cincinnati of which he was president. Both meetings were to be in the same city at the same time. How could he go to one after rejecting the other? Polling the legislative leaders and finding them of his own mind, Madison offered his motion for an election and the following were chosen: George Washington, Patrick Henry, Governor Edmund Randolph, John Blair, James Madison, George Mason and George Wythe.[15]

Now Madison turned once more to the wooing of Washington. "It was the opinion of every judicious friend whom I consulted," he told the general, "that your name could not be spared from the deputation." The critical importance of the convention's work should reconcile it with his feeling about the army officers. The advantage of his name "as a mark of the earnestness of Virginia" and a drawing power throughout the Confederacy, ought not to be given up. These sentiments, he flattered himself, would "at least apologize for my departure from those held out in your letter."

Upon receipt of this appeal, which lay "locked up by ice" for many days, Washington gave his real reason for avoiding the meeting of the Cincinnati. Seeking to modify its constitution to meet the widespread attacks upon it as a suspected scheme to set up a hereditary American nobility, he had been caught in a cross fire between army officers who resisted the changes and civilians worried over republican principles. Unwilling to be charged with dereliction toward either group, he was resigning as president for sound and just reasons of financial necessity and health. What might develop before May 1, to relieve him from his embarrassment, he could not say, but he thought some other appointment should be made. At this slight sign of yielding, Madison replied that there was no need for this action, since the executive could fill vacancies. It was better to leave a door open for future acceptance, "in case the gathering clouds should become so dark and menacing as to supersede every consideration but that of our national existence and safety."[16]

This was the period of closest consultation between Washington and "my particular friend Mr. Madison," as the general called him. For the next year and a half they exchanged letters almost as fast as the post could carry them. Fearing that he could not sustain his part of the writing contract, Washington suggested that if he fell behind, he would be so much in debt to Madison that he might feel a disposition to pay him off in depreciated paper, "which being a legal tender . . . you can not refuse. You will receive the nominal value, and that you know quiets the conscience, and makes all things easy, with the debtor."[17]

With Virginia's indorsement of the Philadelphia Convention, Madison's three-year devotion to state affairs came to an end. Desire and necessity united to carry him back into the national field. There had been calls in that direction before. "Mr. Madison has been nominated for [ambassador to] Spain, and is much approved by the southern states," wrote Richard Henry Lee after Jay's shift to the foreign secretaryship at the end of 1784. Madison must have smiled when that letter reached him at Richmond, for he had just heard from Monroe that Lee "earnestly advocated the appointment of Jefferson to the Court of Spain" in order to open the British and French posts to himself and brother Arthur. Madison had his name withdrawn, but nobody was appointed, for the coming of Gardoqui shifted the Mississippi negotiations to America. A few months later, calling for dignity and the power of compulsion in the federal government, Delegate Jacob Read of South Carolina wrote to Madison: "We want! Greatly want!! the assistance of your abilities and experience in Congress. I would not be thought to derogate from the merits or abilities of the present delegation, but one cannot help drawing comparisons between the language of 1783 and 1785."[18]

A task more immediate than revision of government called Madison back to the expiring federal body. He wanted "to bring about, if possible, the cancelling of the project of Mr. Jay for shutting the Mississippi."[19] Monroe was retiring so there was no need to disturb anybody in the five-man delegation. But when the assembly came to choose, on November 7, it ousted Henry Lee and named Madison and Joseph Jones to the two vacancies. Nothing could have been more embarrassing. Lighthorse Harry had been Madison's friend from college days. He was dropped, moreover, for the exact reverse of the reason Madison was put in. Obeying his instruction on roll calls but not in speech, he had indorsed the surrender of the Mississippi in exchange for a trade agreement with Spain.[20] Realizing that this blow might come, Madison tried to soften it by advance notice of the developing opposition and of the movement for himself. Lee took this as evidence that Madison, whom he worshiped, was trying to supplant him to gratify his own "temporary wishes." His letter saying so is missing from Madison's papers, but is quoted in the latter's protestation of continuing regard.

Madison had not been aware of the full force of the prejudice felt in the assembly, and supposed another name would be withheld or withdrawn.[21] In the second place, without "arrogantly presuming on his own appointment," or demanding to name his own associates, he had done what propriety seemed to admit in his friend's behalf. Whenever Lee's attitude toward the Mississippi was mentioned, "I made it a point to urge the fact that you had invariably obeyed your instructions . . . and that it would be cruel to sacrifice . . . a public servant who was charged with no breach of duty whatever, and who in other respects had gained distinguished honor to himself and to his country. In stating these

facts I discharge a debt due to truth, to candor, and to the friendship which has subsisted between us."[22]

Lee's wound was only beginning to heal when he wrote to
Madison from Alexandria, a month after the bad news reached
him. Nearly drowned in the Potomac "by rashly adventuring to
cross in the night, through bodies of floating ice," he reported that
"providence, kinder to me than my beloved country, rescued my
family and myself. . . . But cruel and ungrateful as I estimate the
treatment I have received from the assembly, I am frank to declare
to you that the opinion I had formed of your dereliction of the
friendship which existed between us rendered my affliction doubly
severe. . . . Your abandonment of a man who loved your character
to excess and who esteemed your friendship among the first
blessings of his life . . . wounded me deeply, and has given me
many melancholy hours." Madison's letter, the lighthorse leader
said, had afforded him some relief, and "strengthens my hope that
you regard me as I have ever esteemed you, and that no difference
in political sentiments ever has or ever can cool the affection which
commenced in our youth, and till very lately has existed in full
vigor. It is my wish that we may ever be united." At the time
he wrote, the assembly already had restored him to his old position,
following Joseph Jones' refusal to serve. The fullness of his recon-
ciliation with Madison was made evident soon after in their Great
Falls land activities.[23]

Planning to leave for New York by mid-December, Madison
asked that his clothes be put in order at Montpelier, so that he
could beat the cold weather by staying only a day or two. However, the law revisal was in jeopardy, there was a chance to dis-
incorporate the Episcopal church, and a rage "to draw all our
revenue from trade" demanded work to "moderate the fury." He
stayed therefore to the end of the session, with success on every
point, though it was the Senate which saved the state's commerce
from this "dreadful blow." The only enjoyment left to the House
was the extravagant idea, as Madison termed it, of squeezing
lawyers by taking ten per cent of their fees and putting a graduated tax on vehicles—two dollars per wheel on two-wheeled chairs,
six dollars per wheel on four-wheeled coaches.[24]

Intent upon the Mississippi crisis, Madison found an opening to deal with it when a memorial "full of consternation and complaint" came in from former army officers and Kentuckians. In a session made turbulent by extremists, he secured unanimous instructions to the delegates in Congress to defend the river's navigation. His resolution—one of the boldest that ever came from his pen—virtually staked the revision of federal government, and thereby the existence of the nation, upon a retreat by Jay and New England from their surrender policy. In a Union based on equal rights, sacrifice of any one part to the real or supposed interest of another would be "a direct contravention of the end for which the federal government was instituted." Virginia's delegates in Congress were to oppose any attempt to barter or surrender the free and common use of the Mississippi, and to protest against the same as a dishonorable departure from the vital principle of the Confederacy.

Such a surrender, the instructions declared, would provoke just resentments in the West and would be regarded "as destroying that confidence in the wisdom, justice and liberality of the federal councils which is so necessary at this crisis, to a proper enlargement of their authority; and finally, as tending to undermine our repose, our prosperity and our Union itself." The United States should negotiate with Spain for such a common use of the river "as may secure the permanent harmony and affection of the two nations." In the Senate, Madison reported to Washington, some thought this language too pointed, but it certainly expressed the sense of the country. "I am entirely convinced from what I observe here," he continued, "that unless the project of Congress . . . can be reversed, the hopes of carrying this state into a proper federal system will be demolished. . . . Mr. Henry, who had been hitherto the champion of the federal cause, has become a cold advocate, and in the event of an actual sacrifice of the Mississippi by Congress will unquestionably go over to the opposite side." Taking these instructions with him to New York, Madison was armed with the most decisive weapon that could be forged against Jay's treaty, and left behind him a record impervious to Patrick Henry's fire.[25]

It was late January 1787 before Madison set out for the seat of Congress. Shifting from horseback to stage at Fredericksburg, he avoided "culpable delay" by omitting a visit with the Monroes, but bad weather held back his arrival in New York until February 9. "From Princeton to Paulus' Hook," he wrote next day to Mrs. Trist, "we had a northeast snowstorm incessantly in our teeth." Rivers "were clogged with ice and a half congealed mixture of snow and water which was more in the way than the ice itself." In New York he found the lone Virginian, William Grayson, somewhat improved after a nervous breakdown with hypochondriac illusions, but "still a frequent prey to his own imagination."[26]

There had been no great need for haste. In more than three months, Congress had mustered a quorum on but four days, and Madison's absence did not block one until two days before he came in. His purpose, now, was to hold aloof from all but crucial matters and devote most of his time to studies for the coming convention. He almost regretted finding himself living in an agreeable group, since that might "expose the unsocial plan I have formed to the greater reproach." The affair of the Mississippi, he quickly learned, was in better train than expected. His missionary work on Dr. Witherspoon and the Jerseyites at Annapolis had borne fruit in a reversal of New Jersey's position. Pennsylvania was expected to act likewise and the Southern states were holding firm. Faced with these odds, Jay had not ventured to proceed in his project and Madison doubted that he would do it. All but three states appeared favorable to the constitutional convention and New York and Connecticut might swing into line. Rhode Island could be relied on for nothing that was good but "must sooner or later bend to Massachusetts and Connecticut." The Virginian's absorption in this subject was evident to his colleagues. "He professes great expectation as to the good effects of the measure," Rufus King reported.[27]

In Congress, Shays' Rebellion was to the fore. Young Charles Pinckney of South Carolina wanted to stop recruiting soldiers to crush an uprising which was already crushed—soldiers who could neither be paid, clothed nor fed and were more likely to be the terror than the support of government. Resuming his notes of debates, Madison recorded both this and King's appeal on the other side. Congress must not withdraw its support now, for Massachusetts planned to disarm and disfranchise the rebels for a limited time, and that would require the help of a federal army. This was disturbing news to Madison. He did not relish the way the anti-Shays recruiting had been ordered in the first place, to deal with a mythical uprising of Shawanese, Puteotamie, Chippewa and other Indians. The rebellion (not of these gentlemen) seemed nearly extinct. If however, he suggested to Washington, the measures "on foot for *disarming* and *disfranchising* those concerned in it should be carried into effect, a new crisis may be brought on." There were reports too of rising monarchist sentiment among terrified New Englanders, but such men were "swayed by very indigested ideas" which might give way to a thorough reform of the existing republican system.

It was one thing to feel worried about this, another thing to deny Massachusetts the begged-for aid. Difficult as it was, Madison said in a speech, to reconcile intervention against a majority with the principles of republican government, respect due to Massachusetts as a suffering member of the federal body required compliance. Popular commotions had to be subdued, therefore every state ought "to submit with cheerfulness to such indulgences to others, as itself may in a little time be in need of." Better wait a few weeks, he advised, before canceling the recruiting order. Congress did wait, thanks not to King and Madison but to the "chaos clause," for only two states stood with Massachusetts on the roll call.[28]

Constitutional revision leaped ahead on February 21 when the New York delegates received instructions to move for congressional approval of a convention. Madison suspected that it was actually a hostile move—an effort, perhaps, to promote a rival convention and defeat both by splitting the attendance. Nevertheless, he saw a chance for clear gain. Let the New York delegates make their motion, then amend it to apply to the Philadelphia Convention, and thus obtain state sponsorship of the final action. This failed because of fear of the New York scheme. However, Nathan Dane, who "was at bottom unfriendly to the plan," brought forward a similar Massachusetts motion, and Madison's idea of a perfecting amendment worked perfectly. Congress approved "a convention," all right, but it was a convention to meet in Philadelphia on the second Monday in May.[29].

Many delegates, Madison commented, considered this resolution as a deadly blow to the existing Confederation. Some of these, including himself, were willing that it should be, but they also viewed it as the harbinger of a better one. In spite of the tone of Boston newspaper articles, he was sure that the great body of the people were "equally indisposed either to dissolve or divide the Confederacy or to submit to any antirepublican innovations." The danger—a grave one—was in a monarchic swing just as the old government was collapsing. It would quickly tumble to the ground, if strong props were not applied to it. "No money is paid into the public treasury; no respect is paid to the federal authority. Not a single state complies with the requisitions." Lacking even "the pittance necessary for the civil list," the government could not last, and if the approaching convention should not agree on a remedy, a very different system would ensue.[30]

The menace was two-fold. "Turbulent scenes in Massachusetts and infamous ones in Rhode Island" had done "inexpressible injury to the republican character," driving leading minds toward monarchy. The bulk of the people, clinging to republicanism, might think it a lesser evil to split the Union into three more energetic governments. So great a hazard, Madison warned Edmund Pendleton, ought to "rouse all the real friends of the Revolution to exert themselves in favor of such an organization of the confederacy as will perpetuate the Union, and redeem the honor of the republican name."

With this feeling already expressed, there could be no doubt about the reaction when infamous Rhode Island, after protecting Shays' refugees, rejected the request to send deputies to Philadelphia. "Nothing can exceed the wickedness and folly which continue to reign there," exclaimed Madison. "All sense of character as well as right is obliterated. Paper money is still their idol, though it is debased to eight for one." That was pallid talk, compared with what Little Rhody's delegates said about their own legislature—the most infamous, licentious, unprincipled set of men who ever disgraced the annals of the world—just after they had been paid their salaries in this paper money, at its face value.[31]

Offered their choice of pardon and disfranchisement, or trial for treason, the Shays party told the government to come on with the treason trials, and straightway carried the Massachusetts elections all the way from constable to governor. As Madison described this, "their wicked measures are to be sheltered under the forms of the constitution," and even though the incoming governor was good old John Hancock, his merits were "not a little tainted by a dishonorable obsequiousness to popular follies." This development, to be sure, built up the support for federal government in the untainted states, but the conflicts between these states, and within them, left plenty of obstructions for the Philadelphia Convention to hurdle.

Madison admitted:

"The nearer the crisis approaches the more I tremble for the issue. The necessity of gaining the concurrence of the convention in some system that will answer the purpose, the subsequent approbation of Congress, and the final sanction of the states, presents a series of chances which would inspire despair in any case where the alternative was less formidable."[32]

In the Mississippi affair, so important in fixing Virginia's attitude, Madison was troubled now by the secrecy Congress had sanctioned. Negotiations with Spain were "entirely behind the curtain." It rests wholly with Jay, he reported to Randolph in March, "how far he will proceed with Gardoqui and how far he will communicate with Congress." Unable to demand information as a matter of right, Madison was unwilling to risk refusal by asking it as a favor. Well then, why not sound out the Spaniard? Two days later: "Memorandum. Called with Bingham today on Mr. Gardoqui, and had a long conversation touching the western country, the navigation of the Mississippi, and commerce; as these objects relate to Spain and the United States."[33]

William Bingham was a wealthy Philadelphian who yearned to be a diplomat, but lived before the era of campaign contributions. He was just back from Europe, followed by a letter from Jefferson (not yet received) describing him to Madison as one who had a rage for being presented to great men but was invited a second time only by those "who were susceptible of impression from the beauty of his wife."[34] From Gardoqui, Madison received strong but agitated assertions of the unyielding nature of Spain's position. If Americans in the West were organizing for action, he was sorry for it as a friend of the United States, but as minister of Spain he had no reason to worry. The Mississippi was closed and would stay so, and if no treaty was signed, American fish would soon be out of the Spanish market. The Virginia instructions (written by Madison) would have no effect except to bring Spanish reinforcements to New Orleans.

Suppose, Gardoqui was asked, Spain held only ten acres at the mouth of the Mississippi. Would she still claim exclusive control? "That was not the case." How much did she own? "After some confusion and hesitation he said she claimed at least as far as the Ohio. We smiled and asked how far eastwardly from the Mississippi? He became still more at a loss for an answer and turned it off by insinuating" that he had talked about it with the foreign secretary. Suppose rumors of intrigues at Detroit proved true, and Britain reclaimed the Western territories. What would Spain do if the Western population was brought into a war against Spanish America? Why, as to that, Spain had it in her power to bend Great Britain to her views. The minister "affected a mysterious air on this point, which only proved that he was at a loss what to say" about the danger, was Madison's comment.

During the interview Gardoqui let fall the information Madison wanted. He had not conferred with Jay on the treaty since October, did not expect to, and would leave for home before long. "The Spanish project sleeps," was the word Madison passed to Jefferson. Sleep, however, was not enough. What it needed was an overdose of narcotics, publicly administered. For Madison received word now that Patrick Henry, whose "disgust exceeds all measure," peremptorily rejected all pleas that he attend the Philadelphia Convention. His evident purpose was to combat or support the result of the convention "according to the result of the

Mississippi business, among other circumstances." With so much at stake, Madison decided to attack the seven-state instruction to Jay.[35]

First, however, he had another chance to talk with Gardoqui, presenting to him a disavowal, by the Virginia executive council, of the looting of Spanish mercantile property in Fort St. Vincennes by George Rogers Clark. To prevent his Ouabache Regiment from starving while on a projected march to drive the Spaniards out of Natchez, Clark had helped himself to taffy, honey and sugar. As these were thirst-producing foods, he took also all the tea, coffee, wine, cordial and French brandy the merchants had in stock. The Virginia delegates were rebuked by Jay for presenting the disavowal direct to Gardoqui instead of "by means of the federal sovereign." Madison's purpose, however, was not to flout national sovereignty but to by-pass a weak defender of it. The disavowal was presented to focus attention on the lawlessness. He was persuading Gardoqui that Spain "has no option but between concession and hostilities."

In this meeting he discovered that the Spaniard believed France was supporting the American position on the Mississippi. This gave force to reports that France might get the Floridas from Spain—something Madison hoped for as he "always wished to see the Mississippi in the hands of France." Gardoqui now seemed uncertain in his position, denying that Spain would make concessions as to the Mississippi, yet not revealing "a real inflexibility." Had Jay been of Madison's mind, a vast change might have been worked in the situation. But he took an exactly opposite view of the Clark looting. It was final evidence that the United States must make a yielding treaty in order to escape war with Spain. This advice to Congress only heightened Madison's feeling that the instructions must be revoked.[36]

First, Jay should be asked to report the state of the negotiations. In so thin a Congress, that meant finessing his supporters into aiding the move. William Pierce of Georgia took the floor and "observed that it had been hinted by Mr. Madison" that a report from Jay would be proper. He moved that Congress call for it. Fish-protector King, whose vote was vital, protested against hasty action in so delicate a matter. Madison did the unexpected by coming to King's support. In the teamwork, Pierce withdrew his motion, reoffered it after the week end, and it went through with the "unwilling but silent assent" of Massachusetts and Connecticut.

The result of the order was a disclosure by Jay that he had treated the seven-state instruction as valid and acted under it. He and Gardoqui had reached an agreement that, since Spanish policy forbade all foreign trade within Spanish territories, the United States would not navigate or use the lower Mississippi during the term of the treaty. That, said Jay, did not concede a Spanish *right* to close the river, but was only a friendly adjustment to the king's policy. Congress knew, of course, that it was a sweeping surrender, placing Mississippi navigation within a permanent Spanish trade and territorial policy. However, Jay revealed, the whole treaty was hung up because he and Gardoqui failed to agree on boundaries. This smoking out by Madison converted Pennsylvania and Rhode Island and virtually killed the treaty. But the absence of five states prevented positive action, so there was still no *corpus delicti* to dangle in front of Patrick Henry.[37]

Seeking a new approach, Madison picked out Jay's warning that the choice was between his treaty and war. He offered a motion which would at least delay such a choice—that the negotiations be transferred to Madrid, and that Jefferson go there from Paris to conduct them. Asked for his comment on this, Jay admitted how deeply it stung him. What was meant by its reference to "the *present state* of the negotiations with Spain and of the affairs of the United States"? (They meant, said Madison in his notes, "the step taken under the spurious authority of seven states" and the menacing temper of the West.) If Congress was dissatisfied with him, Jay asked, why this circuitous way of making a change?

Madison assailed both Jay's reply and his report. The foreign secretary had taken no account of the underlying purpose of the motion, which was "to retract the step taken for ceding the Mississippi, and to do it in a manner as respectful and conciliating as possible to Spain," also to put off the dilemma of "treaty or war" if there was one. This brought the New England motive out into the open, with a blunt statement by Gorham that shutting the Mississippi would benefit the Atlantic states and he wanted to see it shut. Replying, Madison contrasted this illiberal doctrine "with the principles of the Revolution, and the language of American patriots." But nothing was done.[38]

Two days later (April 25, 1787) the Virginian attacked on a third front. He offered a resolve that the 1786 instruction, because adopted by seven states when nine were necessary, did not authorize "any suspension of the use of the River Mississippi." Here he had to act in defiance of a special rule, passed to protect the instruction, that a subject set aside by the previous question could not be revived unless an equal or greater number of states were present. King at once invoked this rule, whereupon Madison expressed surprise that anybody should call up so improper an outgrowth of past intolerance, and moved its repeal. The subject of the Mississippi, he said, had been set aside seven states to five. Under the rule, eleven states unanimously for repeal could not bring it up. In the ensuing debate, not one word was said in defense of the rule, but the opposition assailed Madison's main motion. It was improper, they said, for Congress to make any exposition of their own powers or the validity of their acts. Madison and his allies answered that Congress had just made a sweeping exposition and vindication of its powers in an address to the states on the nature of the peace treaty. With the opposition unyielding, action on Madison's motion was held up to await the coming of new delegates. On their arrival some days later, the obstructive rule was repealed, but a motion to rescind the instruction fell one state short of the needed seven.

In these successive efforts, Madison achieved his immediate aim, which was to establish a formal record of "the paucity of states who abet the obnoxious project." Technically, the issue remained unsettled, but on the whole, he felt that the attempt to surrender the Mississippi was at an end, a point "of great importance in reference to the coming convention."[39]

The address to the states referred to by Madison, in which Congress expounded and vindicated its treaty power, was written by Jay and adopted on April 13. Madison was "not unaware of the bitterness of the pill" to many Virginians, "but national considerations overruled that objection." In every view, he said again, "Congress seem to have taken the most proper course for maintaining the national character." The paper which he thus indorsed was a sweeping assertion of national supremacy over the states in all matters having an international cast.

"Our national constitution having committed to us the management of the national concerns with foreign states and powers, [declared this utterance of Congress] it is our duty to take care that all the rights which they ought to enjoy . . . by the laws of nations and the faith of treaties remain inviolate. . . . When therefore a treaty is constitutionally made, ratified and published by us, it immediately becomes binding on the whole nation and superadded to the laws of the land, without the intervention of the state legislatures."[40]

Thus, on the eve of Madison's departure for the convention which was to write a new constitution, the concept of national sovereignty to which he had always subscribed received the authoritative sanction of the federal legislature—a limited sovereignty, but supreme (in the words of Congress) "for the general and national purposes specified in the constitution." Power, not will; instruments, not organization, were lacking in the nation created by the Revolution. It was to fill these fatal gaps that Madison directed his attention to the coming convention.

CHAPTER XXVI

PROLOGUE TO THE CONSTITUTION

THE studies which Madison engaged in, prior to the Federal Convention, began long before his return to Congress. At bottom, they were unbroken from his college days, but the intensive period began with the streaming in of books which he purchased through the friendly agency of Thomas Jefferson in Paris. He had asked Jefferson, before the latter received his European appointment, for the name of "a fit bookseller both in London and Paris," but that was nothing compared with having Jefferson himself as literary explorer, buyer and shipper.

Their traffic was not confined to book print. Madison asked for a combined walking stick and telescope, and got them separately. A watch, specially made for 600 livres, was delivered by the new French ambassador, M. de Moustier. Warville de Brissot brought across a made-to-order pedometer. "A little itch to gain a smattering in chymistry" resulted in the arrival of a chemistry box. New wonders of the old world were described or sent—a method of printing on engraved plates instead of loose type, a copying press for letters which Madison could not afford but thought needful in all public offices, a package of phosphoretic matches which "were a great treat to my curiosity," a newly invented lamp so wonderful that he did not begrudge the two guineas it cost.[1]

The flow was not all westward. At Jefferson's request, Madison sent him a box of pecan nuts planted in sand. Asked to ship some pippin apple trees, he ventured to expand the order to "half a dozen sorts of apples," twenty sugar maples and seven other kinds of American trees (plums, live oaks, myrtles, honeysuckles, acacias, rhododendrons, dogwoods) plus two barrels of Newtown pippins and two of cranberries. One hundred twenty-two trees of sixteen varieties answered the request for a few of one. If Jefferson would like to "gratify particular characters of merit" with "some of our animal curiosities," Madison could send the skins of all common and some rare quadrupeds and have them stuffed if desired. Studies of Indian languages were sent (through Jefferson and Washington) to aid French researchers and for Catherine the Great's universal dictionary. Most valuable, perhaps, was the urgent advice that Jefferson enlarge his plan for printing his "Notes on Virginia" and send copies for distribution over the state. Many men would be offended by its free strictures on their measures, but the assembled facts and remarks were too valuable not to be made known.[2]

Jefferson's book buying for Madison led off with the great new *Encyclopédie Méthodique,* of which thirty-seven volumes had then been published. He sent notice that he had bought also the *Dictionaire* of Treviux, Wicquefort's *De l'Ambassadeur,* Marti on morals and Mariana's history of Spain. Madison replied with a request for Felice's *Code de l'Humanité* in thirteen volumes, De Thou, Moreri, Pascal, Don Ulloa, French translations of "the historians of the Roman Empire during its decline," tracts on economics and books of natural science.

By the time a shipping opportunity arrived the purchases were multiplied—not only the books Madison asked for, but works of Burlamaqui, Wolfius, d'Albon, Mably, Voltaire, Mirabeau, Diderot, a dozen histories—the whole running to almost 200 volumes. So perfectly did the collection fit his needs, the recipient said, that "no suggestions are necessary as to your future purchases." The cost of the books, 1,164 livres or about $222, was quickly discharged. Madison marked off what was left of Jefferson's old debt to him, made a requested advance to a French visitor, and devoted the remainder to Jefferson's nephews, Peter and Dabney Carr, whose education he was supervising.[3]

This literary cargo, as Madison called it, made an immediate impact upon his constitutional studies. Home from legislative duties in the late winter of 1785-86, he plunged at once into a study of ancient and modern confederacies. What were their elements of strength? Of weakness? Why did the old ones fall, why were the modern feeble? He took them up one at a time—the Lycian Confederacy, the Amphictyonic, the Achaean; the Helvetic, the

Belgic, the Germanic. Out of this work came a manuscript booklet of forty-one pages, describing these confederacies, analyzing their federal authority, and concluding each analysis (after the Lycian) with a section on "The Vices of the Constitution." A vast part of this essay, even the wording of many sentences, was carried by him into Nos. 18, 19 and 20 of the *Federalist Papers*.

The value of the books received from Europe is evident in the innumerable citations of authority which he set down—more than a hundred from Felice alone, many from the *Encyclopédie,* D'Albon, Treviux, Mably. Even more striking is the range of sources he was able to cite—Polybius, Ubbo Emmius, Plutarch, Stanyan, Temple, Potter, Gillie, Raleigh, Montesquieu. The painstaking annotation of every statement is conclusive evidence that this was written for use in public debate on revision of the Constitution; written, furthermore, half a year before the call for a convention went out from Annapolis. The lessons of the ancient and modern world, covering a sweep of more than two thousand years, were compressed into the verdict on the Achaean League, that want of subjection to the general authority ruined the whole body. Added evils, foreign intrigue and civil war, were but the universal by-product of federal weakness and jealousy among the member states.[4]

Out of Madison's free hours in New York, while he was attending Congress in 1787, came his notable "Vices of the Political System of the United States."[5] Finished in April, on the very eve of the meeting to revise the structure of American government, this brief article not only probed the weaknesses of the state and federal structures, but put into words the thoughts on government which its author had distilled out of the world's past and his own mind. Most of the vices were those against which Madison and others had been fighting for years. He named them one after another in these words:

Failure of the states to comply with constitutional requisitions.
Encroachment by the states on the federal authority.
Violations of the law of nations and of treaties.
Trespasses of the states on the rights of one another.
Want of concert in matters where common interest requires it.

Want of guaranty to the states of their constitutions and laws against internal violence.

Want of sanction to the laws, and of coercion in the government of the confederacy.

Want of ratification by the people of the Articles of Confederation.

Multiplicity of laws in the several states.

Mutability of the laws of the states.

Injustice of the laws of the states.

The impressive fact about this compilation is its emphasis upon the dereliction of the states. To remedy some of these vices, important positive additions would have to be made to the powers of Congress. They add up even more strikingly to a need to bring the states under the thumb—or the fist—of a federal constitution.

The first evil, growing out of dependence on the states for revenue, Madison found to be so typical of confederacies that it must be considered inherent in and fatal to the existing system. The most mildly worded vice—want of concert—called for the widest remedies—federal power over commerce ("how much has the national dignity, interest and revenue suffered" for want of it), national seminaries, copyrights, naturalization, incorporation for national purposes, canals and other works.

Unable to enforce its laws or coerce the states, the federal system lacked "the great vital principles of a political constitution." Under the form of such a constitution, it was in fact "nothing more than a treaty of amity, of commerce and of alliance, between independent and sovereign states" from which "unanimous and punctual obedience . . . to the acts of the federal government ought not to be calculated on." Treaty violations were so widespread that "only the moderation of other nations had saved the United States from public calamities."

Madison's basic thinking came to the fore in his treatment of two related vices, the injustice of state laws and the lack of federal power to protect the states against internal violence. The injustice of laws, he asserted, "brings more into question the fundamental principle of republican government, that the majority who rule in such governments are the safest guardians both of public good and private rights." Men sought legislative office from three motives—ambition, personal interest, public good—but how often those moved by self-interest would mask a perfidious sacrifice of their constituents under pretexts of their welfare. "How frequently too will the honest but unenlightened representative be the dupe of a favorite leader, veiling his selfish views under the professions of public good, and varnishing his sophistical arguments with the glowing colors of popular eloquence?" (What would Patrick Henry say to that?) Yet it was not the studied perversity of ambitious individuals that furnished the chief problem, but the class motive for political faction.

"All civilized societies are divided into different interests and factions, as they happen to be creditors or debtors—rich or poor—husbandmen, merchants, or manufacturers—members of different religious sects—followers of different political leaders—inhabitants of different districts—owners of different kinds of property etc. etc. In republican government the majority, however composed, ultimately give the law. Whenever therefore an apparent interest or common passion unites a majority, what is to restrain them from unjust violations of the rights and interests of the minority, or of individuals?"

He named and rejected the ethical restraints on such conduct—the inclusion of individual interest in the general and permanent good of the community, the desire to be thought of good character, the force of religion. Would the last two operate more forcefully on the multitude than on individuals? Quite the opposite. Men join without remorse in legislative acts against which their consciences would revolt, if proposed separately in their closets. Give two persons an interest opposed to the rights of a third. Will the rights of the third be secure if the interest of each depends on the others? "The prudence of every man would shun the danger." Will two thousand be less likely to encroach on the rights of one thousand? The contrary "is witnessed by the notorious factions and oppressions" in corporate towns and little republics.

Where then was security of private rights to be found without a sacrifice of republican government? In a larger sphere of society.

Not from any reduction in the impulse toward injustice, Madison argued, but because, if enlarged sufficiently: "The society becomes broken into a greater variety of interests, of pursuits, of passions, which check each other, whilst those who may feel a common sentiment have less opportunity of communication and concert." Contrary to the prevailing theory, the evils charged against states ruled by the people "are in proportion not to the extent, but to the narrowness of their limits."

The great necessity in forming a system of government, therefore, was to make the sovereignty sufficiently neutral to prevent one faction from oppressing another, yet sufficiently controlled to be itself subject to the interest of the whole society. In an absolute monarchy, the sovereign was neutral, but unrestrained in ambition or avarice. In a small republic, the sovereign could be restrained, but was not neutral toward the parts composing it. This led him to his ultimate conclusion: "As a limited monarchy tempers the evils of an absolute one; so an extensive republic meliorates the administration of a small republic." Combined with the remedies for other vices, this shaped the outlines of the desired constitution— that of a federal republic strong enough at the center to direct the common interests, maintain republican institutions, and restrain the excesses of the states, but held to moderation in turn by the divergent interests of the various sections and classes within its broad territorial sweep.

It was this outlook on government which held Madison so firmly to republican moorings when Shays' Rebellion and worthless money put others to dreaming of monarchy or drugged them with the nearer allurement of aristocracy in a republican veil. Of the four leading statesmen of the period, Washington clung to republicanism from broad faith in humanity and the sheer depth of his hatred of monarchy, Hamilton accepted as much of it as the people forced him to, Jefferson was swayed by his confidence in the moral worth of a farming population and his sympathy for the oppressed. Madison shared Washington's hatred and Jefferson's faith, in lesser degree his sympathy. But of the four, Madison alone saw the rational basis of a republican system which, without bringing human and property rights into harmony, promised such a compromise between them that it would be safe to give the general government all necessary powers. It was this concept which he took with him to Philadelphia, where it became the very core of the new Constitution.

Madison's political philosophy did not grow in a vacuum. Thought, study, observation and experience united to produce it. Aristotle had told him that a king judges between the people and his avarice much as a wild beast might, that republics go down in the turbulent conflict between rich and poor, that agriculture is the only stable base of popular government. Locke hammered home the doctrine that no government is tolerable unless it is based on the people's sovereignty and majority rule. From David Hume, who saw that social conflicts were infinitely more complex than Aristotle thought them to be, came the idea that stability could be attained by balancing class against class, interest against interest, wherefore a large republic should be more stable than a small one, though harder to organize. Weighing the political teachings of the past, Madison rejected many that were glib phrases in the mouths of those about him—Aristotle's everlasting cycle of democracy and tyranny, Locke's nonsense about the separation of purse and sword, Montesquieu's doctrine that only a small republic is virtuous. He threw aside what Hamilton accepted—the old idea that a mixed government of well born and poor (with the former on top) is the cure for both turbulence and oppression.[6]

Apart from his fundamental devotion to majority rule, Madison's great gift to the country at this time was his ability to measure the forces operating most strongly for good or evil in society and in government, and to visualize the structure called for by the particular conditions found in the United States. What was, must be the basis of what was to be, yet warned also of what must not continue. "The mortal diseases of the existing constitution," he wrote to Jefferson on March 19, "have tainted the faith of the most orthodox republicans, and . . . challenge from the votaries of liberty every concession in favor of stable government not infringing fundamental principles." This, he was convinced, was the only security against a shift to the opposite political pole. It was as a

defender of republicanism, a votary of liberty, that he sought to
control its excesses. Only a republic strong enough to cure anarchy
could prevent monarchy or its counterparts, but that strength must
repose in the majority. "A government resting on a minority is an
aristocracy, not a republic," he wrote in his "Autobiography."

It was in this conviction that Madison turned in April to the
work of outlining, in advance, a plan of government to be offered
to the delegates at Philadelphia—a task made more hopeful by
Washington's decision to attend. To him and to Governor Randolph, Madison presented the ideas which, amplified in detail but
unaltered in substance, became the Virginia Plan upon which, as a
working basis, the Constitution was built.[7] In dealing with the
governor, who feared even his own ideas when they took tangible
form, he spoke softly. For the governor wanted to submit each
amendment separately to the states, and must not be told too suddenly that "my ideas of a reform strike so deeply at the old Confederation, and lead to such a systematic change," that they must
be adopted or rejected in a lump. With Washington he could
adopt a different tone: "Temporizing applications will dishonor
the councils which propose them, and may foment the internal
malignity of the disease" even when they seem to palliate it.
"Radical attempts although unsuccessful will at least justify the
authors of them." To both men he presented his basic idea of
national supremacy in a federal republic—in these words to Randolph:

"I hold it for a fundamental point, that an individual independence of the states is utterly irreconcilable with the idea of an ag-
gregate sovereignty. I think, at the same time, that a consolidation
of the states into one simple republic is not less unattainable than
it would be inexpedient. Let it be tried, then, whether any middle
ground can be taken, which will at once support a due supremacy
of the national authority, and leave in force the local authorities
so far as they can be subordinately useful."

He then proposed a federal government with suffrage based on
population instead of state equality; a two-branch legislature, with
senators to be elected by state legislatures and to go out in rotation;

a national executive and judiciary. With this came his outline of the powers he would give to the new government—powers far-reaching on the positive side, but even more drastic in their curtailment of the authority of the states:

"Let the national government be armed with a positive and complete authority in all cases where uniform measures are necessary. . . .

"Let it have a negative, in all cases whatsoever, on the legislative acts of the states, as the King of Great Britain heretofore had. . . .

"Let this national supremacy be extended also to the judiciary department."

The system was to be rounded out by an article "expressly guaranteeing . . . the states against internal as well as external dangers," and the whole constitution was to be given energy by having it "ratified by the authority of the people, and not merely by that of the legislatures."

It was with these ideas in his mind that the man who became known as the Father of the Constitution entered the hall in which it was drafted. So widely do they differ from impressions created in later years, after he turned to state sovereignty for protection against the policies of the Federalist party, that these nationalistic utterances have often been treated as momentary aberrations, or even ignored, in fixing Madison's place in history and in interpreting the Constitution. Approached from the opposite direction, they stand as the inevitable climax of his seven-year service in Congress and the Virginia legislature—the formative period of his life as a builder of government, and the formative period of the government itself.

All through the outlines and arguments which Madison submitted to Washington and Randolph run the phrases of his established nationalism—national authority, national councils, national government, national jurisdiction, national prerogatives, national supremacy, national tribunals, national executive, national administration, supreme government. To Madison, the word "national" meant pertaining to a nation. Not once did he use it in the artificial sense given to it in later constitutional controversies, as the opposite of a "federal" government—the one bearing directly on the people, the other on the states—a use finally cited as evidence that the ordinary meaning was not then in people's minds.

The government Madison visualized was both national and federal. His aim was to convert the shadow of national power into reality. There was to be "a due supremacy of the national authority," with the local authorities "subordinately useful." That was the extent to which he admitted state sovereignty into his federalism, on the eve of the writing of the Constitution. For seven years Madison had endeavored to establish that national supremacy—first by a return to the original authority Congress lost when it stopped printing money and became financially dependent upon the states, next by recognition of implied powers in the Articles of Confederation, then by the vigorous exercise of powers whose validity could not be challenged, finally by amendment of the articles to confer new powers upon Congress. All failed, while the government sank into coma, and he turned as others did to the framing of a new basic charter.

Even in the failures, however, the germ of victory had been planted. In Madison's ceaseless emphasis upon national dignity, in his faithfulness to the French alliance and the sanctity of treaties, in his calls for military vigor, in his defense of Western territories and the Mississippi, in the transfer of Virginia's empire to the nation, in his attempts to create general revenues and fortify public credit, in his work for inland navigation and regulation of commerce—he was spreading the thought of a common nationhood, a common citizenship, a mutual dependence, throughout the new republic. Even in the Virginia Assembly, he was an American rather than a Virginian.

Independence, union, national supremacy and republican self-government were the four pillars of Madison's American empire. The first was won, the other three were still at stake, when he made the last entry in his congressional journal and closed the book. On May 2, 1787, "I left New York for the convention to be held in Philadelphia." That entry also closed a period in the life of the American nation, and left the wide way open to the future.

NOTES

NOTES

LETTERS cited in the notes are usually identified by dates, with added citation of the sources of those not found in the published chronological collections mentioned below.

Letters of James Madison, if cited by date alone, can be found in Madison's *Writings,* edited by Hunt, or in Burnett's *Letters of the Members of the Continental Congress.*

Letters of Thomas Jefferson, cited only by date, are in either the Ford or Library edition of Jefferson's writings, or in Burnett.

Letters of James Monroe, similarly cited, are in Monroe's *Writings* or Burnett.

Letters of George Washington, cited by date, are in the Fitzpatrick edition of Washington's letters.

Letters of Joseph Jones, if no source is given, are in Burnett or in the *Letters of Joseph Jones.*

Letters of Richard Henry Lee, cited only by date, are in Burnett or in Ballagh's collection of Lee's letters.

All other cited letters for which no source is given can be found in Burnett. Letters of nonmembers of Congress, published by Burnett in footnotes, are cited by volume and page.

Letters from American diplomats published in Wharton's *Diplomatic Correspondence of the American Revolution,* are usually cited first by date, then by location, owing to the fact that many are out of their chronological position in that work.

Diplomatic dispatches of the Chevalier de la Luzerne, the Count de Vergennes and François de Marbois are ordinarily cited by date alone. They are chronologically placed in the Archives des Affaires Étrangères, correspondence politique, États-Unis, transcripts of which are in the Division of Manuscripts of the Library of Congress.

Abbreviations by initials to indicate sources are used as follows in the notes:

JCC: *Journals of the Continental Congress.*

PCC: Papers of the Continental Congress (MS., Library of Congress.)

JVHD: *Journals of the House of Delegates, General Assembly of Virginia.*

Other abbreviations are used in the notes as indicated below:

Burnett: *Letters of the Members of the Continental Congress,* edited by Edward C. Burnett.

Doniol: *La Participation de la France a l'Établissement des États-Unis,* by Henri Doniol.

Gay, *Madison: Life of James Madison,* by Sydney H. Gay.

Hening: *Statutes of Virginia,* edited by W. W. Hening.

Hunt, *Madison: Life of James Madison,* by Gaillard Hunt.

Madison MSS.: Papers of James Madison, Library of Congress.

Madison, *Writings: Writings of James Madison,* edited by Gaillard Hunt.

Madison, *Papers: The Papers of James Madison* (1840), edited by H. D. Gilpin.

Madison, *Letters: Letters and Other Writings of James Madison* (1865).

Madison, Notes of Debates: In *Writings* (Hunt) II, and Appendix to *Journals of the Continental Congress,* 1782, 1783 and 1787.

Rives, *Madison: Life and Times of James Madison,* by W. C. Rives.

Sumner: *The Financier and the Finances of the American Revolution,* by W. G. Sumner.

Thomson, Notes: Summaries of debates by the Secretary of Congress, in Burnett.

Wharton: *Diplomatic Correspondence of the American Revolution,* by Francis Wharton (six-volume edition).

CHAPTER I

[1] That Madison went by chaise to Philadelphia is evident from a request (May 20, 1782) that a certain stallion be prepared for the saddle rather than for a stud. "Neither of the horses I have here is fit for that use."—Madison MSS., II, 65. The Fredericksburg route is indicated by Madison's collection of $2 per mile for a 260-mile trip. (Account for attendance to September 20, 1780.—Burnett, *Letters of Members of the Continental Congress,* V, 381*n.*) A 12-day journey is noted in his bill for readjusted salary, Congressional Papers, Virginia State Library.

[2] Conrad-Alexandre Gerard to Foreign Minister Vergennes, January 17, 1779.

[3] William Shippen to Richard Henry Lee, March 21, 1780, Lee Papers, University of Virginia.

[4] Diary of Thomas Rodney, March 10, 1781, Burnett, VI, 20.

[5] Chevalier de la Luzerne, Liste des Membres du Congrès depuis 1779 jusqu'en 1784, Archives des Affaires Étrangères, Mémoires et Documentes, États-Unis, I, 253-287.

[6] James Duane, Notes of Debates, October 6, 1780, Burnett, V, 409. Max Farrand, *Records of the Federal Convention,* III, 232 (French text).

[7] David Jameson to Madison, September 13, 1780; May 24, 1783; Rives Papers, Library of Congress. Madison to Edmund Pendleton, September 19, 1780.

[8] Madison to Edmund Randolph, September 8, 1783, Madison MSS., IV, 78. Madison to Jefferson, September 7, 1784. Eliza Trist to Jefferson, July 24, 1786, Coolidge-Jefferson Papers, Massachusetts Historical Society.

[9] Jefferson to Madison, August 31, 1783. Jefferson to Martha Jefferson, November 28, 1783, in Sarah N. Randolph, *Domestic Life of Thomas Jef-*

ferson. This letter was presented to Queen Victoria in response to her request for Jefferson's autograph.

¹⁰ Eliza Trist to Jefferson, April 13, 1784, Coolidge-Jefferson Papers.

¹¹ John Walker to Jefferson, June 13, 1780. Griffin, as shown by a letter of December, 1779, to Ephraim Blaine, lived in Third Street near Lombard. Thus Madison set the style for his other colleagues by going to Mrs. House's.

¹² See note 2; also Madison's 1780 recapitulation, Congressional Papers, Virginia State Library.

¹³ *Journals of the Continental Congress,* March 18, 20, 1780.

¹⁴ Madison to James Madison, Sr., March 20, 1780.

¹⁵ Madison to Jefferson, March 27, 1780.

¹⁶ Madison, *Papers,* 1840, I, 44. Madison, *Writings,* I, 60. The correct text is in Burnett, V, 97.

¹⁷ John Mathews to Nathaniel Peabody, October 3, 1780.

¹⁸ *Journal of the Virginia House of Delegates,* December 24, 1779.

¹⁹ Madison to Jefferson, May 6, 1780. Washington to Joseph Jones, May 31, 1780.

²⁰ See Brant, *Madison,* I, chapter 18.

CHAPTER II

¹ George Bancroft, *History of the United States,* X, 399. Luzerne to Vergennes, March 16, 1780. Diary of Samuel Holten, January 19, 1780. Burnett, V, 10*n.*

² *JCC,* March 6, 1779; March 21, 1780. United States *v.* Judge Peters, 5 Cranch 115.

³ William Floyd to Governor Clinton, December 21, 1779. Luzerne to Vergennes, January 7, 1780. Instructions to delegates and letter of T.P., *Pennsylvania Packet,* February 8, 1780. "Life of Margaret Shippen," *Pennsylvania Magazine of History and Biography,* XXV, 24-29.

⁴ *JCC,* March 22, 27, 1780.

⁵ *JCC,* March 21, 22, 1780.

⁶ *JCC,* March 29, April 10, 12, 1780. William Ellery to William Vernon, March 16, 1778.

⁷ Luzerne to Vergennes, June 4, 1780. Vergennes to Luzerne, October 22, 1780. *JCC,* May 27, June 13, 1780.

⁸ *JCC,* June 6, November 24, 1780; May 3, 11, 16, 28, June 23, 26, 1781; September 3, 1782. Diary of Robert Morris, September 3, 1782, Burnett, VI, 468. Wharton, *Diplomatic Correspondence of the Revolution,* V, 695, 747. Luzerne to Vergennes, September 6, October 1, 1782.

⁹ William Ellery to the governor of Rhode Island, May 16, 1780.

¹⁰ Madison's settlement with the state for 1780-1782 was based on an average depreciation of $62 paper for $1 of specie from March 20 to June 23, 1780, $75 paper in August, $78 in October, $92 in November, $100 in December, $110 and $120 in February, 1781, $135 in March, $220 in April. After that date the delegates made out their accounts in Pennsyl-

vania currency. Madison final account, Congressional Papers, Virginia State Library. Theodorick Bland, depreciation table, *ibid.*

[11] Madison and Jones accounts, Burnett, V, 381*n* and 412*n*. Madison and Bland to Governor Jefferson, November 5, 1780. The Virginia delegates to Jefferson, May 22, 1781. Bland to Jefferson, June 3, 1781, Congressional Papers, Virginia State Library. Joseph Jones to Bland, February 4, 1781, *Bland Papers*, 58.

[12] W. G. Sumner, *The Financier and the Finances of the American Revolution*, I, 96, 97. Hening, *Statutes of Virginia*, X, 241, 279, 412, 456. Jaquelin Ambler to Madison, December 22, 1781, Madison MSS., II, 26.

[13] Unable to cash a Treasury warrant for $6,000 ($100 specie), Joseph Hiltzheimer, keeper of the Continental stables, bought hay and grain for sixty horses on his personal credit until he had none. Hiltzheimer worked for two years without collecting his salary, then discovered that the resolutions appointing him failed to provide for any. Burnett, V, 149*n*, 346*n*, 404*n*.

[14] *JCC*, April 5, 25, 1780. Washington to the President of Congress, April 2, 7, May 20, 1780. James Duane to Philip Schuyler, May 26, 1780. Lee's troops were officially known as "partisans." *JCC*, October 21, 31, November 6, 1780.

[15] *JCC*, June 1, 6, 19, 29, 1780. Madison to Jefferson, June 2, 1780. The President of Congress to Washington, June 6, 1780. (Also Burnett's footnotes to these letters.) Robert R. Livingston to Schuyler, May 21, 1780.

[16] *JCC*, June 13, 14, 17, 1780. John Mathews to General Gates, March 14, 1780. John Armstrong to Gates, June 6, 1780. The President of Congress to Washington, June 13, 1780.

[17] Diary of Samuel Holten, July 6, 1779, March 30, 1780, *Essex Institute Historical Collections*, LVI, 25, 91.

[18] William Emmett O'Donnell, *The Chevalier de la Luzerne*, 56-60.

[19] Martha Dangerfield Bland to Frances Bland Tucker, March 20, 1781, Tucker Papers, Williamsburg Restoration. Arthur Lee to Theodorick Bland, September 27, 1781, Bland Papers, II, 77, Library of Congress.

[20] Richard Henry Lee to Thomas Lee Shippen, June 4, 1785. Spanish agent Juan Miralles died suddenly on April 28, 1780, while visiting Washington's headquarters at Morristown, New Jersey (Burnett V, 131.) His secretary, Francisco Rendon, succeeded him.

[21] François de Marbois to Vergennes, April 4, 7, 1782.

[22] Marquis de Chastellux, *Travels in North America* (1787 edition) I, 306. Luzerne, List, *op. cit.*

[23] Margaret Bayard Smith, *First Forty Years of Washington Society*, 235. Thomas Lee Shippen to William Shippen, April 22, 1790, Shippen Papers, Library of Congress.

CHAPTER III

[1] *JCC*, April 13, 1780. Nathaniel Peabody to the President of New Hampshire, March 13, 1780.

[2] Luzerne to Vergennes, April 16, 1780.

[3] Washington to Joseph Jones, May 14, 1780, Headquarters Committee to Congress, Burnett, V, 140 and footnote. Luzerne to Vergennes, April 16, 1780.

[4] William C. Rives, *Life and Times of James Madison*, I, 523. Brant, *Madison*, I, 90. Madison to Jefferson, June 2, 1780. *JCC*, April 11, May 19, 1780.

[5] Hening, X, 539. Washington to the Committee at Headquarters, June 11, 1780. Madison to Jefferson, June 23, 1780.

[6] Washington to Joseph Jones, May 31, 1780. Jones to Washington, undated, but soon after June 21, 1780, *Letters of Joseph Jones*, 12. Madison to Jefferson, June 2, 1780.

[7] *JCC*, February 25, 1780.

[8] *JCC*, March 27, 1780. Washington to the President of Congress, December 22-23, 1777. Thomas Mifflin to Horatio Gates, March 23, 1780; Nathanael Greene to Washington, March 23, 28, 31, 1780; Greene to Udny Hay, June 27, 1780; Burnett, V, 99n, 241n.

[9] G. W. Greene, *Life of Greene*, II, 288.

[10] *JCC*, June 29, July 24, 1780. Charles Pettit to Greene, July 13, 1780, Burnett, V, 267n. Henry Laurens to R. H. Lee, August 1, 1780; Committee at Headquarters to Greene, July 28, 1780. Greene to the President of Congress, July 26, 1780, Burnett, V, 299n.

[11] Committee at Headquarters to President of Congress, July 30, 1780. Same to same (signed only by Mathews, his colleagues being absent), August 6, 16, 1780. *JCC*, August 2, 5, 11, 1780.

[12] Ezekiel Cornell to Greene, July 21, 1780.

[13] *JCC*, July 6, 12, August 11, 1780.

[14] Washington to the President of Congress, July 14, 1780. James Lovell to Benjamin Lincoln, July 19, 1780. John Walker to George Weedon, John Armstrong to John Davis, July 25, 1780.

[15] *JCC*, August 17, 1780. Madison draft, Burnett, V, 333.

[16] Washington to the President of Congress, August 20, 1780.

[17] PCC, No. 154, II, 234.

[18] John Mathews to Philip Schuyler, August 23, 1780. Mathews to Washington, September 15, 1780. James Lovell to Elbridge Gerry, September 5, November 20, 1780. Madison to Pendleton, September 12, 1780.

[19] John Sullivan to the President of New Hampshire, September 16, 1780. Whitmill Hill to Thomas Burke, October 9, 1780. Luzerne to Vergennes, October 4, 1780.

[20] Washington to George Mason, October 22, 1780.

[21] John Mathews to Washington, October 6, 17, 1780.

[22] Madison to Greene, January 13, 1781.

[23] *JCC*, July 27, 1781. Horatio Gates to Jefferson, August 2, 1781, Burnett, VI, 210n.

[24] Madison MSS., I, 84. Burnett, V, 417n.

[25] Madison to Pendleton, November 21, 1780.

[26] Mathews to Greene, December 12, 13, 1780; January 4, 1781. Madi-

son to Pendleton, January 2, 1781. Greene to the President of Congress, December 7, 1780, Greene Letterbook, PCC.

CHAPTER IV

[1] Madison to Joseph Jones, November 14, 1780, Madison MSS., I, 75. R. H. Lee to Samuel Adams, November 10, 1780.

[2] Madison to Joseph Jones, November 21, 1780 (Madison MSS., I, 82), November 28, 1780.

[3] Joseph Jones to Madison, November 18, December 8, 1780.

[4] Same to same, July 22, 1782. Madison to James Madison, Sr., September 8, 1783.

[5] Hening X, 331.

[6] JCC, March 29, April 3, 1779; December 9, 1780. January 2, 1781. Thomas Balch, *Les Français en Amérique*, 124.

[7] Hening, X, 338.

[8] *JVHD*, December 1, 2, 24, 30, 1780. Joseph Jones to Madison, December 2, 1780; January 2, 1781.

[9] Madison to Joseph Jones, December 12, 1780. Madison to Pendleton, January 16, 1781. Jones to Madison, October 17, 24, 1780.

[10] *JCC*, February 13, 20, 1781.

[11] Washington to the President of Congress, February 26, 1781.

[12] Luzerne to Vergennes, April 9, 1781.

[13] Luzerne to Vergennes, April 9, November 25, 1781. Benjamin Harrison to Luzerne, May 11, 1782, *Official Letters of the Governors of Virginia*. *JCC*, June 27, 1782. Robert Morris to Luzerne, April 27, 1782, Wharton, V, 331.

[14] Vergennes to Luzerne, October 7, 1781; January 31, August 12, October 14, 1782. Luzerne to Vergennes, January 26, April 27, December 27, 1782. Benjamin Harrison to Luzerne, February 27, 1782. Joly de Fleury to Vergennes, August 23, 1781. Virginia delegates to Luzerne, January 24, 1782, *Calendar of Virginia State Papers*, III, 47. Maryland's dealings with France are described in Kathryn Sullivan's *Maryland and France*, and by St. George L. Sioussat, in the *Pennsylvania Magazine of History and Biography*, October, 1936.

[15] Madison to Pendleton, September 26, October 10, November 14, 1780.

[16] Madison to Pendleton, September 12, 1780. Madison to Joseph Jones, September 19, 1780. Jones to Washington, Jones to Madison, October 2, 1780.

[17] Madison to Joseph Jones, October 24, 1780. Madison to Pendleton, October 31, 1780.

[18] Madison and Bland to Governor Jefferson, January 1, 1781, Virginia State Library; January 25, 1781, *Calendar of Virginia State Papers*, I, 454.

[19] Theodorick Bland to R. H. Lee, March 5, 1781, Lee Papers, University of Virginia. John Mathews to General Greene, February 10, 1781. Joseph Jones to Governor Jefferson, February 10, 1781. Madison and Jones to Jefferson, February 20, 1781, Burnett, V, 568, 567n, 577.

[20] Luzerne to Destouches, January 16, 1781. Washington to the President of Congress, February 26, March 11, 1781. Washington to Joseph Jones, March 24, 1781 (copy in Madison MSS., I, 109). Washington to Rochambeau, December 13, 1780; February 7, 15, 1781. Rochambeau to Washington, December 19, 1780; February 1, 3, 9, 1781. Henri Doniol, *La Participation de la France a l'Éstablissement des États-Unis*, V, 391, 405, 410, 417. Rochambeau to Luzerne, February 1, 1781, Doniol, IV, 570. *JCC*, February 20, 1781.

[21] *Journal of Claude Blanchard*, March 16, 1781. Luzerne to Castries, March 3, 1781. Madison to Governor Jefferson, April 3, 1781.

[22] Luzerne to Vergennes, March 8, 1781. Washington to Alexander McDougal, John Mathews, John Sullivan (identical letters), March 31, 1781. *JCC*, April 4, 5, 1781.

[23] Madison to Joseph Jones, December 12, 1780; Madison to Pendleton, December (20), 1780 (Madison MSS., I, 89, 94), January 16, 1781. Luzerne to Vergennes, January 21, 31, 1781.

[24] The Rev. James Madison to Madison, March 9, 1781, Madison MSS., I, 107.

[25] *Virginia Gazette*, December 30, 1780. "An Independent American" in the *Pennsylvania Gazette*, March 10, 17, 28, 1781.

CHAPTER V

[1] Secret Committee to Silas Deane, March 1, 1776; Secret Committee of Correspondence to Deane, March 3, 1776. George L. Clark, *Silas Deane*, 40-61.

[2] Wharton, I, 539-541, 654-661.

[3] R. H. Lee to Samuel Adams, September 10, 1780. Benjamin Franklin to William Carmichael, March 31, 1780.

[4] *JCC*, April 30, 1779. Vergennes to Gerard, October 26, 1778.

[5] Madison, *Writings*, I, 67n. John Adams to Thomas McKean, September 20, 1779.

[6] *JCC*, August 1, October 17, 1780.

[7] *JCC*, December 19, 1780.

[8] See Brant, *Madison*, I, Chapter XVIII, note 54, and Appendix.

[9] *JCC*, December 3, 1781.

[10] *JCC*, August 7, October 19, 1780. Ralph Izard to the President of Congress, August 6, 1780, Wharton, IV, 21. Izard to R. H. Lee, October 15, 1780, Burnett, V, 362n. Luzerne to Vergennes, August 6, 1780.

[11] Vergennes to Luzerne, February 5, 1780.

[12] Marbois to Vergennes, October 29, 1780.

[13] *JCC*, December 1, 1780.

[14] Arthur Lee to Elbridge Gerry, November 26, 1780; William Whipple to R. H. Lee, August 23, 1779, Burnett, V, 439n, IV, 385, 385n. Whipple wrote: "Fiddlehead shook, Swivel-Eye nestled and turned pale, the chair changed color at every sentence."

[15] Edmund Pendleton to Madison, October 30, 1780. Madison to Pendleton, November 17, 1780, Burnett, V, 439n, 438.

[16] Luzerne to Vergennes, November 10, 1780.

[17] Witherspoon speech of June 11 (?), 1781, Burnett, VI, 117.

[18] JCC, October 19, December 7, 1780.

[19] John Paul Jones to Robert Morris, June 27, 1780. Franklin to Jones, June 17, 1780. Jones to the Board of Admiralty, March 13, 1781. Franklin to the same, March 17, 1781. Wharton, III, 820, 800; IV, 288, 300.

[20] JCC, November 22, 1780.

[21] JCC, November 28, 1780. Madison to Pendleton, November 7, 1780. Madison to Joseph Jones, November 21, 1780.

[22] JCC, December 8, 11, 1780.

[23] Madison to Joseph Jones, December 12, 1780. Luzerne to Vergennes, December 15, 1780.

[24] JCC, December 11, 21, 1780. That Witherspoon's defeated motion to reconsider (JCC, December 11, 1780) was intended to pave the way to Madison's motion is evident from Luzerne's comment to Vergennes on December 15, following its defeat, that Congress would not change the title of "envoy extraordinary."

[25] Diary of Thomas Rodney, March 10, 1781, Burnett, VI, 20. Luzerne List, M. et D., E-U, Book I, 253-287.

[26] JCC, December 23, 1780. Luzerne to Vergennes, December 28, 1780; January 21, 1781.

[27] JCC, January 2, 1781. Lafayette to Committee of Congress, December 16, 1780, Wharton, IV, 196.

[28] JCC, March 28, 1780. Proceedings, Trial of Captain Landais, Lee Papers, VII, 50, Harvard Library.

[29] Franklin to Vergennes, February 13, March 6, 1780. Franklin to the President of Congress, March 12, 1780.

[30] Wharton, IV, 418, 467, 484, 660, 704, 837; V, 119. Vergennes to Luzerne, May 11, 1781. A full statement by the French government of moneys and goods delivered to Franklin and Laurens is in JCC, September 24, 1781. It shows that, altogether, Franklin obtained 15,693,501 livres before Laurens arrived and after he left. Laurens obtained a French guarantee of a 10,000,000-livre loan in Holland, productive in 1782.

[31] Franklin to the President of Congress, May 14, March 12, 1781.

CHAPTER VI

[1] Official Letters of the Governors of Virginia, I, 227. Hening, X, 537.

[2] JCC, August 14, 1779, January 31, 1780. See also February 23, March 17, 24, June 24, July 22, 29, August 5, 6, 14, September 9, 10, 17, 28, 1779, and December 30, 1776.

[3] Luzerne to Vergennes, March 13, 1780.

[4] Luzerne to Vergennes, August 25, 1780, naming Joseph Jones as the June 11 source.

[5] John Jay to the President of Congress, May 26, 1780.

[6] Luzerne to Vergennes, August 25, 1780.

[7] Luzerne to Vergennes, September 8, 15, 1780.

[8] Marbois to Vergennes, October 10, 1780.

[9] Luzerne, List, M. et D., E-U, Book I, 253-287.

[10] Hening, X, 557. Marbois to Vergennes, October 10, 1780. Gerard to Vergennes, July 9, 1779.

[11] Marbois to Vergennes, October 17, 1780.

[12] Madison MSS., II, 28a.

[13] Marbois to Vergennes, October 17, 1780.

[14] *Ibid*. Madison to Joseph Jones, (October 10, 1780). Misdated November, 1780, in *Writings*.

[15] *JCC*, October 4, 6, 1780. Marbois to Vergennes, October 17, 1780.

[16] Marbois to Vergennes, October 21, 1780.

[17] Madison to Joseph Jones, November 25, 1780.

[18] *JCC*, October 17, 1780.

[19] *JCC*, January 31, 1780.

[20] *JCC*, November 18, 1780. Madison to Joseph Jones, November 25, 1780. George Walton, *Observations*, etc., Burnett, V, 457n. Madison to Pendleton, September 12, 1780. John Adams to the President of Congress, May 9, 1780.

[21] Luzerne to Vergennes, November 26, 1780.

[22] Theodorick Bland to Governor Jefferson, November 22, 1780, Burnett, V, 455. MS. in Congressional Papers, Virginia State Library.

[23] Madison to Joseph Jones, December 5, 1780. Madison and Bland to Governor Jefferson, December 13, 1780. Luzerne to Vergennes, December 15, 1780.

[24] *JCC*, February 15, 1781. Madison, *Writings*, IX, 86, and Burnett, V, 578n.

[25] Marbois to Vergennes, October 21, 1780. Jay to the President of Congress, October 3, 1781, Wharton, IV, 743, 761-762.

[26] *JCC*, May 28, 1781. Madison's letter answered those from Jay dated November 6 and 30, 1780.

[27] Wharton, IV, 748.

[28] *JCC*, March 18, 20, April 22, 30, 1782.

CHAPTER VII

[1] Proceedings of the Maryland Convention of 1776, Force, 5th series, III, 178. Notes of debates, by John Adams and Thomas Jefferson, July 25 to August 2, 1776, in appendix to *JCC*, 1776.

[2] Memorial of George Morgan, *JCC*, September 14, 1779.

[3] Luzerne to Vergennes, February 2, 1781. For the organization of Western land companies, see Thomas W. Alvord, *Mississippi Valley in British Politics*; Thomas P. Abernethy, *Western Lands and the American Revolution*; Albert T. Vorwiler, *George Croghan and the Westward Movement*; Merrill Jensen, *The Articles of Confederation*.

[4] *JCC*, May 21, 1779.

[5] *JCC*, January 6, May 21, 1779. William Whipple to Josiah Bartlett, February 5, 1779.

[6] *JCC*, May 20, 1779.

[7] *JCC*, September 14, October 8, 29, 30, 1779. Diary of John Fell, September 14, 1779; Burnett, IV, 418. Virginia delegates to Speaker Harrison, November 2, 1779. *JCC*, November 27, 1779.

[8] Robert R. Livingston to Governor Clinton, November 30, 1779. Philip Schuyler to the New York Assembly, January 29, 1780. *JCC*, March 1, 1781.

[9] Madison "Autobiography," *William & Mary Quarterly*, April, 1945, 204.

[10] Hening, X, 557.

[11] *JCC*, June 26, 1780. James Duane to Washington, May 4, 1780. Willie Jones to Governor Nash, October 1, 1780. Joseph Jones to Governor Jefferson, June 30, 1780. George Mason to Joseph Jones, July 27, 1780, Kate Mason Rowland, *Life of George Mason*, I, 359-367.

[12] Joseph Jones to Washington, September 6, 1780. James Lovell to Samuel Holten, September 19, 1780.

[13] *JCC*, August 24, 1780.

[14] *JCC*, September 16, 1780. James Duane, Notes of Debates, October 6, 1780, Burnett, V, 408.

[15] Madison to Joseph Jones, September 19, 1780.

[16] Managers of the Indiana Company, seeking British validation of their 1768 deed from the Six Nations, found that English politicians and American speculators were trying to set up the larger colony of Vandalia, including their own Indiana (i.e. West Virginia) lands. Failing to secure a validation, the Indiana group entered the Vandalia speculation, which now put forward the Indiana title as its chief asset. The Vandalia scheme collapsed with the outbreak of the Revolution. The Indiana Company thereupon resumed its independent status, pressing its Indiana title upon Congress, and the punctured Vandalia Company became in turn a satellite of the Indiana outfit.

[17] *JCC*, September 26, 27, 1780.

[18] *JCC*, October 10, 1780. Madison to Joseph Jones, October 17, 1780.

[19] *Ibid*.

[20] Memorial of William Trent, PCC, No. 77, 230-233. George Morgan to the Virginia delegates, November 16, 1780; the Virginia delegates to George Morgan; extracts in Burnett, V, 455*n*.

[21] Madison to Joseph Jones, November 21, 1780. Theodorick Bland to Governor Jefferson, November 22, 1780.

[22] R. H. Lee to Samuel Adams, September 10, 1780. Madison to Pendleton, September 12, 1780. Pendleton to Madison, September 25, 1780, Burnett, V, 370*n*.

[23] Jefferson to Washington, September 26, 1780. Jensen, *The Articles of Confederation*, 122 (on Henry). Thomas Wharton to Thomas Walpole, September 23, 1774, *Pennsylvania Magazine of History and Biography*, XXXIII, 444.

24 Luzerne to Vergennes, February 2, 1781. Jenifer to Luzerne, January 5, 1781, *Pennsylvania Magazine of History and Biography*, October, 1936.

25 Marbois to Vergennes, October 16, 1780. Luzerne to Vergennes, February 2, 1781.

26 Luzerne to Jenifer, January 10, 1781, *Pennsylvania Magazine of History and Biography*, October, 1936.

27 Message of the Maryland Senate to the House of Delegates, February 2, 1781, Kathryn Sullivan, *Maryland and France, 1774-1789*.

28 *JCC*, January 31, March 1, 12, May 26, 1781. Virginia delegates to Governor Jefferson, January 30, 1781.

29 *JCC*, June 26, October 2, 1781.

30 Madison to Jefferson, January 15, April 16, 1782. The committee report of November 3, 1781, is in *JCC*, May 1, 1782.

31 *JCC*, October 16, November 14, 1781. Madison to Pendleton, October 30, November 13, 1781. Madison to Jefferson, January 15, 1782. Randolph to Governor Nelson, November 7, 1781.

CHAPTER VIII

1 *Pennsylvania Packet*, March 3, 1781. Diary of Thomas Rodney and Rodney to Mrs. Rodney, March 1, 1781, Burnett, VI, 1. Ezekiel Cornell to the governor of Rhode Island, March 5, 1781.

2 *JCC*, February 12, 22, 23, 24, March 1, 1781. PCC, Nos. 23, 29.

3 Hamilton to James Duane, September 3, 1780. Duane to Washington, January 29, 1781. Joseph Jones to Washington, February 27, 1781.

4 For the establishment of state governments, and the relationship of this to federal sovereignty, see Brant, *Madison*, I, 254-256.

5 Luzerne to Vergennes, May 18, 1781. Diary of Thomas Rodney, March 5, 6, 1781, Burnett, VI, 7-10. The original draft of the Articles was worded: "unless the delegates of seven colonies vote in the affirmative." *JCC*, July 12, 1776.

6 *JCC*, February 14, 1782.

7 *JCC*, March 6, 16, May 2 (text of report), 1781.

8 Madison to Jefferson, April 16, 1781. *JCC*, June 8, 1778, May 22, June 12, November 16, 21, 1780.

9 Madison to Jefferson, April 16, 1781; May 1, 1781, January 15, 1782, Madison MSS., II, 1, 32. Joseph Jones to Jefferson, April 16, July 24, 1781.

10 Madison to Jefferson, October 3, 1785; Jefferson to Edward Carrington, August 4, 1787. Rives, *Madison*, I, 302-305.

11 Edward McNall Burns, *James Madison, Philosopher of the Constitution*, 44.

12 *JCC*, July 24, 1776, June 8, 1778, March 16, 1780.

13 *JCC*, March 16, 27, 1781. Duane and Madison both worked on the revision of Madison's motion. (PCC, No. 36, I, 127 and 131.) The nationalistic phraseology could have come from the pen of either. Compare another Duane phrase, "the dignity and sovereignty of the United States as a free and independent nation" with Madison's "the dignity of the

United States as a sovereign and independent nation." (*JCC*, December 19, 1780; December 3, 1781.) All of this was at a time when, according to some historians, the United States was not thought of as a nation.

[14] *JCC*, April 5, 12, 1781.

[15] *JCC*, August 14, September 14, December 4, 1781; July 9, 10, 1782.

[16] *JCC*, December 23, 1782. Hamilton and McKean were on the committee with Madison.

[17] *JCC*, December 26, 27, 1776; September 17, November 14, December 10, 1777. Washington to the President of Congress, December 15, 1777.

[18] *Pennsylvania Packet*, March 2, 1779. Statement of William Duer, March 9, 1779, Burnett, IV, 97.

[19] *JCC*, April 16, 18, 28, 1781. Washington to the President of Congress, April 12, 1781. Diary of Thomas Rodney, April 12, 18, 1781, Burnett, VI, 51, 62.

[20] *JCC*, November 24, December 23, 1780. Madison to Governor Jefferson, May 5, 1781. The Virginia delegates to Jefferson, May 8, 1781. Luzerne to Vergennes, June 1, 1781. Rivington's *Royal Gazette*, May 13, 1781, quoted in Burnett, VI, 79*n*.

[21] James Lovell to Samuel Holten, May 8, 1781. Jenifer to John Hall, May 15, 1781.

[22] Luzerne to Vergennes, May 21, 1781.

[23] John Mathews to General Greene, May 20, 1781.

[24] *JCC*, July 20, 1781.

[25] *JCC*, August 22, 1781. The committee—Edmund Randolph, Ellsworth, Varnum.

[26] *JCC*, July 27, August 9, 22, 23, 31, September 7, 1781; January 25, 1782.

[27] *Annals of Congress*, August 18, 1789.

CHAPTER IX

[1] *JCC*, March 20, 21, 29, 31, April 20, 21, 25, 27, 1781. Robert Morris to Daniel Clark, May 30, 1782, Wharton, V, 448.

[2] *JCC*, February 27, 28, March 30, April 16, July 6, 18, August 29, September 7, 28, October 1, 30, 1781; January 17, 1782. James Mitchell Varnum to Washington, August 20, October 21, 1781. John Sullivan to Washington, March 6, 1781. Philip Schuyler to Washington, April 3, 1781. Luzerne to Vergennes, March 25, 1781.

[3] Thomas Burke to William Bingham, January 30, February (6?), 1781. Bingham was a candidate for the foreign secretaryship himself.

[4] Arthur Lee to Samuel Adams, August 13, 1781, Burnett, VI, 176*n*. Luzerne to Vergennes, May 18, 1781.

[5] *Ibid*, and Luzerne to Vergennes, August 11, 1781.

[6] Luzerne, who described the McClurg candidacy in his August 11 letter, made no specific mention of it on May 18. However, he said, "Others

NOTES 433

were placed in nomination." This and the absence of Virginia from the
Lee column clearly point to the use of McClurg at this time.

⁷ See notes 4 and 5. Lee's account to Adams reads as if three ballots
were taken on successive days in August. Luzerne tells of two ballots prior
to May 18, and two afterward, but omits the semifinal one described by
Lee. The first ballot must have been cast between March 21 and April 6—
the only period, prior to Luzerne's account, when all five states named by
Lee as his original supporters were present.

⁸ Madison to Philip Mazzei, July 7, 1781. Chastellux (*Travels*, II, 30,
Robinson translation 1787) puts the French money in circulation in
America in 1782 at 35,000,000 livres, nearly a million and a half pounds
sterling.

⁹ *JCC*, February 27, 28, May 10, 15, 1781.

¹⁰ *JCC*, May 30, June 1, 2, 1781.

¹¹ Madison to Randolph, June 4, 1782.

¹² Madison to Pendleton, January 8, 1782. See also James Wilson, *Works*
(J. D. Andrews), I, 558; Edward S. Corwin, *American Historical Review*,
XXX, 528. Jefferson wrote to the Count von Hogendorp, August 25, 1786,
that the chartering of the Bank of North America by Congress "is perhaps the only instance of their having done that which they had no
power to do."

¹³ Sumner, II, 24-35; tables on pages 32 and 129.

¹⁴ *JCC*, June 21, 22, 1780; February 6, June 22, 1781. Madison to Jefferson, June 23, 1780.

¹⁵ *JCC*, May 26, 1779 (appreciation of currency); September 19, 1775
and December 18, 1778 (Indian education); June 20, 1777 (public tanyards); June 30, 1779 (Continental ferry); April 7, 1779 (road to Nova
Scotia). R. H. Lee to Hall & Sellers, October 17, 1777 (moving press).

¹⁶ Robert Morris to John Jay, July 13, 1781, Wharton, IV, 562. Alexan-
der Hamilton in "The Continentalist" (1781), *Works* (Lodge) I, 266.
Madison to Randolph, July 16, 1782, Madison MSS., II, 93. Luzerne to
Vergennes, June 23, 1782.

¹⁷ *JCC*, June 17, September 18, 1782.

¹⁸ Luzerne wrote to Vergennes, May 18, 1781: "Mr. Lee . . . returned
several days ago, and I expect new intrigues here. He could not succeed
in getting himself elected as a delegate from Virginia to Congress, although
his family enjoys great influence in that state." Lee was named in place
of John Blair on December 28.

¹⁹ *JCC*, July 2, 1782 (including footnote). PCC, Committee Book 186,
November 21, 1782; January 6, March 31, 1783.

²⁰ *JCC*, June 17, 1783.

²¹ Madison to Pendleton, November 4 (5), 1782. Madison to Randolph,
November 5, 1782. Thomas McKean to Samuel Adams, July 8, 1781.
Samuel Huntington to Washington, July 10, 1781. Luzerne to Vergennes,
November 10, 1781. *JCC*, July 9, 10, 1781, November 5, 1781, Novem-
ber 4, 1782. Madison, Notes of Debates, November 4, 1782.

CHAPTER X

[1] Vergennes to Luzerne, December 4, 1780. Letters written by Silas Deane for the purpose of being intercepted were published in New York late in 1781. Their genuineness, Madison reported, was generally doubted, but from other sources (nonintercepted letters) there was "indubitable proof" of his obliquity. "Either from pique, interested projects of trade, or a traitorous correspondence with the enemy, he has certainly apostatized from his first principles." Franklin wrote that Deane had gone to Ghent where he "raves and writes abundance . . . he is changed and his character ruined." Madison to Jefferson, November 18, 1781. Franklin to Livingston, March 4, 1782, Wharton, V, 216.

[2] Vergennes, Memoir on a Truce, February 1781, Archives des Affaires Étrangères, Corr. Pol., E-U, Book 15, 269-278. See also Bancroft, X, 444.

[3] Adams to Vergennes, February 19, June 20, 22, July 17, 26, 1780, Wharton, III, 503, 805, 809, 861; IV, 7. Vergennes to Adams, February 24, June 21, 30, July 25, 1780, Wharton, III, 518, 807, 828, 882. Vergennes' marginal annotations, Wharton, IV, 3.

[4] Adams to Vergennes, July 13, 21, 27, 1780, Wharton, III, 848, 872; IV, 12. Vergennes to Adams, July 20, 1780, Wharton, III, 870.

[5] Vergennes to Adams, July 29, 1780; Vergennes to Franklin, July 31, 1780; Franklin to the President of Congress, August 9, 1780, Wharton, IV, 16, 18, 21. Vergennes to Luzerne, August 7, 1780.

[6] James Lovell to Franklin, March 9, 1781. John Adams to the President of Congress, June 26, August 14, 1780. JCC, December 12, 1780.

[7] JCC, May 25, 26, 28, 1781.

[8] Vergennes to Luzerne, Febuary 19, March 9, 1781. Luzerne to Vergennes, June 1, 1781.

[9] Luzerne to Vergennes, June 8, 1781. JCC, June 8, 1781.

[10] JCC, June 6, 1781.

[11] JCC, June 6, 7, 1781.

[12] Luzerne to Vergennes, June 8, 1781.

[13] JCC, June 7, 8, 1781. PCC, No. 25, I, 447.

[14] JCC, June 8, 1781. Daniel of St. Thomas Jenifer to John Hall, Luzerne to Vergennes, June 11, 1781.

[15] Luzerne to Vergennes, June 13, 1781.

[16] JCC, June 11, 1781. The instruction relative to France, as adopted, read: "For this purpose, you are to make the most candid and confidential communications upon all subjects to the ministers of our generous ally, the King of France; to undertake nothing in the negotiations for peace or truce without their knowledge and concurrence; and ultimately to govern yourselves by their advice and opinion, endeavoring in your whole conduct to make them sensible how much we rely on his Majesty's influence for effectual support in everything that may be necessary to the present security, or future prosperity, of the United States of America."

[17] JCC, June 8 (committee report), 9, 11, 14, 1781.

[18] *JCC*, June 15, 1781. Madison, Notes of Debates, December 30, 1782.
[19] Luzerne to Vergennes, June 23, 1781.
[20] *JCC*, August 13, 1779.
[21] *JCC*, June 9, 19, 29, 1781.
[22] Marbois to Vergennes, July 11, 1781.
[23] *JCC*, July 12, 1781. Marbois to Vergennes, July 14, 1781.
[24] James Lovell to John Adams, July 21, 1781. James Lovell to Abigail Adams, August 10, 1781.
[25] *JCC*, November 17, December 12, 1781; August 23, 1782. James Lovell to Samuel Adams, December 13, 1781.

CHAPTER XI

[1] The report of January 8 is in *JCC*, August 20, 1782.
[2] Luzerne to Vergennes, January 1, 10, 1782.
[3] Luzerne to Vergennes, January 11, 1782. *JCC*, January 22, 1782.
[4] *JCC*, April 18, May 1, 6, 1782. Madison to Randolph, May 1, 1782. Madison to Arthur Lee, May 7, 1782.
[5] Madison to Randolph, May 1, 1782.
[6] Madison, *Papers* (Gilpin), I, 122; Burnett, VI, 340; Sparks, *Writings of Washington*, VIII, App. X, 547.
[7] Madison to Randolph, May 1, 1782 (misdated 1781, and misplaced in *Writings*). Note also the words "we have been mistaken," in Madison to Randolph, April 9, 1782.
[8] *JCC*, June 17, August 8, 1782. Charles Thomson, Notes of Debates, August 16, 1782, Burnett, VI, 444. Madison to Randolph, July 2, 1782. Committee Book 186, PCC, shows the addition of Duane, Williamson, Osgood and Madison to the Carroll-Randolph-Montgomery committee (reduced to Montgomery) on August 5, 1782.
[9] *JCC*, August 15, 1782.
[10] Thomson, Notes of Debates, August 15, 16, 1782, Burnett, VI, 444.
[11] *JCC*, August 20, 1782.
[12] Madison to Randolph, August 20, 1782. Franklin, a stockholder in the Indiana Company, was accused of willingness to surrender the West to Great Britain in order to gain a validation of the company's claim from that power—a charge completely disproved by his negotiations.
[13] Thomson, Notes of Debates, August 20, 1782, Burnett, VI, 447. *JCC*, June 11, 1783 (footnote).
[14] Madison to Randolph, August 27, 1782. Livingston to Franklin, January 7, 1782, Wharton, V, 87.
[15] *JCC*, September 24, October 3, 4, 1782. Madison to Randolph, October 8, 1782. Luzerne to Vergennes, October 6, 1782.
[16] *JCC*, August 27, 1782. Thomson, Notes of Debates, August 27, 1782, Burnett, VI, 456. For 1776 support of federal ownership and sale of Western lands, see newspaper articles in Force, *American Archives*, 4th series, IV, 1170, 1496; V, 855. From New Jersey came a proposal that Congress divide New York and the Southern colonies, on the principle

that "the strength and happiness of America must be continental, and not provincial." New Yorkers were told that land sales "to pay the millions emitted by the Congress . . . will . . . set us free from slavery and taxation to all generations."

[17] JCC, July 31, September 4, 5, 6, 1782. Madison to Randolph, September 10, 1782.

[18] The original draft of Witherspoon's resolves used the language of the Jones-Madison motion of September 6, 1780, directly outlawing Indian deeds. This would have come more naturally from Madison than from Witherspoon, who could not afford to be so blunt in attacking a land company which ruled his legislature. An earlier related motion by Witherspoon, on territorial claims, is in Madison's handwriting.

[19] JCC, September 25, October 29, 30, 1782. Madison to Randolph, November 5, 1782.

[20] Madison to Governor Harrison, November 15, 1782.

[21] JCC, April 23, June 4, 6, 20, 1783. Madison, Notes of Debates, June 10, 20, 1783.

[22] JCC, September 13, 1783. Virginia delegates to Governor Harrison, November 1, 1783. On June 17 Washington transmitted a petition of army officers (read in Congress on July 1) for lands northwest of the Ohio.

CHAPTER XII

[1] Madison to Philip Mazzei, July 7, 1781. John Walker to Jefferson, June 13, 1780. H. J. Eckenrode, *The Story of the Campaign and Siege of Yorktown.*

[2] *Journal of the Council of the State of Virginia,* July 18, 1781.

[3] JCC, September 20, 27, October 1, 1781. Two years earlier, Congress had ordered Franklin to "employ incendiaries" to burn London (particularly the royal palace), Bristol, Liverpool, Glasgow and Edinburgh as "objects of national retaliating resentment." *JCC,* August 2, 1779. Marine Committee to Franklin, July 19, 1779.

[4] JCC, October 26, December 3, 1781.

[5] Madison to Pendleton, August 14, September 18, 1781, Madison MSS., II, 8, 11. John Mathews to General Greene, August 23, 1781.

[6] Madison to Pendleton, September 3, 1781.

[7] Samuel Livermore to the president of New Hampshire, September 4, 1781. Ezra L'Hommedieu to the governor of New York, September 8, 1781.

[8] Diary of Robert Morris, September 5, 1781; Washington to Morris, September 6, 1781, Wharton, IV, 693, 699.

[9] Thomas McKean to Arthur Lee, September 4, 1781. Madison to Pendleton, September 3, 1781.

[10] *Journal of Claude Blanchard,* September 3-7, 1781. Blanchard was Luzerne's house guest.

[11] Diary of Robert Morris, September 5, 1781; Morris to Rochambeau, September 6, October 2, 1781, Wharton, IV, 700, 737.

[12] Madison to Pendleton, September 18, October 2, 1781.

[13] JCC, October 24, 29, 1781. Pennsylvania Packet, October 5, November 1, 1781 (in Burnett, VI, 250n). Thomas McKean to Washington, October 18, 1781. Elias Boudinot to Elisha Boudinot, October 23, 1781, Shippen Papers, Pennsylvania Magazine of History and Biography, XXV, 27.

[14] Madison to Pendleton, October 30, 1781.

[15] JCC, October 29, November 23, 1781. Madison to Pendleton, November 13, 1781. JVHD, December 17, 1781; December 1, 1784.

[16] Franklin's Journal, May (9?), 1782, Franklin to Livingston, Lafayette to Livingston, June 25, 1782, Wharton, V, 553, 511, 519. Lafayette to Vergennes, November 22, 1782, John Adams, "Journal of Negotiations," November 23, 1782, Franklin to Livingston, December 5, 1782, Franklin to Robert Morris, December 25, 1783; Wharton, VI, 67, 70, 111, 745. Adams disbelieved Lafayette's statement to Vergennes that he had been asked to delay his departure to aid in diplomacy, and said Franklin and Jay both denied asking him to. It would have been strange indeed if Franklin denied it to Adams, since he and Lafayette already had reported the request to Livingston, both on the same day, June 25, 1782.

[17] Madison and Bland to Washington, December 21, 1780, Emmet Collection, New York Public Library. Judging young Thornton by his family, they advised that he be allowed to come through the American lines.

[18] JCC, November 28, 1781, March 21, 1782. Madison to Pendleton, November 27, 1781. Diaries of Washington, May 13, 1787.

[19] JCC, May 24, 29, 1782. Madison and Bland to Governor Harrison, June 4, 18, 1782. Luzerne to Vergennes, March 24, April 23, May 29, 1782. See also references in Burnett, VI, 367n.

[20] Madison to Randolph, Madison to Arthur Lee, May (7), 1782. Marbois to Vergennes, April 7, 1782.

[21] Hening, XI, 545. Randolph to Madison, May 16, 21-24, 1782, Madison MSS., II, 62, 68. Madison to Randolph, May 28, 1782. Luzerne to Vergennes, May 24, 1782.

[22] JCC, May 2, 7, 10, 13, 1782. Livingston to the Secretary of Congress (two letters) and the latter to Livingston, May 8, 9, 1782, Burnett, VI, 346-347. Diary of Robert Morris, May 13, 1782, Wharton, V, 410n. Luzerne to Vergennes, May 14, 1782. Luzerne to Washington, June 10, 1782, Wharton, V, 483.

[23] Luzerne to Vergennes, Madison to Randolph, May 14, 1782. JCC, May 14, 1782.

[24] JCC, May 14, 28, 1782.

[25] JCC, May 31, 1782. Madison to Randolph, May 28, 1782. Luzerne to Vergennes, June 3, 1782.

[26] Madison to Randolph, June 11, 1782. Madison's English version of the Marbois letter is in Madison Papers, III, xxxvi. Jaquelin Ambler appealed to Madison to write anonymous articles for the Virginia Gazette,

saying: "Oh sir we want some publications that will rouse our citizens. I sincerely wish you could spare an hour now and then to this salutary work." Madison himself thought a new newspaper should be established in Virginia for patriotic propaganda. Madison, *Writings*, I, 329n.

CHAPTER XIII

[1] *JCC*, October 25, December 3, 1781.

[2] *JCC*, June 14, 1781; February 18, 23, 1782.

[3] Madison to Jefferson, April 3, 1781. Madison and Bland to Governor Jefferson, Madison and Bland to Luzerne, April 2, 1781, *Calendar of Virginia State Papers*, II, 8, 4. *JCC*, December 30, 1777.

[4] *JCC*, February 8, 11 (two entries), 1782.

[5] Madison to Randolph, July 2, 1782. Madison to Randolph, Madison to Arthur Lee, May 28, 1782.

[6] Madison to Randolph, May 29, June 4, 6, 1781. *JCC*, May 29, 30, 1781.

[7] *JVHD*, June 14, 1782. Madison to Randolph, June 11, 1782; Randolph to Madison, June 15, 20, 1782, Madison MSS., II, 78, 83.

[8] Madison to Randolph, July 2, 1782.

[9] Madison to Randolph, June 18, 1782.

[10] *JCC*, June 14, 17, 21, 1782.

[11] *JCC*, June 10, 11, 17, 28, July 1, 15, 29, 1782. Madison to Randolph, August 9, September 3, 1782.

[12] *JCC*, June 5, 1782. Luzerne to Vergennes, May 24, 1783.

[13] *JCC*, August 12, 1782.

[14] Madison to Randolph, July 16, 1782, Madison MSS., II, 93. See also Washington to the President of Congress, April 4, 1778; Thomas Burke to the governor of North Carolina, April 9, 1778.

[15] *JCC*, October 16, November 5, 7, 1782. Madison, Notes of Debates, November 5, 7, 1782.

[16] Madison to Randolph, May 1, 1782 (misdated 1781 in *Writings*).

[17] Wharton, V, 463n. Balch, *Français en Amérique*, 55. *JCC*, October 1, December 3, 1781; April 29, 1782. Washington to Nathanael Greene, December 15, 1781.

[18] Madison to Randolph, July 16, 1782.

[19] Lady Asgill to Vergennes, July 18, 1782, Wharton, V, 635.

[20] Madison to Randolph, July 16, August 27, October 29, 1782. *Reminiscences of Elias Boudinot*, quoted in Burnett, VI, 539n.

[21] Marbois to Vergennes, April 12, 1782.

[22] Henry Laurens to the President of Congress, May 30, 1782, Wharton, V, 445.

[23] Luzerne to Vergennes, September 22, 1782.

[24] Richard Oswald to Franklin, June 5, 1782, Wharton, V, 478.

[25] Henry Laurens to Franklin, April 7, 30 (misdated 20 in Wharton), May 17, June 24, 1782, Wharton, V, 536, 546, 559, 503. Franklin to Shelburne, April 18, 1782; Shelburne to Franklin, April 30 (misdated 20

in Wharton), 1782, Wharton, V, 538, 547. Franklin to Henry Laurens, April 20, May 25, 1782, Wharton, V, 543, 561. The two letters misdated April 20 were in answer to letters received after that date. Both contain references to events of April 27. It is impossible to follow the Laurens-Shelburne-Franklin activities without knowledge of this misdating.

[26] *JCC*, September 17, 1782. Madison to Randolph, September 24, 1782.

[27] Franklin to Livingston, June 29, 1782, Wharton, V, 553.

[28] *JCC*, September 25, 1782 (footnote). Cornell's departure made Madison chairman of the Cornwallis committee. Montgomery was added to it.

[29] *JCC*, September 20, 1782. Thomson, Notes, September 19, 20, 1782, Burnett, VI, 481-488.

[30] Madison to Randolph, September 24, 1782. Laurens petition, Wharton, V, 744, Madison MSS., II, 24a.

[31] *JCC*, September 20, 1782. Samuel Osgood to John Adams, December 7, 1783.

[32] *JCC*, September 25, 26, 1782. Luzerne to Vergennes, October 20, 1782.

[33] *JCC*, November 22, 25, 26, 1782. Madison, Notes of Debates, November 22, 25, 1782. Franklin to Livingston, March 4, 1782, Wharton, V, 216.

[34] Madison, Notes of Debates, November 25, 1782.

[35] Vergennes to Washington, July 29, 1782; Washington to the President of Congress, October 25, 1782, Wharton, V, 634, 833. Vergennes' letter, sent on a British packet, was delivered to Washington under a flag of truce.

[36] *Reminiscences of Elias Boudinot*, quoted in Burnett, VI, 539n.

[37] Madison to Randolph, November 5, 1782. Madison, Notes of Debates, November 7, 1782.

[38] *JCC*, November 7, 8, 1782. Madison, Notes of Debates, November 7, 1782.

[39] *JCC*, November 8, 1782. Madison, Notes of Debates, November 7, 8, 1782.

CHAPTER XIV

[1] *JCC*, May 9, 1782. Luzerne to Vergennes, April 27, 1782.

[2] *JCC*, May 24, 1782. Robert Morris to the President of Congress, May 23, 1782, Wharton, V, 438.

[3] *JCC*, May 28, 29, 1782.

[4] Jackson-Franklin letters, Wharton, IV, 529, 530, 531, 543, 544, 545, 557, 838. Franklin to the President of Congress, July 11, 1781; Franklin to Robert Morris, July 26, 1781, Wharton, IV, 559, 605. Franklin to John Adams and to John Laurens, November 7, 8, 1781, Wharton, IV, 835. A letter from Jackson to Congress, dated July 25, 1782, was referred to the Bland Committee but is not among the PCC.

[5] *JCC*, July 12, 25, 29, 1782. Arthur Lee to Samuel Adams, August 6, 1782. Luzerne to Vergennes, August 12, 1782.

[6] Madison ordinarily used the official Virginia cipher, in which different numbers were used to represent letters, syllables and words. On July 5, 1782, following a mail robbery, Randolph suggested that they use the cipher of James Lovell of Massachusetts, in which a five-letter word known only to them would serve as key to the alphabet written in five columns, each one beginning with a letter of the key word. Thus each letter had five different numbers, employed through consecutive use of the columns— first letter of the message from first column, second letter from second column, etc. Their key was Cupid, the name of the Negro boy who waited on the Reverend James Madison of William and Mary College. Randolph was unable to decipher the letters written in it. Dr. E. C. Burnett has done that. See Randolph to Madison, July 5, Madison to Randolph, August 20, 1782, and footnotes in Burnett, VI, 384, 452. Also, Burnett, "Ciphers of the Revolutionary Period," *American Historical Review*, XXII, 331.

[7] *JCC*, August 5, 8, 1782. Luzerne to Vergennes, August 12, 15, 1782. Madison to Randolph, July 16, 23, September 3, 1782.

[8] Thomson, Notes, July 24, 1782, Burnett, VI, 391. Madison to Randolph, July 30, 1782. Arthur Lee, draft of motion, Lee Papers, Harvard.

[9] Thomson, Notes, August 2, 1782. *JCC*, August 2, 6, 8, 1782. Madison to Randolph, August 5, 1782.

[10] *JCC*, June 17, 1782. Madison to Randolph, July 2, 1782.

[11] Thomson, Notes, August 8, 1782. *JCC*, August 8, 1782.

[12] Footnote to *JCC*, November 18, 1782.

[13] Arthur Lee to James Warren, July (23?), 1782. *JCC*, May 29, August 6, 1781, June 19, 26, July 12, 14, 19, August 5, November 18, 1782. Thomson, Notes, July 25, 1782. Lee's Memorial is in PCC, No. 41, V, 281. The July 12 *JCC* footnote recording it should be June 12. Papers were lacking for sixteen shipments of goods by Lee, but his accounts were approved: "Mr. Lee having declared upon his honor in writing that his accounts of expenses, ordinary and extraordinary, are to the best of his knowledge justly charged."

[14] *JCC*, July 29 (footnote), November 18, 1782.

[15] *JCC*, September 14, November 20, 1782. Luzerne to Vergennes, August 12, 1782.

[16] *JCC*, September 19, 28, 1782. Madison to Randolph, October 8, 1782.

[17] *JCC*, November 1, 1782. Madison to Randolph, October 15, 1782. Committee Book 186 shows the appointment of Madison and Carroll.

[18] *JCC*, August 14, 1782. Luzerne to Vergennes, September 18, 1782.

[19] Madison to Randolph, October 8, 1782. Randolph to Madison, November 2, 1782, Madison MSS., III, 28. *Freeman's Journal*, Philadelphia, August 7, 1782. *Independent Gazetteer*, September 28, October 5, 19, 1782. Luzerne to Vergennes, November 16, 1782; February 12, 1784.

[20] Randolph to Madison, November 2, 29, December 13, 20, 27, 1782, Madison MSS., III, 28, 40, 47, 50, 52. The Reverend James Madison to Madison, January 16, 1783, Madison MSS., III, 65. Arthur Lee to T. L. Shippen, April 25, 1790, Shippen Papers, Library of Congress.

[21] Luzerne to Vergennes, August 12, 1782.

²² R. H. Lee, *Life of Arthur Lee*, II, 390-391.

²³ Francis Dana to the President of Congress, March 24, 28, 31, April 4, 1781, Wharton, IV, 325, 333, 344, 349. Dana to Vergennes, March 31, April 2, 1781; Vergennes to Dana, April 1, 1781, Wharton, IV, 343, 348. Dana to Franklin, April 6, 1781; Franklin to Dana, April 7, May 11, 1781, Wharton, IV, 352, 353, 407.

²⁴ Dana to John Adams, Adams to Dana, April 18, 1781, Wharton, IV, 367, 368. Dana to the President of Congress, May 13, July 28, September 15, October 15, 1781, Wharton, IV, 407, 610, 710, 773. The Marquis de Verac to Dana, September 2, 12, 1781; Dana to Verac, September 1, 4, 13, 1781; Wharton, IV, 683, 684, 695, 705, 707.

²⁵ Madison to Randolph, April 23, May 14, 1782; Randolph to Madison, May 5, 1782, Madison MSS., II, 52a, 61, 57. The original of the May 14 letter has disappeared. Somebody who had access to it in 1858 made a copy of the expurgated version published by Gilpin in 1840 and interlined the omitted text.

²⁶ Samuel Osgood to John Adams, December 7, 1785. Jacob Read to the Secretary of Congress, August 16, 1784, Burnett, VIII, 860.

²⁷ *JCC*, May 27, 1782. Livingston to Dana, May 10, 1782, Wharton, V, 411.

²⁸ Samuel Osgood to John Adams, December 7, 1783. Madison's resolution was missing from the packet Dana received, presumably lost by Russian agents who abstracted a set of government ciphers from it. This led to a false charge that Livingston sent the letter before the resolution was adopted. Dana to Livingston, September 29, 1782; Dana to John Adams, October 15, 1782; Wharton, V, 780, 815. Delivery of the letter to Luzerne is shown by the endorsement in Livingston's Letterbook, PCC, No. 79.

²⁹ Madison to Randolph, October 8, 22, 1782, Madison MSS., III, 15, 34; Burnett, VI, 514n. Dana to the President of Congress, June 28, 1782, Wharton, V, 528. Dana to Livingston, September 5, November 18, December 27, 30, 1782, Wharton, V, 700; VI, 54, 170, 171. *The Nation*, June 11, 1868, quoted in Wharton, V, 414n.

³⁰ *JCC*, April 22, 1783. Madison, Notes of Debates, April 12, 1783. Livingston to Dana, May 1, 1783; Wharton, VI, 403.

³¹ Livingston to the President of Congress, May 19, 1783, PCC, No. 79, III, 221. *JCC*, December 19, 1780. Dana's instructions lacked the usual order to sign the treaty. His commission, however, carried the pledge of Congress to "confirm whatsoever shall by him be transacted in the matter."

³² Stephen Higginson to Theodorick Bland, January 1, 1784.

³³ *JCC*, May 21, 22, 1783. Madison, Notes of Debates, May 21, 1783. Dana to Livingston, July 27, August 8, 1783; Dana to John Adams, July 29, 1783, Wharton, VI, 597, 635, 617. PCC, No. 36, II, 121 (Madison motion), 123-125 (Hamilton motion). That Madison's motion was written first, though introduced last, is evident from the fact that some of its provisions are interlined in Hamilton's paper, while Hamilton's pre-

amble is appended to Madison's motion. Catherine finally refused to recognize Dana because his credentials were of earlier date than the peace treaty. Dana's own friends aided his recall by a mild permission to come home. *JCC*, April 1, 1783.

[34] Madison to Jefferson, May 13, 1783. Madison to Randolph, May (20), 1783.

[35] *JCC*, May 21, 1783. PCC, No. 36, II, 123-125.

[36] *JCC*, June 12, 1783. PCC, Committee Book 186. Madison, Notes of Debates, June 12, 1783. The original May 21 resolve against foreign commitments was taken up once more and formally approved, on October 29, 1783, by inclusion in a set of general instructions to American ministers in Europe.

[37] Madison to Monroe, June 21, 1786.

[38] Vergennes to Luzerne, July 21, 1783.

CHAPTER XV

[1] Randolph to Madison, April 26, 1783, Madison MSS., IV, 11. Hening, X, 465. E. Bancroft to W. Frazer, November 8, 1783, George Bancroft, *History of the Constitution*, I, 333.

[2] David Jameson to Madison, March 9, 1782, Rives Papers. Hening, XI, 31.

[3] James Madison account as delegate in Congress, December 1779 to November 7, 1782, Congressional Papers, Virginia State Library. Gaillard Hunt, in Madison, *Writings*, II, 178n, summarizes Madison's receipts from the state as £2,000 before he left Virginia and £500 up to November, 1782. The latter figure actually included the former, which was inflated paper money with a specie value of 32 pounds 5 shillings.

[4] Randolph to Madison, April 11-13, 1782; Ambler to Madison, May 11, 1782, Madison MSS., II, 49b, 60. State Treasurer Brooks died April 6, 1782. Historians have quoted Treasurer Ambler's remark of May 11, "We have not had ten pounds specie in it [the treasury] since my coming into office," without noting that he had been in office less than five weeks.

[5] Madison to James Madison, Sr., August 1, 1781, (Madison MSS., II, 7); February 12, March 30, May 20, 1782.

[6] Madison to Randolph, August 27, September 30, 1782.

[7] Ambler to Madison, May 3, 10, 17, 1783, Madison MSS., IV, 14, 19, 23. Draft of Madison's final account as delegate, Madison MSS., XC, 23-24.

[8] Madison to Ambrose Madison, January 2, 1781. Madison to Pendleton, May 29, 1781. *JCC*, February 1, 3, 7, 1781. Madison's amendment is in a footnote, page 113. A finance committee report of November 8, 1780, recommending a 2½ per cent impost, is said by the *JCC* editor to be in Madison's handwriting, but is actually in that of John Henry of Maryland.

[9] For dates of impost ratifications, see Burnett, VI, 372. *JCC*, April 19, 1781. Jesse Root to the governor of Connecticut, December 27, 1780.

[10] Robert Morris to the governors of the states (draft of a proposed letter), May 16, 1782, Wharton, V, 423.

[11] *JCC*, May 20, 1782.

[12] *JCC*, May 20, 22, 1782. Diary of Robert Morris, May 20, 1782, Wharton, V, 426*n*.

[13] Madison to Randolph, May (7), 1782.

[14] David Howell to the governor of Rhode Island, July 30, October 15, 1782.

[15] *JCC*, August 30, September 26, 28, October 1, November 12, 20, December 4, 1782.

[16] Madison, Notes of Debates, December 4, 1782.

[17] *Ibid*, January 24, 1783.

[18] John C. Hamilton, *History of the Republic . . . in the Writings of Alexander Hamilton*, II, 361-363 (1857). PCC, No. 20, II, 445-452 (Fitzsimons report).

[19] *JCC*, July 22, 1782, January 7, 1783. Madison, Notes of Debates, November 26, December 7, 24, 1782. J. C. Hamilton, *History of the Republic*, II, 353, 356.

[20] Rives pointed this out in *Madison*, I, 437-443.

[21] Madison, Notes of Debates, November 26, 1782.

[22] Madison to Randolph, November 19, 26, 1782.

[23] Madison, Notes of Debates, December 6, 1782. *JCC*, December 6, 1782.

[24] *JCC*, December 12, 1782. Madison, Notes of Debates, December 12, 13, 1782.

[25] *JCC*, May 2, 1781; December 12, 16, 1782. Madison to Jefferson, April 16, 1781. Hamilton to Governor Clinton, February 24, 1783.

[26] Madison, Notes of Debates, January 28, 1783. Claude H. Van Tyne, *The American Revolution*, 180. The specific comparison was with the 1821 Congress of Laibach. See Brant, *Madison*, I, 393.

[27] *JCC*, December 12, 17, 18, 1782. Madison, Notes of Debates, December 17, 18, 1782. Luzerne to Vergennes, December 19, 1782. Jonathan Arnold to the governor of Rhode Island, December 6, 18, 1782.

[28] *JCC*, December 18, 20, 1782. Madison, Notes of Debates, December 20, 1782.

[29] Osgood of Massachusetts, Mifflin of Pennsylvania, Nash of North Carolina made up the deputation to Rhode Island.

[30] *JCC*, December 6, 12, 17, 1782. Madison and Joseph Jones to Governor Harrison, Madison to Randolph, December 10, 1782. Madison, Notes of Debates, December 24, 1782.

[31] Samuel Osgood to Benjamin Lincoln, January 1, 1783. Madison, Notes of Debates, December 24, 1782. Madison to Randolph, December 24, 30, 1782. *JCC*, December 24, 31, 1782; January 2, 3, 14, 1783.

[32] Madison to Randolph, January 22, 1783 (misdated 1782 and misplaced in *Writings*).

[33] Benjamin Harrison to Madison, January 4, 1783, Madison MSS., III, 60. Randolph to Madison, February 7, 1783, Burnett, VII, 21*n*.

[34] Hening, XI, 171.

[35] Madison to Randolph, December 30, 1782. Madison, Notes of Debates, January 6, 7, 1783.

[36] *JCC*, September 14, 1782. Madison to Randolph, September 24, 1782. Madison, Notes of Debates, January 8-9-10, 1783.

[37] *Ibid. JCC*, January 10, 1783. Luzerne List, M. et D., E-U, I, 253-287.

[38] Madison, Notes of Debates, January 13, 17, 1783.

[39] *Ibid*, January 10, 13, 1783. Madison to Randolph, January 22, 1783. Diary of Robert Morris, January 14, 1783. Luzerne to Vergennes, January 26, 1783.

[40] *JCC*, May 15, 1778; October 21, 1780; December 15, 1782. Charles Thomson, Notes, July 31, 1782, Burnett, VI, 406. Madison, Notes of Debates, January 13, 1783.

[41] *JCC*, January 25, 1783. Madison, Notes of Debates, January 24, 25, February 4, 1783.

[42] *Ibid*, January 25 (cost of pay plan), February 4, 27, March 22, 1783. *JCC*, March 22, 1783. Burnett, *The Continental Congress*, 568.

[43] *JCC*, January 25, 1783. Madison, Notes of Debates, January 24, 1783. The important words "general and" are omitted from the report as published in the *Journals*.

[44] Madison, Notes of Debates, January 27, 1783.

[45] Virginia Assembly resolution of May 28, 1782 (on land valuation). Hening, XI, 171 (impost repeal).

[46] Madison, Notes of Debates, January 8, 14, 31 (including footnotes), 1783.

[47] *Ibid*, January 27, 1783.

[48] Madison to Randolph, January 28, 1783.

[49] John C. Hamilton continued his grotesque attacks on Madison by charging (*History of the Republic*, II, 399) that he invented the story of Wilson's motion, and his own remodeling of it, to take credit away from Alexander Hamilton and bestow it on himself. Hamilton's authorship, his son said, was proved by the existence in the State Department (i.e., in the PCC) of a copy of it in his handwriting. Rives (*Madison*, I, 437) exploded that by pointing out that the copy in Hamilton's handwriting is of the Wilson motion *after it was amended by Gorham*.

[50] Madison, Notes of Debates, January 28, 1783. Madison to Randolph, February 4, 1783.

[51] *JCC*, February 6, 7, 1783. Madison, Notes of Debates, January 28, 29, 31, February 5-6, 7, 1783.

[52] *Ibid*, February 7, 10, 11, 14, 17, 1783. *JCC*, February 14, 17, 1783.

[53] *JCC*, February 12, 1783. Madison, Notes of Debates, February 18, 19, 20, 1783. Madison to Randolph, February 18, 1783. Mercer led the move in the Virginia Assembly to oust Arthur Lee from Congress—Randolph to Madison, December 20, 1782, Madison MSS., III, 50.

[54] Madison, Notes of Debates, February 20, 1783. Hamilton to Washington, February 7, 1783.

[55] Madison, Notes of Debates, February 21, 1783. Madison to Randolph, February 25, 1783. Jefferson, *Autobiography*.

[56] Madison, Notes of Debates, February 21, 26, 27, 28, March 3, 4,

1783. *JCC*, March 4, 6, 1783. To keep the abatement plan within the general project, Madison on March 4 helped to defeat Hamilton's motion for its separate adoption.

[57] Madison to Randolph, February 25, 1783. Madison to Jefferson, April 22, 1783.

[58] Jefferson to Madison, May 7, 1783. PCC, No. 26, 438-440. Madison, Notes of Debates, February 26, March 7, 1783.

[59] Robert Morris to the President of Congress, January 24, 1783, Wharton, VI, 228. Madison, Notes of Debates, January 24, 1783.

[60] *Ibid*, March 4, 5, 1783. *JCC*, March 5, 1783. Robert Morris to the President of Congress, February 26, 1783, Wharton, VI, 266.

[61] Madison, Notes of Debates, March 17, 1783. Washington to the President of Congress, March 12, 1783. John Armstrong, Jr., to General Gates, April 29, May 9, 30, 1783, Burnett, VII, 155*n*, 160*n*, 175*n*.

[62] Madison, Notes of Debates, March 17, 1783. Washington to Joseph Jones, Washington to Hamilton, March 12, 1783. In that loving masterpiece of historical distortion, *The Conqueror*, page 235, Gertrude Atherton squarely reverses the attitudes of Madison and Hamilton on the use of army unrest in 1783 to aid the public creditors. She presents an imaginary conversation in which Madison asks whether it would not "be patriotic to push things from bad to worse as quickly as possible," and Hamilton replies that "it might lead to anarchy and the jaws of Europe." In reality, Hamilton urged Washington (February 7, March 17, 1783) to utilize the army spirit of revolt to frighten the states into granting general revenues, while Madison wrote to Edmund Randolph on February 25: "The discontents and designs of the army are every day taking a more solemn form. . . . Unless some amicable and adequate arrangements be speedily taken for . . . discharging the public engagements, a dissolution of the Union will be inevitable . . . and this country be made subject to the wars and politics of Europe."

[63] Luzerne to Vergennes, March 5, 1783.

[64] Madison, Notes of Debates, March 17, 1783. *JCC*, March 17, 18, 22, 1783. Burnett, (*The Continental Congress*, 568) surmises that Madison "if not the principal, was at least *particeps criminis* in . . . this bit of grim humor." Madison, too, would have been most likely to choose the harmless Mercer for the joke, rather than trouble-making Arthur Lee, who deserved the place far more. The subject was transferred on March 22 to a new committee.

CHAPTER XVI

[1] Madison to Randolph, March 4, 1783.

[2] Stephen Higginson to Theodorick Bland, October 6, 1783. That Higginson aimed the epithet "aristocratic junto" at Madison is evident from

his letters to Gorham and Bland, August 5, 1783 and January 1, 1784, Burnett, VII, 251, 387n.

[3] Stephen Higginson to Theophilus Parsons, Sr., April (7?), 1783.

[4] Madison to Randolph, September 10, 1782. *JCC*, April 23, June 4, September 13, 1783.

[5] *JCC*, January 30 (on 1782 receipts), March 11, 18, 20, 21, 1783. Madison, Notes of Debates, March 18, 20, 21, 1783. Luzerne to Vergennes, February 13, 1783.

[6] Madison, Notes of Debates, March 26, 1783. Luzerne to Vergennes, October 6, 1782. Vergennes to Luzerne, December 21, 1782.

[7] Madison to Randolph, March 25, 1783. Madison, Notes of Debates, March 22, 1783.

[8] *Ibid*, March 27, April 17, 1783.

[9] *Ibid*, March 27, 28, April 1, 1783. *JCC*, March 28, April 1, 1783.

[10] *JCC*, April 18, 1783. Madison, Notes of Debates, April 18, 1783. Madison to Jefferson, April 22, 1783. Theodorick Bland to Washington, April 16, 1783. Hamilton to Governor Clinton, May 14, 1783.

[11] Madison, Notes of Debates, April 21, 1783. Madison to Jefferson, April 22, 1783.

[12] Madison to Randolph, February 25, April 1, 1783. Randolph to Madison, March 7, 22, 29, 1783, Madison MSS., III, 94, 102, 106.

[13] *JCC*, April 22, 23, 28, 1783. Arthur Lee to Samuel Adams, March 5, 1783. Robert Morris to the President of Congress, March 8, 17, May 1, 3, 1783.

[14] *JCC*, April 26, 29 (appendices to Madison letter), 1783.

[15] *JCC* bibliographical notes for 1783.

[16] Luzerne to Vergennes, May 16, 1783.

[17] Washington to the governors of the states, June 8, 1783.

[18] Madison to Randolph, May (20), June 10, 1783. Madison to James Madison, Sr., June 5, 1783, Madison, *Letters*, I, 65. Jefferson to Madison, May 7, 1783. Randolph to Madison, April 26, May 9, 1783, Madison, MSS., IV, 11, 18.

[19] Randolph to Madison, May 15, 24, 1783, Madison MSS., IV, 22, 27. Jefferson to Madison, June 1, 1783. Joseph Jones to Madison, May 25, 1783.

[20] Randolph to Madison, May 24, 1783 (*op. cit.*) Richard Henry Lee to General William Whipple, July 1, 1783, Ballagh, II, 284.

[21] Joseph Jones to Madison, June 14, 1783.

[22] Luzerne to Vergennes, July 15, 1783.

[23] Randolph to Madison, May 24, 1783 (*op. cit.*)

[24] Jaquelin Ambler to Madison, June 1, 1783, Madison MSS., IV, 33.

[25] Joseph Jones to Madison, May 31, June 8 (Madison MSS., IV, 39), June 14, 1783.

[26] Washington to the governors of the states, June 8, 1783. Joseph Jones to Madison, June 28, 1783. Madison to Randolph, July 8, 1783.

[27] Madison to Randolph, May 27, July 8, 1783.

[28] Luzerne to Vergennes, May 24, 1783. The Reverend James Madison to Madison, June 15, 1782, Madison MSS., II, 79. Madison to Randolph, September 3, 1782. Madison, Notes of Debates, February 13, 1783.

CHAPTER XVII

[1] Franklin's Journal from March 21 to July 1, 1782, Wharton, V, 535-538, 549-551, 582.

[2] *JCC*, September 10, 1782. Madison to Randolph, May 14, 29, August 9, 1782; September 10, 1782, Madison MSS., III, 4. Edmond Fitzmaurice, *Life of Shelburne*, III, 219.

[3] Madison to Randolph, September 11, 1782. Franklin to Livingston, June 25, 1782; Jay to Livingston, June 25, 28, 1782, Wharton, V, 510, 516, 527.

[4] *JCC*, September 24, 1782. Vergennes to Luzerne, April 9, May 2, June 28 (Nos. 35 and 36), 1782. Lafayette to Livingston, June 25-29, 1782, Wharton, V, 517. Madison to Randolph, September 30, 1782.

[5] *JCC*, September 23, 24, 1782. Committee Book 186, September 25, 30, 1782. *Parliamentary History of England*, XXIII, 189, 193. Vergennes' notes of conferences with Grenville, June 15, 21, 1782, Doniol, V, 117.

[6] *JCC*, October 3, 4, 1782. Luzerne to Vergennes, October 6, 1782. Madison to Randolph, October 8, 1782.

[7] Franklin's Journal, Wharton, V, 540-542, 548-549, 572, 581-584.

[8] Franklin to Oswald, June 27, 1782, Wharton, V, 584.

[9] Fox to George III, May 18, 1782, in Lord Russell's *Memorials and Correspondence of Charles James Fox*, I, 352. Fox to Grenville, May 21, June 10, 1782; Richard Brinsley Sheridan to Grenville, May 26, 1782, Wharton, V, 431, 484, 440. Arthur Lee to Francis Dana, July 6, 1782.

[10] *JCC*, October 17, November 12, 1782. Madison to Jefferson, April 3, 1781, Madison MSS., I, 111; January 15, 1782. Madison to Pendleton, December 25, 1781; January 8, 1782. Sarah N. Randolph, *The Domestic Life of Thomas Jefferson*, 59, 62-68. Madison to Randolph, September 30, 1782, Madison MSS., III, 14.

[11] Madison to Randolph, December 3, 1782; February 11, 1783. Randolph to Madison, February 1, 22, 1783, Madison MSS., III, 70, 90. Madison, Notes of Debates, November 28, 1782.

[12] *JCC*, December 3, 21, 1782. Madison, Notes of Debates, December 21, 1782. Madison to Randolph, December 30, 1782. Luzerne to Vergennes, January 2, 1783. Madison submitted a schedule of diplomatic salaries on May 28, 1782, cutting Franklin, Jay and Adams from $11,111 10-90ths to $3,000 per year plus $4,000 for household expenses of the minister, his private secretary and the secretary of the embassy. On November 21, he dissented from the report of a committee of three upholding the old level and secured a reference of the matter to a new, economy-minded committee.

[13] Madison to Randolph, December 17, 24, 1782. Franklin to Livingston, September 26, October 14, 1782; Secretary of State Townshend to Oswald (inclosed by Franklin), September 20, 1782, Wharton, V, 764, 747, 811. Oswald's two commissions, dated July 25 and September 21, are in Wharton, V, 613, 748.

[14] Jay to Livingston, September 18, 28, October 13, 1782; Jay to Robert Morris, October 13, 1782, Wharton, V, 740, 779, 809, 810.

[15] Marbois to Vergennes (translation), March 13, 1782, Wharton, V, 238. "Fly out" was a copyist's slip for "cry out."

[16] Madison, Notes of Debates, December 23, 24, 1782. Madison to Randolph, December 24, 1782.

[17] Jay to Livingston, December 30, 1782. See also Luzerne's statement in *JCC*, September 24, 1782, and Franklin's Journal, Wharton, V, 564.

[18] Madison, Notes of Debates, December 30, 1782; January 1, 3, 1783.

[19] Madison to Jefferson, May 13, 1783. Vergennes to Luzerne, August 12, 1782. The diplomatic historian Wharton (V, 241-242*n*) attached such importance to Marbois' disavowal, recorded by Madison, that he refused to accept an oral account, years later, of the diplomat's admission that the intercepted letter was genuine. Doniol informed Wharton that the original dispatch (if it existed) was not in the French Archives. It is there now. The French wording disproves the charge that Marbois' position was exaggerated through mistranslation. On the contrary it was toned down. His disparaging statement about the Samuel Adams party, *"les intrigants ne pourront nourrir les espérances des peuples"* became a mere "the hopes of the people could not be supported."

[20] Jay to Livingston, November 17, 1782, Wharton, VI, 11-49, especially 24-32.

[21] Fitzmaurice, *Shelburne*, III, 263-268. Rayneval instructions and report, Wharton, VI, 49-51.

[22] JCC, December 31, 1782. Madison, Notes of Debates, December 30, 1782.

[23] *Ibid*, January 16, 1783.

[24] *Ibid*, January 6, 1783. JCC, January 2, 1783.

[25] JCC, July 8, 17, 1782; January 23, 1783. Madison, Notes of Debates, January 29, 1783. Madison to Randolph, January 28, 1783. The ceremonial for reception of foreign ministers (*JCC*, October 25, 1783) says all replies "shall be in the language of the United States."

[26] Jefferson to Madison, January 31, February 7, 1783. Madison to Jefferson, February 11, 1783. Ralph Izard to Franklin, June 28, 1778, Wharton, II, 624. For previous identifications of "Mr. Z" see Burnett, VII, 40*n*; Madison, *Letters*, I, 63*n*.

[27] Madison to Jefferson, February 11, 1783. Jefferson to Madison, February 14, 1783, Madison MSS., III, 83. John Adams to Livingston, February 19, September 4, 1782; Adams to Dana, September 17, 1782; Franklin to Livingston, July 22, 1783, Wharton, V, 185, 692, 732; VI, 582. Jefferson's "give the same fair play" appears in his published letters as "give them some fair play," the error arising from Madison's decipherment of "the" as "them" and his failure to make a complete erasure of the extra letter.

[28] Madison to Jefferson, May 6, 1783. John Adams to Livingston, February 5, 1785, Wharton, VI, 242. Gilpin's directions are penciled on the manuscript of Madison's letter.

[29] Madison to James Madison, Sr., February 12, 1783. *Parliamentary History of England*, XXIII, 206.

[30] Madison, Notes of Debates, February 13, 1783. Madison to Randolph, February 13, 1783.

[31] Madison to Randolph, March 12-15, 1783. Adams, Franklin, Jay and Laurens to Livingston, December 14, 1782, Wharton, VI, 131. The provisional peace treaty is in *JCC*, April 15, 1783.

[32] Franklin to Livingston, December 5-14, 24, 1782; John Adams to Livingston, November 8, 11, 18, 1782, Wharton, VI, 110, 163; V, 864, 875; VI, 52.

[33] John Adams, Journal of Negotiations, November 10, 11, 1782, Wharton, V, 874, 880; Adams, *Works*, III, 306, 309. Besides Adams and Franklin, those present at the little dinner party, as chronicled by Adams, were the Abbés Chalut and Arnoux (nineteen of whose letters to Franklin are in the latter's papers); Chalut the farmer-general, a Franklin intimate; Franklin's banker M. Grand; their families; Franklin's secretary-grandson and the Maryland state agent Ridley; an unnamed French youth.

[34] Jay to Livingston, November 17, December 12, 1782, Wharton, VI, 11-49, 130.

[35] Madison to Randolph, March 12, 18, 1783. Madison, Notes of Debates, March 12-15, 1783.

[36] *Ibid.* Vergennes to Luzerne, December 19, 21, 1782.

[37] Arthur Lee to Randolph, March 11, 1783. Lee to James Warren, March 12, 1783. Lee dated these two letters December 11 and 12, 1782.

[38] Madison to Randolph, March 12, April 1, 1783. Randolph to Madison, March 24, 1783, Burnett, VII, 120*n*.

[39] John Adams, Journal of Negotiations, November 30, 1782, Wharton, VI, 91. Oswald to Franklin, September 5, 1782; Franklin to Lord Grantham, September 11, 1782, Wharton, V, 699, 717. Jay to Livingston, November 17, 1782, Wharton, VI, 11, 22, 48.

[40] John Adams, Journal of Negotiations, November 3, 1782; Adams to Livingston, October 31, 1782, Wharton, V, 845, 838. Bancroft, X, 583. Adams reached Paris on Saturday, October 26, conferred at once with Jay, met the British commissioners at Jay's house in the forenoon of October 29 and saw Franklin for the first time in the evening of that day. Franklin learned from the British, on October 30, of Adams' promise to them.

[41] Franklin to Oswald, November 26, 1782; John Adams, Journal of Negotiations, November 28, 30, 1782; Oswald to Secretary of State Townshend, November 30, 1782, Wharton, VI, 85, 90, 93.

[42] Vergennes to Luzerne, August 12, October 14, November 23, 1782.

[43] Franklin, Journal of Negotiations, May 29, 1782, Wharton, V, 564.

[44] Referring to the October 30 conference with Oswald and Strachey, John Adams wrote in his November 30 notes: "In considering one point and another, Dr. Franklin turned to Mr. Jay and said: 'I am of your opinion, and will go on with these gentlemen in the business without consulting this court.'" Wharton, VI, 91.

[45] Jay to Livingston, November 17, 1782. Vergennes to Luzerne, October 14, November 23, 1782.

[46] Franklin to Livingston, July 22, 1783, Wharton, VI, 570.

[47] Vergennes to Rayneval, December 4, 1782, Wharton, VI, 107. Fitz-maurice, *Shelburne*, II, 202n. Clarence W. Alvord, "Virginia and the West, an Interpretation," *Mississippi Valley Historical Review*, June, 1916.

[48] Luzerne to Vergennes, March 19, 1783.

[49] John Adams to Livingston, November 6, 1782, Wharton, V, 857. Madison, Notes of Debates, March 18, 19, 22, 1783.

[50] *Ibid*, March 26, 1783.

[51] Madison to James Maury for James Madison, Sr., March 24; Madison to Randolph, March 24, 25, 1783; other letters in Burnett, VII, 93-106.

[52] Madison, Notes of Debates, March 24, 1783.

[53] *Ibid*, March 31, 1783. Luzerne to Vergennes, April 12, 1783.

[54] *JCC*, April 11, 1783. Madison, Notes of Debates, April 10, 11, 1783. Randolph to Madison, April 26, 1783, Madison MSS., IV, 11. Madison to Randolph, May 6, 1783.

[55] *JCC*, September 25, 1783.

[56] *JCC*, April 15, 16, 1783. Madison, Notes of Debates, April 14, 15, 16, 1783.

[57] Madison's recording of Hamilton's change of position on release of prisoners brought the usual charge by the latter's son-biographer that Madison made a false record of the debate. Alexander Hamilton, he asserted (*History of the Republic*, II, 508-509, 532-535), believed at all times in the binding force of the treaty and consistently opposed release of prisoners except in proportion to the evacuation of British posts. To prove this, he quoted Hamilton's letter of April 15, 1783, to Washington, advocating the step-by-step policy, and his letter of June 1 to Governor Clinton describing as "plain subterfuge" the claim of "some men that the operation of this treaty is suspended till the definitive treaty." Actually, the first of these was written just at the time he changed his views. The second relates to an entirely different matter—the claim of British property confiscators that the *act of ratification* did not bring the provisional treaty into effect. Hamilton's change of position is recorded in the manuscript of his own motion (PCC, No. 25, II, 197) where he scratched out the word "necessary" and wrote in "preparatory"—the exact change Madison ascribed to him.

CHAPTER XVIII

[1] Jefferson to Madison, April 14, 1783, Madison MSS., IV, 5.

[2] Madison to Jefferson, April 22, 1783, Madison, MSS., IV, 9. Cipher uncovered by Hazeldean Brant.

[3] Jefferson to Madison, May 7, 1783, Madison MSS., IV, 17.

[4] Madison to Jefferson, September 20, 1783.

[5] Madison to Jefferson, May 6, 1783; Jefferson to Madison, June 1, 1783, Madison MSS., IV, 15, 31.

[6] Madison to Jefferson, May 20, 1783. Madison to Randolph, June 3, 1783. Jefferson to Madison, May 7, June 17, 1783. Randolph to Madison, May 24, 1783, Burnett, VII, 178n.

[7] Madison to Jefferson, July 17, August 11, 1783, Madison MSS., IV, 58,

67. At the request of the Library of Congress, the Federal Bureau of Investigation attempted in 1945 to bring out the underlying writing, in the letter of August 11, by photography, but was unsuccessful because the two inks were of the same original color.

[8] Jefferson to Madison, August 31, 1783.

[9] Hamilton, 26; Hawkins, 29; Madison, 32; these were the youngest members of Congress in 1783: at the other extreme, Dyer, 62; Clark, 57; Joseph Jones, 56; Carroll, 53; Floyd, 49; average age, 43.

[10] Gay, *Madison*, 43-46. Hunt, *Madison*, 68-70. John Hall and Samuel Clarkson, *Memoirs of Mathew and Geraldus Clarkson*, (1890). William was the son of Geraldus. Catherine died August 7, 1832. *D.A.R. Lineage, Book*, XLI, 75.

CHAPTER XIX

[1] PCC, Committee Book 186. *JCC*, January 24, 1783. Bland (undoubtedly at Madison's request) made the motion for appointment of the committee on purchase of books, and Bland and Williamson served with Madison on it. There is no likelihood that either of them contributed to the list Madison prepared for Congress.

[2] "Mr. Jefferson is here awaiting further instructions of Congress." Madison to Randolph, March 4, 1783.

[3] Madison book list for Congress, PCC, Misc. Portfolio 103.

[4] Madison, Notes of Debates, January 23, 1783. The list is endorsed January 24, so has been inserted in the *JCC* of that date.

[5] Madison to Randolph, February 18, 25, 1783, Madison MSS., III, 88, 91. Madison to Jefferson, September 20, 1783.

[6] Madison, Notes of Debates, April 3-6, 1783. PCC, Committee Book 186, April 4, 1783.

[7] *JCC*, April 21, September 20, October 15, 30, 1783; May 28, 1784. Brooke Hindle, "The March of the Paxton Boys," *William & Mary Quarterly*, October, 1946. "An account of a terrible massacre of the Moravian Indians has been put into my hands. I send you the papers that you may see how the fact is represented in Europe." Franklin to Livingston, August 12, 1782. That was nineteen years after the massacres of the Moravian Christian Indians at Conestoga and Lancaster, Pennsylvania, by the "Paxton Boys."

[8] Livingston to Lafayette, September 18, 1782, Wharton, V, 743.

[9] *JCC*, April 23, May 23, 26, 1783. Madison, Notes of Debates, April 23, May 20, 23, 26, 1783.

[10] Submitted on June 18, the army report was recommitted and is in *JCC*, October 23, 1783.

[11] Madison to Randolph, August 12, 1783.

[12] Madison to Randolph, June 17, 1783.

[13] *Ibid.* Luzerne to Vergennes, June 18-25, 1783.

[14] Madison, Notes of Debates, June 19, 20, 21, 1783. *Pennsylvania Packet*, June 24, *Pennsylvania Gazette*, June 25, 1783.

[15] Luzerne to Vergennes, June 22, 1783. Madison, Notes of Debates, June 21, 1783.

[16] *Ibid.* Elias Boudinot to Elisha Boudinot, June 23, 1783. *JCC,* June 21, 1783.

[17] John Armstrong to Horatio Gates, June 26, 1783, Burnett, VII, 199*n.* Madison to Randolph, June 30, 1783. Madison, Notes of Debates, June 21, 1783.

[18] Henry Carberry to Major William Nichols, June 29, 1783; John Sullivan to Colonel Moylan, June 30, 1783; also other papers; PCC, No. 38. Thomas Stone to Maryland Assembly, January 11, 1785; Pennsylvania delegates to President of Pennsylvania, June 30, 1786. *JCC,* September 13, 1783.

[19] Madison to Randolph, July 8, 1783. Madison to Jefferson, July 17, 1783, Madison MSS., IV, 58. *JCC,* July 29, 1783. Schoepf, *Travels in the Confederation,* I, 42.

[20] Hamilton to Madison, June 29 (unsent), July 8, 1783. Madison to Hamilton, October 16, 1783.

[21] Madison to Jefferson, July 17, 1783; John Francis Mercer to Madison, August 14 (15?), 1783; November 14, 1784, Madison MSS., IV, 58, 69, V, 29. Madison to Randolph, August 18, 1783. Joseph Jones to Madison, August 4, 1783. See *JCC,* August 1, 13, 14, 1783, and Burnett, VII, 264*n.* Mercer made a $400 salary assignment to Madison on November 12, 1784, as partial payment on this and other loans; Madison MSS., V, 29.

[22] Madison to Randolph, August 30, October 13, 1783. Madison to Joseph Jones, August 30, 1783. Madison to Jefferson, September 20, 1783.

[23] Jefferson to Madison, August 31, 1783. Madison to Jefferson, September 20, 30 (Madison MSS., IV, 86), 1783. To his father Madison wrote on September 8: "The favorable turn of my mother's state of health is a source of great satisfaction to me, and will render any delay in my setting out for Virginia the less irksome to me."

[24] Madison to Jefferson, September 20, 1783. Arthur Lee to James Warren, September 17, 1783. *JCC,* September 16, 1783.

[25] *JCC,* October 1, 1782; July 28, 1783.

[26] *JCC,* September 16, 17, 18, 25, 1783. Madison to Randolph, September 8, 1783.

[27] Madison to Jefferson, August 11, 1783; Madison to Randolph, August 18, 1783.

[28] PCC, No. 20, I, 151, 155. The first insert is in Madison's handwriting, the second in that of J. F. Mercer. If Mercer wrote the second, he picked both thought and wording out of Madison's "The North American No. 1," published a few days earlier in the *Pennsylvania Journal* (September 13, 1783). See *infra* in this chapter.

[29] *JCC,* September 19, 25, 1783.

[30] *JCC,* July 8, September 22, 1783.

[31] Madison to Randolph, July 28, 1783.

[32] Madison to Randolph, August 30, October 13, 1783.

[33] *JCC,* October 17, 18, 20, 21, 1783. Elias Boudinot to R. R. Living-

ston, October 23, 1783. Abiel Foster to the President of New Hampshire, October 23, 1783. Massachusetts delegates to the Massachusetts Assembly, October 23, 1783. Elias Boudinot to Robert Morris, October 23, 1783. Jefferson to Governor Harrison, November 11, 1783.

[34] *Ibid.*

[35] The "North American" No. 1 and No. 2 were republished for the first time in the *William & Mary Quarterly*, October, 1946.

[36] Madison wrote to Jefferson on September 30, 1783, that he was sending him "The North American No. 1," "leaving the author to your conjectures"—the conventional method of piercing anonymity for a friend.

[37] This refers to Sheffield's pamphlet, *Observations on the Commerce of the American States*, published in England in 1783, which Madison described to Randolph and Jefferson on August 20 and September 20, 1783.

[38] Jefferson reached Princeton on November 4, 1783, the day Congress adjourned to meet in Annapolis on November 26. He spent the interval with Madison in Philadelphia. *JCC*, November 4, 1783. Jefferson to Monroe, November 18, 1783. Madison to Jefferson, December 10, 1783.

CHAPTER XX

[1] Madison to Jefferson, December 10, 1783. Jefferson wrote on the eleventh: "I pitied your probable situation in the tempestuous season which immediately succeeded your departure."

[2] Orange County Deed Book 17, March 22, 1781. Madison to James Madison, Sr., May 20, 1782; Madison MSS., II, 65.

[3] Draft, partly in Madison's writing, of letter to Bart. Dandridge, February 28, 1785, Madison MSS., V, 65.

[4] Diary of Francis Taylor, February 14, 15, 25, March 1, 1788, Virginia State Library.

[5] Madison to Jefferson, December 11, 1783; February 11 (in Gilpin), March 16, 1784. David Jameson to Madison, May 21, 1780, Rives Papers.

[6] Madison to Jefferson, December 10, 1783; April 25, May 12, June 19, 1786. Jefferson to Madison, February 20, 1784. Madison's meteorological record is held by the American Philosophical Society, Philadelphia.

[7] Madison to Jefferson, December 10, 1783; March 16, May 15, 1784. Jefferson to Madison, January 1, February 20, July 1, 1784.

[8] Stephen Higginson to Henry Knox, February 8, 1787, *American Historical Ass'n Report*, 1896, I, 745.

[9] Madison to Jefferson, December 10, 1783. Joseph Jones to Madison, July 28, 1783.

[10] Madison to Jefferson, December 10, 1783. Jefferson to Madison, April 25, 1784.

[11] Madison to Randolph, March 10, 1784. Madison to Jefferson, March 16, 1784. Randolph's letter of January 27 to Madison has been lost, but must have been much the same as Randolph to Jefferson, January 30, 1784, Conway, *Randolph*, 51.

[12] Notably James Brown Scott, *The United States of America: A Study in International Organization.* See Brant, *Madison*, I, 392-393.

[13] Madison to James Madison, Sr., June 24, 1784. The words "as before," in a request for a chaise, indicate that he went to Richmond in the same fashion.

[14] Madison to James Madison, Sr., May 13, June 5, 1784. James Madison, Sr. to Madison, June 4, 1784, Madison MSS., V, 6.

[15] Randolph to Jefferson, May 15, 1784; Conway, *Randolph*, 55.

[16] Madison to Jefferson, April 25, May 15, 1784.

[17] Schoepf, *Travels in the Confederation*, II, 55, 64.

[18] *JVHD*, May 13, 14, 20, 1784.

[19] Randolph to Jefferson, May 15, 1784; Conway, *Randolph*, 55. Madison to Jefferson, July 3, August 20, 1784. *JVHD*, May 28, June 17, 1784.

[20] Hening, XI, 401, 402, 415. Rives, *Madison*, I, 303n. L. G. Tyler in Bruce, *History of Virginia*, II, 271.

[21] *JVHD*, May 19, 22, 28, June 1, 1784. *JCC*, April 30, 1784. Madison to Jefferson, September 20, 1783. Madison's sponsorship of most of these propositions is shown by his handwriting in Papers of the House of Delegates, 1784, Virginia State Library.

[22] Madison to Jefferson, July 3, August 20, 1784. Madison to James Madison, Sr., June 15, 1784; Madison, *Letters*, I, 81. A. Stuart to Wm. Wirt, August 25, 1816, *William & Mary Quarterly*, (2) VI, 340.

[23] *JVHD*, June 26, 1784. Madison to Randolph, August 12, 1783. Randolph to Jefferson, May 15, 1784, *op. cit.* Madison to Jefferson, July 3, 1784.

[24] *JVHD*, May 29, 1784. Madison to Jefferson, July 3, 1784.

[25] *Ibid. JVHD*, June 21, 1784. Madison, Notes of Speech, *Writings*, II, 54n. For Madison and Jefferson on revision of the Virginia Constitution, see Brant, *Madison*, I, 260-271.

[26] *JVHD*, June 7, 14, 22, 23, 1784. Madison, Proposition on British Debts, *Writings*, II, 55n (but see Madison MSS., V, 5, for correct wording as to installments).

[27] Washington to Madison, June 12, 1784. Jefferson sent a similar proposal to Madison, in Paine's behalf, on May 25, 1784.

[28] Madison to Washington, August 12, 1784. The footnote about Arthur Lee is in Madison MSS., V, 12, the draft of letter lost in transmission.

[29] *JVHD*, May 15, June 5, 8, 22, 1784.

[30] *Diaries of George Washington*, October 12, 14, 18, 1785. Jefferson to Madison, February 8, 1786.

[31] Rives, *Madison*, I, 572. Madison to Jefferson, May 12, 1786. Jefferson's authorship of the substitute Houdon inscription is indicated also by his proposal to depict the "primum," "iterum" and "ultimum" of Washington's military exploits as decorations for three sides of the statue. No Frenchman would have been likely to specify "capture of the Hessians."

[32] *JVHD*, June 28, 1784. Papers of the House of Delegates, 1784, Virginia State Library.

[33] *JVHD*, May 15, 1784 (Warwick petition). Madison to Jefferson, July 3, 1784.

[34] *Ibid.* John B. Smith to Madison, June 21, 1784, Madison MSS., V, 9 (part in Madison, *Writings*, II, 213n). *JVHD*, May 26, June 4, 8, 16, 21, 1784.

CHAPTER XXI

[1] Jefferson to Madison, December 11, 1784. Madison to Jefferson, March 16, August 20, 1784. Orange County Deed Book 17, 316.

[2] Madison to Jefferson, September 7, October 17, 1784. Madison to Samuel House, May 29, 1784, Gilmer Papers, University of Virginia. Eliza Trist to Jefferson, April 13, 1784, March 12, 1785, Coolidge-Jefferson Papers, Harvard University.

[3] Madison to James Madison, Sr., September 6, 1784. Madison to Jefferson, September 7, 1784.

[4] Madison to Jefferson, August 20, September 15 (Madison, *Letters*, I, 101), 1784; April 27, 1785. Washington to Henry Lee, June 18, 1786. Washington to Richard Henry Lee, July 19, 1787. Lafayette sailed for France on *La Nymphe*, December 21, 1784. His unpreserved letter, quoted by Madison, was dated December 15-17.

[5] Lafayette to Washington, March 19, April 16, 1785, *Letters of Lafayette to Washington*, 293, 295.

[6] Madison to Jefferson, September 15, 1784, Madison, *Letters*, I, 101. Diary of Griffith Evans, September 14, 1784, Huntington Library.

[7] *Lafayette in America Day by Day*, 225.

[8] Marbois' letter-journal of the trip to the Indian country is in his letters (*Our Revolutionary Forefathers*, 117-214). A copy of it, with some verbal changes, was sent as an official report to the French government and is in Book 28, Archives des Affaires Étrangères, Corr. Pol., E-U. The Chevalier de la Luzerne married Mlle. Angran d'Alleray, sister of his sister-in-law, the Countess de la Luzerne. (O'Donnell, *Luzerne*.) Marbois addressed his fiancée as Mlle. de Montry d'Alleray, and referred to her and the Countess de la Luzerne as the ladies of the household. Jefferson told of the Chevalier's deep grief after his wife's death in 1788.

[9] Utica, N. Y., *Herald*, June 14, 1825.

[10] Madison to Jefferson, October 11, 17, 1784. Lafayette to Washington, October 8, 1784, *Letters of Lafayette to Washington*, 286.

[11] Diary of Griffith Evans, October 3, 1784, *op. cit.*

[12] *Ibid.* Madison to Monroe, November 27, 1784. Marbois to Vergennes (with accompanying memoir on commerce), September 30, October 9, 1784. Also Marbois Journal, *Our Revolutionary Forefathers*.

[13] Madison to Jefferson, October 17, 1784.

[14] Augustus J. Foster, "Notes on the U. S. A.," Library of Congress.

[15] *JHVD*, October 30, November 1, 9, 14, 15, 16, 18, 19, December 1, 1784. Madison to Monroe, November (20), December 4, 1784. Madison

to Lafayette, March 20, 1785. Madison to Jefferson, August 20, 1785. *JHVD*, October 28, November 1, 1785. Franklin's Journal (on Lafayette's dual citizenship), May 9, 1782, Wharton, V, 553.

[16] Madison to Jefferson, October 17, 1784; August 12, 1786.

[17] Madison to Jefferson, January 22, 1785, Madison MSS., V, 60. Madison to Lafayette, March 20, 1785. Madison to Randolph, July 26, 1785. A misreading of this last letter caused Gaillard Hunt to conclude that Madison wished to become a lawyer in order to escape dependence on slaves. (Hunt, *Madison*, 70.)

[18] Jefferson to Madison, December 8, 1784. Madison to Jefferson, April 27, 1785. Madison to Lafayette, March 20, 1785.

[19] Caleb Wallace to Madison, July 12, 1785, Madison MSS., V, 98. Madison to Wallace, August 23, 1785.

[20] Monroe to Madison, July 12, 1785. Madison to Jefferson, August 20, October 23, 1785. Eliza Trist to Jefferson, March 12, May 4, 1785, Coolidge-Jefferson Papers. The tobacco contract with House is revealed by Madison's letter of September 8, 1786, to his brother Ambrose.

[21] *Diaries of Washington*, September 3, 5, October 2, 12, 13, 14, 18, 1785. Washington to Mary Washington, February 15, 1787. Washington to George Clinton, April 5, 20, 1785; November 5, 1786; June 9, July 11, 1787. Washington to John Francis Mercer, September 9, 1786.

[22] Monroe to Madison, February 9, 16 (lost), 1786. Madison to Monroe, February 24, March 14, 1786, Madison MSS., VI, 39, 41, 45. Monroe to Jefferson, January 19, 1786.

[23] Henry Lee to Madison, February 16, 1786. William Grayson to Madison, March 22, 1786, Madison MSS., VI, 50.

[24] Madison to Monroe, March 19, April 9, May 13, July 11 (Madison MSS., VI, 65), 1786. Arthur Breeze to Madison, April 11, 1794; contract of sale, Madison MSS., XVII, 50; XIX, 1.

[25] Madison to Jefferson, March 18, May 12, June 19, 1786. Madison to Monroe, June 4, July 11 (*op. cit.*), 1786. Madison to Ambrose Madison, September 8, 1786.

[26] Madison to Jefferson, August 12, 1786. Jefferson to Madison, December 16, 1786. Madison to Monroe, October 5, 1786. After Monroe became minister to France, he proposed the raising of a loan in Europe to be invested by Madison—Monroe to Madison, November 30, 1794.

[27] Hunt, *Madison*, 137. Henry Lee to Madison, October 19, 1786.

[28] Madison to Monroe, December 21, 1786. Bond of Joseph Thompson to Samuel House, Madison MSS., VI, 13.

[29] Madison to James Madison, Sr., December 17, 1786. Madison to Monroe, December 21, 1786; April 17, May 14 (settlement of account), June 1, 1790, Madison MSS., XIII, 10, 58, 84. Monroe to Madison, March 5, June 7, 1790. Contract of sale by James Madison to Theodorus Bailey and John B. Van Wyck, January 5, 1796, Madison MSS., XIX, 1.

[30] Madison to Arthur Breeze, May 13, 1796; Arthur Breeze to Madison, December 17, 1796, Madison MSS., VI, 56 (misplaced among 1786 letters); XIX, 108.

[31] Arthur Breeze to Madison, January 28, April 11, 16, 1794, Madison MSS., XVII, 8, 50, 53.

CHAPTER XXII

[1] *JVHD,* October 30, November 2, 4, 1784.

[2] *JVHD,* November 11, 12, 1784. R. H. Lee to Madison, November 26, 1784.

[3] Madison, "Essay on Monopolies," *Harper's Magazine,* March, 1914, and *William & Mary Quarterly,* October, 1946. Notes of Speech, Madison MSS., V, 12*a,* published in Madison, *Writings,* II, 88. The article on monopolies, submitted to Harper's shortly after Madison's death, was mislaid and came to light seventy-five years later.

[4] Rives, *Madison,* I, 605.

[5] *JVHD,* November 11, 17, December 11, 1784.

[6] *JVHD,* November 17, 1784. Madison to Monroe, November 14, 1784. Jefferson to Madison, December 8, 1784. Madison to Jefferson, January 9, 1785.

[7] *JVHD,* November 19, 20, 22, December 2, 1784. Madison to Monroe, November 27, December 4, 1784.

[8] *JVHD,* December 1, 1784.

[9] Madison to Jefferson, January 9, 1785. Andrews, *Virginia, the Old Dominion,* 357. The text of the assessment bill is in Papers of George Washington, V, 231, Library of Congress.

[10] Jefferson, Notes on Virginia, *Writings* (Ford in ten volumes), III, 252-253.

[11] *JVHD,* December 11, 18, 22, 23, 24, 1784. Madison to James Madison, Sr., January 6, 1785, Madison MSS., V, 56. Madison to Jefferson, January 9, 1785. The assessment bill lost five delegates (enough to decide the issue) who voted for the measure on November 11. The year's postponement reflected the abolition, after 1784, of the spring legislative session.

[12] Madison to Monroe, April 12, 1785. Madison to Jefferson, April 27, 1785. George Nicholas to Madison, April 22, 1785, Madison MSS., V, 79. The Nicholas letter is published, with the sentence about a revolution omitted, in Madison, *Writings,* II, 183*n.*

[13] Madison to Jefferson, January 9, April 27, 1785. Madison to Monroe, April 28, May 29, June 21, 1785.

[14] A petition for repeal of the Episcopal incorporation act, in Madison's handwriting, is among his papers. It is marked "copy," and is bizarrely addressed "To the Honorable the Speaker & Gentlemen the General Assembly of Virginia" (as if there were only one speaker). The protest contains arguments which would come naturally from Madison, though couched in more violent language than he was accustomed to use. It sounds on the whole as if he wrote it with the intention of disguising its origin. It does not appear among the numerous petitions on the subject recorded in the *JVHD* or preserved in the petition records of the assembly. This paper is in Madison MSS., V, 52, and *Writings,* II, 213.

[15] Randolph to Madison, July 17, 1785, Madison MSS., V, 100. Gaillard Hunt, "Madison and Religious Liberty," *American Historical Ass'n Report,* 1901, I, 170.

[16] John B. Smith to Madison, May 1785; Madison to Smith, May 27, 1785, Madison MSS., V, 87, 82.

[17] George Nicholas to Madison, July 7, 24, 1785, Madison MSS., V, 97, 102. For the influence of Dr. Witherspoon's disciples in the Shenandoah Valley, in this contest, see F. H. Hart, *The Valley of Virginia in the American Revolution,* 141.

[18] Madison, Essay on Monopolies, *op. cit.* Madison to Jefferson, January 22, 1786.

[19] Madison, *Writings,* II, 183-191.

[20] "The people of the U. S. owe their independence and their liberty to the wisdom of descrying in the minute tax of 3 pence on tea, the magnitude of the evil comprised in the precedent." Madison, "Essay on Monopolies," *op. cit.*

[21] Madison to Randolph, July 23, 1782.

[22] Madison to Monroe, June 21, 1785.

[23] *JCC,* April 23, 1785. Madison to Monroe, May 29, 1785.

[24] Hening, XII, 84. *JVHD,* October 26, 27, 29, November 2, 3, 17, 26, December 17, 29, 1785; January 9, 13, 16, 1786. Madison to Jefferson, January 22, 1786.

[25] Madison, "Essay on Monopolies," *op. cit.*

CHAPTER XXIII

[1] Joseph Jones to Madison, May 30, 1786.

[2] *JVHD,* November 27, December 2, 10, 1784. Madison to Jefferson, January 9, 1785. Madison to Monroe, December 4, 1784.

[3] *JVHD,* November 22, 26, December 13, 1785; January 2, 3, 5, 1786. Joseph Jones to Jefferson, February 21, 1786. Madison to Monroe, December 24, 30, 1785. Madison to Washington, December 24, 1786. Madison to Pendleton, January 9, 1787. Madison to Jefferson, August 20, 1785.

[4] *JVHD,* October 31, December 14, 15, 1785. Madison to Washington, November 11, December 9, 1785. Madison to Jefferson, January 22, 1786.

[5] Madison to Jefferson, December 4, 1786; February 11 (15 in *Writings*), 1787.

[6] Madison to Washington, November 1, 1786. Madison to Pendleton, January 9, 1787. Madison to Jefferson, February 11, December 9, 1787.

[7] *JVHD,* November 30, December 1, 1784; January 5, 1785. Madison to Jefferson, January 9, 1785.

[8] *Ibid.* Patrick Henry to R. H. Lee, January 9, 1785. *JVHD,* December 22, 1784; January 6, 7, 1785. Hening, XI, 446. Madison tells of a three-day wait for the absent legislators; the Journals record but two.

[9] Madison draft of bill, Legislative Papers, Virginia State Library. *JVHD,* December 14, 20, 28, 1785. Madison to James Madison, Sr., December 24, 1785. Madison to Monroe, December 30, 1785.

[10] Madison to Washington, February 21, 1787. Madison to Randolph, April 15, 1787. Madison to Pendleton, April 22, 1787.

[11] *JVHD*, November 3, 12, 20, 22, 23, 26, 27, 1784. Madison to Jefferson, January 9, 1785. Madison to Monroe, November 27, December 24, 1784.

[12] *JVHD*, December 2, 15, 16, 1785. Hening, XII, 47. Madison to Jefferson, January 22, 1786.

[13] *JVHD*, December 14, 23, 1785; January 17, 1786. Madison to Washington, November 11, 1785. Madison to Ambrose Madison, December 15, 1785. The manumission statute is in Hening, XI, 39; a portion in Madison, *Writings*, II, 203n.

[14] Hening, XI, 362. *JVHD*, May 21, 27, 1784.

[15] *JVHD*, December 13, 18, 28, 29, 1784; November 11, 21, 22, 23, 25, December 1, 2, 1785. Madison to Jefferson, January 9, 1785; January 22, 1786.

[16] Madison, "Notes of Speech Against Paper Money," *Writings*, II, 279. Madison to Jefferson, May 12, 1786. Madison to Monroe, June 4, 1786.

[17] *JVHD*, November 1, 1786. Madison to James Madison, Sr., November 1, 1786. Madison to Pendleton, April 22, 1787. Madison to Jefferson, June 6, 1787, Madison, *Letters*, I, 332.

[18] Madison to James Madison, Sr., December 24, 1785; November 16, 24, 1786. Madison to Monroe, May 29, 1785. Washington to Madison, December 16, 1786. Madison to Washington, December 24, 1786.

[19] Madison to Jefferson, August 12, 1786.

[20] Washington to Timothy Pickering, August 6, 1783. Washington to Chastellux, October 12, 1783. Washington and Madison were both in Princeton on October 12, but had no later contact before Madison entered the legislature. Madison to Randolph, October 13, 1783.

[21] Jefferson to Madison, February 20, 1784. Madison to Jefferson, April 25, July 3, 1784. Jefferson to Washington, March 15, 1784. Washington to Jefferson, March 29, 1784. Advertisement, dated March 10, 1784, Washington, *Writings* (Fitzgerald), XXVII, 353.

[22] Washington to James Craik, Washington to Gilbert Simpson, July 10, 1784. Washington to Governor Harrison, October 10, 1784. Washington to Robert Morris, February 1, 1785.

[23] *Ibid*. Washington to George William Fairfax, November 10, 1785. Washington to Randolph, September 16, 1785. Washington to Richard Butler, January 10, 1788. Madison to Jefferson, August 12, 1786. For batteaux, see Maryland Subscription Paper, *American Historical Review*, XXVIII, 507.

[24] Washington to Madison, November 28, 1784.

[25] *JVHD*, December 4, 7, 9, 10, 13, 1784. Madison to Jefferson, January 9, 1785. Washington to the Secretary at War, January 5, 1785. Madison to Washington, January 1, 1785.

[26] Madison to Jefferson, April 25, 1784.

[27] Washington to Madison, December 28, 1784. Washington to Randolph, September 16, 1785. For Washington's papers relative to the Po-

tomac see Corra Bacon-Foster, *Patomac Route to the West* and "Washington and the Potomac: Manuscripts of the Minnesota Historical Society," *American Historical Review*, XXVIII, 497-519, 705-722.

[28] Hening, XI, 450, 510. *JVHD*, December 15, 18, 21, 24, 31, 1784; January 1, 3, 4, 5, 1785. Madison to Jefferson, January 9, 1785; June 19, 1786. For road bill see Madison, *Writings*, II, 101n.

[29] *Ibid*. *JVHD*, December 13, 14, 21, 22, 28, 29, 30, 1784; January 1, 1785. Madison to Washington, January 1, 1785; Madison, *Letters*, I, 120. Washington to Patrick Henry, November 30, 1785.

[30] *JVHD*, January 4, 5, 1785. Madison to Jefferson, January 9, 1785. *JCC*, May 12, 1786.

[31] Washington to George William Fairfax, February 27, 1785. Washington to William Grayson, April 25, 1785. Madison to Jefferson, April 27, 1785.

[32] Madison to Jefferson, October 3, 1785. Washington to Madison, October 29, 1785.

[33] *JVHD*, November 11, 15, 16, 18, 1785. Madison to Washington, November 11, 1785. Madison to Jefferson, January 22, 1786. Washington to Jefferson, September 26, 1785. Rives, *Madison*, I, 628n.

[34] Madison to Jefferson, January 9, 1785. Washington certificate, *Writings* (Fitzgerald), XXVII, 468. Washington to Governor Harrison, October 10, 1784. *Diaries of Washington*, September 6, 1784. Hening XI, 502.

[35] Madison to Jefferson, October 3, 1785; January 22, 1786. James T. Flexner, *Steamboats Come True* (description of pole boat), 68, 98, 384. Bacon-Foster, *Patomac Route to the West*, 63, 72, 76-80, 89-90.

[36] *JVHD*, November 15, 18, 1785. *JCC*, May 11, 1785; February 5, March 5, 1788. Hening, XII, 616. For evidence that Washington knew of Rumsey's steamboat activities as early as November 1784, when the two men (and Madison) were together in Richmond, see Rumsey to Washington, March 10, 1785, in *Maryland Historical Magazine*, XXXII, 18, and Washington to Rumsey, Jan. 31, 1786.

[37] *JCC*, March 26, May 2, 1783. *JVHD*, November 15, 18, 21, 1785. Noah Webster to Madison, July 5, 1784, Madison MSS., V, 14. Madison, "Essay on Monopolies," *op. cit.*

[38] Madison to Jefferson, January 9, 1785; January 22, 1786. Madison to Monroe, May 29, 1785.

[39] Caleb Wallace to Madison, July 12, 1785, Madison MSS., V, 98. Madison to Wallace, August 23, 1785. Madison to John Brown, October 12, 1788. See Brant, *Madison*, I, 265-271 for Madison's views on a Kentucky constitution.

[40] *JVHD*, October 28, November 14, 22, 1785. Hening, XII, 37 (article three being Madison's amendment), 240. Madison to Richard Henry Lee, July 7, 1785. Madison to Monroe, Madison to Washington, December 9, 1785.

[41] Madison to Jefferson, August 12, 1786.

[42] Henry Lee to Madison, October 29, November 19, 1788, Madison MSS., X, 35, 50.

[43] Madison to Washington, November 5, December 2, 1788. Washington to Madison, November 17, 1788.

[44] Madison to Henry Lee, November 30, 1788; April 13, 1790, Madison MSS., X, 57, XIII, 7. Henry Lee to Madison, December 8, 17, 1788; January 14, 1789, April 22, 1790, December 8, 1791, Madison MSS., X, 63, 69, 84, XIII, 12, XIV, 83. Madison, "Remarks on Great Falls," *Writings*, V, 321.

CHAPTER XXIV

[1] Madison to Jefferson, April 27, 1785. Randolph to Madison, July 17, 1785, Madison MSS., V, 100. Joseph Jones to Madison, June 12, 1785.

[2] Madison to Randolph, July 26, 1785. George Mason to Madison, August 9, 1785, Madison MSS., V, 106.

[3] Hening, XII, 50. *JVHD*, December 5, 13, 22, 26, 27, 29, 30, 1785.

[4] *JVHD*, November 7, 1785. George Mason and Alexander Henderson to the Speaker, March 28, 1785, Madison MSS., V, 71. Edward Coles to W. C. Rives, June 19, 1857, *William & Mary Quarterly*, 2d series, VII, 171.

[5] *JVHD*, December 13, 21, 1784. Madison to Jefferson, January 9, 1785. Rufus King to Elbridge Gerry, May 1, 1785. William Grayson to Madison, May 1, 1785. Boston *Gazette*, April 18, May 9, 1785.

[6] Madison to Monroe, June 21, August 7, 1785.

[7] *Ibid*. Richard Henry Lee to Madison, August 11, 1785.

[8] Madison to Monroe, August 7, 1785. Madison to Jefferson, October 3, 1785.

[9] *JVHD*, October 31, November 1, 4, 5, 1785. Madison to Washington, November 11, 1785. Madison to Jefferson, January 22, 1786.

[10] Madison, *Writings*, II, 194.

[11] Jefferson to Monroe, June 15, 1785.

[12] *JVHD*, November 7, 14, 1785. Rives, *Madison*, II, 53-54. Draft of resolution, Madison MSS., VI, 85c. A note by Payne Todd, "Date uncertain—supposed about the time of convention at Annapolis," caused this paper to be marked "September 1786" when it should be November 14, 1785.

[13] Madison to Washington, November 11, December 9, 1785. Madison to Jefferson, January 22, 1786.

[14] *JVHD*, November 30, December 1, 1785. By an error in drafting, the thirteen-year limitation was made to apply to regulatory acts of Congress, instead of the basic power to regulate. This was corrected next day (December 1), but failure to notice the correction has caused historians to treat the miswritten clause as the one which caused the bill to be abandoned.

[15] *JVHD*, January 21, 1786. Madison to Jefferson, Madison to Monroe, January 22, 1786.

[16] Madison to Monroe, January 22, March 19, 1786.

[17] George Tucker, *History of the United States*, I, 343n. L. G. Tyler, *Letters and Times of the Tylers*, I, 130-134, III, 179-180. Madison to Noah Webster, October 12, 1804. Madison, "Origin of the Constitutional Convention," *Writings*, II, 397.

[18] Madison to Jefferson, March 18, 1786.

[19] Monroe to Madison, March 18, 1786. Madison to Monroe, April 9, June 4, July 11, (Madison MSS., VI, 65), 1786. Madison to Jefferson, August 12, 1786.

[20] Rufus King to Jonathan Jackson, September 3, 1786.

[21] Madison to Ambrose Madison, August 7, 1786. Madison to Jefferson, August 12, 1786. Madison to Monroe, March 19, 1786.

[22] Madison to Jefferson, May 12, August 12, 1786. See Burnett, VIII, 389n, for state actions.

[23] Madison to Ambrose Madison, September 8, 1786. Stephen Higginson to John Adams, July 1786, *American Historical Ass'n Report* 1896, I, 734. Madison to Monroe, September 11, 1786. "Colonel Madison's bill 1786," receipted by George Mann, covers the period from September 4 to September 15, but with the first day's expenses placed with those of September 13. In a total bill of £14.7.2, Madison's meals and lodgings cost £4.12.8, his servant's £3.15, liquors 19/6, feed and stabling of horses £5.10. Madison, *Writings*, II, 271n.

[24] Madison, Debates of Federal Convention, June 6, 1787.

[25] *JVHD*, January 13, 1786. Tench Coxe to the Virginia Commissioners, September 13, 1786, *Calendar of Virginia State Papers*, IV, 168.

[26] Draft by Randolph, Madison MSS., VI, 85b. Madison to Monroe, May 13, 1786. Madison to Noah Webster, October 12, 1804.

[27] John T. Morse, *Hamilton*, I, 167. Randolph to Madison, February 12, 1785, Madison MSS., V, 63. Richard Price, *Observations on the Importance of the American Revolution* (chapter "Of Peace").

[28] *JCC*, September 20, 1786. Eliot, *Debates*, I, 116-118.

CHAPTER XXV

[1] Madison to James Madison, Sr., November 1 (Madison MSS., VI, 92), December 17, 1786. Robert Hunter, MS., Journal of Travels in North America, 1785-86 (February 28, 1786), Huntington Library. Schoepf, *Travels in the Confederation*, II, 65. To anchor the capital at Richmond, Madison in the spring of 1784 helped to frame a bill to sell surplus state lands in that city to obtain funds for public buildings. State lands at Williamsburg were given to William and Mary College, which in the following February (though by no means for that reason) handed Madison an LL.D.—Madison to Jefferson, July 3, 1784. *William & Mary Quarterly* (1) XXII, 297. Legislative papers show amendments in Madison's writing.

[2] *JCC*, August 25, 1785, February 2, May 31, August 1, 3, 1786. Mon-

roe to Madison, May 31, 1786. Rufus King to Elbridge Gerry, August 13, 1786.

[3] Madison to Monroe, June 21, August 12 (Burnett, VIII, 419n), August 15 (Madison MSS., VI, 71), 1786.

[4] Madison to Jefferson, August 12, 1786.

[5] JCC, August 29, 1786. Minutes of proceedings and Virginia motions, Burnett, VIII, 427, 431, 438, 440. Monroe to Madison, August 14, 30, September 1, 1786. Madison to Jefferson, March 16, 1784.

[6] Madison to Jefferson, August 12, 1786. Madison to Monroe, September 11, October 5, 1786.

[7] Charles Thomson, Minutes, August 16, 1786, Burnett, VIII, 427.

[8] Madison to Monroe, October 30, 1786. Madison to James Madison, Sr.; Madison to Washington, November 1, 1786.

[9] Henry Lee to Madison, October 19, 1786. Washington to Madison, November 5, 1786. Madison to James Madison, Sr., November 1, 1786.

[10] Madison to Washington, November 8, 1786. Jefferson to Madison, October 28, 1785.

[11] Madison to Jefferson, June 19, 1786.

[12] Jonathan Smith, "Features of Shays' Rebellion," *Clinton (Mass.) Historical Society Papers*, I, 9-20. Diary of Nathaniel Ames, January 21, 1787, published in Charles Warren, *Jacobin and Junto*.

[13] Madison to Washington, November 8, 1786.

[14] *JVHD*, November 9, 1786.

[15] Washington to Madison, November 18, 1786.

[16] Madison to Washington, December 7, 24, 1786. Washington to Madison, December 16, 1787. Madison did not share the widespread fear of the Cincinnati. Presumably at Washington's request, he introduced a resolution in the fall of 1784 for incorporation of the society in Virginia. No action was taken.

[17] Madison to Washington, February 21, 1787. Washington to Madison, March 31, 1787. Washington to D. Humphries, December 26, 1786.

[18] JCC, January 31, 1785. Monroe to Madison, December 18, 1784. Madison to Jefferson, August 20, 1785. R. H. Lee to Madison, December 27, 1784. In a semireturn to congressional affairs, Madison accepted an appointment in the fall of 1786 as judge in a South Carolina-Georgia boundary dispute, but the two states settled the affair. In 1782, Madison declined a request to act for Virginia in a joint commission to settle the boundary with Pennsylvania, saying that the place should go to someone able to make astronomical observations. It went to Madison of the College. JCC, September 13, 14, 1786, February 3, 1787. Charles Pinckney to the Secretary of Congress, May 30, 1787. David Jameson to Madison, February 23, 1782, Rives Papers.

[19] Madison, "Autobiography."

[20] Henry Lee to Washington, July 3, 1786. Monroe to Madison, October 2, 1786.

[21] Richard Henry Lee did not attend Congress for a single day in 1786, and might have been expected to withdraw, but did not. He also was

willing to abandon the Mississippi. R. H. Lee to Washington, July 15, 1787.

[22] Madison to Henry Lee, November 9, 23, 1786. Madison's first letter about hostility to Lee is missing.

[23] *JVHD*, December 1, 1786. Henry Lee to Madison, December 20, 1786, Madison, *Writings*, II, 284n. Madison to Washington, November 8, 1786.

[24] Madison to James Madison, Sr., December 12 (*Letters*, I, 266), 17, 1786. Madison to Washington, December 24, 1786. Madison to Pendleton, January 9, 1787. Hening, XII, 283.

[25] *JVHD*, November 29, 1786. Madison to Jefferson, December 4, 1786. Madison to Washington, December 7, 1786.

[26] Madison to Eliza Trist, February 10, 1787, Emmet Papers, N. Y. Public Library. Madison to Monroe, February 11, 1787, Madison MSS., VII, 30.

[27] Madison to Eliza Trist, *op. cit.* Madison to Jefferson, February 11 (misdated 15), 1787. Rufus King to Elbridge Gerry, February 11, 1787.

[28] *JCC*, October 20, 1786, February 14, 16, 19, 1787. Madison, Notes of Debates, February 19, 1787 (in *JCC* Appendix). Madison to Washington, February 21, 1787.

[29] *JCC*, February 21, 1787. Madison, Notes of Debates, February 21, 1787.

[30] *Ibid.* Madison to Pendleton, February 24, 1787.

[31] *Ibid.* Madison to Randolph, April 2, 1787. James Manning to Hezekiah Smith, January 18, 1787. James M. Varnum to Washington, June 18, 1787, *Documentary History of the Constitution*, I, 277.

[32] Madison to Jefferson, March 19, 1787. Madison to Pendleton, April 22, 1787.

[33] Madison to Randolph, March 11, 1787. Jefferson to Madison, March 19, 1787. Madison, Notes of Debates, March 13, 1787.

[34] *Ibid.* Jefferson to Madison, January 30, 1787.

[35] Madison to Jefferson, March 19, 1787. Madison to Washington, March 18, 1787. Randolph to Madison, March 1, 1787, Madison MSS., VII, 43.

[36] *Ibid. JCC*, April 13, 1787. Madison to Randolph, March 25, April 2, 1787. Madison, Notes of Debates, March 29, 1787.

[37] *JCC*, April 13, 1787.

[38] *JCC*, April 13, 20, 1787. Madison, Notes of Debates, April 18, 19, 23, 1787.

[39] *Ibid*, April 25, 26, 1787. *JCC*, August 29, 30, 31, 1786, May 10, 11, 1787. Madison to Jefferson, April 23, 1787.

[40] Madison to Pendleton, April 22, 1787. Madison to Randolph, April 15, 1787. *JCC*, April 13, 1787.

CHAPTER XXVI

[1] Madison to Jefferson, February 25, 1784, April 27, 1785, March 18, May 12, June 19, 1786, August 10, 1788. Jefferson to Madison, Febru-

ary 8, December 16, 1786, January 30, June 20, August 2, October 8, 1787. Jefferson to George Wythe, August 13, 1786.

[2] Madison to Jefferson, November 15, 1785, January 22, May 12, 1786, June 6, December 9, 1787, September 21, 1788. Jefferson to Madison, May 25, 1784, May 11, 1785, February 8, 1786, August 2, 1787. Madison to Washington, March 18, 1787.

[3] Jefferson to Madison, November 11, 1784, March 18, 1785, February 8, 1786. Madison to Jefferson, April 27, 1785, March 18, April 27, May 12, 1786. Jefferson continued to send books to Madison, and entrusted him with deliveries to Franklin, Washington, Congress and the colleges in Philadelphia and Williamsburg. See Madison to Jefferson, October 24, 1787, and as to the Carr boys, April 27, 1785, January 22, May 12, 1786, February 15, 1787.

[4] Madison, "Of Ancient and Modern Confederacies," *Writings*, II, 369-390. This must have been written between February and July, 1786, the only period, after receipt of the book shipment from Paris and before the constitutional convention, when he had the necessary access to his library.

[5] Madison, *Writings*, II, 361-369.

[6] Aristotle, *Ethics and Politics*. Montesquieu, *Spirit of Laws*. Locke, *Second Treatise on Government*. Hume, *Essays:* "Parties in General," "Of the Independency of Parliament," "First Principles of Government," "Perfect Commonwealth." Douglass Adair, "Intellectual Origins of Jeffersonian Democracy," MS., Yale Library.

[7] Madison to Randolph, April 8, 1787. Madison to Washington, April 16, 1787.

INDEX

INDEX

Jefferson, Thomas—*cont.*
354; law, 356, 357, 358; river navigation, 364, 366, 368; Annapolis Convention, 375; on commercial treaties, 379; conditions in France, 392; appraises Bingham, 404; letters from Madison, 19, 20, 29, 35, 36, 109, 128, 308, 310, 311, 315, 318, 323, 328, 341, 372, 378, 383, 389; mentioned, 58, 158, 247, 248, 325

Jenifer, Daniel of St. Thomas, 72, 73, 74, 75, 76, 77, 78, 80, 90, 92, 99, 100, 116, 138, 140, 144

Joe, servant of Madison, 388

Johnson, Thomas, 90, 92, 99, 100, 366, 373

Johnston, Zachariah, 343

Jones, John Paul, 25, 65. 67-69, 104, 160

Jones, Joseph, in Virginia delegation, 15; in Trist-House home, 17; in debt, 27; described, 33; need for strong powers, 35, 36; slavery, 47, 48-49; French aid, 50, 53, 54, 55; Western lands question, 71, 72, 73, 78, 79, 83, 92-96, 98; need for strong government, 105; distrust of Arthur Lee, 122; the impost, 213, 214, 220, 228, 235; criticism of Madison's address, 249, 250, 251, 252; peace negotiations, 262, 277; at Princeton, 296, 297; Lafayette statue, 335; for religious assessment, 343; legal reforms, 357, 358; Robertson bill, 361; mentioned, 44, 137, 174, 365, 375, 397, 398

Jones, S., 307, 313

Jones, Walter, 381

Jordan, Nicholas, 332

Jouett, Jack, 158

Journal de Paris, 330

Journals of Congress, 63, 73, 76, 77, 150, 197, 216, 220, 243, 262, 283

Kaskaskia, 12

Kayewla, *see* Lafayette, Marquis de

Kentucky, 94, 95, 139, 140, 153, 200, 238, 315, 336, 338, 372, 374

King, Rufus, 340, 383, 389, 400, 401, 405, 406, 407

King's Mountain, 44, 45

Kinloch, Francis, 29, 30, 158

Kirkland, missionary, 331, 333

Kiskeminetas   Moghulbughkitum (Tobey's Creek), 365

Knox, Henry, 310, 391, 393

Koscuisko, Col. Thaddeus, 113

Lafayette, Marquis de, promise of naval aid, 24, 52; ordered to Virginia, 55; in Virginia, 115, 117, 158; wine presented to, 159; Yorktown, 163, 166; northward trip with Madison, 325-334; statues of, 334-335; appraised, 335, 336; mentioned, 67, 256, 270, 291, 337

Lake Champlain, 364

Lake George, 364

Lake of the Woods, 365

Lake Ontario, 364

L'Ambassadeur, de, Wiequefort, 410

Landais, Capt., 65, 67-68

La Nymphe, 335

Laurens, Henry, 60, 66, 142, 172, 182, 183, 184, 185, 187, 188

Laurens, John, 66, 67, 68, 69, 128, 163, 193, 270

Le Clerc, Jean, 289

Lee, Maj., 307

Lee, Arthur, elected Paris commissioner, 58; diplomatic battle in Paris, 59-69; candidate for post of Secretary for Foreign Affairs, 122-124; investigation of Morris, 126, 130, 131; article in *Freeman's Journal,* 143; Western lands, 148, 150, 151, 152, 155; attacks finance measures, 173-176, 298; exchange of prisoners, 182, 185, 187; attack on Frank-